INSURANCE

FUNDAMENTALS, ENVIRONMENT AND PROCEDURES

INSURANCE

FUNDAMENTALS, ENVIRONMENT AND PROCEDURES

B.S. BODLA • M.C. GARG • K.P. SINGH

Reader   Sr. Lecturer   Sr. Lecturer

Department of Business Management,
Guru Jambheshwar University, Hisar

DEEP & DEEP PUBLICATIONS PVT. LTD.

F-159, Rajouri Garden, New Delhi-110027

INSURANCE:
FUNDAMENTALS, ENVIRONMENT AND PROCEDURES

ISBN 81-7629-462-4

Typeset by ASHISH TECHNOGRAPHICS,
3190, Mohindra Park, Shakur Basti, Delhi-110034.

Printed in India at ELEGANT PRINTERS,
A-38/2, Maya Puri, Phase-I, New Delhi-110064.

Published by DEEP & DEEP PUBLICATIONS PVT. LTD.
F-159, Rajouri Garden, New Delhi-110027.
Phones: 25435369, 25440916
E-mail: ddpbooks@yahoo.co.in • deep98@del3.vsnl.net.in
Showroom:
2/13, Ansari Road, Daryaganj New Delhi-110002 • Telefax: 23245122

DEDICATED
TO
OUR
WORTHY
TEACHERS

CONTENTS

FOREWORD

Insurance Business has emerged as one of the prominent areas of financial services during recent times particularly in developing economies where it could not grow much prior to globalisation. The pace of growth of insurance sector has accelerated with the process of opening up of such economies to outside world under WTO regime. Insurance performs remarkable functions by insuring the insurable public and property located at different places. In view of its great significance in economic operations it has comprehensively networked itself in almost all parts of the society today. From academic angles, the insurance sector provides a vast and discrete scope for a textbook reflecting on its fundamentals and procedural imperatives *vis-a-vis* the current economic environment in the country. The need for a good textbook on the subject therefore cannot be taken as an exaggerated option in the present times.

This book on 'Insurance: Fundamentals, Environment and Procedures' is an icy shower in the hinterland of insurance and written by persons having long and solid exposure to the subject. The book, which has been divided into three parts, contains twenty-one chapters in total. It gives comprehensive coverage to broad areas of insurance fundamentals, insurance environment and procedures for insurance in India in a coherent and systematic manner. The book is an upshot of an incredibly absolute scholarly exercise. It is unique in many ways. Firstly, it has been written in a very down-to-earth language and different concepts have been lucidly explained. With a minimum of sagacious backdrop, a person who reads can follow its compassion without a set twist. Secondly, the book explains at length about the fundamentals of insurance. It clarifies the rules and general guidelines for insurance policy-takers as well as companies offering policies. The economic environment for insurance business has also been bejeweled in a splinter section. Thirdly, in one docile volume the authors have condensed the spirit of the subject matter without going off beam from any imperative linkage and facet. In fact, Dr. Bodla, Dr. Garg and Dr. Karam Pal Singh have made me to appreciate their well-heeled experience of teaching and research in the most sought after subject. They have covered in the book just what is considered necessary in the civic of insurance.

I value their academic endeavour and this book is a significant accrual to the accessible citations on Insurance Business. As a result, it will serve as a genuine textbook on the subject. In my opinion the book will be precious to all individuals including students, teachers, insurance takers, professionals, and others who have a modest curiosity to learn the subject of insurance business.

PROF. H.L VERMA
Former Pro-Vice-chancellor
G.J. University,
Hisar (Haryana)

PREFACE

It was in the 14th century in which the idea of insurance was first conceptualized. At that time it was used more as a tool for protection against financial loss of sea fearers involved in foreign trade. Since then this concept has undergone several changes. It is basically the unforeseen contingencies of human life that has given a very new look to the insurance industry. Gradually as competition increased the benefits given by the industry to its customers improved by leaps and bounds. It was the breakup of the traditional extended family system that provided a natural umbrella to each and every member of the family, which gave the insurance (life and non-life institutions an impetus to excel.

With the growth of industry, trade and commerce the insurance also grew over a period of time and gained maturity. In terms of insurance premium collection, presently, India stands fifth in Asia with, Japan. having 40 times more premium collection than India. Despite a double digit growth in last two years, the ratio of insurance premium to GDP has remained low in China and India. Currently, only 70 millions people are insured in India out of the overall population of over one billion. On the other hand, the non-life insurance business has vital role to play to safeguard the properties of the nation. The gross domestic premium income of general insurance business in India has increased to Rs. 9522 crores in 2000 from Rs. 184 crore in 1973. This speaks about the volume of growth in non-life insurance business in the country.

In India, the general insurers started working since 1850 with the establishment of the Triton Insurance, Calcutta. Again in 1861, the North British and Mercantile catered the requirements of insurance business. The general insurance in India could not progress much. The slow growth of joint-stock enterprise and mechanized production was another reason for the low level of general insurance business. In India, some Europeans started the first life insurance company in Bengal Presidency, viz., the Orient Life Insurance Company in 1818. The year 1870 was a landmark in the history of Indian Insurance separating the early period of pioneering attempts at life insurance from the subsequent period of steady development at the establishment of Indian Life Office, viz., Bombay Mutual Life Assurance Society in 1871. The next important life office was Oriental Government Security Life Assurance Co. Ltd., which started its operations since 1874.

Insurance Business is one of the fast emerging financial services, predominantly in the developing nation like ours, in terms of the population it serves. It performs remarkable feats by insuring the insurable public and its properties in metro cities, big towns, and even in most inaccessible rural areas. In view of its crucial significance, the insurance business (life and non-life insurance) has been comprehensively networked in almost all parts of the country. The insurance sector, obviously, provides a vast and discrete scope of a textbook in terms of its fundamentals and procedural imperatives *vis-a-vis* the economic environment dictating change. The call for a textbook on Insurance Business, therefore, cannot be glorified in this swift changing age.

This present book on ***Insurance: Fundamentals, Environment and Procedures*** is an icy shower in the hinterland of Insurance, The book, which has been alienated into three parts that contain twenty-one chapters in total. It provides a comprehensive coverage on the subject matter of insurance fundamentals, environment, and procedures for insurance in India in a coherent and systematic manner. The book has been divided into three parts. First part contains the fundamentals of insurance and has been alienated into ten chapters. The second part is devoted to insurance environment and consists of eight chapters and finally the third part discusses about the procedural aspects of insurance that has been elucidated all the way through three comprehensive chapters. All the chapters have been designed into a consistent manner and all particulars provided in the text are in self-instructional mode.

At the very outset, we place on record our special and sincere thanks to former Pro-Vice-Chancellor Professor H.L. Verma for agreeing to write a Foreword for this book. We are dutybound to place our special gratitude to Prof. M.S. Turan, Dean, Faculty of Management Studies, G.J. University, Hisar. His great contribution in terms of proficient observations, competent support, and academic inspiration has indeed imbibed value to the book. We would like to acknowledge the scholastic hand provided by Dr. S.K. Munjal from New India Assurance, New Delhi, Dr. J.N. Dhankhar, Executive Director, Jaipur Stock Exchange, Prof. D.P.S. Varma, Delhi School of Economics, University of Delhi, Prof. L.N. Dahiya, Prof. R. Vinayek, Prof. S.S. Chahal, and Prof. Daleep Singh from M.D. University, Rohtak. Prof. B.S. Bhatia, Punjabi University, Patiala, Prof. R.P. Hooda and Prof. S.L. Gupta from Kurukshetra University, Kurukshtra, Prof. Bal Krishan, H.P. University, Shimla, Prof. R.D. Sharma, University of Jammu, Prof. Subhash Sharma, G.N.D. University, Amritsar, Prof. L.K. Bansal, Panjab University, Chandigarh.

We would like to put on record our bizarre gratefulness to Dr. R.K. Chauhan, the Hon'ble Vice-Chancellor, G.J. University, Hisar, who has been a continuous source of stimulus to us all the way through this project.

We are also indebted to all our colleagues in the department for their constructive suggestions from time to time. We are also beholden to all our nearers and dearers especially who made considerable academic involvement in this at hand work. We sense gratefulness to the officers and officials of the university libraries in this part of the country who provided all cooperation to us in the effecting of this bookwork. We have parallel zeal to express our heartfelt appreciation to countless others who have contributed to this piece of knowledge both unequivocally and unconditionally. Therefore, we would like to show gratitude to all of them.

Hisar (Haryana) Authors

PART A

FUNDAMENTALS OF INSURANCE

1

CHAPTER

INTRODUCTION TO INSURANCE

LEARNING OBJECTIVE

The main objective of this chapter is to make the learners understand about the meaning, nature, functions, types, and evolution of insurance.

1.1 INTRODUCTION

Insurance is a tool by which fatalities of a small number are compensated out of funds (premium payment) collected from plenteous. Insurance companies pay back for financial losses arising out of occurrence of insured events, e.g. in personal accident policy death due to accident, in fire policy the insured events are fire and other allied perils like riot and strike, explosion, etc. Hence, insurance is safeguard against uncertainties. It provides financial recompense for losses suffered due to incident of unanticipated events, insured within policy of insurance. Moreover, through a number of Acts of Parliament, specific types of insurances are legally enforced in our country, e.g. third party insurance under Motor Vehicles Act, public liability insurance for handlers of hazardous substances under Environment Protection Act, etc.

Insurance, essentially, is an arrangement where the losses experienced by a few are extended over several who are exposed to similar risks. Insurance is a protection against financial loss arising on the happening of an unexpected event. Insurance companies collect premium to provide security for the purpose. As loss is paid out of the premium collected from the insuring public and the insurance companies act as trustees to the amount so collected. Insurance companies have standard proposal forms, which are to be filed up giving the details of insurance required and presented to insurance company. Depending upon the answers given in proposal form insurance companies assess the risk and quote the premium. On payment of premium and acceptance thereof by insurance company the insurance is affected. Nonetheless, there is no insurance cover if premium is not paid.

1.2 MEANING OF INSURANCE

It is a commonly acknowledged phenomenon that there ... e countless risks in every sphere of life. For property, there are fire risks; for shipment of goods, there are perils of sea; for human life there are risks of death or disability; and so on. The chances of occurrences of the events causing losses are quite uncertain because these may or may not take place. Therefore, with this view in mind, people facing common risks come together and make their small contributions to the common fund. While it may not be possible to tell in advance, which person will suffer the losses, it is possible to work out how many persons on an average out of the group, may suffer losses. When risk occurs, the loss is made good out of the common fund. In this way, each and every one shares the risk. In fact, they share the loss by payment of premium, which is calculated on the likelihood of loss. In olden time, the contribution by the persons was made at the time of loss. The following examples make clear the above-stated notion of insurance.

Example 1

In a town, there are 2000 persons who are all aged 60 and are healthy. It is expected that of these 20 persons may die during the year. If the economic value of the loss suffered by the family of each dying person were taken to be Rs. 50,000, the total loss would work out to Rs. 10,00,000. If each person of the group contributes Rs. 500 a year, the common fund would be Rs. 10,00,000. This would be enough to pay Rs. 50,000 to the family of each of the 20 dying persons. Thus, the risks in cases of 20 persons are shared by 2000 persons.

Example 2

In a village, there are 250 houses, each valued at Rs. 2,00,000. Every year one house gets burnt, resulting into a total loss of 2,00,000. If all the 250 owners come together and contribute Rs. 800 each, the common fund would be Rs. 2,00,000. This is enough to pay Rs. 2,00,000 to the owner whose house got burnt. Thus, the risk of one owner is spread over 250 house-owners of the village.

1.3 DEFINITION OF INSURANCE

As stated in the very beginning, insurance companies bear risk in return for a fee called premium. Thus, insurance companies are risk bearers. They accept or underwrite the risk in return for an insurance premium. Accordingly, the term insurance may be defined as a co-operative mechanism to spread the loss caused by a particular risk over a number of persons who are exposed to it and who agree to ensure themselves against that risk. Risk is, in fact, an uncertainty of a financial loss. Risk must not be confused with loss itself that is the unintentional decline in or disappearance of value arising from a contingency. The function of insurance include providing certainty, protection, risk sharing, prevention of loss and capital formation. Wherever there is uncertainty with respect to a probable loss there is risk. The insurance is also defined as a social apparatus to accumulate funds to meet the uncertain losses arising through a certain hazard to a person insured for such hazard.

Insurance has been defined to be that in which a sum of money as a premium is paid by the insured in consideration of the insurer's bearing the risk of paying a large sum upon a given contingency. The insurance, thus, is a contract whereby:

(a) certain sum, termed as premium, is charged in consideration,
(b) against the said consideration, a large amount is guaranteed to be paid by the insurer who received the premium,
(c) the compensation will be made in a certain definite sum, i.e., the loss or the policy amount whichever may be, and
(d) the payment is made only upon a contingency.

More specifically, Insurance may be defined as a contract wherein one party (the insurer) agrees to pay to the other party (the insured) or his beneficiary, a certain sum upon a given contingency (the risk) against which insurance is required.

1.4 NATURE OF INSURANCE

On the basis of the definition of insurance discussed above, one can observe its following characteristics:

Risk Sharing and Risk Transfer

Insurance is a mechanism adopted to share the financial losses that might occur to an individual or his family on the happening of a specified event. The event may be death of earning member of the family in the case of life insurance, marine-perils in marine insurance, fire in fire insurance and other certain events in miscellaneous insurance, e.g., theft in burglary insurance, accident in motor insurance, etc. The loss arising from these events if insured are shared by all the insured in the form of premium. Hence, risk is transferred from one individual to a group.

Co-operative Device

Insurance is a cooperative device under which a group of persons who agree to share the financial loss may be brought together voluntarily or through publicity or through solicitations of the agents. An insurer would be unable to compensate all the losses from his own capital. So, by insuring a large number of persons, he is able to pay the amount of loss. Like all co-operative devices, there is no compulsion here on anybody to purchase the insurance policy.

Risk Assessment in Advance

Insurance companies are risk bearers. Therefore, the risk is evaluated before insuring to charge the amount of share of an insured, herein called, consideration, or premium. The probability theory is used to evaluate the risks. Probability theory is that body of knowledge concerned with measuring the likelihood that something will happen and making estimates on the basis of this likelihood. The likelihood of an event is assigned a numerical value between 0 and 1, with those that are impossible assigned a value of 0 and those that are inevitable assigned a value of 1. The higher values are assigned to those events estimated to have a greater likelihood or probability of occurring.

Compensation at the Occurrence of Contingency

The compensation is made at a certain contingency insured. If the contingency occurs, payment is made. Since the life insurance contract is a contract of certainty, because the contingency the death or the expiry of term, will certainly occur, the payment is certain.

Similarly, in certain types of life policies, payment is not certain due to uncertainty of a particular contingency within a particular period. For example, in term insurance the payment is made only when death of the assured occurs within the specified term, may be one or two years. Similarly, in Pure Endowment payment is made only at the survival of the insured at the expiry of the period.

Amount of Payment

On the occurrence of the contingency, the insurer is legally bound to make good the financial loss suffered by the insured. The amount of payment depends upon the value of loss occurred due to the particular insured risk provided insurance is there up to that amount. In life insurance, the purpose is not to make good the financial loss suffered. The insurer promises to pay a fixed sum on the happening of an event. It is immaterial in life insurance what was the amount of loss at the time of contingency. But in the property and general insurance, the amount of loss, as well as the happening of loss, are required to be proved.

Huge Number of Insured Persons

To make the insurance cheaper, it is essential to insure larger number of persons or property because the lesser would be cost of insurance and so, the lower would be premium. In past years, tariff associations or mutual fire insurance associations were found to share the loss at cheaper rate. In order to function successfully, the insurance should be joined by a large number of persons.

Insurance must not be Confused with Charity and Gambling

The uncertainty is changed into certainty by insuring property and life because the insurer promises to pay a definite sum at damage or death. In the absence of insurance, the property owners could at best practice only some form of self-insurance, which may not give him absolute certainty. Thus, the family is protected against losses on death and damage with the help of insurance. From the company's point of view the life insurance is essentially non-speculative, in fact, no other business operates with greater certainties. From the insured point of view, too, insurance is also the antithesis of gambling. Failure of insurance amounts gambling because the uncertainty of loss is always looming. In fact, the insurance is just the opposite of gambling. In gambling, by bidding the person exposes himself to risk of losing, in the insurance, the insured is always opposed to risk, and will suffer loss if he is not insured.

Insurance is not possible without premium. Charity is given without consideration. It provides security and safety to an individual and to the society although it is a kind of business because in consideration of premium it guarantees the payment of loss.

Investment Portfolio

Since insurers' collect premiums initially and make payment later when (e.g., the insured person's death) or if (e.g., an automobile accident) an insured event occurs, insurance companies maintain the initial premiums collected in an investment portfolio, which generates a return. Thus, the insurers have two sources of income: the insurance premium and the investment income, which occurs over time.

1.5 FUNCTIONS OF INSURANCE

Insurers provide insurance policies, which are legally binding contracts for which the policy-holder pays insurance premium. Under an insurance contract, insurance companies promise to pay specified sum contingent on the occurrence of future events. Based upon this, the functions of insurance may be discussed as follows:

Certainty

Insurance provides certainty of payment for the risk of loss. There are different types of uncertainty in a risk. The risk will occur or not, when will occur, how much loss will be there? In other words, there are uncertainty of happening of time and amount of loss. Insurance removes all these uncertainty and the assured is given certainty of payment of loss. The insurer charges premium for providing the said certainty.

Protection

The main function of the insurance is to provide protection against the probable chances of loss. The insurance guarantees the payment of loss and thus protects the assured from sufferings. The insurance cannot check the happening of the event but can compensate for losses arising at the happening of the risk event.

Risk Sharing

When risk takes place, the loss is shared by all the persons who are exposed to the risk. The share is obtained from each and every insured in the shape of premium without which the insurer does not guarantee protection.

Assists in Capital Formation

The insurance provides capital to the society. The accumulated funds are invested in productive channel. The scarcity of capital of the society is minimized to a greater extent with the help of investment of insurance.

Prevention of Loss

The insurance companies assist financially to the health organization, fire brigade, educational institutions and other organizations, which are engaged in preventing the losses of the masses from death or damage. The insurance joins hands with these institutions in preventing the losses of the society because the reduction in loss causes lesser payment to the assured and so more saving is possible which will assist in reducing the premium. Lesser premium invites more business and more business causes lesser share to the assured. The reduced premium will stimulate more business and more protection to the masses.

On the basis of discussion made above, it can be concluded that the primary function of insurance is the creation of the counter balance for risk, which is security. Insurance does not eliminate or decrease the uncertainty for the individual as to whether or not the event will occur, nor does it alter the possibility of occurrence, but it does reduce the extent of financial loss connected with the event. From the individual's point of view, the purchase of an adequate amount of insurance on a house reduces the financial loss in the event of the house catching fire.

A number of times one might think that he has wasted his money in purchasing insurance policy if loss does not occur and consequently, no financial returns are received. Some even feel that if they have not had a loss during the policy term, their premium should be returned. Both viewpoints constitute the inadequate understanding of the insurance concept. Relative to the first, it is already known that the insurance contract provides a valuable feature in the relief from the burden of uncertainty. Even if a loss is not sustained during the policy term, the insured has received something for the premium in the form of freedom from the worry of financial loss. With respect to the second, one must appreciate the fact that the operation of insurance principle is based on the contributions of the many paying the losses of the unfortunate few. If the premiums were returned to the many who did not have losses, there would be no funds available to pay for the losses of the few who did. Basically, then, the insurance device is a method of loss distribution. What would be devastating loss to an individual is spread in an equitable manner to all members of the group, and it is on this basis that insurance can exist. In other words, insurance meets the social commitment every member of the society has to provide relief to those who necessitate it.

1.6 TYPES OF INSURANCE

Insurance occupies an important place in the modern world because the risk, which can be insured, have increased in number and extent owing to the growing complexity of the present day economic system. It plays a vital role in the life of every citizen and has developed on an enormous scale leading to the evolution of many different types of insurance. In fact, now a days almost any risk can be made the subject matter of contract of insurance. The different types of insurance have come about by practice within insurance companies, and by the influence of legislation controlling the transacting of insurance business. Broadly, insurance may be classified into the following categories:

1. Classification on the basis of nature of insurance:
   (a) Life Insurance,
   (b) Fire Insurance,
   (c) Marine Insurance,
   (d) Social Insurance, and
   (e) Miscellaneous Insurance.
2. Classification from business point of view:
   (a) Life Insurance, and
   (b) General Insurance.
3. Classification from risk point of view:
   (a) Personal Insurance,
   (b) Property Insurance,
   (c) Liability Insurance, and
   (d) Fidelity Guarantee Insurance.
   (For detail please refer to Chapter-III)

1.7 EVOLUTION OF INSURANCE

Marine insurance is the oldest form of insurance followed by life insurance and fire insurance. The history of insurance can be traced back to the early civilization. As civilization progressed, the incidence of losses started increasing giving rise to the concept of loss sharing. The Aryans through their village co-operatives practiced loss of profits insurance. The Mediterranean merchants also practised it in the 14th century through the issue of Bottomry Bonds. The Code of Manu indicates that there was the practice of marine insurance carried out by the traders in India with those of Srilanka, Egypt, and Greece.

The earliest transaction of insurance as practiced today can be traced back to the 14th century A.D. in Italy when ships were only being covered. This practice of Marine Insurance gradually spread to London and during the 16th century it was established in the mercantile transactions. The history of Marine Insurance is closely linked with the origin and rise of the Lloyds Shipowners. The Lloyd's Act was framed to set-up the Lloyd's by whom they were empowered to transact other classes of insurance. Today, Lloyd's is regarded as the largest insurance underwriter in the World.

The origin and growth of General Insurance and Life Insurance are given below:

I. Evolution of Non-Life Insurance in India

The boycott of British goods and British institutions, which occurred because of the nationalist movement, encouraged formation of Indian-owned commercial and business houses. By 1907, the Indian Mercantile, the first of the long lasting General Insurance Companies to be established with Indian capital, had started functioning. Five offices, The New India, Vulcan, Jupiter, British India General and the Universal, were established in 1919 almost simultaneously for transacting general insurance business.

In 1928, prominent insurance men of Bombay met and formed the Indian Insurance Companies Association to protect the interest of Indian insurers. Leaders of the insurance industry began to organize conferences, educate public on the benefits of insurance, focus attention on the annual remove of national wealth through 'invisible exports', and arise public interest in favour of Indian insurance.

In 1950, the Planning Commission was set-up to formulate plans for successive five years. This five-year plan brought about large scale economic development and increased insurance consciousness among the people. As insurance business increased the number of claims for compensation against losses also naturally increased. Settlement of too many large claims meant a severe demand on the funds of insurance companies. So to prevent this situation the practice of 'Reinsurance' was adopted. According to which insurers themselves reinsured portions of the insurances they had undertaken. So Indian insurance companies with their expanding business wanted to reinsure for which they had to seek foreign reinsurance markets.

Since the need for conserving foreign exchange was felt in India, all the insurers (Indian as well as foreign) operating in India formed the India Reinsurance Corporation in 1956. This corporation provided reinsurance facilities. It was compulsory for insurers in India to reinsure a fixed percentage of their insurances with the Corporation.

The Insurance Amendment Act, 1950 imposed certain limitations on expenses of management. The commission payable to principal agents was also restricted. Further a statutory association called the Insurance Association was also formed with two councils—Life Insurance Council and General Insurance Council. The General Insurance Council constituted what was called the Tariff Committee to control and regulate terms and conditions of business.

There was a general demand for nationalization of the industry. The government introduced only some more 'social control' measures in 1968 like licensing of surveyors, guidelines on investments, maintenance of statutory accounts, tighter control by the controller of insurance, payment of premium in advance before insurance can be accepted. On 13-5-1971, finally an ordinance was declared by the President of India to take over the management of general insurance companies by the Government.

In 1972, the General Insurance Business (Nationalization) Act, 1972 was passed. Under the provisions of this Act, the General Insurance Corporation of India was established for the purpose of directing, controlling and carrying on the general insurance business and all the 106 insurers were merged with one or the other four subsidiaries of the General Insurance Corporation of India, namely:

- National Insurance Company Ltd., with its head office at Calcutta.
- The New India Assurance Company Ltd., with its head office at Bombay.
- The Oriental Insurance Company Ltd., with its head office at Delhi.
- The United India Insurance Company Ltd., with its head office at Madras.

The Government of India set-up these four subsidiary companies with the following twin objectives:

- To ensure that these are so situated as to render their combined services effectively and in all parts of India; and
- To ensure proper service to the public through mutual competition.

Marine Insurance

The marine insurance is the oldest form of insurance. Under Bottomry bond, the system of credit and the law of interest were well developed and were based on a clear appreciation of the hazard involved and the means of safeguarding against it. If the ship was lost, the loan and interest were forfeited. The contract of insurance was made a part of the contract of carriage, and Manu shows that Indians had even anticipated the doctrine of average and contribution. Freight was fixed according to season and was expected to be reasonable in the case of marine transport, which was then very much at the mercy of winds and elements. Travelers by sea and land were very much exposed to the risk of losing their vessels and merchandise because the piracy on the open seas and highway robbery of caravans were very common. Besides there were several risks. Many times, it might have been captured by the king's enemies or robbed by pirates or got sunk in the deep waters. The risk to owners of such ships was enormous and, therefore, to safeguard them the marine traders which could not be conveniently borne by the unfortunate individual victims. The co-operative device was quite voluntary in the beginning, but now in modern it has been converted into modified shape of premium.

The oldest and the earliest records of marine policy relates to a Mediterranean voyage in 1347. In the year 1400, a book written by a merchant of Florence, indicates premium rates charged for the shipments by sea from London to Pisa. Marine Insurance spread from Italy to trading routes in other countries of Europe. Later on, in the year 1556, Philip II made marine insurance regulations for Spain and in 1563 for Antwerp (America) insured three ships on a voyage from Hawaii to Central America.

In 1575, during the reign of Queen Elizabeth I, opened the Chamber of Assurance in the Royal Exchange for the registration of marine parcels. Following this, an act of parliament was passed in 1601 to deal with disputes relating to marine insurance. During the period 1720-1824 the two-chartered companies viz., London Assurance and Royal Exchange Assurance enjoyed dominant position in the field of marine insurance. With the introduction of steamship and growth of international trade, specialized marine services were introduced. Following this the Lloyd's Association founded in 1692 and originated from coffee house run by Edward Lloyd became the major centre of marine insurance.

Marine Insurance in India

About India, there are evidences that marine insurance was practiced here about three thousand years ago. In earlier days travelers by sea and land were exposed to risk of losing their vessels and merchandise because of piracy on the open seas. Moreland has maintained that the practice of insurance was quite common during the rule of Akbar to Aurangzeb, but the nature and coverage of insurance in this period is not well known. It was the British insurers who introduced general insurance in India, in its modern form. The Britishers opened general insurance in India around the year 1700. The first company, known as the Sun Insurance Office Ltd. was set-up in Calcutta in the year 1710. This was followed by several insurance companies in different parts of the world, in the field of marine insurance. In 1972, the government of India nationalized the general insurance business by forming General Insurance Corporation (GIC).

Fire Insurance

Fire insurance was observed in Anglo-Section Guild form for the first time where the victims of fire hazards were given personal assistance by providing necessaries of life. It had originated in Germany in the beginning of sixteenth century. The fire insurance got momentum in England after the great fire in 1666 when the fire losses were tremendous. About 85 per cent of the houses were burnt to ashes and property worth of sterling ten crores were completely burnt off. Fire Insurance Office was established in 1681 in England. With colonial development of England, the fire insurance spread all over the world in current form.

In India, fire insurance was started during the British regime. The oldest of these companies include the Sun Insurance Office, Calcutta (1710), London Assurance and Royal Exchange Assurance (1720), Phoenix Assurance Company (1782), etc. At present, fire insurance business is in the hands of subsidiaries of General Insurance Corporation of India. Prior to Nationalization of General Insurance business, out of 106 branches of General Insurance Companies, 92 are doing fire insurance business in the country.

Miscellaneous Insurance

Owing to the increasing demand, different forms of insurance have been developed. Industrial Revolution of 19th century had facilitated the development of accidental insurance, theft and dacoity, fidelity insurance, etc. In 20th century, many types of social insurance started operating, viz., unemployment insurance, crop insurance, cattle insurance, etc. This way the business of insurance developed simultaneously with human and social development. Today, the use of computers in the field of insurance is frequently increasing. Insurance is becoming an inseparable part of human development and its scope is increasing with the advancement of society.

2. Evolution of Life Insurance

The first insurers of life were the marine insurance underwriters who started issuing life insurance policies on the life of master and crew of the ship, and the merchants. The early insurance contracts took the nature of policies for a short period only. The underwriters issued annuities and pension for a fixed period or for life to provide relief to widows on the death of their husbands. The first life insurance policy was issued on 18th June 1583, on the life of William Gibbons for a period of 12 months.

It was in the eighteenth century, societies began to be formed for issuing life insurance policies. Among such societies the Amicable Society (1705), The Equitable Life Assurance Society (1762), the Westminster Society (1792) was the important societies. The premium rates were varied in view of reputation and the health condition of the insured. During the early years of nineteenth century, a large number of life insurance companies were formed in India. Some of these companies preferred to amalgamate their business with other companies and a good number failed to function effectively. In order to stabilize and strengthen the insurance business, Life Insurance Companies Act, 1923 was passed and later amended it in 1946, 1958 and 1967.

Life Insurance in India

Life insurance in its current form came in India from United Kingdom (UK) with the establishment of a British firm, Oriental Life Insurance Company in 1818 followed by Bombay Life Assurance Company in 1823, the Madras Equitable Life Insurance Society in 1829 and Oriental Life Assurance

Company in 1874. Prior to 1871, Indian lives were treated as sub-standard and charged an extra premium of 15% to 20%. Bombay Mutual Life Assurance Society, an Indian insurer that came into existence in 1871, was the first to cover Indian lives at normal rates. The Indian Life Assurance Companies Act, 1923 was the first statutory measure to regulate life insurance business. Later, in 1928 the Indian Insurance Companies Act was enacted, *inter alia,* to enable the government to collect statistical information about life and non-life insurance business transacted in India by Indian and foreign insurers, including the provident insurance societies.

In order to protect the interest of insuring public, earlier legislation was consolidated and amended by Insurance Act, 1938 with comprehensive provisions for detailed and effective control over the activities of insurers. In turn to administer the aforesaid legislation, an insurance wing was established and attached first with the Ministry of Commerce and then Ministry of Finance. This ministry was administratively responsible for policy matters pertaining to insurance. The actuarial and operational matters relating to the insurance industry were looked after by an attached office in Shimla, headed first by Actuary to the Government of India, then by Superintendent of Insurance and finally by the Controller of Insurance. The act was amended in 1950, making far-reaching changes such as requirement of equity capital for companies, carrying on life insurance business, ceilings on shareholdings, stricter control on investment of life insurance companies, submission of periodical returns relating to investments and such other information to the Controller as he may call for, appointments of administrators for mismanaged companies, ceilings on expenses of management and agency commission, incorporation of the Insurance Association of India and formation of councils and committees thereof.

By 1956, 154 Indian insurers, 16 non-Indian insurers and 75 provident societies were carrying on life insurance business in India. Life insurance business was conformed mainly to cities and better-off segments of the society.

With a view to spread insurance to rural areas, to operate it systematically, and to achieve the objectives of socialistic pattern of society, the Government of India decided to nationalize the life insurance business. Resultantly, after considerable controversy with people both for and against nationalization, the President of India declared an ordinance on 19.1.1956 taking over management and control business of Life Assurance in India including foreign business of Indian insurers and Indian business of foreign insurers and then nationalized on 1.9.1956 when the Life Insurance Corporation came into existence. More specifically, the main aims of nationalization were:

- To spread insurance to rural areas;
- To encourage public savings to finance the Five-Year Plans;
- To provide complete security to policy-holder;
- To prevent malpractices, misuse of powers and positions, etc.;

- To avoid wasteful efforts in competition and conduct the business with utmost economy;
- To regulate insurance on scientific basis; and
- To achieve the goal of the socialistic pattern of society.

1.8 WHY LIFE INSURANCE?

It Covers the Risk of Death

The risk of death is covered under insurance scheme but not under ordinary savings plans. In case of death, insurance pays full sum assured, which would be several times larger than the total of the premiums paid. Under ordinary savings plans, only accumulated amount is payable.

It Encourages Compulsory Saving

After taking insurance, if the premium is not paid, the policy lapses. Therefore, the insured is forced to go on paying premium. In other words, it is compulsory. A savings deposit can be withdrawn very easily.

Easy Settlement and Protection Against Creditors

Once nomination or assignment is made, a claim under life insurance can be settled in a simple way. Under M.W.P. Act, the policy moneys become a kind of trust, which cannot be taken away, even by the creditors.

It helps to Achieve the Purpose of the Life Assured

If a lump sum amount is received in the hands of anybody, it is quite likely that the amount might be spent unwisely or in a speculative way. To overcome this risk, the life assured can provide that the claim amount be given in instalments.

Insurance Facilitates Liquidity

If a policy-holder is not in a position to pay the premium, he can surrender the policy for a cash sum.

Loan Facility and Tax Relief

He can also take a loan for a temporary period to tide over the difficulty. Some times, a life insurance policy is acceptable as security for a commercial loan. By paying the insurance premium, the assured obtains significant reliefs in Income tax and wealth tax.

1.9 SUMMARY

Insurance is a tool to spread the loss caused by a particular risk over a number of persons who are exposed to it and who agree to ensure themselves against that risk. Risk is uncertainty of a financial loss. Risk must not be confused with loss itself that is the unintentional decline in or disappearance of value arising from a contingency. The function of insurance include providing certainty, protection, risk sharing, prevention of loss and capital formation.

Broadly, insurance may be classified as Life and Non-Life Insurance.

The origin of insurance is lost in antiquity. The earliest traces of insurance in the ancient world are found in the form of marine trade loans or carriers' contracts, which included an element of insurance. Evidence is on record that arrangements embodying the idea of insurance were made in Babylonia and India at quite an early period. The codes of Hummurabi and of Manu had recognized the advisability of provision for sharing the future losses. However, there is no evidence that insurance in its present form was practiced prior to the 14th century.

In India, the general insurer started working since 1850 with the establishment of the Triton Insurance, Calcutta. Again in 1861, the North British and Mercantile catered the requirements of insurance business. The general insurance in India could not progress much. The slow growth of joint-stock enterprise and mechanized production was another reason for the low level of general insurance business.

In India, some Europeans started the first life insurance company in Bengal Presidency, viz., the Orient Life Insurance Company in 1818. The year 1870 was a landmark in the history of Indian Insurance separating the early period of pioneering attempts at life insurance from the subsequent period of steady development at the establishment of Indian Life Office, viz., Bombay Mutual Life Assurance Society in 1871. The next important life office was Oriental Government Security Life Assurance Co., Ltd., which started its operation since 1874. Since then, for life insurance several offices developed in India.

The miscellaneous insurance took the present shape in the later part of nineteenth century with the industrial revolution in England. Accident insurance, fidelity insurance, liability insurance and theft insurance were the important forms of insurance at that time. Now, insurances such as cattle insurance, crop insurance, profit insurance, etc. are taking place.

Insurance particularly the life insurance is sought after because:

(i) It is superior to an ordinary saving plan.
(ii) Insurance encourages compulsory saving and forces thrift.
(iii) Easy Settlement and Protection Against Creditors.
(iv) It helps to achieve the purpose of the life assured.
(v) Enhances Marketability and Liquidity.

1.10 REVIEW QUESTIONS

1. What is insurance? What are different functions of insurance?
2. Bring out the main characteristics of insurance. Why one should have insurance cover?
3. The latest and the oldest form of insurance is marine insurance. Illustrate.
4. Write a note on the evolution of life insurance business in India.
5. What are the main benefits of having a life insurance policy? Elaborate.

2

CHAPTER

PRINCIPLES OF INSURANCE

LEARNING OBJECTIVE

The main objective of this chapter is to make the apprentice understand about the principles of insurance and the essentials of a valid insurance contract.

2.1 INTRODUCTION

In Chapter 1, the term insurance has been defined as the device in which a sum of money as a premium is paid in consideration of the insurer's incurring the risk of paying a large sum upon a particular eventuality. The insurance, accordingly, is a contract whereby:

(a) certain sum, called premium, is charged in consideration,
(b) against the said consideration, a large sum is guaranteed to be paid by the insurer who received the premium,
(c) the payment will be made in a certain definite sum, i.e., the loss or the policy amount whichever may be, and
(d) the payment is made only upon a contingency.

More explicitly, Insurance may be defined as a contract in which one party (the insurer) agrees to pay to the other party (the insured) or his beneficiary, a certain sum upon a particular unforeseen event (the risk) against which insurance is wanted.

Every subject or discipline has certain generally accepted and systematically laid down standards or principles to achieve the underlying objectives. Insurance is not exception to this general rule. In insurance, there is a body of doctrines commonly associated with the theory and procedures of insurance, serving as an explanation of current practices and as a guide for all stakeholders for making choice among procedures where alternatives exit. These principles may be defined as the rules of action or conduct that are universally adopted by the different stakeholders involved in the insurance business. These principles may be classified into following categories:

- General Principles or essentials of Insurance Contract.
- Specific Principles of Insurance Contract.
- Miscellaneous Principles of Insurance Contract.

A deliberation on these categories of principles follows in the forthcoming pages in this chapter.

2.2 GENERAL PRINCIPLES OR ESSENTIALS OF INSURANCE CONTRACT

An agreement enforceable by law is called a contract. In other words, any agreement between two parties or more than two parties to perform or to abstain from performing an act, with an intention to create a legally binding relationship is termed as contract. Specifically, one can define the term insurance as a contract in which one party agrees to pay a given sum on the happening of a particular event contingent upon the duration of human life/property in consideration of the payment of a sum.

It is obvious from the above that there are two main parties, the insurer, who undertakes to pay the sum guaranteed on the happening of an unforeseen event and insured, who pays the premium for insurance protection. The valid insurance contract, like any other contracts, according to Section 10 of Indian Contract Act, 1872, must hang upon the following principles:

- Offer and acceptance.
- Legai consideration.
- Competent to make contract.
- Free consent.
- Legal object.

Offer and Acceptance

The intimation of the proposer's intention to buy insurance is the 'offer', while the insurer's readiness to undertake the risk stated, is the 'acceptance'. The offer in case of insurance is called proposal. If other party accepts this proposal, it is transformed into an agreement. The offer for entering into contract may generally come from the insured. The insurer may also propose to make the contract. Whether the offer is from the side of insurer or from the side of insured, the main fact is acceptance. Any act that precedes it is an offer or a counter-offer. All that precede the offer or counter-offer is an invitation to offer. In insurance, the publication of prospectus, the canvassing of other agents are invitations to offer. When the prospect (the potential policy-holder) proposes to enter the contract it is an offer and if there is any alteration in the offer that would be a counter-offer. If this alteration or change (counter-offer) is accepted by the proposer, it would be an acceptance. At the moment, the notice of acceptance is given to other party; it would be a valid acceptance.

Legal Consideration

In insurance contract, the premium is the consideration on the part of the insured. Certainly, the insurer who promise to pay a fixed sum at a given contingency must have some return for his promise. It need not be money only but it must be valuable. It may be sums, right, interest, profit, or benefit. Premium being the valuable consideration must be given for starting the insurance contract. The amount of premium is not important to begin the contract. The fact is that without payment of premium, the insurance contract cannot be initiated.

Competent to make Contract

The parties to the contract should be competent to contract. Every person is competent to contract:

(a) who is of the age of majority according to the law,
(b) who is of sound mind, and
(c) who is not disqualified from contracting by any law to which he is subject.

A minor is not competent to contract. A contract by a minor is void excepting contracts for necessaries. A person is said to be of sound mind for the purpose of making a contract if at the time when he makes it, he is capable of understanding it and of forming a rational judgement as to its effect upon his interest. An alien enemy, an undischarged insolvent and criminals cannot enter into contract. Contract made by incompetent party/ parties will be void.

As far as the insurance contracts are concerned, only those insurers can grant insurance policies who have been issued licenses by Insurance Regulatory and Development Authority (IRDA). Similarly, minor, people of unsound mind and criminal background cannot take on insurance. This applies to bankrupt persons. In case of minor, the natural guardians can enter into a valid contract on behalf of the minor, till the minor attains 18 years of age.

Free Consent

When both the parties have agreed to a contract on the terms and conditions of the agreement in the same sense and spirit, they are said to have a free consent. The consent will be free when it is not caused by:

(1) coercion,
(2) undue influence,
(3) fraud, or
(4) misrepresentation, or
(5) mistake.

When there is not free consent except fraud the contract becomes voidable at the option of the party whose consent was so caused. In case of fraud the contract would be void. The proposer for free consent must sign a declaration to this concern.

Legal Object

The object of the agreement should be lawful. An object that is:

(i) not forbidden by law, or
(ii) is not immoral, or
(iii) opposed to public policy, or
(v) which does not defeat the provisions of any law, is lawful.

In proposal form the object of insurance is asked which should be legal and the object should not be concealed. If the object of an insurance, like the consideration is found to be unlawful, the policy is void. Moreover, the object of the contract should not be based on gambling nature.

How to Translate General Contract into Insurance Contract

As stated above, insurance is a contract between (two parties) the insurer and the policy-holder, to perform a particular service. The practical aspects of the insurance contract are proposed to be dealt with here. The nature of insurance transaction can be represented by the following triangle:

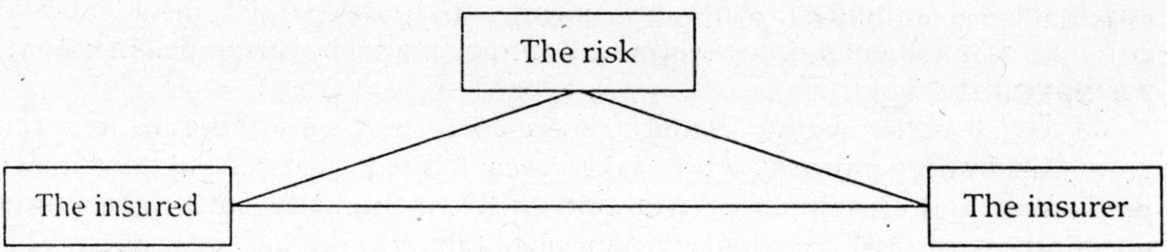

At the apex of this triangle there is the risk insured against. The insured—policy-holder—is the person or company entering into the insurance contract and the insurer is the insurance company that has contracted with the insured to provide cover for the risk insured against.

Looking at this triangle from the insured's side one could say that:

(a) the insured knows the nature of the risk;
(b) the insured has to describe the risk to the insurer. At this stage

insured could more properly be termed the proposer as he, she or the firm is at the point of describing the risk to the insurer in order to obtain insurance;

(c) the proposer will look for acceptable protection. He may have a particular form of insurance cover in mind or want a special clause included or even excluded. The proposer knows, or should know, what he wants, and will get into the market place in an effort to satisfy his needs; and

(d) an important determinant in selecting an insurer will be price. The proposer will also, of course, be concerned with service and security, but price will be extremely important.

From the Insurer's side, one could say that:

(a) it will be told about the risk by the proposer;

(b) in many cases the insurer will not rely on this source of information alone but will make its own inquiries. This may imply using skilled risk surveyors to look at proposals and make physical inspection or doctors to carry out medical examination for a life or permanent health insurance proposal;

(c) the insurer will decide on the level of cover which it is prepared to offer to the proposer; and

(d) finally, the insurer will have to determine the price to be charged for the cover it is willing to offer. This price will have to reflect a number of relevant factors.

However, the triangle does not reveal the whole story. At the "insured" end of the triangle, there is the intermediary. The intermediary—the agent or broker—will assist insured or proposer at various stages in the transaction of insurance. For any large industrial insured, the use of a broker is almost essential as the role, he performs, is of crucial importance.

2.3 SPECIFIC PRINCIPLES OF INSURANCE CONTRACT

Besides, the essentials of a valid insurance contract discussed in the previous section, there are certain specific principles, which are of paramount significance to the contract of both the life and non-life insurance. The specific principles of the contract of insurance consist the following:

- Uberrima fides or Utmost Good Faith
- Insurable Interest
- Indemnity
- Proximate Cause
- Subrogation

I. Uberrima Fides or Utmost Good Faith

In life insurance, the nature of the subject matter the product of a contract, is an intangible one and the circumstances surrounding the subject matter are known by one of the parties, namely, the proposer. Only the proposer knows, or should know, all the relevant facts about the risk being proposed for insurance. It is true that the underwriter can have a pre-survey for fire insurance or medical examination for life or health insurance, carried out, but even then there are certain aspects of the risk which are not apparent at the time of pre-survey or medical examination, for example, the previous loss or medical history and so on.

Because of the aforesaid reasons the law imposes a greater duty of disclosures on both the parties to an insurance contract than to other commercial contracts. This is called uberrima fides [utmost good faith]. A summary of the doctrine of utmost good faith was given in the case of *Rozanes* v. *Bowen* [1928] as follows:

As the underwriter knows nothing and the man who comes to him to ask him to insure knows everything, it is the duty of the assured . . . . to make a full discloser to the underwriter without being asked of all material circumstances. This is expressed by saying it is a contract of the utmost good faith.

Definition of Utmost Good Faith

> Utmost good faith may be defined as a positive duty voluntarily to disclose, accurately and fully, all facts material to the risk being proposed, whether requested or not.

Here, one may note that every circumstance is material, which would influence the judgement of a predent insurer in fixing the premium or determining whether he will take the risk.

In life insurance contracts, material facts are: age, income, type of occupation, habits, health, family history, earlier policies and loss, if any, suffered in the past. As the material facts are determined not on the basis of opinion, the proposer should disclose not only those matters which the proposer may feel are material but all facts which are material.

Duty of Disclosure on Both the Parties

The duty of full disclosure rests on both parties. Since the decision to ensure is taken on the basis of subject matter, the life to be ensured in life insurance, and the material facts are known by proposer, it is much more responsibility of the proposer to disclose the material facts. It is easier to see where the proposer might be in breach of the duty rather than the insurer. In practice, there are fe·· breaches of the duty by the insurer. Examples are:

(a) Withholding from the proposer the fact that the sprinkler system in his premises entitles him to a substantial discount on his fire insurance premium—may be, similarly, non-smoker's discount for life insurance premium;

(b) Accepting an insurance, which the insurer knows, is unenforceable at law, or, which it is not registered to underwrite; and

(c) Making untrue statements during the negotiations for the contract.

The Extent of the Duty

The responsibility to disclose material facts ends at the moment when the proposal form has been fully and correctly fulfilled provided there is no such facts which he considers or expects to be considered material and have not been disclosed. It must be noted in this regard that the proposer can not defend on the ground that he had omitted to disclose it by carelessness or by mistake or that he did not consider it material to the contract.

Facts which must be Disclosed

Those facts, which must be disclosed, are any circumstances which would influence the insurer in accepting or declining a risk or in fixing the premium or terms and conditions of the contract. The fact must be material at the date at which it should be communicated to the insurer. A fact, which was immaterial when the contract was made, but becomes material later on, need not be disclosed. There is one exception to the rule and it occurs when there is a policy condition requiring continuous disclosure. This would be an usual condition to find in most general insurance policies. The categories of facts which must be disclosed are:

(a) Facts, which show that the particular risk represents a greater exposure than, would be expected from its nature or class;

(b) External factors which make the risk greater than would normally be expected;

(c) Previous losses and claims under other policies;

(d) Any special terms imposed on previous proposals by other insurers;

(e) The existence of other non-idemnity policies such as life and accident; and

(f) Full facts relating to the description of the subject matter of insurance.

Some examples of such facts in case of various types of insurances are:

(a) *Fire Insurance*: The construction of the building, the nature of its use, fire detection, and firefighting equipment.

(b) *Theft Insurance*: The nature of stock, its value and other nature of security precautions.

(c) *Motor Insurance*: The type of car, whether it has been specially adapted, details of regular drivers, and the model.

(d) *Marine Insurance*: Cargo insurance—the terms of sale, mode o carriage, whether containerized.

(e) *Life Insurance*: Age, previous medical history, occupation, anc smoking/drinking habits.

(f) *Personal Accident Insurance*: Age, height, weight, previous medica history, and occupation.

Facts need not be Disclosed by the Insured

The following facts, however, are not required to be disclosed by the insured:

(i) Facts, which tend to lessen the risk.
(ii) Facts of public knowledge.
(iii) Facts, which could be inferred from the information, disclosed.
(iv) Facts waived by the insurer.
(v) Facts governed by the conditions of the policy.
(vi) Facts of Law.
(vii) Facts, which are superfluous to disclose by reason of a conditior or warranty.

Legal Consequence

It is worth mentioning that in the absence of utmost good faith the contract would be voidable at the option of the person who suffered loss due to non-disclosure. The inadvertent concealment will be treated as fraud anc it *void ab initio*. However, as and when the voidable contract has beer validated by the party not at fault, the contract can not be avoided by him later on.

2. The Principle of Insurable Interest

Inspite of the popular belief that everything can be insured, not all risks are insurable. They must have certain characteristics. For example, they must be capable of financial measurement and there must be sufficient number of similar risks for rating purposes, they must be pure and particular risks. The occurrence of the event insured against must not be against public policy, the premium has to be reasonable and finally and importantly, there must be insurable interest on the part of the person insuring.

The subject matter of insurance can be any type of property or any event that may result in a loss of legal right or the creation of a legal liability. In this way the subject matter of insurance under a fire policy can be a building, stock or machine; under a liability policy it can be a person's legal liability for injury or damage; with a life assurance policy, the subject matter of insurance is the life being assured; in marine insurance it could be the ship, its cargo or legal liability arising from the ownership of the vessel or its cargo, for injury to third parties or damage to their property.

To identify insurable interest in all of this, it is vital to grasp one fundamental fact. It is not the house, ship, machinery, potential liability of life that is insured but it is the pecuniary interest of the insured in that house, ship, machinery, etc. which is insured.

Subject Matter of the Contract

The subject matter of the contract is the name given to the financial interest which a person has in the subject matter of the insurance. The concept is at the very root of the doctrine of insurable interest and was stated clearly in the case of *Castellian* v. *Preston* (1883) as follows:

> What is it that is insured in a fire policy? Not the bricks and materials used in building the house but the interest of the insured in the subject matter of insurance.

Thus, it is the interest of the insured in the subject matter of the insurance, which is insured. This is what demonstrates the importance of insurable interest.

Definition

There is no single definition of insurable interest, which is universally accepted, but it can be similar to the following:

> The legal right to insure arising out of a financial relationship recognised under law, between the insured and the subject matter of insurance.

The essentials of a valid insurable interest are the following:

(i) There must be subject-matter to be insured.
(ii) The policy-holder should have monetary relationship with the subject-matter.
(iii) The relationship between the policyholders and the subject-matter should be recognized by law. In other words, there should not be any illegal relationship between the policy-holder and the subject-matter to be insured.
(iv) The financial relationship between the policy-holder and subject-matter should be such that the policy-holder is economically benefited by the survival or existence of the subject-matter and/or will suffer economic loss at the death or existence of the subject-matter.

Insurable Interest in Life Insurance

Insurable interest is the pecuniary interest. In life insurance, insurable interest may be classified into two categories:

(a) Insurable interest in own's life, and
(b) Insurable interest in other's life.

The later can further be sub-divided into two categories—where the proof is required and where the proof is not required. Moreover, the insurable interest requiring the proof may arise due to business relationship or family relationship.

Insurable Interest in Own's Life

Every such individual who is otherwise competent to enter into a contract has an insurable interest in his own life. Its presence is not required to be proved. Buyon says, "Every man is presumed to possess an insurable interest in his estate for the loss of his future gains or savings which might be the result of his premature death." According to the definition of insurable interest it is also evident that the person will continue to gain financially while he is surviving and will suffer loss if he is dead because he will be unable to earn or protect the property.

Regarding the extent of the insurable interest in own life it may be said that this interest is unlimited because the loss to the insured or his dependent cannot be measured in terms of money and, therefore, no limit can be placed to the amount of insurance that one may take on one's own life. Thus, theoretically, a person can take a policy to any unlimited amount on his own's life; but in practice no insurer will issue a policy for an amount larger than amount seems suitable to the circumstances and means of the applicant. Generally, it is mentioned that one cannot purchase policy usually more than ten times of his one year's income. The premium can be paid by third party provided there was no intention to speculation. If there is possibility of wager contract it would be void.

Insurable Interest in Other's Life

According to the principle of insurable interest, life insurance can be affected on the lives of third parties provided the proposer has insurable interest in the third party. There are two types of insurable interest in other's life. First where proof is not required and second, where proof is required.

Proof not Required

In the following two cases, the presence of insurable interest is legally presumed and therefore need not be proved.

1. Wife has Insurable Interest in the Life of Husband

Wife is presumed to have insurable interest in the life of her husband because husband is legally bound to support his wife. The wife will suffer financially if the husband is dead and will continue to gain if the husband is surviving. Since, the extent of loss or gain cannot be measured in this case, the wife has insurable interest in the husband's life up to an unlimited extent.

2. Husband has Insurable Interest in the Life of his Wife

It was decided in the case of *Griffith* v. *Flaming* (1909) that the husband has insurable interest in his wife's life because of domestic services performed by the wife. If the wife is dead husband has to employ other person to render the domestic services and certain other financial expenditures will involve at her death, which are not calculable. The husband is benefited at the survival of his wife, so it is self-proved that husband has insurable interest in his wife's life. Since the monetary loss at her death or monetary gain at her survival cannot be measured, there is unlimited insurable interest in the life of wife.

Proof is Required

In the following cases, the presence of the insurable interest has to be proved:

1. Business Relationship

The insurable interest may be present in the life of assured due to business or contractual relationship between them. Here, the amount of insurable interest corresponds with the amount of risk involved. Some of such examples are described hereunder:

(a) A Creditor has Insurable Interest in the Life of his Debtor

If the debtor dies before the loan is repaid, the creditor may lose money. The continuance of debtor's life is financially meaningful to the creditor because the latter will get all his money repaid at the former's survival. The maximum amount of loss to a creditor may be the amount of outstanding loan plus interest thereon and the amount of premium paid. So, the maximum amount of insurable interest is limited to the outstanding loan, plus interest and amount of premium expected to be paid. The interest is calculated on the estimation of duration of debt to be paid. The maximum amount of interest does not say about the payment of policy amount, it, merely, determines the chances of speculation. The full amount of policy is payable irrespective of the payment of loan and interest. In view of the fact that it is life insurance, the full policy amount is paid.

(b) Trustee and Interest Protected

A trustee has insurable interest in respect of the interest of which he is trustee because at the survival of the other person the trustee is benefited and at his death he will suffer.

(c) Surety and Principal

A surety has insurable interest in the life of his principal. If the principal (the debtor) is dead, the surety is responsible for payment of outstanding loan, or obligated amount. At the survival of principal, he will not suffer this loss. The insurable interest is limited up to the amount of outstanding loan, interest and premium paid.

(d) A Partner's Interest in Life of other Partner

As per the provisions of Partnership Act, at the death of a partner, the partnership will be dissolved and the surviving partner will lose financially. Even if the firm continues at the death of the partner, the firm has to pay deceased partner's share to his dependent. This will involve a huge financial loss to the partnership. Therefore, the firm collectively can purchase insurance policies in the life of each partner of the firm. Since the firm part of money up to the extent of deceased partner goodwill, capital, share of profit and reserve, the firm has insurable interest up to the extent in each partner. Similarly, all the partners have insurable interest in life of each partner because they will financially suffer at a death.

(e) An Employer's Interest in the Life of a Key-man

The person whose presence or potential cause profit to the business may be termed as a keyman of the employer. If the key-man is dead, the business will reduce profit up to a certain extent. The business suffers reduced profit, expenses involved in appointing and training new persons and the amount to be given to the dependent of key-man at his death. So the business has insurance interest up to such extent in the key-man's life.

(f) An Insurer has in the Life Assured

The insurer suffers at the death of life assured and therefore, he can get reinsurance of the assured persons by him. The insurable interest is limited up to the policy amount.

2. *Family Relationship*

Besides, the business relationship discussed above, the insurable interest may arise due to family relationship if pecuniary interest exists between the policyholders and life assured because mere relationship or ties of blood and of affection does not constitute insurable interest. The proposer must have a reasonable expectation of financial benefit from the continuance of the life of the person to be insured or of financial loss from his death. The interest must be based on value and not on mere sentiments. Similarly, mere moral obligation is not sufficient to warrant existence of insurable interest although legal obligation to get support will form insurable interest of the person who is supported in life of the person who is supporting. Thus, a son can insure his father's life only when he is dependent on him and the father can take insurance policy on his son's life only when he is dependent on his son.

Universal Rule of Insurable Interest in Life Insurance

Following are some vital and universal rules for insurable interest:

1. *Point in Time of Insurable Interest*

The insurable interest must exist at the time of proposal. Policy, without insurable interest, will be wager. It is not essential that the insurable interest must be present at the time of claim.

2. Various Services

Except the services of wife, services of other relatives will not essentially form insurable interest. There must be financial relationship between the proposer and the life assured. In other words, the services performed by the son without dependence of his father, will not constitute insurable interest of the father in the life of his son. *Vice-versa* is not essential for forming insurable interest.

3. Insurable Interest has to be Precious

In business relationship the value or extent of the insurable interest must be determined to avoid wager contract of the additional insurance. Insurance is limited only up to the amount of insurable interest.

4. Insurable Interest is Supposed to be a Legal Binding

Insurance interest should not be against public policy and it should be recognized by law. Therefore, the consent of life assured is very essential before the policy can be issued.

5. The Legal Liability may be Basis of Insurable Interest

Given that the person will suffer financially up to the extent of responsibility, the proposal has insurable interest to that extent. For instance, a person will be under legal responsibility to expense at the funeral of his wife and children, he can purchase insurance in their lives up to that extent.

6. Insurable Interest has to be Crystal-Clear

The insurable interest must be present definitely at the time of proposal. Mere expectation of gain or support will not constitute insurable interest.

7. Legal Consequence

The insurable interest must be there to form legal and valid insurance contract. Without insurable interest, it would be unacceptable and invalid.

Universal Rules of Insurable Interest in Property Insurance

Insurable interest normally arises out of ownership where the insured is the owner of the subject matter of insurance, for example, a house. There are, however, other situations and financial interests that will give rise to insurable interest but which do not involve full ownership. They include:

(a) A Part or Joint Owner

Any person who has a partial interest in some property is entitled to insure to the extent of full value of the property, rather than just the extent of the actual interest: A part or joint owner is treated as a trustee for the other owner(s). If any claim monies are received and they exceed his own financial interest then he holds that money as an agent for the others.

(b) Mortgagees and Mortgagors

Mortgagees are most common in the area of house or vehicle purchase. They involve a lender (normally a bank or other financial institution) known as mortgagee and the purchaser known as the mortgagor. Both parties have an insurable interest. The purchaser's interest arises from the ownership of the house or the vehicle and the financial institution's as a creditor that is limited to the extent of the loan.

(c) Executors and Trustees

They are legally responsible for the property in their charge and it is this which gives rise to insurable interest.

(d) Bailees

A bailee is a person legally holding the goods of another, which may be for payment or gratuitously. Motor garages, launderers and watch repairers are examples of bailees and in each case, they have responsibility to take reasonable care of the goods which are in their custody and to look after them as if their own.

(e) Agents

Where a principal has insurable interest, his agent can affect insurance on his behalf.

(f) Husband and Wife

Each has an unlimited interest in each other's life and they have mutual insurable interest in each other's property.

3. Principle of Indemnity

Next specific principle of insurance is that all insurance contracts except personal insurance are contracts of indemnity. According to this principle, the insurer undertakes to put the insured, in the event of loss, in the same position that he occupied immediately before the happening of the event insured against. In certain form of insurance, the principle of indemnity is modified to apply. For example, in marine or fire insurance, sometimes, certain profit margin that would have earned in absence of the event, is also included in the loss. In true sense of the indemnity, the insured is not entitled to make a profit of his loss.

Merits of the Principle of Indemnity

The principle of indemnity offers the following advantages:

(i) The principle of indemnity is an essential feature of an insurance contract, in absence whereof this industry would have the hue of gambling and the insured would tend to effect over-insurance and then intentionally cause a loss to occur so that a financial gain could be achieved. So, to avoid this intentional loss, only the actual loss becomes payable and not the assured sum (which is higher in over-insurance). If the propriety is under-insured, i.e. the assured amount is less than the actual value of the propriety insured, the insured is generally regarded his own insurer for the amount if under-insurance and in case of loss he shall share the loss himself.

(ii) This principle helps in avoidance of anti-social act. If the assured is allowed to gain more than the actual loss, which is against the principle of indemnity, he will be tempted to gain by destruction of his own property after getting it insured against a risk. Thus, the whole society will be doing only anti-social act, i.e., the persons would be interested in gaining after destruction of the property. So, the principle of indemnity has been applied where only his loss will be compensated.

(iii) The principle of indemnity helps to maintain the premium at low-level. If the principle of indemnity is not applied, larger amount. will be paid for a smaller loss and this will increase the cost of insurance and the premium of insurance will have to be raised.

Certain Conditions for Indemnity Principle

The following conditions are supposed to be satisfied in full for the application of the principle of indemnity:

(i) The insured has to prove that he will suffer loss on the insured matter at the time of happening the event and the loss is actual monetary loss.

(ii) The amount of compensation will be the amount of insurance. Indemnification cannot be more than the amount insured.

(iii) If the insured gets more amount than the actual loss, the insurer has right to get the extra-amount back.

(iv) If the insured gets some amount from third party after being fully indemnified by insurer, the insurer will have right to receive the entire amount paid by the third party.

4. The Principle of Proximate Cause

According to the principle of proximate cause an insurance policy is designed to provide compensation only for such losses as are caused by the perils, which are stated in the policy. The liability of the insurer arises only if the loss is caused by a peril, which is specifically covered under the policy. However, the loss is not payable if it is caused by a peril, which is excluded under the policy or is not mentioned. It is thus necessary to ascertain the cause of the loss to decide whether it is payable under the policy or not. In life insurance, the doctrine of *Causa Proxima* is not applied because the insurer is bound to pay the amount of insurance whatever may be the reason of death. It may be natural or unnatural. So, this principle is not of much practical importance in connection with life insurance. However, this principle is observed in life insurance too in the following circumstances:

Suicide

When suicide occurs within one year of the policy or there was intention to commit suicide then the payment of policy would be restricted, only up to the interest of third party in the policy provided the interest was expressed at least one month before the suicide.

Accident Benefits

In accident benefit policy, double of the policy amount is paid. So, the cause of death in this policy is of very high importance.

War-Risk

If a policy is issued on exclusion of war-risk, the principle of the proximate cause becomes important because the insurer waives its liability in case death occurred due to war. In this case, only premium paid or surrender value whichever is higher is payable. However, in our country on social grounds, this principle is ignored and full benefit of a policy is given to the person killed in the field of war.

Perils relevant to an insurance claim can be classified under three headings:

(a) Insured Perils

Those named in the policy as insured, e.g. fire, lightening, storm and theft.

(b) Excepted or Excluded Perils

Those stated in the policy as excluded either as causes of insured perils, e.g. riot, earthquake or war or a result of insured perils, e.g. certain types of explosion.

(c) Uninsured or other Perils

Those perils not mentioned in the policy at all. Smoke and water may not be excluded nor mentioned as insured in a fire policy.

Need for the Doctrine of Proximate Cause

When the loss is the result of two or more causes, operating simultaneously or one after the other in succession, it becomes necessary to ascertain what is known as the proximate cause, which brought about the loss.

If, however, the excepted perils relate to a loss "directly or indirectly" arising out of their operation, the insurer may not be liable, as illustrated in the following case:

Coxe v. *Employer Liability Assurance Corporation* (1916). An army officer while visiting sentries posted along the railway line was killed by a passing train. The policy excluded death or injury "directly or indirectly caused by wary, etc." The passing of the train was the proximate cause of the accident, but the indirect cause was war, for that was the reason why the officer was present on the railway line. In view of the words used in the policy, the insurers were not liable.

Meaning of Proximate Cause

The principle of the legal doctrine of 'proximate cause' may be explained as follows:

The doctrine is based on the principle of cause and effect, which states that having proved the effect and traced the cause, it is not necessary to go further. "The law does not concern itself with the cause of causes." The law provides the rule. *Cause proxima non-remota spectatur*—"the immediate cause not the remote or distant one should be regarded which was evolved by courts to solve the difficulty."

To be proximate, therefore, a cause must be immediate cause. The expression 'immediate' does not mean that it should be the cause nearest to the loss in point of time. The expression immediate should be understood in terms of effectiveness or efficiency. Thus, from a number of causes, if one has to be selected as the proximate cause, the choice will be "upon the one which may be variously ascribed the qualities of reality,. predominance, efficiency." In other words, it is the cause, which is effectual in producing that result.

To summarise, the proximate cause means the direct, the most dominant and most effective cause of which the loss is the natural consequence. It is the cause, which is most closely and directly connected with the loss, not necessarily in time but in efficiency and effectiveness. Once this cause is identified, it is not necessary to go further into the cause of causes. Finally, this cause has to be selected by applying commonsense standards, i.e. the standards of a man in the street.

Proximate cause has been defined in the English case of *Pawsey* v. *South Union & National Insurance Co.* (1907) as follows:

> "The active efficient cause that sets in motion a train of events which bring about a result, without the intervention of any force started and working actively from a new and independent source."

Proximate in Efficiency, and not in Time

It is also noteworthy that the time which elapses between cause and result may be long or short, but this in no way affects the issue, so long as the relationship of cause and effect is established. For example, a ship was torpedoed, while her final loss was due to a storm. It was held that it was the torpedo that proximately caused her loss:

> "To treat proximate cause as if it was the case which is proximate in time is out of the question. The cause, which is truly proximate, is that which is proximate in efficiency. That efficiency may have been preserved although other causes may in the meantime have sprung up which have not yet destroyed it, or truly impaired it, and it may culminate in a result of which it still remains the real efficient cause to which the event can be ascribed."

It is then, not the latest, but the direct, dominant, operative, and efficient cause that must be regarded as proximate.

Practical Application of the Doctrine

In theory, the doctrine is clear. To entitle an insured to recover, the train of events, leading from the insured peril to the actual financial loss suffered by the insured, must be unbroken. If a train of events from an excepted or uninsured peril breaks the train of event from an insured event, then only the loss up to the break is covered. Its practical application is difficult since several events acting simultaneously or one after the other may cause loss. Moreover, it is necessary to differentiate between the insured peril, the excepted peril and the unimbursed peril.

5. Doctrine of Subrogation

The principle of subrogation refers to the right of the insurer to stand in the place of the insured, after settlement of a claim, as far as the insured's right of recovery from an alternative source is involved. If the insured is in a position to recover the loss in full or in part from a third party due to whose negligence the loss may have been precipitated, his right of recovery is subrogated to the insurer on settlement of the claim The insurers, thereafter, recover the claim from the third party. The right of subrogation may be exercised by the insurer before payment of loss but not in marine cargo insurances. The principle of subrogation is just a corollary to the principle of indemnity. The insured can realize only actual value of the loss or damage to the property as per the principle of indemnity.

Essentials of Doctrine of Subrogation

The following aspects elucidate the essentials of Doctrine of Subrogation:

(i) Corollary to the Principle of Indemnity

The doctrine of subrogation is the supplementary principle of indemnity. The latter doctrine says that only the actual value of the loss of the property is compensated, so the former follows that if the damaged property has any value left, or any right against a third party the insurer can subrogate the left property or right of the property because if the insured is allowed to retain, he shall have realised more than the actual loss, which is contrary to principle of indemnity.

(ii) Subrogation is the Substitution

The insurer, according to this principle, becomes entitled to all the rights of insured subject matter after payment because he has paid the actual loss of the property. He is substituted in place of other persons who act on the right and claim of the property insured. It must be noted here that the right of subrogation is exercisable at common law after the insurer has paid the claims made against it.

(iii) Subrogation only up to the Amount of Payment

The insurer in subrogated all the rights, claims, remedies and securities of the damages insured property after indemnification, but he is entitled to get these benefits only to the extent of his payment. The insurer is thus, subrogated to the alternative rights and remedies of the insured, only up to the amount of his payment to the insured. In the same way if the insured is compensated for his loss from another party after he has been indemnified by his insurer he is liable to part with the compensation up to the extent that the insurer is entitled to. In one U.S. case it was made clear, "If the insurer, having paid the claim to the insured, recovers from the defaulting third party in excess of the amount paid under the policy, he has to pay this excess to the insured though he may charge the insured his share of reasonable expenses incurred in collecting."

(iv) The Subrogation may be Applied before Payment

If the assured got certain compensation from third party before being fully indemnified by the insurer, the insurer can pay only the balance of the loss.

(v) Personal Insurance

The doctrine of subrogation does not apply to personal insurance because the doctrine of idemnity is not applicable to such insurance. The insurers have no right of action against the third party in respect of the damages. For example, if an insured dies due to the negligence of a third party his dependent has right to recover the amount of the loss from the third party along with the policy amount. No amount of the policy would be subrogated by the insurer.

How Subrogation Arises

Subrogation rights arise in four ways as under:

(a) Tort;
(b) Contract;
(c) Statute; and
(d) Subject matter of insurance.

Tort

Where the insured has sustained some damage, lost rights or incurred liability due to atrocious acts of some other person then the insurer, having indemnified for the loss is entitled to take action to recover the outlay from the wrongdoer.

This may arise in a number of ways:

(a) a lorry driver may back into your building;
(b) an employee may leave the factory door open so that thieves can steal stock; and
(c) a painter may drop a ladder onto a machine as .. result the machine breaks down and production is lost.

There are policies which could be arranged to cater for each of these events. As well as the indemnity to which he is entitled from his insurers, the insured would have a right, in tort, against the individuals involved. Insurers will assume these rights and attempt to recover their outlays from the guilty party. When an action is taken by insurers in this situation they use the name of the insured and his permission would be sought if legal action were considered necessary.

There is a further practical reason why the insured will be asked for permission before legal action is taken and that is he may well have an uninsured claim, which he wishes to include. The law only allows one to sue a person once for an event.

Contract

Subrogation relates to rights, which arise out of certain contracts. This may arise where there is a custom of the trade to which the contract applies—for example, hotel proprietors who properly display the declaration regarding the relevant law. The other situation where Subrogation may arise from contract is where a person has contractual right to compensation regardless of fault. Insurers will assume the benefits of these rights.

Statute

In the UK, where damage to property is sustained by an insured as the result of a riot and the insurers indemnify that person they are empowered to recover their outlay from the police authority of the district in which the riot occurred. They may do so in their own name. This right of recovery originates from the Riot (Damages) Act, 1886.

Subject Matter of Insurance

Sometimes a situation will arise where an insured has been indemnified and the subject matter treated as lost. Once this has happened the insured cannot claim the salvage as this would give him more than an indemnity. It can be argued, therefore, that when insurers sell salvage, as in situations where they dispose of damaged cars, they are really exercising their subrogation rights in support of the principle of indemnity.

When Subrogation Arises

Now the question that comes to our mind is when does the

subrogation arises? The general law right of subrogation only arises once the insurers have admitted the insured claim and paid it. This might give rise to some problems because the insurers would not have complete control from the date of the loss. Their eventual position could be seriously prejudiced by delay or some other action taken by the insured. To make sure that they are in control of the situation, insurers place a condition in the policy giving themselves subrogation rights before the claim is paid. The only limitation is that the insurer cannot recover from a third party before he has actually settled with his own insured. Nonetheless, the express condition allows the insurer to hold the third party liable pending indemnity being granted to the insured.

There is a side effect which subrogation brings. Although it is strictly in support of the principle of indemnity, many individuals once their insurer has paid for damage to be repaired will lose interest in pursuing any recovery rights they may have. Subrogation condition has the effect of ensuring that those who are negligent are not able to get away with it because of the existence of insurance. The rights, which pass, to the insurers by virtue of Subrogation are the rights that the insured has. The condition, therefore, place certain obligations upon the insured in these circumstances—to assist the insurers in enforcing claims and to do nothing which would prejudice the insurer's chances of recovery.

Modification of Subrogation

There are situations in which, by virtue of subrogation operating, insurers would be claiming back from each other very frequently. The Motorist who drives into a wall, one motorist driving into another—these are frequent occurrences and a mountain of correspondence would be involved each time an insurer sought to exercise subrogation rights against another. Because of these situations most insurers become parties to the 'knock for knock' agreement. This agreement operates between companies and simply means that insurers will not exercise subrogation rights against each other for damage to their own insured vehicles. Such an agreement exists amongst the insurers in India. Subrogation may also be waived where an employee suffers injury at the workplace as the result of negligence of another employee.

2.4 MISCELLANEOUS PRINCIPLES

Besides the general and specific principles, there are certain miscellaneous principles for insurance that should usually be presumed in practice:

Contribution

Contribution is the right of an insurer who has paid claim under a policy, to call upon other insurers liable for the same loss to contribute to the payment. As is the case of subrogation it also supports the principle of indemnity. There is, therefore, no contribution in personal accident policies under which insurers contract to pay specific sums on happening of a certain event. Such types policies are not contract of indemnity.

Contribution doctrine operate in the following circumstances:

(i) The concerned policies must always cover the same perils which caused the loss.
(ii) They must cover the same subject matter.
(iii) They must protect the same interest.
(iv) They must be enforced at the time of loss.

As already discussed the principle of indemnity put a stop to the insured to recover more than his loss. In the absence of contribution condition in the policy, there is nothing to prevent an insured that is holding policies covering the same risk with different insurers the whole of his loss from one insurer if the sum insured is adequate. The insurer who has paid the loss would then have the right and trouble of obtaining a contribution to the loss from other insurers. To avoid this situation all the non-marine policies contain a contribution condition which provides that where two or more policies covering the same risk, the insured must claim under all policies, recovering a rateable proportion only from each of the insures concerned. All non-marine cargo claim form invariably require the claimant to disclose the details of any other policies held by him on the same subject matter. This enables the insurer to check that the terms of contribution condition are observed.

Special Clause—More Specific Insurance

Sometimes a clause is included in the policy to the effect that in case the property is insured by any other more specific insurance, then the policy will not insure the same subject matter except only as regards any excess of value beyond the amount of the more specific insurance.

Different Interests

The principle of contribution applies only where the sure risk is insured. There is a possibility that under certain circumstances two insurers will have to pay the same loss in full because different interests are involved. Two cases, "*The Scottish Amicable Heritable Securities Association* v. *Northern Insurance Co.* (1883) and *The Glargow Provident Investment Society* v. *Westminster Fire Office* (1887) are closely connected with this issue. In these cases the material property was the same but also where the interests were different.

Messrs Hay as Mortgagors and the Scottish Amicable as Mortgagers are jointly insured in respect of Messers Hay's property and the 'Glasgow Provident' were second mortgagees. In the first case it was decided that the mortgagors and the first mortgagers could recover in full and the insurance held by the second mortgagees did not affect their right to a full indemnity for their insurers. In the second case, it was ruled that the second mortgagers were also entitled to a full indemnity from their insurers, as they had not benefited from the result of the previous act.

From the above decisions it will be observed that in these circumstances contribution did not apply, as the interests were entirely different and each insured recovered to the full amount of his respective interest.

Principle of Assignment

Marine and life policies can be freely assigned but assignment under fire and accident policies are not valid without the prior consent of the insurers—except changes of interest by will or operation of law. Moreover, assignments under fire and accident policies must be made before the insured parts with his interest. Once he has lost the interest, the policy is void and can not be assigned.

The policy in life insurance can be assigned freely for a legal consideration or without consideration in case of love and affection. The assignment shall be complete and effectual only on the execution of such endorsement either on the policy itself or by a separate deed. Notice for this purpose must be given to the insurer who will acknowledge the assignment. Once the assignment is complete, it can not be revoked by the assignor because he ceases to be the owner of the policy unless re-assignment is made by the assignee in favour of the assignor. The life policies are the only policies, which can be assigned whether the assignee has an insurable interest, or not. Life policies are frequently charged, assigned, or otherwise dealt with, for they are valuable securities.

A marine cargo policy is freely assignable unless it contains terms expressly prohibiting assignment. It assigned either before or after loss. A marine cargo policy may be assigned by endorsement thereon or in other customary manner. In practice, a marine cargo policy is frequently endorsed in blank and becomes in effect a quasi-negotiable instrument. Thus, it will be appreciated, adds considerably to the convenience of mercantile transactions as the policy can be negotiated through a bank along with other documents of title. Marine Hull Policies can not be assigned without the consent of the insurers.

Assignment in fire insurance cannot be recognized without prior consent of the insurer, change of interest in fire policies (unless by will or operation of law) are not valid unless and until the consent of the insurer has been given. The fire policies are not in the nature of assignment for intended to be assigned from one person to another without the consent of the insurer. Assignment in fire insurance constitutes a new contract.

Principle of Return of Premium

Ordinarily the premium once paid cannot be refunded. However, in the following cases the refund is allowed.

(i) By Agreement in the Policy

The assured may pay full premium while effecting the insurance but it may be agreed to return it wholly or partly in the happening of certain events. For example, special packing may reduce the risk.

(ii) For Reasons of Equity

Equity implies a condition that the insurer shall not receive the price of running a risk he bears. Thus, the contract does not come into effect in this case or it is held to be void *ab initio*. It is established by the following points:

(a) Non-attachment of Risk

Where the subject-matter insured or part thereof, has never been imperilled for example, term insurance with returnable premium where premium is returned to the policy-holder if death does not occur during period of insurance.

(b) Undeclared Balance of an Open Policy

The policy may be cancelled and premium may be returned for short interest allowed provided there was no further interest in the policy.

(c) Payment of Premium is Apportionable

The apportioned part of the consideration is refundable when a part of policy interest is not involved. For example, insurance may be taken for a voyage in stages, each stage being rated separately. In such a case if some stages are not completed the premium relating to incomplete stage is returnable.

(d) Where the assured has no insurable interest throughout the currency of the risk, the premium is returnable provided the policy was not attached by way of wagering.

(e) Unreasonable delay in commencing the voyage may also entitle the insurer to cancel the insurance by returning the premium.

Principle of Over-insurance by Double Insurance

If there is over-insurance by double insurance, a proportionate part of the several premium is returnable provided that if the policies are taken at different times and any earlier policy has at any time born the entire risk or if a claim has been paid. On the policy in respect of the full insured thereby, no premium is returnable in respect of that policy and when double insurance is effected knowingly by the assured no premium is returnable.

Legal Principles

Life Insurance is a contract and therefore, the provisions of the Contract Act, 1872 apply. Other enactments like Transfer of Property Act, Estate Duty Act, Indian Stamps Act, Law of Limitation, Succession Act, etc. also are applicable. All the essentials of contract have to be fulfilled in the insurance contract also.

Auxiliary Principles

Life Insurance contracts have the following additional principles: Life insurance contract is:

(i) an Aleatory contract,
(ii) a unilateral contract,
(iii) a conditional contract,
(iv) a contract of Adhesion, and
(v) not a contract of indemnity.

Indemnity Contract is not Applied

The indemnity principle is not applicable in life insurance contract because the value of loss at death cannot be ascertained. It is not possible to ascertain .the time up to which the insured would have survived and it is also difficult to ascertain the amount of money to be earned by him during life-time. So, the doctrine of subrogation is also not applicable. In life insurance a fixed sum is paid which may be the sum assured and bonus if the policy is participating one.

Conditional Contract

Life insurance contract is conditional. It is due to the fact that the insurer shall pay the assured sum only when the contract is continuing by payment of premium. In addition, the insurer's promise to pay the sum assured is also conditional upon the furnishing of satisfactory proof of death and other conditions mentioned in the policy.

Contract of Adhesion

Contract of adhesion means that the terms of the contract are not arrived by mutual negotiations between the parties as in the case of ordinary contracts. The proposer is not in a position to bargain about the terms of contract because these terms are already determined. The only course open to the proposer is whether to accept or not a particular policy.

Aleatory Contract

Aleatory contract refers that contract depends on chance. In ordinary contract approximately equal value is exchanged by both parties; but in life insurance contract, the full sum assured may be payable even if all premiums are not paid. Thus, on the chance of death, higher amount is payable. It should be clear, here, that, this does not make the contract of wager because of insurable interest.

Unilateral Contract in Nature

Life insurance contract is unilateral contract because, here, only the insurer makes an enforceable promise. The proposer had already performed his duty of payment of premiums. If the first premium is paid, the insurer is bound to accept subsequent premium and to pay the amount claim when it arises except on the ground of fraud.

2.5 SUMMARY

Insurance is mantra to broaden the loss caused by a particular risk over a number of persons who are exposed to it and who agree to ensure themselves against that risk. Risk is uncertainty of a financial loss. Risk must not be confused with loss itself that is the unintentional decline in or disappearance of value arising from a contingency. The function of insurance include providing certainty, protection, risk sharing, prevention of loss and capital formation.

The valid contract, according to Section 10 of Indian Contract Act, 1872, must have the following essentialities:

(a) Agreement (offer and acceptance).
(b) Legal consideration.
(c) Competent to make contract.
(d) Free consent.
(e) Legal object.

Besides, the insurance contract observes the subsequent principles:

Utmost Good Faith

Utmost good faith may be defined as a positive duty voluntarily to disclose, accurately and fully, all facts material to the risk being proposed, whether requested or not

Insurable Interest

The legal right to insure arising out of a financial relationship recognized under law, between the insured and the subject matter of insurance. The insurable principle is that all insurance contracts except personal insurance are contracts of indemnity. According to this principle, the insurer undertakes to put the insured, in the event of loss, in the same position that he occupied immediately before the happening of the event insured against.

Principle of Proximate Cause

According to the principle of proximate cause, an insurance policy is designed to provide compensation only for such losses as are caused by the perils, which are stated in the policy.

Doctrine of Subrogation

It refers to the right of the insurer to stand in the place of the insured, after settlement of a claim, as far as the insured's right of recovery from an alternative source is involved. Subrogation rights arise in four ways as follows:

(a) Tort;
(b) Contract;

(c) Statute;
(d) Subject matter of insurance.

Assignment or Transfer of Interest

Marine and life policies can be freely assigned but assignment under fire, accident, and marine hull policies are not valid without the prior consent of the insurers—except changes of interest by will or operation of law.

Return of Premium

Ordinarily the premium once paid cannot be refunded.

Provisions of Other Laws

Life Insurance is a contract and therefore, the provisions of the Contract Act, 1872 shall apply. Other enactments like Transfer of Property Act, Estate Duty Act, Indian Stamps Act, Law of Limitation, Succession Act, etc. also are applicable.

Life insurance policies have the following auxiliary principles: Life insurance contract is:

(i) indemnity contract is not applied in life insurance,
(ii) a conditional contract,
(iii) a contract of Adhesion,
(iv) an aleatory contract, and
(v) a unilateral contract.

2.6 REVIEW QUESTIONS

1. Discuss the following principles of insurance with suitable examples:
   (a) Insurable Interest,
   (b) Uberrima Fides, and
   (c) Doctrine of Subrogation.
2. Explain the essential features of life insurance contract.
3. Elucidate in detail how insurable interest, utmost good faith, and proximate cause are applicable in life insurance.
4. 'The policies are freely assignable in case of life insurance'. Discuss.
5. 'Proximate cause is not very indispensable in case of life insurance contract'. Put in plain words the detail with examples.
6. Write short notes on the following:
   - Principle of Contribution,
   - Principle of Assignment,
   - Principle of Return of Premium, and
   - Principle of Over-insurance by Double Insurance.

3

CHAPTER

CLASSIFICATION OF INSURANCE

LEARNING OBJECTIVE

After going all the way through this chapter the student would be able to comprehend the categorization of insurance from different point of views.

3.1 INTRODUCTION

As discussed in the previous chapter, the origin of insurance is lost in antiquity. The earliest traces of insurance in the ancient world are found in the form of marine trade loans or carriers' contracts, which included an element of insurance. Evidence is on record that arrangements embodying the idea of insurance were made in Babylonia and India at quite an early period. In Rigveda, the most sacred book of India, references were made to the concept 'Yogakshema' more or less akin to the well-being and security of the people. The codes of Hummarabi and of Manu had recognized the advisability of provision for sharing the future losses. However, there is no evidence that insurance in its present form was practiced prior to the twelfth century.

The hazards, which can be insured, have amplified in number and extent owing to the growing complexity of the present day economic system. Insurance, thus occupies an important place in the modern world. It plays a vital role in the life of every citizen and has developed on an enormous scale leading to the evolution of many different types of insurance. In fact, now a days, almost every risk can be made the subject matter of contract of insurance.

The different types of insurance have come about by practice within insurance companies, and by the influence of legislation controlling the transactions of insurance business. By and large, insurance may be classified as follows:

- Classification on the basis of nature of insurance.
- Classification from business point of view.
- Classification from risk point of view.

Let us talk about these classifications taking one by one.

3.2 CLASSIFICATION ON THE BASIS OF NATURE OF INSURANCE

On the basis of nature, insurance may be of the following categories:

- Life insurance.
- Fire insurance.
- Marine insurance.
- Social insurance.
- Miscellaneous insurance.

I. Life Insurance

Life insurance may be defined as a contract in which the insurer, in consideration of a certain premium, either in a lump sum or by other periodical payments, agrees to pay to the assured, or to the person for whose benefit the policy is taken, the assured sum of money, on the happening of a specified event contingent on the human life or at the expiry of certain period. For life insurance, the risk ensured against is death. The life insurance company pays the sum assured to the insured in the event of death. There are several types of insurance products/policies, which have been discussed in later chapter.

At present, life insurance enjoys maximum scope because the life is the most important property of the society or an individual. Each and every person requires the insurance. This insurance provides protection to the family at the premature death or gives adequate amount at the old age when earning capacities are reduced. The insurance is not only a protection but is a sort of investment because a certain sum is returnable to the insured at the death or at the expiry of a period.

Fundamental of Life Insurance Contract

Life insurance contract is based on certain fundamental principles. These principles are outlined hereunder:

Essentials of a Valid Contract

The life insurance contract must have all the essentials of a valid contract. According to Indian Contract Act, 1872, a valid contract must contain the following essentials:

(i) Offer and acceptance.
(ii) Capacity to contract.
(iii) Free consent of parties.

(iv) Lawful consideration.
(v) Lawful object.

The detail discussion on the essentials of a valid contract has been made in previous chapter.

Principle of Utmost Good Faith

The contract of life insurance is a contract of utmost good faith. The insured should be honest and truthful in giving information to the insurance company. He knows more about the subject matter of the contract than the other party (the insurer). Consequently, he is under a duty to disclose accurately all material facts known to him to the insurer. Concealment of any fact will entitle the insurer to deprive the assured of the benefit of the contract.

Principle of Insurable Interest

In life insurance, the insured must have insurable interest in the life assured. Without insurable interest the contract of insurance is void. In case of life insurance, insurable interest must be present at the time when the insurance is affected. It is not necessary that the assured should have insurable interest at the time of maturity also.

In the following three cases insurable interest is presumed and no proof is necessary, viz.:

(i) Own life,
(ii) Husband in the life of wife, and
(iii) Wife in the life of husband.

The following persons have been held to have insurable interest:

(i) A person is presumed to have an interest in his own life and every part of it.
(ii) A creditor has an insurable interest in the life of his debtor.
(iii) A proprietor of a drama company has an insurable interest in the lives of actresses.
(iv) A servant engaged for a term of years has insurable interest in the life of his employer.

Principle of Indemnity

The life insurance contract is not a contract of indemnity. The loss of life cannot be compensated and only a specified sum of money is paid. That is why the amount payable in life insurance on the happening of the event is fixed in advance. Once the sum of money payable is fixed, it is constant invariable. A contract of insurance, therefore, is not a contract of indemnity. The loss resulting from the death of life assured cannot be estimated in terms of money and only a fixed amount is paid.

2. Fire Insurance

A fire insurance is a contract whereby the insurer, in consideration of the premium paid, undertakes to make good any loss or damage caused by fire during a specified period. Normally, the fire insurance policy is for a period of one year after which it is to be renewed from time to time. A claim for loss by fire must satisfy the following two conditions:

(i) there must be actual loss; and
(ii) fire must be accidental and non-intentional.

The risk covered by a fire insurance contract is the loss resulting from fire or some cause, which is the proximate cause of the loss. If damage is caused by overheating without ignition, it will not be regarded as a fire loss within the meaning of fire insurance and the loss will not be recoverable from the insurer.

Fundamental Principles of Fire Insurance Contract

Fire insurance contract is based on certain fundamental principles. These principles are:

Insurable Interest

In fire insurance, the assured must have insurable interest in the subject matter of the insurance. Without insurable interest the contract of insurance is void. In case of fire insurance, unlike life insurance insurable interest must be present both at the time of insurance and at the time of loss. In case of goods, insurable interest arises on account of:

(i) ownership,
(ii) possession, and
(iii) contract.

The following persons have insurable interest in the subject matter of insurance in case of a fire policy:

(i) A person has insurable interest in the property he owns.
(ii) A businessman has insurable interest in his stock, plant and machinery and building.
(iii) Agent has an insurable interest in the property of his principal.
(iv) Partner has insurable interest in the property of partnership firm.
(v) Mortgagee has insurable interest in the property, which is mortgaged.

Utmost Good Faith

Similar to the life insurance contract, the contract of fire insurance is a contract of utmost good faith. The insured should be truthful and honest in giving information to the insurance company. Insured knows everything about the subject matter of the insurance. He is under a duty to disclose accurately all factual information known to him. The insurance company should also disclose the facts of the policy to the proposer. So utmost good faith on the part of both the parties is a must.

Indemnity

The contract of fire insurance is a contract of strict indemnity. The assured can, in the event of loss, recover the actual amount of loss from the insurer. This is subject to the maximum amount for which the subject matter is insured. The value of the policy undertaken is fixed at the time of contract. The actual amount of loss suffered is compensated and the sum insured is reduced by the amount paid. Value of policy is only the maximum limit.

If a person has insured his house for Rs. 4,00,000 the insurer is not necessarily liable to pay that amount, although the house may have been totally destroyed by fire; but he will pay the actual loss after deducting depreciation within the maximum limit of Rs. 4,00,000.

Difference between Life and Fire Insurance.

Basis of Difference	*Life Insurance*	*Fire Insurance*
1. Subject Matter	The subject matter of insurance is human life.	The subject matter is any physical property or assets
2. Object	The object of life insurance is to protect the human life form future uncertainties.	The object of fire insurance is to protect the assets or property from fire.
3. Element	Life insurance has the elements of protection and investment, both.	Fire insurance has only the element of protection and not the element of investment.
4. Insurable interest	Insurable interest must be present at the time of effecting the policy but need not necessary at the time when the claim falls due.	Insurance interest on the subject matter must be present both at the time of effecting policy as well as when the claim falls due.
5. Duration	The duration of life insurance policy usually exceeds a year.	The duration of the fire insurance policy usually does not exceed a year.
6. Indemnity	Life insurance is not an indemnity insurance. The sum assured is paid either on the happening of certain event or on maturity of the policy.	The fire insurance is an indemnity insurance. The loss due to fire is indemnified subject to the maximum limit of the policy amount.
7. Classification of risk	Classification of risk in life insurance is much easier.	Classification of risk in fire insurance is very difficult.

8. Surrender value	Life insurance policy has surrender value.	Fire insurance does not have any surrender value.
9. Policy amount	One can insure for any in life insurance. amount.	In fire insurance, the amount of the policy cannot be more than the value of the subject matter.
10. Payment of premium	Payment of premium is made in instalments.	Lump sum payment of premium is made.
11. Moral hazard	Life insurance lacks moral hazard.	In fire insurance, moral hazard is more influential.

3. Marine Insurance

A marine insurance contract is an agreement whereby the insurer undertakes to indemnify the insured in the manner and to the extent thereby agreed against marine losses. Marine insurance is an arrangement by which the insurer undertakes to compensate the owner of a ship or cargo for complete or partial loss at sea.

Marine insurance provides protection against loss of marine perils. The marine perils are collision with rock, or ship attacked by enemies, fire and capture by pirates, etc. These perils cause damage, destruction or disappearance of the ship and cargo and non-payment of freight. So, marine insurance insures ship (Hull), cargo and freight.

Fundamental Principles of Marine Insurance

The following are fundamental principles of marine insurance:

Contract of Indemnity

Unlike life insurance, the contract of marine insurance is a contract of indemnity. The assured can, in the event of loss recover the actual amount of loss from the insurer. Under no circumstances, the insured is allowed to make profit out of the marine insurance contract, so far Hull insurance is concerned. However, in Marine Cargo policies the principle of indemnity is modified since it is not possible to adhere to strict indemnity in these policies due to fluctuation in market. Cargo policies provide commercial indemnity rather than strict indemnity. The insurers promise to indemnify the insured "in the manner and to the extent agreed."

In case of 'Hull Policy', the amount insured is fixed at a level rather above the current market value. In case of 'Cargo Policy', the amount insured also includes an amount for certain charges and profit when the policy is taken on CIF basis.

Contract of Good Faith

Similar to life and fire insurance, the contract of marine insurance is a contract of uberrima fides, i.e., utmost good faith. Both the insured and insurer must disclose everything, which is in their knowledge and can affect the insurance contract. The insured should be truthful and honest in giving information to the insurance company. He is under a duty to disclose accurately all factual information known to him. The insurer should also disclose the facts of the policy to the proposer. If utmost good faith is not observed by either party, the contract may be avoided by the other party. So utmost good faith on the part of both the parties is a must.

4. Social Insurance

Social insurance has developed to provide economic security to weaker sections of the society who are unable to pay the premium for adequate insurance. Pension plans, disability benefits, unemployment benefits, sickness insurance, and industrial insurance are the various forms of social insurance. With the increase of the socialistic ideas, the social insurance is an obligatory duty of the nation.

5. Miscellaneous Insurance

The process of fast development in the society gave rise to a number of risks or hazards. To provide security against such hazards, many other types of insurance also have been developed. The important among them are:

A. *Motor Insurance*

Motor insurance has been classified according to types of vehicles, viz. Scooter/Motor cycles, Private cars, commercial vehicles—private and public goods or passengers and miscellaneous vehicles.

No motor vehicle or any mechanically propelled vehicle can ply in a public place unless it is insured against third party liability prescribed under Motor Vehicles Act, 1988. After the amendment in the Act in 1988 the liability for personal injury/death to any person is unlimited and third property damage is limited to Rs. 6,000. However this liability can be increased on payment of extra premium. The insured has the option to cover his vehicle against own damage to the extent of its market value. The most comprehensive policy is of private car. In addition to the above provisions of the Motor Vehicle Act some of the other liabilities are also covered under this Act:

In case of Motor Insurance the liability incurred is in respect of:

(i) Death or personal injury to owner of the goods or his authorised representative in a goods vehicle.

(ii) Liability incurred in respect of death or bodily injury of any passenger of a public service vehicle.

(iii) Liability arising under Workmen Compensation Act, 1923 in respect of death or bodily injury of:
- Paid driver in a vehicle;
- Conductor or ticket examiner in a public service vehicle; and
- Workers carried in a goods vehicle.

(iv) Liability in respect of death/injury to passengers who are carried for hire or by reason of or in pursuance of contract of employment.

The insurance of Motor Vehicle against damage is not made compulsory but the insurance of third party liability arising out of the use of motor vehicles in a public place is made compulsory.

Under own damage section of the policy the following risks are covered:

(a) Fire, explosion, self-ignition, or lighting.
(b) Burglary, Housebreaking or theft.
(c) Riot and Strike, Earthquake, Flood, Storm, hailstorm and frost.
(d) Accidental external means, malicious damage, terrorist risk.
(e) Transit by Rail/Road, Inland Waterway, lift, elevator or air.
(f) Landslide/rockslide.

B. Accident Insurance

An accident is an unanticipated event, which brings forth unfortunate consequences. An accident may happen with respect to self, property or where an unanticipated liability is imposed. Accident insurance consists of three kinds of coverage, namely:

- Personal accident insurance, which includes insurance against sickness;
- Property insurance, which covers fidelity insurance, burglary and solvency etc.; and
- Liability insurance.

Personal Accident Insurance

A contract of personal accident insurance is a contract whereby a sum of money is payable to the assured or his legal representative in the event of his disablement or death resultant of an accident. It provides coverage against injury resulting from accident.

Personal accident insurance may be regarded as a variant of life insurance as it provides against loss to persons in case of temporary or permanent injuries or disablement by a cause falling in the category of accident.

A personal accident policy is an annual policy renewable from year to year. Upon the payment of the premium for each year an entirely new contract arises for that year only and the amount payable under it on the accidental death of the assured.

Policies of accident insurance do not cover death due to natural causes. Such policies generally provide for insurance against the event of bodily injury caused by violent accident, external and visible injury which independent of other causes becomes the sole cause of death. For liability of insurer to sustain the injury or death must not only be accidental but also be caused by accidental means.

Property Insurance

The risk insured by property insurance is damage to various types of properties. Specially, it is insurance against financial loss caused by damage, destruction, or loss to property as a result of an identifiable event that is sudden, unexpected or unusual.

The policies of insurance against burglary, house-breaking theft provide for indemnity of damage caused by the specified events. Such policies may be categorized as accident insurance for protection of property. A policy of insurance of such a nature is a contract of strict indemnity; therefore, it is necessary for the assured to establish that he has sustained a loss.

A policy of such nature would exclude damage or loss, which are capable of being covered by any other kind of insurance. For instance, a loss by theft, which follows a fire, may be excluded from coverage in a policy of theft.

Liability Insurance

With liability insurance, the risk insured is litigation, or the risk of law suits against the insured due to actions of the insured or others. Any lawful liability arising out of an incident may take a person by surprise. Liability arises when a defective product is sold; a person is injured by a motor vehicle or where an industrial accident occurs. Liability may be insured. Liability insurance may be prescribed by law or be subscribed voluntarily. Liability insurance hence is a form of accident insurance.

C. Duty Insurance

This policy is normally taken by an importer to cover the payment of actual duty on the imported goods. When imported cargo arrives in India, certain duty is leviable by the custom authorities. This duty can be insured either by including it in the marine cargo policy's sum insured or by purchasing a separate duty policy. It forms a part of Cargo Policies and also agreed value policies but the claim is payable 75% of the assured claim.

D. Erection All Risks Insurance

Erection All Risks (EAR) insurance has become an indispensable part of progress in all industrialized countries. Large projects such as the erection of Thermal Power Stations, Fertilizer Plants, Oil Refineries or the installation of complete factory facilities, bring about many risks for both the contractors and the principal that is only possible to bear these risks in an economical manner by taking out an EAR insurance.

An Erection All Risks Insurance is an insurance on property against accidents resulting in damage to machinery and steel structures while in the normal course of erection or construction.

EAR insurance is a fairly recent branch of engineering insurance, which became popular all over the world. The basic concept of EAR insurance is to offer comprehensive and adequate insurance protecting against all risks involved in the erection of machinery and plant as well as steel structures of any kind. Before EAR insurance was introduced, protection against the main risks arising during erection activities could only be provided by concluding a number of individual policies insurance covering the risks of fire, windstorm, flood, third party liability, theft, burglary, etc. Even after inclusion of numerous covers it was often found that protection offered by these insurance policies were inadequate. In other words, the cover granted by these separate policies did not afford protection against hazard inherent in engineering projects. Further the various insurance covers frequently overlapped so that in the event of a loss the insured was faced with various complications, such as double insurance, subrogation procedure, etc. It must be evident that the total premium to be paid for an erection project under the several policies was quite excessive.

E. Contractor's All Risk Insurance (CAR)

This insurance has been specially designed to protect the interest of civil contractors against the damage to or destruction of various civil engineering projects undertaken by them and includes accidental damage to civil construction work, contractor's plant and machinery at the construction site and damages/defects during the subsequent period of maintenance for which the contractor is liable under the terms of the agreement between the contractor and the principal. All types of civil engineering works ranging from small buildings to massive dams are susceptible to damage by fire, water, storm, impact and internal defects.

It provides an all risks cover, i.e. every hazard is covered unless specifically excluded. This means that any sudden and unforeseen loss or damage occurring during the period of insurance to the property insured on the construction site will be indemnified.

Normally, the CAR insurance policy covers the following perils:

- Fire and lighting;
- Accidental damage during construction, e.g. due to dropping or falling or defective workmanship and material, lack of skill, negligence, malicious act or human error,
- Water damage, flood storm, tempest, inundation, earthquake;
- Collapse, collision, impact;
- Theft and burglary, malicious damage;
- Subsidence, landslide, rockslide.
- Act of terrorism. This policy can be extended to cover third party liability on payment of extra premium.

F. Machinery Breakdown Insurance

Basically, the machinery breakdown insurance was developed to grant industry specific insurance cover for expensive plant, machinery and mechanical equipment.

This Insurance can be taken to cover any type of machinery, plant, mechanical equipment and apparatus whether mobile or stationary which is subject to mechanical or electrical stresses.

Interestingly, Machinery Breakdown Insurance is important for everyone who operates machinery, i.e. not only for large industrial enterprises using large units or fully automated production plants but also equally important for all medium sized and small enterprises where a machinery failure may have serious financial and economic consequences. All types of machinery, plant, mechanical equipment and apparatus may be covered under Machinery Breakdown Insurance, such as for example power generating units (boilers, turbines, generators), power distribution plant (transformers, high and low tension equipment) as well as production machinery and auxiliary equipment (machine tools, weaving looms, paper machines, kneaders pumps, compressors, tanks pipes and tubes, etc.).

G. Product Liability Insurance

This is a variant of liability insurance. It is affected by the manufacturers of products traded commercially when they are susceptible to claims on account of defects in their products. This is a specialized policy for manufacturers' legal liability if defective product arises under the provisions of Consumer Protection Act, 1986.

The product insurance covers legal liability arising out of defective product manufactured. There are two types of limits of liability provided in this policy, namely, any one accident and Any one year ratios of limits can be 1:1, 1:2, 1:3, 1:4. Maximum limit of indemnity under the policy is restricted to Rs. 3.5 crores in any one-year and applies to liability arising within India. This policy can be taken by exporters also. The compulsory excess is 0.5% of any one accident limit but for export to U.S.A. and Canada it is 1% with minimum of Rs. 4000.

H. Refrigeration Plant Insurance

We know that processed food, canned juices, ready to eat preparation can be consumed only when preserved and transported at very low temperatures. Cryogenic preservation of perishable commodities is also an industry. Technical progress and consumer market requirements have led to the increasing storage of stock at low temperature. Technological, chemical and biological know-how are involved in developing cold storage techniques.

Deterioration of stock (DOS) in cold storage insurance was introduced to meet the requirements of those who wanted to insure themselves against deterioration of goods they stored in cold storage, which might arise due to a breakdown of refrigerating machinery. The event resulting in deterioration of stock in cold storage must always be an indemnified breakdown of machinery, i.e. loss of or damage to refrigerating equipment which is covered under machinery breakdown insurance policy. Deterioration of stock in cold storage insurance is therefore regarded as a complement to the cover provided by machinery, breakdown insurance and a DOS Policy can only be taken out in connection with a MB Cover. The policy includes deterioration damage due to refrigerants escaping or leaking as a consequence of an indemnifiable machinery breakdown.

I. Machinery Loss of Profits Policy

On account of rapid industrialization in recent years the machinery that is used has gradually become more and more complex with the result that repairs entail delays and complications. Sometimes when a small but vital part of the machine fails the entire work comes to a stand still and it is essential for the industrialist to insure against such a contingency. It is apparent that machinery breakdown insurance policy to cover the consequential losses that may be suffered by individuals using the machinery following breakdown is necessary. This is because the carrying out of repairs to machinery following breakdown has become not only costly but time taking. Sometimes the time lag between their breakdown and completion of repairs is too long and though the insured may get indemnified full in respect of cost of repairs to his machinery under a machinery breakdown policy yet they will be left unprotected as to the losses consequent upon the breakdown of his machinery. Many a time consequential loss is more than the cost of repairs to machinery. The machinery loss of profits policy covers consequentional loss suffered by insured as an inevitable consequence of breakdown of any machinery or boiler due to an accident.

J. Cash Insurance

Cash insurance policy intends to protect banks and industrial business establishments against loss of money which may be carried by messengers and which may be in transit from one place to another. Cash Insurance is essentially a modified version of burglary insurance. "Cash" unless otherwise stated means current coin, bank and currency notes, cheques, postal orders, and current postage stamps.

K. Business Premises Burglary Insurance

This insurance policy covers contents of business premises against the risk of loss or damage by burglary and house-breaking only. The issue of a separate fire policy must cover fire risk. The property insured is covered only if loss or damage takes place whilst contained in the premises described in the schedule.

The properties which are covered under this policy are:

- Stock in trade (excluding any class of stock specifically insured);
- Goods-in-trust or on commission for which the insured is responsible;
- Fixtures, fittings and utensils in trade; and
- Cash and currency notes secured in locked safe.

This policy excludes the following properties from its cover:

Articles made of gold or silver, watches or jewellery or precious stones or deeds, bonds, bills of exchange, promissory notes, cash, treasury notices and bank notes, cheques, securities for money stamps, stamp collection, books of account, documents of any kind, manuscripts, medals and coins, motor vehicles and accessories or live stock (unless specially mentioned in the policy).

L. Office Protection Insurance

This is a very comprehensive policy that seeks to provide protection to offices against different kinds of risks and perils. By opting for this single policy the office-owner covers the risks his business is likely to encounter, while concentrating on his business activity.

About the suitability of this policy, it may be stated that it is beneficial for large offices owned by big companies as well as small and medium size offices like travel agencies, professionals like chartered accountants, consultants, architects, interior decorators, engineers or any other service provider.

M. Shopkeeper's Insurance Policy

This policy is designed to cover various risks and contingencies faced by small shopkeepers under a single policy. It provides protection for property and interests of the insured and his partners in the shop. The shop premises must conform to specification of Class-A construction as per fire tariff.

The shops where value at risk (including the value of the building if owned the insured) is not exceeding Rs. 10 lacs at any time during the policy year are eligible to buy this policy. The insurers would not permit this policy in case the value of risk is more than Rs. 10 lacs at the time of taking insurance or is likely to exceed this limit any time during the period of insurance.

N. Personal Package Insurance Policy for Executives/Businessmen

This package policy is designed keeping in mind the specific insurance needs of an executive/businessman. The major sections of this policy are as follows:

Section I—Laptop Portable Computer

According to this section of personal package insurance policy for executives the insurer will indemnify the insured in the event of any unforeseen sudden physical loss or damage due to any cause, to the portable computer belonging to the insured and in the personal custody of insured.

Section II—Cellular Phone

In this section, the insurance company will indemnify the insured for the loss of or damage to cellular phone by theft and burglary, fire, lighting explosion, malicious or accidental damage due to external means, earthquake, flood, storm, electrical and mechanical breakdown.

Section III—Loss of Cash

In the event of loss of cash due to accident or misfortune happening when the insured is on official duty or on outstation tour, the insurer will pay to the insured the amount of such loss not exceeding the sum Insured and up to a maximum of Rs. 5,000 during the policy period.

Section IV—Baggage Insurance

In the event of damage to baggage due to accident or misfortune whilst on journey, anywhere in the world, the company will indemnify the insured in respect of such damage up to the actual value at the time of happening of damage but not exceeding the sum insured in any one period of insurance.

Section V—All Risks (Jewellery and Valuables)

The insurer will indemnify the insured in respect of loss or damage to valuables caused by accident or misfortune whilst anywhere in India.

Section VI—Personal Accident Insurance

It provides a scale of benefits for lump sum payment for accidental injuries resulting into various disabilities defined in the policy including transportation of insured's dead body to the place of residence, clothing of the insured due to an accident, reimbursement of ambulance charges.

Section VII—Mediclaim

It provides for reimbursement of hospitalization/domiciliary hospitalization expenses incurred for illness/diseases or injury sustained.

Section VIII—Personal Liability

Under this section, the insurer will indemnify the insured against legal liability in respect of accidental death or injury to a third Party or his property caused by fault or negligence of the insured.

O. Rural Insurance

The various important schemes under rural insurance category are as follows:

Cattle Insurance

This policy is meant for milk cows, milk buffaloes, bullocks, and claves/heifers. It provides risk cover of death due to accident including natural calamities, strikes, riots, and terrorisms. Maximum sum assured cannot be in excess to market value of the cattle concerned.

Sheep and Goat Insurance

This policy covers the risk of death from diseases or accident including natural calamities. Maximum sum assured is limited to the market value.

Camel/Horse/Mule/Pony/Donkey/Yak Insurance

Here the risk covered and the sum assured are similar to that of cattle insurance.

Plantation/Horticulture Insurance

This policy can be issued to cover: Grape, Citrus, Chicoo, Pomegranate, Banana, Rubber, Eucalyptus, Popar, Teak work, Tea, Apple, Oil palm, Betelvine, Floriculture, Kadam and Coconut. The policy shall cover and indemnify the insured to the extent of loss or damage to the insured trees/fruits due to any one or more of these: fire, lightening, storm, hailstorm, cyclone, tempest, tornado, flood, riots and acts of terrorism. Sum insured would be determined on the basis of cost of cultivation. Rate of premium varies from crop to crop. For example, in case of horticulture, it ranges from 1.25 percent to 5 percent of sum assured.

Sericulture (Silkworm) Insurance

Sericulture insurance is applicable to univoltline/bivoltine/multivoltine/pure or hybrid races of mulberry silkworm crops reared by the sericulturists as declared by the farmer/department/agency. Under this scheme, the risk cover commences from the place and time the eggs leave premises of the licensed supplier (grainane) and covers loss by fire, lighting, flood, storm, tempest inundation, earthquake, landslide, rock slide, impact by rail/road/aircraft and riot and strike damage. The insurance will also cover the death of silkworm due to diseases like flachgerie, mascardine, pebrine.

Agriculture Insurance (Cultivation of Beehives)

Honey is a key ingredient in many Ayurvedic formulations. Cultivation of beehives has therefore emerged as a profitable venture with ample scope of monetary benefits. The scheme for providing this insurance cover has been designed taking into consideration the special requirements of this trade. The scheme is applicable to beehives and/or colonies belonging to individuals, co-operative societies and those sponsored and subsidized under various projects or respective state and central government. Bee colonies of Indian Honey bee and Italian Honey bee are covered. A minimum of five bee colonies shall be covered and it shall be compulsory to have hives/colonies together.

The policy provides coverage for total loss, damage to beehives and for bee colonies as a result of fire, flood, inundation, storm, tempest, cyclone, hurricane, tornado. Additional coverage can be extended to loss of beehives and/or colonies due to theft, total loss damage to bee colonies due to specified viral diseases, transit loss during migration of the bee colonies as a result of accident of the vehicle carrying the beehives or crumbling of honey combs or destruction due to summer heat.

Hut Insurance

This insurance applies only to those huts used for dwellings and constructed in rural areas with financial assistance from Banking/Co-operative/Government Institutions. It can also apply to a selected area or cluster of huts for.

The scope of cover of this policy is against loss or damage due to fire, (including fire resulting from explosion and short circulating) lightening, explosion of boiler or gas used for domestic purpose only, earthquake, flood, inundation, stork, tempest, cyclone and other allied perils, riot and strike damage, malicious, damage, aircraft and impact damage.

P. House Holders' Insurance Policy

Householders' Insurance (HHI) policy is designed to cover various risks and contingencies faced by householders under a single policy. It provides protection for property and interests of the insured and his family members who permanently reside with the insured.

Q. Domestic Travel Insurance

A traveler is exposed to risk factors in the course of his travel. This policy provides risk coverage, against accident, emergency expenses, which are incurred on account of events happening during the course of travels.

R. Rajeshwari Mahila Kalyan Bima Yojna

This policy has been designed to provide relief to the family members of insured women in case of their death or disablement arising due to all kinds of accidents and/or death and/or disablement arising out of problems incidental to women only.

S. Special Contingency Policy

Ordinarily, the risks of fire and lighting are covered by the fire department and the other risks such as burglary, accidental external damage, etc. are covered by the accident department of the insurance company. However, to cater to the requirements of clients who desire to have all these risks in respect of their machinery and equipment or any other property covered under a single policy there is a growing tendency on the part of the insurers to issue special contingency policies in the accident department.

The perils normally covered are fire, lighting, burglary and accidental external damage, but other perils can also be covered, if required. It is usual only for machinery and/or equipment to be covered under these policies, but there is no hard and fast rule in this regard and any property can be covered. If the insured property is fragile, an excess is imposed in respect of each and every loss arising from accidental external means.

T. Sports Insurance

This policy assures a comprehensive cover available to amateur sportsmen covering their sporting equipment, personal effect, legal liability and personal accident risks. If desired the cover can also be made available in respect of the named member of insured's family residing with him. This cover is not available to professional sportsmen. The cover is available in respect of any one or more of the following sports: Angling, Badminton, Cricket, Golf, Lawn tennis, Squash, Use of sporting guns.

U. Amartya Siksha Yojana Insurance Policy

This policy offered by the General Insurance Company secures the education of dependent children. If the insured parent/legal guardian shall sustain any bodily injury resulting solely and directly from accident, caused by external violent and visible means and if such injury shall within twelve calendar months of its occurrence be the sole and direct cause of his/her death or permanent total disablement, the insurer shall indemnify the insured student, in respect of all covered expenses to be incurred from the date of occurrence of such accident till the expiry date of policy or completion of the duration of covered course whichever first occurs and such indemnity shall not exceed the sum insured as stated in the policy schedule.

V. Engineering Insurance

Advance Loss of Profits Policy

This policy is also known as delay in start up policy. It covers the loss of profit which will be caused due to non-completion of project in time due to accidental damage to the project material. It is issued on the same lines of Machinery Breakdown Loss of Project Policy but is issued before hand of the actual commencement of the business. The idea of this policy is to safeguard the principal or the owner of the project against the actual loss caused due to delay in commencement of new project under construction. The delay must be caused by direct physical loss mainable under material damage CAR/EAR insurance covering the contract work. Since it is a highly specialized type of policy hence is drafted specifically in every case.

Marine-Cum-Erection (MCE) Policy

Under EAR the risk commences with the delivery of first consignment of machinery at the site of erection. It requires that a separate Marine transit policy has to be taken for imported equipments and Inland policy for indigenous equipments both up to the site of the project. Under Marine-Cum-Erection Policy cover starts from the time the equipments leave the warehouse of manufacturers overseas or within the country and continues during the voyage up to the port of entry, unloading at the port, inland transit to the site of erection, storage and thereafter during erection, testing and finally commissioning.

3.3 CLASSIFICATION OF INSURANCE FROM BUSINESS POINT OF VIEW

From business point of view, insurance can be classified into two broad categories:

A. Life insurance; and
B. General Insurance.

A. Life Insurance

Life insurance may be defined as a contract in which the insurer, in consideration of a certain premium, either in a lump sum or by other periodical payments, agrees to pay to the assured, or to the person for whose benefit the policy is taken, the assured sum of money, on the happening of a specified event contingent on the human life or at the expiry of certain period.

B. General Insurance

General insurance business refers to fire, marine and miscellaneous insurance business whether carried on singly or in combination with one or more of them.

3.4 CLASSIFICATION OF INSURANCE FROM RISK POINT OF VIEW

From risk point of view, insurance can be classified into four categories:

1. Personal insurance;
2. Property insurance;
3. Liability insurance; and
4. Fidelity guarantee insurance.

The description of each is as follows:

1. Personal Insurance

Personal insurance refers the loss to life by accident, or sickness to individual, which is covered by the policy. The insurer undertakes to pay the sum insured on the happening of certain event or on maturity of the period of insurance, and sickness insurance. Life insurance contains the element of investment and protection, while the accidental, sickness or health insurance contains the element of indemnity only.

2. Property Insurance

Contract of property insurance is a contract of indemnity. Proof by the assured of loss is an essential element of property insurance. The policies of insurance against burglary, home breaking or theft, etc. fall under this category. The assured is required to protect the insured property. After the loss has taken place, the assured usually required notifying the police as to losses.

3. Liability Insurance

Liability insurance is the major field of general insurance whereby the insurer promises to pay the damage of property or to compensate the losses to a third party. The amount of compensation is paid directly to third party. The fields of liability insurance include: workmen compensation insurance, third party motor insurance, professional indemnity insurance. There may be various reasons for the arising of liability, viz., accident of a worker at the workplace, defective goods, explosion in the factory during the process of production and formation of poisonous gas within the factory due to the uses of chemicals and other such substances in the manufacturing process.

4. Fidelity Guarantee Insurance

In this type of insurance, the insurer undertakes to indemnify the assured (employer) in consideration of certain premium, for losses arising out of fraud, or embezzlement on the part of the employees. This kind of insurance is frequently adopted as a precautionary measure in cases where new and untrained employees are given position of trust and confidant.

3.5 SUMMARY

A contract of insurance is a device wherein one party in consideration of the price paid to him proportionate to the risk provides security to the other party that he shall not suffer loss damage or prejudice by the happening of certain specified events. Insurance is meant to protect the insured against uncertain events, which may cause disadvantage to him. Insurance may be classified into different categories. The classification of insurance into different categories can be on the basis of nature of insurance, from business point of view and from risk point of view. The subject matter of life insurance is life of the assured. In a life policy the life is covered for a certain amount which is payable on the maturity of the policy or on the death of policy-holder whichever is earlier. General insurance can be categorized according to the uncertainties and events covered by the respective policies.

According to the nature of business, insurance may be classified into— Life insurance, Fire insurance, Marine insurance, Social insurance, and Miscellaneous insurance. From business point of view, insurance can be classified into two broad categories viz., Life insurance and General Insurance. On the other hand, from risk point of view, insurance can be classified into four categories viz., Personal insurance, Property insurance, Liability insurance and Fidelity guarantee insurance.

3.6 REVIEW QUESTIONS

1. Describe the different types of insurance and examine briefly the nature of risks protected by each kind of insurance.
2. What is life insurance? How is it different from fire insurance?
3. Write detailed note on miscellaneous insurances.
4. Explain and illustrate the following:
   (a) Agricultural insurance;
   (b) Health insurance;
   (c) Cash insurance;
   (d) Motor car insurance; and
   (e) Accident insurance.
5. What is marine insurance? Discuss the principles of marine insurance.
6. Discuss briefly, the various insurance schemes covered under rural insurance category.

4

CHAPTER

INSURANCE INTERMEDIARIES

LEARNING OBJECTIVE

The main objective of this chapter is to acquaint the readers about the functions and code of conduct for various insurance intermediaries who bring the insurer and insured together. The training schedule and structure necessary for becoming an agent is also discussed in this chapter.

4.1 INTRODUCTION

Insurance mediators or intermediaries are autonomous populace or firms who carry the insurer and the insured together and act as the mediator. Some groups of intermediaries also act as a distribution channel for bringing the product of the Insurance to the customers as in the case of brokers. An insurance intermediary acts either on behalf of the client or the insurance company. In India, the insurance intermediaries except surveyor were not in existence till 1999 but with liberalization, privatization and globalization (LPG) of insurance sector the distribution channels have also been widened and the IRDA Act, 1999 included the term "Insurance Intermediaries" in the Insurance Act, 1938. Up to 1999, the insurance product was sold either through an Agent or the company directly through Development Officers and the Branch Managers. Prior to 1950, the Chief Agent, Special Agent, and Principle Agent were also in existence but the practice was discontinued after 1950.

In India the insurance intermediaries have been defined in the IRDA Act, 1999 and section 2(1)(f) of the act states:

"Intermediaries or Insurance intermediary includes Insurance brokers, reinsurance brokers, insurance consultants, surveyors and loss assessors."

Though the insurance sector has been privatized the insurers can deal with intermediaries only if they are holding valid license issued by the Authority and the authority has laid down the norms for licensing of intermediaries. Some, which have already been passed by the Parliament and others, which are awaiting clearance, are being discussed in this chapter.

4.2 INSURANCE BROKER

The insurance brokers are such individuals who contribute maximum share of insurance business. A high standard of professional skills and conduct is expected of the broker. The Insurance Broker can be issued license under section 42-D of the Insurance Act, 1938 but the regulations about their qualifications, capital and functions are yet to be passed by the parliament. Though the bill was introduced it was referred to Finance Committee for review before being passed by the Parliament, however, the draft regulations put up in Parliament are discussed in the following paras:

Who can become an Insurance Broker

Any person, may be an individual, a partnership firm or a company formed and registered under the companies Act, 1956 can apply for grant of license to be a broker. (In case of a company the aggregate holding of equity shares by a foreign company either by itself or through its subsidiaries or nominees or persons should be within the prescribed limits laid down by the Reserve Bank of India).

How to Apply

The application is to be sent to the insurance regulatory and development authority in prescribed form and it can be made for any one of the following categories.

Category I

(a) Direct General Insurance Broker, or
(b) Direct Life Insurance Broker.

This means a person who is registered in respect of either general Insurance business or life Insurance business but not for reinsurance business. Such individuals contribute maximum share of business in life insurance.

Category II

Reinsurance Broker, which is different from category one and is also called indirect broker.

Category III

Composite Broker whose functions will consist of both that of Direct Insurance Broker and Reinsurance Broker.

Category IV

Others—Insurance Consultants, Risk Management consultant or any other nomenclature as may be approved by the Authority. Such intermediaries create awareness among the people about the importance of insurance and also provide consultancy as to how to invest in the insurance.

Functions Brokers

The functions of brokers are defined as follows:

1. Obtaining a detailed knowledge of the client's business and philosophy;
2. Maintaining clear records of the client's business so that this can be explained to an insurer and other parties;
3. Provision to the client of technical advice and advice on developments in the insurance market and the law;
4. Maintaining a detailed knowledge of available markets;
5. Selection and recommendation of an insurer or group of insurers;
6. Negotiating with insurers on the client's behalf;
7. Acting promptly on instructions from a client and providing written acknowledgements and progress reports;
8. Collecting and remitting premiums and claims;
9. Where appropriate and dependent on the size of both the client and broker, providing additional services such as Insurance consultancy services, risk management services and uninsured loss recoveries;
10. Assisting in the negotiation of claims;
11. Maintaining precise records of past claims; and
12. Providing services such as Insurance consultancy services, risk management services and uninsured loss recoveries.

4.3 PROCESSING OF APPLICATION FOR BROKERSHIP

While processing the Application for grant of license the Authority will satisfy itself towards the following aspects:

(i) Availability of infrastructure, i.e. adequate office space, equipment and manpower.

(ii) Applicant should have minimum 2 persons in his employment who have the experience to conduct the business of Insurance broker.

(iii) Applicant should have no direct or indirect connection with a person whose application has been rejected earlier.

(iv) Applicant should have a net worth of Rs. 25 lakhs in case of Category I, Rs. 100 lakhs for Category II, Rs. 125 lakhs for Category III, and Rs. 10 lakhs for Category IV.

(v) The Applicant (individual); any partner (in case of firm); Director or Principal Officer (in case of company) should not be a minor; should not be of unsound mind; should not have been found guilty of criminal misappropriation, breach of trust, cheating or forgery or abatement of or attempt to commit such an offence unless five years have elapsed since the completion of the sentence imposed on the applicant.

(vi) The applicant or minimum of two Partners/Directors in a firm and principal officer have a minimum qualification as an Associate of Insurance Institute of India or its equivalent or any other professional qualification recognized by the Government in finance, law, engineering or business management and has undergone theoretical and practical training for a specified period to be conducted by the National Insurance Academy, Pune. However, the Authority may relax the qualification criteria in case of applicants who have been carrying on reinsurance business and/or Insurance consultancy for 10 years or who have sufficient experience of running Insurance business with any insurer but the training as prescribed will be compulsory.

Licensing Procedure

On being satisfied that the applicant is eligible the authority will issue a license in prescribed form and shall send intimation to the applicant mentioning the category for which the license has been given. In case the category awarded to him is not the one he had applied for, the applicant can again apply after one year from the date of grant of license and the authority can grant license for the other category.

On grant of license the applicant will have to pay the fee for the category for which the license has been granted.

Renewal of License

The application for renewal of license in prescribed form should be submitted at least 30 days before the date on which the license ceases to remain in force. If the application for renewal does not reach the authority at least 30 days before the date of expiry of license it may be accepted with payment of late fee of Rs. 100 only. The authority will entertain no application if it reaches after the date of expiry of license but if however it is proved to the satisfaction of the authority that the applicant would suffer undue hardship then it may consider the application for renewal on payment of penalty of Rs. 750.

Payment of Fees

The licensing fee or the renewal fee is to be paid as follows:

First instalment within 15 days from the date of intimation from the authority and subsequent instalments including renewal fee on or before expiry of 12 months from the date of license.

If Fee is Not Paid

If the broker fails to pay the fee within the stipulated period, the Authority may suspend his license and the Insurance Broker shall cease to function as an Insurance broker for the duration of the suspension period. Any person who acts as an insurance broker without holding a license shall be punishable by the Authority with a fine, which may extend to Rs.1 lakh. Where the person is a company or a firm without prejudice to the action taken against the company the Authority can take action against every director, manager, secretary or other officer of the company and every partner of the firm who is knowingly a party to such contravention and shall be punishable with a fine which may extend to Rs. 10,000 each. Any insurer who appoints a broker not licensed by the authority or transacts business in India through such a person shall be punishable by the Authority with a fine, which may extend to Rs. 5 lakhs.

Remuneration to Brokers

Brokers belonging to Category I will be paid brokerage not exceeding 17.5% of the premium payable on the policy. In other categories the market forces will determine the remuneration.

4.4 CODE OF CONDUCT FOR BROKERS

The Code of Conduct is required to establish a recognized standard of professional conduct of which all insurance brokers should, in the interest of the public and in the performance of their duties, conform and in doing so they should bear in mind this objective and the underlying spirit of this Code in the matter of regulation of their professional standard.

Claims against Insurance Broker for compensation arising from acts or omissions amounting to negligence are matters for determination by the Courts. Nevertheless, acts of gross negligence or repeated acts of negligence may amount to unprofessional conduct and notwithstanding that the matters be the subject of legal proceedings, the Authority may still investigate the conduct of the Insurance Brokers. The Code of Conduct will cover the following:

(I) Relationship with Clients

Insurance Brokers must:

- deal with their clients with utmost good faith and truthfulness at all times;
- act with care and meticulousness;
- make sure that the client understands his relationship with the broker and on whose behalf the broker is acting;
- treat all information supplied by the prospective clients as completely confidential to themselves and to the Insurer(s) to which the business is being offered;

- take appropriate steps to maintain the security of confidential documents in their possession;
- understand the type of clients that they are dealing with and the extent of the clients' awareness of risk and Insurance. This knowledge should be taken into account in their dealings with their client, and
- avoid conflicts of interest.

(2) Sales Practices

Insurance Brokers must:

- authenticate that they are members of the Insurance Brokers Association of India (IBAI); as approved by the Authority;
- make out who they are and explain as soon as possible the degree of choice in the products that they are able to offer;
- ensure that the policy proposed is suitable to the needs of the prospective clients;
- offer advice only on those matters in which they are knowledgeable and seek or recommend other specialist advice when necessary;
- not make inaccurate or unfair criticisms of any insurer or IBAI member;
- enlighten why a policy or policies are proposed and provide comparisons in terms of price, cover and/or service where they are able to offer more than one choice of product;
- explain the period for which the quotation remains valid if cover is not affected immediately;
- put in plain words when and how the premium is payable and how it is to be collected. Where another party is financing all or part of the premium, full details should be given to the client including any obligations that the client may owe to that party; and
- clarify the procedures to follow in the event of a complaint.

(3) Duty to Disclose Information

Insurance Broker must:

- make certain that the consequences of non-disclosure and inaccuracies are pointed out to the prospective client;
- stay away from influencing the prospective client and make it clear that all the answers or statements given are the latter's own responsibility. The client should always be asked to check the details of information given;
- appeal their client to make true, fair and complete disclosure where they believe that the client has not done so. If further disclosure is not forthcoming they should consider declining to

act further;

- explain to their clients the importance of disclosing all subsequent changes that might affect the Insurance throughout the duration of the policy; and
- disclose on behalf of their client all material facts within their knowledge and give a fair presentation of the risk.

(4) Explanation of the Contract

Insurance Brokers must:

- categorize the insurer or insurers. Any changes once the contract has commenced must be advised immediately;
- explain all the essential provisions of the cover afforded by the policy(ies), they are recommending so that, as far as possible, the prospective client understands what is being purchased;
- draw attention to any major or unusual restrictions and exclusions in the policy, explain how the contract may be cancelled;
- present the client with prompt written confirmation that Insurance has been effected. If the full wording of the contract is not included with this confirmation, it should be forwarded as soon as possible;
- notify changes to the terms and conditions of any Insurance contract and give reasonable notice before any changes take effect;
- advise their clients of any Insurance proposed on their behalf which will be effected with an insurer outside India and, if appropriate, of the possible risks involved; and
- advise their client that any non-insurance product will not be subject to IBAI and, if appropriate, the implications in terms of consumer redress and solvency.

(5) Renewal Procedures

Insurance Brokers must:

- promise that their clients are aware of the expiry date of the Insurance even if they choose not to offer further cover to the client;
- make certain that renewal notice contains a warning about the duty of disclosure including the necessity to advise changes affecting the policy, which have occurred since the policy inception or the last renewal date;
- ensure that renewal notices contain a warning that the proposer should keep a record (including copies of letters) of all information supplied to the insurer for the purpose of renewal of the contract; and
- assurance that their client always receives the insurer's renewal

invitation (unless they have delegated authority from an Insurer to issue one on their behalf).

(6) Claims

Insurance Brokers must:

- put in plain words to their clients their obligations to notify claims promptly and to disclose all material facts and advise subsequent developments as soon as possible;
- request their clients to make true, fair and complete disclosure where they believe that the client has not done so. If further disclosure is not forthcoming they should consider declining to act further for the client;
- give prompt advice to the client of any requirements concerning the claim;
- forward any information received from the client regarding a claim or an incident that may give rise to a claim without delay, and in any event within three working days; and
- inform the client without delay of the insurer's decision or otherwise of a claim; and on request give all reasonable assistance to a client in pursuing his claim.

(7) Complaints

Insurance Brokers must:

- ascertain that letters of instructions, policies and renewal documents contain details of complaints handling procedures;
- accept complaints either by phone or in writing;
- acknowledge a complaint not later than 14 days from the receipt of correspondence; advise the member of staff who will be dealing with the complaint and the timetable for dealing with it;
- ensure that response letters inform the complainant of what they should do if they are unhappy with the response;
- ensure that they have a procedure so that complaints are dealt with at a suitably senior level; and
- have in place a system for recording and monitoring complaints.

(8) Documentation

Insurance Brokers must:

- make sure that any documents issued by them comply with all statutory or regulatory requirements from time to time in force;
- send policy documents without avoidable delay;
- make available, with policy documentation, advice that the documentation should be read carefully and retained by the client;

- not withhold documentation from their clients without their consent, unless adequate and justifiable reasons are disclosed in writing and without delay to the client. Where documentation is withheld, the client must still receive full details of the Insurance contract;
- acknowledge receipt of all money received in connection with an Insurance policy;
- ensure that they reply promptly or use their best endeavours to obtain a prompt reply to all correspondence;
- ensure that all written terms and conditions are fair in substance and set out clearly and in plain language client's right and responsibilities; and
- subject to the payment of any monies owed to them, make available to any new Insurance Broker instructed by the client all documentation to which the client is entitled and which is necessary for the new Insurance Broker to act on behalf of the client.

(9) Handling Client's/Insurer's Money

Insurance Brokers must:

- make certain that the moneys belonging to clients or insurers are not mixed with their/his own;
- separate accounts are properly maintained in regard to those amounts and proper information is periodically made to the client/insurer;
- ensure that these moneys are banked in a proper manner;
- ensure that moneys belonging to others are kept with them for a reasonable period only; and
- ensure strict compliance of the provisions of regulation 17 (i.e. Segregation of Insurance moneys).

(10) Advertising

Insurance Brokers must:

- undertaking that statements made when advertising are not misleading or extravagant;
- where appropriate, distinguish between contractual benefits, which the Insurance is bound to provide, and non-contractual benefits which may be provided;
- ensure that advertisements shall not be restricted to the policies of one insurer except where the reasons for such restrictions are fully explained with the prior approval of that insurer obtained;
- ensure that advertisements should contain nothing which is in breach of the law nor omit anything which the law requires;
- ensure that advertisements should not encourage or condone

defiance or breach of the law;

- ensure that advertisements should contain nothing which is likely, in the light of generally prevailing standards of decency and propriety, to cause grave or widespread offence or to cause disharmony;
- ensure that advertisements should not be so framed as to abuse the trust of client or exploit their lack of experience or knowledge; and
- ensure that all descriptions, claims and comparisons which relate to matters of objectively ascertainable fact should be capable of substantiation

(11) Remuneration

Insurance Brokers must:

- reveal all fees or charges (not commission) they propose to charge the client, which will be in addition to the insurance premium. Score back of commission will be considered as a charge for these purposes;
- recommend the client in writing of the Insurance premium and any fees or charges separately and the purpose of any related services;
- if requested by a client, disclose the amount of their commission or other remuneration they receive as a result of effecting Insurance for that client. This will include any payment received as a result of securing on behalf of the client any service additional to the arrangement of the contract of Insurance; and
- advice their clients prior to effecting the Insurance of their intention to make any deductions from the amount of claim collected for a client where this is a recognized practice for the type of Insurance concerned.

(12) Competence and Training

Insurance Brokers must:

- make certain that their staff are aware of and adhere to the standards expected of them by this Code;
- make sure that staff are competent, suitable and have been given the necessary training as required by the Authority;
- ensure that there is a system in place to monitor the quality of advice given by their staff; and
- ensure that members of staff are aware of legal requirements including the law of agency affecting their activities; and only handle classes of business in which they are competent and/or are licensed by the Authority.

(13) Display on the Notice Board

Insurance Brokers must:

- display in any office where they are carrying on business and to which the public have access a notice to the effect that a copy of the Code of Conduct is available upon request and that if a member of the public wishes to make a complaint and requires the assistance of the Authority in resolving a dispute, he may write to the Authority;
- an Insurance Broker as described in these regulations under categories IA and IB, II, III and IV above shall not act as an Insurance Agent of any Insurer under regulation 42 of Insurance Act, 1938; and
- Insurance Brokers shall abide by the provisions of the Insurance Act, 1938, IRDA Act, 1999, rules and regulations made thereunder which might be applicable and relevant to the activities carried on by them as Insurance Brokers.

4.5 INSURANCE AGENTS

The business of insuring people against perils is done by insurance companies whose main business is to club people sharing the same risk, collect the share of contribution from all of them, and then pay out the compensation to the sufferers. The business of insurance companies both life and non-life is procured through an individual who is appointed as an agent. An agent is a person licensed by the IRDA to do insurance business. Agents are not the regular employees of the insurer; they work on commission basis in a freelance manner. There are some qualifications and procedural formalities, which have to be fulfilled for grant of a license of agent.

All agents, in order to obtain a license, have to go through a training programme and appear for an examination. The purpose of licensing course is designed to prepare an individual to work as an insurance agent. It provides a foundation of knowledge, terminology, and concepts upon which an individual can build a successful career as an agent.

Common Licensing Provisions

Evidence of all of the following have to be made available to the authority before registration as an agent:

1. Section 42(4) of the amended Insurance Act, 1938 states an agent to be one who is not:
   (a) A minor;
   (b) Found to be of unsound mind by a court of competent jurisdiction;
   (c) Found guilty of criminal misappropriation or criminal breach

of trust or cheating or forgery or an abetment of or attempt to commit such offence by a court of competent jurisdiction; and

(d) Found guilty of having knowingly participated in or connived at any fraud, dishonesty or misrepresentation against an insurer or an insured.

2. And who:-

(a) possesses a pass in 12th standard (reduced to 10th standard for rural agents);

(b) has been trained for a minimum period of four weeks; and

(c) has a pass in an examination prescribed by the Authority.

The expectations from an agent are:

- Agent should offer consumers good service by responding to customer's needs in terms of grant of cover, advice, conduct, etc.
- Agent should be willing to promote products in personal lines market making the best use of their professional ability

Need of Agent's Training

Agents are provided training to:

(a) Instruct him (her) complete knowledge of products;

(b) Imbibe in him (her) the importance of Pre-and-Post sale service to customers;

(c) Equip him (her) as a trusted professional capable of advising persons on "Insurance";

(d) Make him (her) as an efficient salesperson;

(e) Enable him (her) to master various techniques in the area of sale of insurance products; and

(f) Instill in him (her) an ethical code which will inform all his (her) dealings.

Training Schedule and Structure

I. Training Modus Operandi

(i) The classroom training may be by means of lectures, discussions, speeches/seminars, question-answer sessions, case studies, role playing, exchange of experiences, team training, replication of real life situation in the classroom, open house, self-study, etc.

(ii) The use of various audio-visual devices while taking the lectures like slides, overhead projectors, computers, markers, etc. may be encouraged

(iii) The training institute may ask the faculty to give handouts/written material on the proposed lecture to the participants in advance.

(iv) The training institute will arrange to supply every agent an agents manual, service manual, list of all the products available in the market, a handbook containing specimen copies of proposal form, policy form, claim form, etc. from the insurance company who has nominated the agent for the training course.

2. *Examinations for Agents*

(i) All agents on completion of their training will have to appear in a written examination.
(ii) The exam will consist of objective type questions only.
(iii) The exam will be of maximum 100 marks.
(iv) The time for examination will be 2 hours.
(v) 10% of Questions will be numerical.
(vi) This will be followed by an interview of 25 marks, conducted by the insurance company.
(vii) Every agent will have to score at least 50% marks in the written exam and 60% in the interview for qualifying in the agent's examination and for award of a certificate.

3. *Practical Training*

(i) Every person aspiring to take up agency as a career will have to undergo on the job practical training with the designated company where he will work under the supervision of a sales functionary.
(ii) The sales functionary will teach the trainee the nuances of creating the need in the mind of the customer, understanding the wants of the clients, proposing 2 or 3 solutions for satisfying the want and finally helping him decide the best option and closing the deal.
(iii) In addition, administrative matters, documentation, etc. will also be taught to the trainee.

The syllabus for examination for agents in life insurance and non-life insurance is given hereunder:

Syllabus for Agent Training—Life Insurance

1. *Introduction to Insurance*

(a) Purpose and Need of Insurance.
(b) Insurance as a social security tool.
(c) Role of Insurance in the development of economy.
(d) Pooling of risks and resources.

2. *Fundamentals of Agency Law*

(a) Agency Law including definition of who is an agent, what are his functions, who can become an agent, the kind of business he can procure, etc.
(b) Agents' Regulations.
(c) Contract Act.
(d) Various intermediaries in the insurance market—agents, brokers, surveyors, consultants, etc.
(e) Difference between an agent, a broker, and other intermediaries.
(f) Methods of remunerating the agent.

3. *Leguskatuve and Regulatory Matters*

(a) Insurance Act, 1938.
(b) LIC Act, 1956.
(c) Insurance Regulatory and Development Authority Act, 1999.
(d) Consumer Protection Act, 1986.
(e) Ombudsman Scheme.
(f) Various other Acts such as Income Tax Act, etc. connected with conduct of Life Insurance Business.
(g) Code of conduct in Advertisement and Publicity areas.

4. *Procedure for Becoming an Agent*

(a) Pre-requisite for obtaining a license.
(b) Insurance company sponsorship.
(c) Obtaining a license—minimum age, educational qualification, practical training.
(d) Maintenance and Duration of license.
(e) Termination of License: revocation or suspension/termination of appointment.
(f) Unfair Practices: Rebates; Prohibited Inducements and Discrimination; twisting and poaching, Misrepresentations and incomplete comparison; False statements regarding insurance companies' financial condition.

5. *Functions of the Agent*

(a) Proposal Form and other forms for grant of cover.
(b) All material and relevant information.
(c) Financial and medical underwriting.
(d) Family history, medical examination, special medical reports, etc.
(e) Admission of Age.
(f) Special reports, Moral Hazard report, etc.
(g) Advance payment of premium before acceptance of the risk: Sec.

64VB of the Insurance Act.

(h) Ensuring delivery of policy to the insured.
(i) Revivals.
(j) Nomination and Assignment.
(k) Procedure regarding settlement of benefits.

6. *Company Profile*

(a) Organizational Set-up of the company.
(b) Corporate Mission.
(c) Strengths of the company.
(d) Market Share.
(e) Product details.
(f) Promotion Strategy.
(g) The Actuarial Profession—Role in life insurance companies.
(h) Product Pricing—Actuarial aspects.
(i) Distribution Channels which the insurer has—other distribution channels—their relative merits and demerits.
(j) Hierarchical structure for agents—Trainee Agent, Junior/Senior Agent, etc.

7. *Fundamentals/Principles of Life Insurance*

(a) Utmost Good Faith.
(b) Insurable Interest.
(c) Pooling of similar risks.

8. *Financial Planning and Taxation*

(a) Trends in Financial Services Market.
(b) Other Savings Instruments like shares, units, capital markets, mutual funds, etc. *vis-a-vis* insurance.
(c) Tax benefits under insurance policies.
(d) Life cycle—Needs.
(e) Solutions—Matching of the customers' needs and requirements to that of the products available.
(f) Comparison between different products offered *vis-a-vis* premium chargeable, coverage, etc.

9. *Insurance Salesmanship: Selling Techniques*

(a) Salesmanship—An Introduction.
(b) Selling Process.
(c) Pre-Approach.
(d) Interview.
(e) Objection.

(f) Closing.
(g) Service.
(h) Consumer Education.

10. Computation of Premiums/Bonuses

(a) Use of premium table in calculating premiums.
(b) Premium rebates—mode rebates, large sum assured policies rebate.
(c) Computation of premium, extra premium, rider premiums.
(d) Computation of benefits—Surrender Value, Paid up Value, etc.

11 Insurance Documents

(a) Proposal Forms and other relevant forms.
(b) First Premium Receipt/Renewal Premium Receipt.
(c) Policy Contract.
(d) Endorsements.
(e) Renewal Notice/Bonus notices.
(f) Other Insurance Documents related to insurance.

12. Life Insurance Products

(a) Traditional/Unit Linked policies.
(b) Individual and Group Policies.
(c) With Profit and Without Profit Policies.
(d) Different types of insurance products—whole life products, Interest sensitive products, Term, Annuities, Endowment, Combination plans and variations.
(e) Policies for Females, Children, Physically Handicapped.

13. Options, Guarantees and Riders

(a) Policy riders.
(b) Policy options.
(c) Policy guarantees.

14. Group Insurance and Superannuation Schemes/Pension Plans

(a) Special legal/other Features of group Insurance/Superannuation schemes.
(b) Group insurance schemes—Employees' Deposit Linked Scheme (EDLI) and Non-EDLI Schemes.
(c) Gratuity schemes.
(d) Superannuation Schemes—Money purchase and Defined benefit Schemes.

(e) Savings linked insurance policies
(f) Group annuity Schemes.
(g) Voluntary Retirement Schemes.

15 Health Insurance

(a) Critical Illness/Dreaded Disease Plans.
(b) Health Insurance riders.
(c) Permanent Health Insurance.
(d) Notification of claim, doctor's report, claim form, payment of claims.

16. Government Schemes/Programmes on Insurance

(a) Details of different Government insurance schemes.
(b) Subsidy provided by the Government for underwriting the schemes—SSGS, RGLIS, IRDP Scheme.

17. Rural Insurance

(a) Definition of rural area.
(b) Rural Insurance Schemes—SSGS, RGLIS, IRDP Scheme.
(c) Targets in terms of total premium which should be completed by the agent.
(d) Penalties for not meeting the laid down stipulations.
(e) Special skills to market rural insurance schemes.
(f) Details of schemes specially designed for the rural areas.

18. Claims

(a) Intimation Procedure.
(b) Claims Documents—Forms.
(c) Settlement Procedures.

19. Agency Commission Structure

20. Personal Development

(a) Personal Business Goals—Understanding the competition and enhancing time management skills, future prospects within the company.
(b) Marketing and Sales opportunities—Identify target markets and build relationship skills in the total planning sale.
(c) Target Marketing—Develop the prospect customer's profile and focus on new profitable target markets.
(d) Review the expanding market of aging adults.

(e) Business Continuity—Emphasis on retaining the client by providing him upto date information on the changes taking place, the benefits that he may enjoy because of changes in rules/regulations/change in company policy, sending out renewal notices, etc.

21. Behavioural Aspects

(a) Motivation.
(b) Morale.
(c) Communication Skills.
(d) Persuasive Skills.
(e) Analytical Ability.
(f) Behaviour with other Agents/Employees of Insurer.

22. Feedback to Companies on Customer's Requirements with Regard to their Insurance needs and Miscellaneous Matters

(a) New requirements of the customers.
(b) Modifications on the coverage, rates, etc. of the customers.
(c) Code of conduct laid down by IRDA.
(d) Penalties.
(e) Dispute resolution forum set-up by IRDA for adjudication of disputes between the Agent and customer/insurer.
(f) Feedback to IRDA on the nature of disputes and methods of resolution.

Syllabus for Agent Training—Non-Life Insurance

I. Introduction to Insurance

1. Purpose and Need of Insurance.
2. Insurance as a social security tool.
3. Role of Insurance in the development of economy.
4. Pooling of risks and resources, spread of risks.

2. Fundamentals of Agency Law

1. Agency Law including definition of who is an agent, what are his functions, who can become an agent, the kind of business he can procure, etc.
2. Agent's Regulations.
3. Contract Act.
4. Various intermediaries in the insurance market—agents, brokers, surveyors, consultants, etc.

5. Difference between and agent and a broker and other intermediaries.
6. Methods of remunerating the agent.

3. *Legislative and Regulatory Matters*

1. Insurance Act, 1938.
2. Marine Insurance Act, 1963.
3. General Insurance Business Nationalisation Act, 1972.
4. Insurance Regulatory and Development Authority Act, 1999.
5. Carriers Act, 1865.
6. Indian Stamp Act, 1899.
7. Public Liability Insurance Act, 1991.
8. Motor Vehicles Act, 1988.
9. Consumer Protection Act, 1986 and Ombudsman Scheme.
10. Workmen's Compensation Act, 1923.
11. Sale of Goods Act, 1930.

4. *Procedure for Becoming an Agent*

1. Pre-requisite for obtaining a license.
2. Insurance company sponsorship.
3. Obtaining a licence-minimum age, educational qualification, practical training.
4. Maintenance and Duration of license.
5. Termination of License: Revocation or Suspension/Termination of Appointment.
6. Unfair Practices: Rebates; Prohibited Inducements and Discrimination; Misrepresentations and incomplete comparison; False statements regarding insurance companies financial condition.

5. *Functions of the Agent*

1. Proposal Form and other forms of grant of cover.
2. Gathering all material and relevant information to the risk including signature of the customer on the proposal form.
3. Explaining the terms, conditions, coverages, exclusions under the policy.
4. Advance payment of premium before acceptance of the risk: Sec. 64VB of Insurance Act, 1938.
5. Ensuring delivery of policy to the insured.
6. Helping the customer in lodging the claim and completing all formalities.

6. *Company Profile*

1. Organizational Set-up of the company.
2. Corporate Mission.
3. Strengths of the company.
4. Market Share.
5. Product details.
6. Promotion Strategy.
7. Product Pricing.
8. Distribution Channels available with insurer—their relative merits and demerits.

7. *Fundamentals/Principles of General Insurance*

1. Utmost Good Faith.
2. Indemnity.
3. Insurable Interest.
4. Subrogation.
5. Contribution.
6. Proximate Cause.

8. *Financial Planning and Taxation*

1. Premium rates charged in policies.
2. Tax benefits under selected insurance policies.
3. Comparison between different products offered by various insurers *vis-a-vis* premium chargeable, coverages, etc.

9. *Insurance Salesmanship: Selling Techniques*

1. Salesmanship—An Introduction.
2. Selling Process.
3. Pre-Approach.
4. Interview.
5. Objection.
6. Closing.
7. Service.
8. Consumer Education.

10. *Proper Use of General Insurance Products*

1. Products available in the general insurance market.
2. Scope of coverage some of the important policies.
3. Matching of the customer's needs and requirements to that of the products available.
4. Code of Advertisement and Publicity.

11. Rating

1. Tariffs.
2. Basis of Rate Making.
3. Market Agreements.
4. Importance of Data Base.
5. Role of TAC.

12. Insurance Documents

1. Insurance Forms.
2. Proposal Forms.
3. Cover Notes.
4. Certificate of Insurance.
5. Policy Forms.
6. Endorsements.
7. Renewal Notice.
8. Other Insurance Documents related to insurance.

13. Underwriting

1. Fire Policies: Scope; Coverage; Exclusions; Conditions; Premium.
2. Marine Policies: Scope; Coverage; Exclusions; Conditions; Premium.
3. Miscellaneous Policies: Scope; Coverage; Exclusions; Conditions; Premium.
4. Motor Policies: Scope; Coverage; Exclusions; Conditions; Premium.
5. Engineering Policies: Scope; Coverage; Exclusions; Conditions; Premium.
6. Basis of fixing the sum insured under different policies.
7. Discount, Loadings, etc.
8. Management of Risks.

14. Health Insurance

1. Long Term/Short-Term Policies.
2. Annual Policies.
3. Unit Linked Policies.
4. Post-Retirement (Bhavishya Arogya) Type plans.
5. Group Medical Insurance Schemes.
6. Basic Hospital, Medical and Surgical Policies.
7. Coverages, Exclusions, Premium, Cumulative Bonus.
8. Time limit on certain defences, reinstatement, Grace period for renewal.
9. Pre-existing disease clause, maternity benefit.

10. Notification of claim, doctor's report, claim form, payment of claims.

15. Government Schemes/Programmes on Insurance

1. Details of different Government insurance schemes like Crop insurance, PASS, Landless Agricultural Scheme, Solatium Fund.
2. Subsidy provided by the Government for underwriting the schemes.

16. Rural Insurance

1. Definition of rural areas.
2. Rural Insurance Schemes.
3. Targets in terms of total premium, which should be completed by the agent.
4. Penalties for not meeting the laid down stipulations.
5. Special skills to market rural insurance schemes.
6. Details of Schemes specially designed for the rural areas.

17. Claims

1. Preliminary Procedure.
2. Investigation and Assessment.
3. Surveyors and Loss Assessors.
4. Claim Documents.
5. Arbitration.
6. Limitation.
7. Settlement.
8. Loss Minimization and Salvage.

18. Provisions and Differences in Policy Contracts

1. Important differences to be highlighted.
2. Difference between Breach of Warranty and Condition.
3. Endorsement.
4. Drafting of a Cover Note.

19. Agency Commission Structure

20. Personal Development

1. Personal Business Goals—Understanding the competition and enhancing time management skills.
2. Marketing and Sales opportunities—Identify target markets and build relationship skills in the total planning sale.

3. Target Marketing—Develop the prospect customer's profile and focus on new profitable target markets.
4. Review the expanding market of aging adults.
5. Business Continuity—Emphasis on retaining the client by. providing him up to date information on the changes taking place, the benefits that he may enjoy because of changes in rules/regulations/change in company policy, sending out renewal notices, etc.

21. Behavioural Aspects

1. Motivation.
2. Morale.
3. Communication Skills.
4. Persuasive Skills.
5. Analytical Ability.

22. Feedback to Companies on Customer's Requirements with Regard to their Insurance needs and Miscellaneous Matters

1. New requirements of the customers.
2. Modifications on the coverages, rates, etc. of the customers
3. Code of conduct laid down by IRDA.
4. Penalties.
5. Dispute resolution forum set-up by IRDA for adjudication of disputes between the Agent and customer/insurer.
6. Feedback to IRDA on the nature of disputes and methods of resolution.

4.6 SURVEYOR AND LOSS ASSESSORS

This category of intermediaries is related to only non-life business. Their main functions are to survey and assess any mis-happening or disaster and evaluate the financial loss to the insurance companies. The insurance companies make financial assistance on the basis of the evaluation made surveyor. More specifically, the functions of any Surveyor and Loss Assessor will be as follows:

- Conduct inspection, re-inspection, pre-inspection of the property in question suffering a loss;
- Examine, inquire, investigate, verify and check upon the causes and the circumstances of the loss in question including their nature and extent of loss and related factors/documents;
- Estimate—measure—determine: the quantum—description—valuation of the subject under loss;
- Initiate immediate measures to protect damage property and to

prevent aggravation of losses;

- Advise the insurer and the insured about the loss minimization, loss control, security, and safety measures, where appropriate to avoid further losses;
- Check the admissibility of the loss whether it falls within the scope of the policy contract, to point out about the adequacy or inadequacy of the sum insured, and whether the amount claimed are: fair, reasonable and necessary;
- Survey and assess the loss on behalf of insurer or insuring public;
- Recommend the net liability in terms of insurance contract;
- Point out the discrepancy, if any, and the aspects, which the policyholders might have over-looked;
- Advise on repair and replacement techniques;
- Checking the ownership—insurable interest—indemnity-related proofs;
- Declare whether the surveyor/loss assessor has an interest in the subject matter in question or whether it pertains to any blood relation, business partners or through shareholding, and if so refrain from carrying out the survey and loss assessment in that respect;
- Conduct himself within professional code of conduct while discharging the services, maintain the confidentiality and the independent-neutral position without: bias, prejudice, and without jeopardizing the liability of the insurer and claim of the insured;
- Perform balancing act to represent the best interests of all parties concerned in the event of a claim and determine the liability of the insurer, obtain necessary statements, documents for the purposes of preserving the recovery and legal rights of the insurer;
- Satisfy queries of the insured/insurer and of persons incidental thereto in respect of the loss/claim;
- Conduct: spot survey—interim survey—preliminary survey—final survey—joint survey, etc. as and when called for;
- Accord approval—consent before actually carrying out the repairs as well as loss minimization and damage control measures;
- Render assistance to inquiries of average Assessors and also to other: civil, Government, and Court agencies if there is any investigation or the litigation in respect of subject matter of loss in which he has rendered the services;
- Discuss various matters connected with the loss with the insured and the insurer as well as other connected persons such as repairers;
- Comment upon the franchise, excess, under insurance, co-insurance, double insurance;
- Report on the financial loss of the damage suffered by the insured to the insurer. The reporting must be intelligently communicated,

so that, adequate information and the supporting documents and statements satisfy beyond doubt that the recommendations are substantiated and that he has thoroughly discharged his duties expected of him;

- Recommend about the applicable depreciation and the basis on which a particular amount of depreciation has been arrived at;
- Report about unfair claim handling practices, observed during discharge of duties;
- Comment on duties of the insured after the loss and their compliance by him;
- Comment at the circumstances leading to abandonment by the insured;
- Preserve the evidences with relation to loss and comment on the circumstances showing that the burden of proof has been discharged by the person concerned;
- Comment any happening in the process of discharge of duties if it is against the law of the land;
- Recommend about the total loss, partial loss, constructive total loss, whether the subject in question is repairable or beyond repairs, or replaceable, and other alternative choices for indemnification;
- Comment whether the claim is worth repudiation and the grounds thereof;
- State that there has been no professional negligence in discharge of the service;
- Comment the steps which will ensure complete discharge of insurers' liability in the claim in question;
- Obtain a certificate of consent/satisfaction about the settlement of the claim from the insured and in absence thereof releases its report with reasonable grounds at his end and report about the controversies;
- Report about the damages to the Third Parties and the properties which are not parties to the contract of insurance;
- Take expert opinion, if required;
- Adjust the loss, after it is assessed, taking into account: the policy conditions, exclusions and other factors, e.g. customs duty, usage of items, expenses for which others may be responsible and salvage position;
- Scrutinize and identify the property under loss with the property insured under the contract;
- Comment about the salvage realization efforts; and
- Recommend about the part payment, i.e. on account payment.

Eligibility for becoming Surveyor

Any person who holds any of the following qualifications can become a Surveyor and Loss Assessor:

1. Degree of a recognized university in any branch of Engineering;
2. Fellow or Associate member of Institute of Chartered Accountants of India or Institute of Cost Works Accountants of India;
3. Actuarial qualifications or holds a degree or diploma of any recognized university or institute in relation to insurance; and
4. Holds a Diploma in insurance granted or recognized by the Government.

Modus Operandi for License

Any person possessing the abovementioned conditions can apply to the Insurance Authority in a prescribed format provided he is not disqualified on the following grounds:

1. That a person is minor;
2. That he is found to be unsound mind by a court of competent jurisdiction;
3. That he has been found guilty of criminal misappropriation or criminal breach of trust or cheating or forgery or an abetment of or attempt to commit any such offence by a Court of competent jurisdiction; and
4. That he does not poses the requisite qualifications and practical training for a period not exceeding twelve months.

4.7 CODE OF CONDUCT FOR SURVEYOR AND LOSS ASSESSORS

Like the brokers and agents, every surveyor and loss assessor including the Company/Firm of Surveyor and Loss Assessors shall abide by the code of conduct specified by the Authority from time to time. In particular and without prejudice to the generality of the foregoing the code of conduct shall include the following:

(a) To exhibit the identity card and/or the license issued by the Authority while carrying out the job of survey and loss assessment and be physically fit to undertake the rigorous of the job.

(b) To conduct the survey job in a manner and behaviour which is transparent, honest, sincere, fair, objective and free from personal interest and ensure that the professional, technical standards of competence are upheld.

(c) To endeavor to keep abreast with professional standards and advancements by attending professional courses, trainings, seminars, and workshops meant for upgrading the required skills.

(d) To uphold not only ethical behaviour but professional reputation and credibility while refraining from making remarks, comments or grievances in the public or to the press without exhausting internal professional and legal avenues.

(e) No Surveyor and Loss Assessor shall agree or take the work of survey and loss assessment where he or his family members are interested through shareholding or employment or business dealings.

(f) No Surveyor and Loss Assessor shall act as an insurer or an insurance agent or a insurance broker or an insurance consultant, owner or partner or otherwise connected with motor garage or workshop taking accidental jobs and be an employee or Director of any of these.

(g) Not to advertise or solicit directly or indirectly or through middlemen for work or receive remuneration from both insured and insurer simultaneously for the same work or seek any discount or trade commission or favour in connection with the discharge of professional work.

(h) Not to share and exchange with others the confidentiality of the information of the insured and insurer or other parties connected with the job, which is gained by him during the course of discharge of duties.

(i) Not to render professional services as a second surveyor for re-survey/reassessment unless and until it is called by the instructions of the Authority or its Designated Officer or by an insurer with specific written terms of reference to do so. The intimation and information of such jobs rendered must be furnished to the Surveyors and Loss Assessors' Committee

(j) To issue survey and loss assessment report including the annexures duly signed and stamped after due verification and satisfaction.

(k) Every licensed surveyor and loss assessor shall provide practical training to any aspiring applicant for the period not less applicant. The certificate issued on completion of training shall be in the form and manner specified by the Authority. The refusal to do so shall be deemed as misconduct unless and until the refusal is with valid and cogent reasons to the satisfaction of the Authority.

(l) To maintain a register of survey work containing the relevant information as specified in the prescribed form and keep important records of the survey reports, photographs and other important documents for a period of six years and furnish the same and such other specified returns as and when called for by the Authority or by any investigating authority or the insurer.

(m) Not to allow the use of his name, license number to any other person or lend his survey reports and other documents for direct or indirect use by the said person or to any other licensed surveyors whether for consideration or reward or for any other purpose.

(n) Not to suppress any material fact known to him in his capacity as a surveyor and loss assessor but disclose all the relevant facts and figures known to him in conduct of the survey and loss assessment work. The disclosures should be conducive to the purpose of loss assessment and not misleading or negligent in any form and manner in the conduct of professional duties.

(o) Any conduct of surveyor and loss assessor which is not: professional, proper, right, efficient, good behaviour, efficient or contains deliberate disobedience, unlawful behaviour, neglect of duty, conduct amiss, malfeasance, will include among other matters to be misconduct and violative of the code of conduct. The Authority, before imposing any penalty, fine or suspension or cancellation of a licence because of misconduct shall cause an enquiry and provide reasonable opportunity to the licence-holder of being heard.

4.8 THIRD PARTY ADMINISTRATORS—HEALTH SERVICES

A Third Party Administrator (TPA) means who, for the time being, is licensed by the Authority, and is engaged, for a fee or remuneration, by whatever name called as may be specified in the agreement with an insurance company, for the provision of health services:

"Health Services" means all the services to be rendered by a TPA under an agreement with an insurance company in connection with "health insurance business" or 'health cover' as defined in regulation 2(f) of the IRDA (Registration of Indian Insurance Companies) Regulations, 2000, but does not include the business of an insurance company or the soliciting, directly or through an insurance intermediary including an insurance agent, of insurance business.

Conditions of and Procedure for Licensing of TPA

The following conditions must be fulfilled for getting licensing of PTA:

(1) Only a company with a share capital and registered under the Companies Act, 1956 can function as a TPA.

(2) The main or primary object of the company shall be to carry on business in India as a TPA in the health services, and on being licensed by the Authority, the company shall not engage itself in any other business.

(3) He shall not be:

(a) A person of unsound mind;

(b) An undischarged insolvent; and

(c) A person who had been subjected to a term of imprisonment for a period of three months by a court of competent jurisdiction on grounds of misconduct, misfeasance, forgery, etc.

(4) The qualifications referred to in sub-regulation (2) are:

(a) A degree in arts, science or commerce or management or health or hospital administration or medicine; and
(b) A pass in the Associateship examination conducted by the Insurance Institute of India or such equivalent examination as may be recognised by the Authority and notified from time to time; and
(c) Completion of practical training, as may be specified by the Authority, not exceeding one hundred hours with an institution recognized by the Authority, for these purposes, from time to time.

The Authority may grant, on an application made to it, by the CAO or CEO through the TPA, time not exceeding twenty four months from the date of the coming into force of these regulations for fulfilling the qualification, requirements as stated in sub-clauses (2) and (3) of this sub-regulation.

4.9 CODE OF CONDUCT FOR TPA

A third party administrator licensed under insurance regulations shall act in the best professional manner as underlined in the lisense. In particular and without prejudice to the generality of the provisions contained above, it shall be the duty of every TPA, its Chief Administrative Officer or Chief Executive Officer and its employees or representatives to:

(a) Ascertain its identity to the public and the insured/policy-holder and that of the insurance company with which it has entered into an agreement;
(b) Make known its license to the insured/policy-holder/prospect.
(c) Disclose the details of the services it is authorized to render in respect of health insurance products under an agreement with an insurance company;
(d) Bring to the notice of the insurance company with whom it has an agreement, any adverse report or inconsistencies or any material fact that is relevant for the insurance company's business;
(e) Obtain all the requisite documents pertaining to the examination of an insurance claim arising out of insurance contract concluded by the insurance company with the insured/policy-holder;
(f) Render necessary assistance specified under the agreement and advice to policyholders or claimants or beneficiaries in complying with the requirements for settlement of claims with the insurance company;
(g) Conduct itself/himself in a courteous and professional manner;
(h) Refrain from acting in a manner, which may influence directly or indirectly insured/policy-holder of a particular insurance company to shift the insurance portfolio from the existing

insurance company to another insurance company;

(i) Refrain from trading on information and the records of its business;

(j) Maintain the confidentiality of the data collected by it in the course of its agreement;

(k) Refrain from resorting to advertisements of its business or the services carried out by it on behalf of a particular insurance company, without the prior written approval by the insurance company;

(l) Abstain from inducing an insured/policy-holder to omit any material information, or submit wrong information;

(m) Desist from demanding or receiving a share of the proceeds or indemnity from the claimant under an insurance contract; and

(n) Pursue the guidelines/directions that may be issued down by the Authority from time to time.

4.10 INSURANCE INTERMEDIARIES IN INDIA: AN INTROSPECTION

In terms of sheer numbers, the strength of LIC's distribution channel comprising over 5.90 lakh active Agents and over 18,800 Development Officers appears to be phenomenal. This is indeed a diverse in nature and spread, for which a strong marketing network is imperative. The network duly supported by 2048 servicing branches no doubt gives us the confidence in terms of numbers. Let us examine the Indian intermediaries channel:

(a) Since the reorganization in 80s, LIC has been laying a lot of emphasis on professionalising its field force. Prior to these attempts, most of the training needs were left to the Agent's instructors and this arrangement had many shortcomings, which included:

  (i) Lack of professional approach, technical and material know-how on part of the instructor himself;

  (ii) Fewer number of instructors in comparison to the training requirements of agents;

  (iii) Lack of proper infrastructure and training facilities; and

  (iv) Lukewarm approach on the part of the Development Officers in promoting professionalism amongst their agents.

(b) Even today, some of the agents do not have adequate product knowledge and their sales skills have not been developed beyond a certain level. One of the inhibiting factors possibly is ensuring that the agency force remains dependent on sales supervision or in other words, fear of independence of the agency force is predominant. As such, the phenomenon of dependency was and is being encouraged to maintain a firm grip/hold over the agency force. One of the best indicators of this phenomenon is the fact that when the umbrella of sales supervision is somehow not available, a majority of agents get terminated due to lack of guidance which they had got used to. This has also given rise to a situation where a majority of agents never visit the office, as the need to do so is never emphasized upon them by their sales supervisor.

(c) However, with training becoming a major focus of the re-organization especially for the field force with the creation of a network of ZTCs and STCs to provide both knowledge and professional inputs to the agents as well as the Development Officers, the situation has been slowly changing for the better. However, a lot still needs to be done in terms of qualitative improvement of our agents, which cannot be achieved just through training but also requires qualitative improvement in selection/recruitment itself.

(d) Life Insurance requires need-based selling. For need-based selling, we need to emphasize on the customer's need distinct from the salesman's need. The picture of life insurance selling has to be in conformity with the customer aspirations. Some of the agents have a tendency to sell products that they want to sell rather than the products that the customer actually needs. This leads to a lot of wrong selling and consequently a high degree of lapsation. A correct sale will guarantee a regular inflow of premium for the insurance organization. Some of the main reasons that contribute to this wrong system of selling, viz. distribution of the life insurance products is attributable to the existing remuneration pattern for the agents (i.e., commission structure). The commission structure somehow has been designed to give the agents the incentive to promote certain prodcucts, which would guarantee a bulkier commission initially, rather than those products wherein the commissions are spread out over a period of time. To overcome this lacuna, it is essential that the basic rate of commission itself is restructured so that the agents do not derive any benefit in so far as promoting a product for their own short-term financial gain. This will lead to a situation where the customer is more assured of being sold a product of his choice rather than being misled into buying a product that he does not need.

Suggestions for Strengthening the Intermediaries

Market dynamics are changing fast. Openness is the buzz world. With the opening up of the insurance sector for private sector competition is knocking at the doors. The need for strict regulations and/or controls on the operation of insurance business was not felt earlier and the present framework is provided by the Legislature through the Insurance Act, 1938 and the LIC Act, 1956. The setting up of the IRDA has given a clear cut signal of what we should expect in the future. A regulated insurance regime will see things changing both with regard to the control of overall life insurance business as also every facet connected thereto. Insurance intermediaries will also be governed by various regulations and these regulations will cover aspects starting from the basic eligibility conditions to the more detailed conditions of ceilings on commission structure, promotional channels, loyalty of agents, etc. Let us look at each of these factors individually.

Eligibility Conditions/Selection/Confirmation

(a) The present conditions should certainly be made more stringent and the minimum qualification level for rural and urban agents needs to be raised. This is necessary because insurance is not a simple product but a complex service that will require a certain degree of understanding to ensure correct sale.
(b) The present standards of testing the ability of an agent to permit him with a licence to do insurance business are minimal.
(c) A foolproof system of recruitment after training of 100 hours to be passed by the agent within one year from recruitment.

Supervisory Cadre

The present supervisory cadre comprises of the Development Officers. There is no doubt that this cadre has contributed its mite to the growth of life insurance in our country. The cadre in its present set-up is perceived to be an appointment cadre rather than a promotional one for existing agents. As such, this cadre is not perceived as a promotional opportunity by a majority of the field force. Some of the other factors which do not seem to be on the side of the present cadre are the present system of incentives which is perceived to be based on quantity, i.e. the new business done by his team of agents and does not have sufficient weightage for quality, i.e. developing professionalism amongst the team members and rendering adequate post-sales service to the customers.

One school of thought is of the opinion that it would also be more beneficial for the agents, customers, as well as the organization to have an additional level of supervisory cadre for the agents to be termed as Special Agents or Chief Agents.

Role Perceived for Special Agents/Chief Agents

The Chief Agent would be a promotional cadre for the agent. The chief Agent himself will be an agent of standing and repute and apart from doing his regular business of selling insurance, he would also be responsible for recruitment of agents, training of agents and ensuring their retention. He would normally be a member of the highest professional club and pass a professional examination.

Special Facilities Envisaged for the Chief Agents

Like providing support for an office, computer and limited access to the office network to obtain information about his own agency force as well as the policies serviced by him and his agency force. The Chief Agent would also be entitled to a limited credit as a small percentage of the commission earnings by his agency force subject to conditions such as minimum number of five agents and premium income generated. Credit would also be available for generating professionals within his agency force. The measure of professionalism can be the membership of various clubs as is prevalent today. Incentive patterns on these broad guidelines may have to be worked out by the insurance organisation.

Restructuring of Commission Structure

To ensure correct and need-based selling while keeping in mind the customer need, retention of customers, etc., it is imperative that the present remuneration pattern is restructured. The new pattern should be so based that:

(i) There is equal weightage for all products.
(ii) There is more weightage for renewal premium rather than first premium, i.e., there is a more uniform spread of commission over the term of the policy to ensure retention of customers.
(iii) There is definite need to change the present pattern of bonus commission structure. One of the suggestions being mooted in this regard is the payment of bonus commission in respect of policies which run for a minimum period of three years.

Enhancing Standards for Membership to Professional Clubs

The present rules governing club membership also need to be looked at afresh. It is being felt that after a certain stage, viz. a certain stretch of maintaining membership of a club leads to a situation where retention of club membership loses its relationship with generation of new business. One should not lose track of the fact that the primary aim of an insurance intermediary is promotion of insurance business through enlargement of market and no system should be encouraged which overlooks this aspect.

Strengthening of Training Infrastructure

As an organisation, LIC has a certain advantage in so far as it would have a head start where basic training infrastructure is concerned. LIC needs to concentrate on strengthening the existing infrastructure rather than expanding it further. What is implied by this statement is the fact that there is a need to build a cadre of professional trainers from both within the organisation as well as to tap the market for expert/specialised hands in the field of marketing of financial instruments. Total dependence on in-house training apparatus may not suffice. If insurance organisations work in this direction, it would be possible to expand the horizon of our training institutes to such an extent that they may serve as professional training institutes to players in insurance market as well provide help in making possible a further diversification of our operations.

Contemplating Multi-channels of Distribution, viz. Insurance Intermediaries

The future Indian insurance market scenario will see faster changes and possibly faces of many international players, besides several Indian players leading to a scenario where insurance companies would have graduated from being just a Life or General Insurance Company into a financial service conglomerate providing various financial services apart from insurance such as banking, housing, mutual funds, etc., from under the same roof. The success or the future of the insurance organisation would largely depend upon how it uses information technology as a major facilitator and will also depend on factors such as:

- Range of services;
- Innovation of products; and
- Market innovation and professionalism.

Such an organisation would have to develop into what can be termed as Financial Super market with a sophisticated product range that will be able to address world class standards and expectations as well as a sophisticated distribution system and servicing standards to match international levels.

World over, the concept of *Bancassurance* seems to be gaining ground. Studies have shown that with the financial institutions other than insurance competing increasingly to mop up domestic savings in competition with life insurance, a situation emerges where a loss of insurance market share as a percentage of Gross Domestic Savings (GDS) leads to an increase in percentage share of bank deposits. The concept of Bancassurance has been largely envisaged to overcome this situation and it is expected to get a fillip in our country in not very distant future.

In the above background of world standard products, the present system of distribution channel with the changes as envisaged earlier in terms of increased emphasis on professionalism and with the possible introduction of concepts like Chief Agent and Agency Manager, an insurance organisation may have to focus on the multi-channel distribution system of insurance intermediaries to encompass the following modes:

1. To overcome the challenges of the banking system taking a share of the life insurance market, think in terms of either setting up a subsidiary for banking/non-banking financial functions or entering into joint ventures with an existing banking chain. This would help the organization in targeting the large customer base of banks as also use the vast banking network of the partner(s) resulting in a very low cost of distribution.

2. Agency to Co-operative Societies, Panchayats and Registered Societies This is to take the advantage of the regional/rural presence of these co-operative societies, Panchayats and Registered Societies.
3. Direct Marketing:
   (a) World-wide, insurance is largely sold through various direct marketing techniques. With the information technology explosion, direct marketing has grown beyond the common Direct Mail to the following as well:
   - Tele Marketing; and
   - Cyber/Internet Marketing.

   (b) Besides, Insurance Companies may also consider setting-up of Direct Sales Force (DSF) with specially trained executive personnel such as product manager, field area manager and area manager who will be assigned specific jobs for direct marketing and will be supported by the Direct Marketing Department. The DSF will use the above mentioned tools of direct marketing besides encouraging Over the Counter (OTC) sale of the product.

   To encourage direct marketing, companies may consider giving discount to the clients for interacting directly with the marketing officials resulting in low cost insurance sales.
4. Agencies to independent financial brokers and housing finance companies.
5. Agencies to Professional Bodies like Medical Association: It is a fact that both insurance and medical science go together. It would not be out of place for the companies to enter into business agreement with hospitals and other associations. These intermediaries could in turn have liaison with various authorities like hospitals and other research institutes for promotion of insurance. To tap/encourage these distribution channels, specialized health products, disability products and critical care product will have to be exclusively marketed through these distribution channels.

However, many of the above modes of distribution would warrant amendments to the existing legal provisions. Hence, the insurance regulations must be updated without further delay.

4.11 SUMMARY

Keeping in view the world scenario the Authority has defined the term insurance intermediaries but practically except for surveyors they have yet to come in existence.

The Broker concept has been included because the private sector players may not be able to open the offices in every nook and corner of the country. The Broker will not act only for one insurance company but he can represent more than three companies at a time. The concept of broker is very well entrenched in the developed countries and more than 40% of Insurance Business is conducted through brokers.

In General insurance, the claims are settled on the basis of the report submitted by the independent agency, which is known as Surveyor or Loss Assessor and they are qualified persons, having expertise in this field. If the insurance company employs its own experts then they may be biased toward the claim as they are employees of the insurance company therefore to avoid any conflict of interest independent surveyors are necessary.

Third Party Administrator in Health Services will also play an important role in insurance sector but Health insurance is not very popular in India as people are not taking health insurance because it is a costly proposal. Furthermore there is lack of awareness amongst the people about the benefits they can derive from health Insurance. At present, health Insurance is being purchased by those people who are affluent and can afford to pay the medical bills whereas it is actually required by those who can ill-afford the costly medical treatment. With the entry of the TPAs this concept will spread and more people will go in for health Insurance.

4.12 REVIEW QUESTIONS

1. Define the functions of the Insurance Broker.
2. Who can become the Surveyor and Loss Assessor?
3. Explain the various provisions related to Third Party Administrator in Health Service.
4. Explain and illustrate the strengths and weaknesses of insurance intermediaries in India. Suggest some improvement in it.

5

CHAPTER

INSURANCE AND SOCIAL SECURITY

LEARNING OBJECTIVE

The main objective of this chapter is to make the students familiar with the role of insurance in terms of providing social security and expose them to various situations in which insurance fulfils the expectations of the society.

5.1 INTRODUCTION

In general connotation, insurance is a mechanism in which losses of few are compensated out of funds (insurance premium) collected from many insured. Insurance provides economic security for such losses arising out of happening of insured event, e.g. in personal accident policy death due to accident, in fire policy the insured events are fire and other allied perils like riot and strike, explosion, etc. Insurance is protection against uncertainties of life. It provides monetary compensation for losses suffered due to happening of unforeseen events, insured under the policy of insurance. Insurance is no more an optimal activity. Moreover, in India, the Government has notified some of the insurances as compulsory, e.g. third party insurance under Motor Vehicles Act, public liability insurance for handlers of hazardous substances under Environment Protection Act, etc.

Insurance, in fact, is an arrangement by which the upset suffered by a few are broadened over many, who are exposed to analogous risk. Insurance is a shelter against financial loss arising on the occurrence of an unanticipated incident. Insurance companies collect premia to offer security for the purpose. As loss is paid out of the premia collected from the insuring community and the insurance companies act as trustees to the amount so collected. Insurance companies have set proposal forms that are to be filed up by supplying the particulars of insurable interest for which the insurance is required and then it is presented to insurance company. Depending upon the answers specified in proposal form insurance companies evaluate the risk and estimate the premium. On payment of premium and acceptance thereof by insurance company, the insurance is affected. However, unless premium is paid there is no insurance cover.

In India, till recently, Insurance safety measures were available only through public sector insurance companies, namely, Life Insurance Corporation of India (LIC), General Insurance Corporation of India (GIC). The Life Insurance Corporation of India offered all life insurance schemes, while the General Insurance Corporation of India through its four subsidiaries, viz. National Insurance Company, New India Assurance Company, Oriental Insurance Company, and United India Insurance Company offered all non-life insurance schemes. But after the passing of the IRDA Act (Insurance Regulation Development Authority), the insurance sector has been opened up for private companies to take on insurance business. As a result, in about three years, more than a dozen of private companies have already entered the insurance business in our country with a variety of new insurance products.

Nowadays, the major wrangle of the insurance in India is whether privatization would erode the "social cause" of the Indian insurance industry by making profitability the main goal as a replacement for of social welfare and development. The LIC and GIC own a total fund of more than Rs. 1,80,000 crore together and invest a combined Rs. 25,000 crore in the social sectors, for social safety measures and development says Gurudas Dasgupta. Privatization of insurance will elevate premium, monopolize business, and result in net outflow of funds by foreign companies, he adds. However, on the other hand, the LIC and GIC have enormous rural exposure with about 40 per cent of their premia collected from the rural areas countrywide. LIC for instance, administers two of the world's largest social security schemes, viz. Lalgi under which 1.2 crore landless agricultural labourers draw benefits of life insurance and the social security scheme for IRDP beneficiaries covering 1.28 crore. Besides this, LIC has as many as 24 social security group insurance schemes for occupation groups like beedi workers, brick-kiln workers, carpenters, cobblers, lady tailors, and papad workers.

The IRDA Act stipulates that funds of policyholders should be retained within the country besides essential exposure to rural and social sector, which will be predetermined by the authority. The Act, which was finally passed, has already incorporated three amendments that include giving priority to health insurance, policyholders' funds investing in social sector and infrastructure and a penalty of Rs. 2.5 million on insurers that fail to fulfil social sector obligations. It becomes pretty clear from the discussion made so far that the social security has turn out to be one of the central goals of insurance business in the country.

5.2 EVOLUTION OF INSURANCE ORGANIZATIONS

With a view to serve the society, the insurance organizations have been developed in different forms with the innovation of insurance practices for social welfare and development. Some of these forms are outlined here.

(a) Self-Insurance

The arrangement in which an individual or concern sets up a private fund out of which the losses, if take place, are paid, is termed "Self-insurance." The person lays aside, periodically, convinced sum to meet the losses of any contemplated risk. While it may be called "self-insurance," it is not, as a matter of fact, insurance at all because there is no hedge, no shifting, or distributing of the burden of risk among larger persons. It is merely a provision for meeting the unforeseen event. Here the insured himself becomes the insurer for the particular risk. But, it can be effectively worked only when there is wide distribution of risks subject to the same hazard. It may be lesser expensive, provided the amount of loss is terrific. The fund, as it accumulates, belongs to the insured and he can invest it, as he may deem prudent. He pays no commission to agents, no extra expenses for maintaining office. So, on the one hand, the return of an investment will be higher and on the other, the cost of operation will be lesser.

The self-insurance will be successfully operated where:

(i) there are several properties such as, machine, motor vehicle, house, factories, etc.,
(ii) the properties or units are widely distributed,
(iii) these are under the influence of varied risks, and
(iv) the risks are greater at one place and lesser at another place.

So a shipping company owning a larger number of ships can profitably employ this scheme or an automobile firm having numerous motor vehicles can successfully operates this scheme. Certainly a concern of limited risk and resources should not attempt to operate this scheme. The self-insurance cannot be effectively utilized by those concerns where the losses cannot be easily estimated, in proper management of the accumulated funds can be practiced, and the accumulated funds prove to be inadequate at the contingency insurer provided he has sufficient resources and talent of insurance business. However, the individual organization has been rarely present in the field of insurance.

(b) Partnership

A partnership firm may also carry on the insurance business for the sake of profit. Since it is not an entity distinct from the persons comprising it, the personal liability of partners in respect of the partnership debts is unlimited. In case of huge loss the partners have to pay from their own personal funds and it will not be profitable to them to start insurance business. In the early period before the advent of joint stock companies many insurance undertakings were partnership firms or unincorporated companies. They were constituted by deed of partnerships, which regulated the business. Before formation of joint stock companies, the Crown had empowered to grant an application letter patent to such unincorporated companies to operate the business with limited liabilities. Sometimes, the policyholders were permitted to share the management of the concern. This form of insurance has completely disappeared with the advent of joint stock companies.

(c) Joint Stock Companies

The joint stock companies are those, which are organized by the shareholders who subscribe the necessary capital to start the business. These are formed for earning profits for the stockholders who are the real owners of the companies. The management of a company is entrusted to a Board of Directors who is elected by the shareholders from amongst themselves. The company can operate insurance business and the policyholders have nothing to do with the management of the concern. But, in life insurance, it is the practice to share certain portion of profit among the certain policyholders. The participating policyholders are getting the bonus. Before nationalization, according to Insurance Act, 1938, the policyholders had a right to elect their representatives to the Board of Directors to the extent of one-fourth of the total number of directors of the company. The provision enabled the policyholders to have an effective voice in the management of the company. Most of the insurance businesses were done on joint stock basis before nationalization. They were operating through the memorandum of association and articles of association framed by them.

(d) Mutual Fund Companies

The mutual fund companies are co-operative associations formed for the purpose of effecting insurance on the property of its members. The policyholders are themselves the shareholders of the companies. Each member is insurer as well as insured. They have power to participate in management and in profit sharing to the full-extent. Whenever the income is more than the expenses and claims, it is accumulated in the form of saving and is entitled in reducing the rate of premium. Since the insured are insurers also, they always try to reduce the management expenses and to keep the business at sound level.

The theoretical base of the mutual companies is issuing of participating policies, i.e., the policyholders had full power in management and profit, whereas the joint stock companies, strictly are to issue non-participating policies. But, in practice, the joint-stock companies are also issuing participating policies. It makes them mixed companies, i.e. where the features of both the joint stock companies and the mutual fund companies are present.

(e) Co-operative Insurance Organization

Co-operative insurance organizations are those concerns, which are incorporated and registered under Indian Co-operative Societies Act. The concerns are also called 'Co-operative Insurance Societies'. These societies like mutual fund companies are non-profit organizations. The aim is to provide insurance protection to its members at the lowest reasonable net cost. The Indian Insurance Act, 1938, has provided special provisions for the co-operative insurance societies, but after nationalization the societies have ceased to exist.

(f) Lloyd's Association

Lloyd's Association is one of the greatest insurance institutions in the world. Taking its name from the Coffee House of Edward Lloyd where underwriters assembled to transact business, and pick-up news. The organization traces its origin to the latter part of the seventeenth century. So, it is the oddest insurance organization in existing form in the world. In 1871, Lloyd's Act was passed incorporating the members of the association into a single corporate body with perpetual succession and a corporate seal. The powers of Lloyd's Corporation were extended from the business of marine insurance to other insurances and guarantee business. The Lloyd's association is an association of individual insurers known as 'underwriters'. They are also termed as 'Syndicates'; or 'Names'. Any insurer who wants to become a member of such association has to deposit a certain fee as security for the regular payment of his liabilities. The association before enrolling the insurer as a member of the association will inquire about the financial position of the concern, business reputation, and experience. On satisfactory proof the association admits him into the association. The insurers called underwriters, syndicates, or names affect the business. The association is merely a controlling and guiding body. Anybody desirous of taking insurance will approach the 'underwriters' and not the association. Each underwriter will be responsible for his business underwritten of a policy. Thus, several underwriters will underwrite a policy but their share or portion of business is fixed individually. When the policy becomes a claim, the insured realizes money from all the underwriters who had underwritten the policy according to their respective shares. If an underwriter fails to pay his share of claim, the association will pay from his security, which he had taken at time of enrolment of the underwriter. Never is one member or underwriter liable for the losses of other members either on a policy or in a syndicate. Underwriters assumes liability 'each for himself and not for another'. Lloyd's as a corporation is never liable on a policy. It does supervise the conditions under which its members may issue policies; it undertakes to provide collective protection for the commercial and maritime interest of its members.

The Lloyd's has done commendable work not only in the field of marine insurance but in other insurances also. War risk, election risk, exports risk, aeroplane risk, etc., have been insured by the Lloyd's Association. The association also publishes, 'Lloyd's List' and 'Register of Shipping' for the information of insuring public and the insurers.

(g) State Insurance

The government of a nation, sometimes, owns the insurance and runs the business for the benefit of the public. The state insurance is defined as that insurance which is under public sector. France had nationalized larger insurance companies in 1946. In Brazil, Japan, and Mexico, the insurances are largely nationalized. Previously, the State undertook only those insurances, which were regarded to be vital for the public interest or where private companies were not able or willing to enter the field of insurance. Social development, unemployment, crop insurance, war risk insurance, export credit insurance, aeroplane insurance were generally under state insurance.

In India, the life insurance business was nationalized in 1956 and the general insurances were nationalized In 1971. Thus, the insurance business in India, till recently, was under the control and ownership of the Central Government although they were in different forms of insurances. But recently, the government has started privatizing the insurance business in India.

5.3 INSURANCE ORGANIZATIONS IN INDIA

(a) Departmental Organization

Departmental insurances are prevalent in different departments of the Central and State governments. The postal department of the country has its own system of insurance under which the employees of post-offices are insured. Similarly, the postal deportment as a carrier of goods has also provided insurance for the goods to be dispatched. These insurances are not compulsory in India. The Government of different states has provided life insurance to their respective employees. Apart from this, the State Governments have also provided sickness, maternity, disability, medical and pension insurances to their employees.

(b) Corporations

In India, at the time of nationalization of insurance business in the country, the following corporations were established under separate Acts to deal with the insurance business.

(i) The Life Insurance Corporation of India Act, 1956

Insurance legislation for life insurance business conducted by the Life Insurance Corporation of India established under the said Act. It started its functions since Sept. 1, 1956. It owns all the life insurance business (including annuities) in India.

(ii) The General Insurance Corporation of India

Established under the General Insurance Corporation of India Act, 1972 has four distinct companies which are:

(i) National Insurance Company Ltd.,
(ii) New India Assurance Company Ltd.,
(iii) Oriental Fire and General Insurance Company Ltd., and
(iv) United India Fire and General Insurance Company Ltd.

These companies work separately through their distinct entitles but they are controlled and guided by the General Insurance Corporation of India. This is a neo-techno scheme of nationalization where the companies are also to work freely in the market. They will suffer and gain their own losses and profits. The monopoly of the concern, may be corporation, has gone in this new technique. These companies will be the subsidiaries of the G.I.C. (The General Insurance Corporation).

(iii) Employees State Insurance Corporation

This corporation was established in 1948. This corporation provides social security in the course of insurance to labourers of factories who are getting less than four hundred rupees per month. They are provided a definite assistance in case of sickness, maternity, disability, medical expenses and assistance to dependents.

(iv) Deposit Insurance Corporation

This corporation was established in 1962. It provides protection to the depositors of a bank. In case the bank fails, the depositors can get their deposits back up to rupees ten thousand.

(c) Government Companies

The government according to the provision of Indian Companies Act established certain Insurance Companies. In 1957, Export Risks Insurance Corporation was established to insure the export risks. The name of this company was converted to Export Credit and Guarantee Corporation in 1964. Now the above said four government companies conduct all the general insurance business.

5.4 INSURANCE AND SOCIAL SECURITY

The path of insurance has been evolved to look after the interests of people from uncertainty by providing certainty of compensation at a given contingency. The insurance principle comes to be more useful in modern affairs. It not only serves the ends of individuals, or of special groups of individuals, but also tends to spread through and renovate modern social order.

(A) Social Security to Individuals

(i) Insurance Provides Security and Safety

The insurance provides safety and security against the loss on a particular event. In case of life insurance, payment is made when death occurs or the term of insurance is expired. The loss to the family at a premature death and payment in old-age are adequately provided by insurance. In other words, security against premature death and old-age sufferings are provided by life insurance. Similarly, the property of insured is secured against loss on a fire in fire insurance. In other insurance, too, this security is provided against the loss at a given contingency. The insurance provides safety and security against the loss of earning at death or in old-age, against the loss at fire, against the loss of damage, destruction or disappearance of property, goods, furniture and machines, etc.

(ii) Insurance Offers Peace of Mind

The security wish is the prime motivating factor. This is the wish, which tends to stimulate to work more. If this wish is unsatisfied, it will create a tension which may manifest itself in the form of an unpleasant reaction causing reduction in work. The security banishes fear and uncertainty. Fire windstorm, automobile accident and death are almost beyond the control of human agency and on occurrence of any of these events may frustrate or weaken the human mind. By means of insurance, however, feeling of insecurity may be eliminated.

(iii) Insurance Protects Mortgaged Property

At the death of the owner of the mortgaged property, the property is taken over by the lender of money and the family is deprived of the use of the property. At the damage or destruction of the property, he will lose his right to get the loan repayed. The insurance will provide adequate amount to the dependents at the early death of the property-owner to pay-off the unpaid loans. Similarly, the mortgagee gets adequate amount at the destruction of the property.

(iv) Insurance Eliminates Dependency

What would happen at the death of the husband or father, the annihilation of family needs no elaboration. Similarly, at destruction of property and goods, the family would suffer a lot. It brings reduced standards of living and the suffering may go to any extent of begging from the relatives, neighbours, or friends. The economic independence of the family is reduced or, sometimes, lost totally. What can be more pitiable condition than this that the wife and children are looking at others more benevolent than the husband and father in absence of protection against such dependency? The insurance is here to assist them and provide adequate amount at the time of sufferings.

(v) Life Insurance Encourages Saving

The elements of protection and investment are present only in case of life insurance. In property insurance, only protection element exists. In most of the life policies elements of saving predominates. These policies combine the programs of insurance and savings. The saving with insurance has certain extra advantages:

(i) Systematic saving is possible because regular premia are required to be compulsorily paid. The saving with a bank is voluntary and one can easily omit a month or two and then abandon the program entirely.

(ii) In insurance the deposited premium cannot be withdrawn easily before the expiry of the term of the policy. In contrast to this, the saving which can be withdrawn at any moment will finish within no time.

(iii) The insurance will pay the policy-holder money irrespective of the premium deposited while in case of bank-deposit, only the deposited amount along with the interest is paid. The insurance, thus, provides the wished amount of insurance and the bank provides only the deposited amount.

(iv) The compulsion or force to pay premium in insurance is so high that if the policy-holder fails to pay premiums within the days of grace, he subjects his policy to lapsation and may get back only a very nominal portion of the total premia paid on the policy.

For the preservation of the policy, he has to try his level best to pay the premium. After a certain period, it would be a part of necessary expenditure of the insured. In absence of such forceful compulsion elsewhere life insurance is the best mode of saving.

(vi) Life Insurance Provides Profitable Investment

Individuals unwilling or unable to handle their own funds have been pleased to find an outlet for their investment in life insurance policies. Endowment policies, multipurpose policies, deferred annuities certainly offer better type of investment. The element of investment, i.e. regular saving, capital formation, and return of the capital along with certain additional return are perfectly observed in life insurance. In India, the insurance policies carry special exemption from income tax, wealth tax, gift tax and estate duty. An individual, on his own may not be able to invest regularly with enough of security and profitability. The life insurance fulfils all these requirements with a lower cost. The beneficiary of the policyholder can get a regular income from the life-insurer.

(vii) Life Insurance Fulfils the needs of a Person

The needs of a person are divided into:

(a) Family needs,
(b) Old-age needs,
(c) Re-adjustment needs,
(d) Special needs, and
(e) The clean-up needs.

(a) Family needs

Death is certain, but the time is uncertain. So, there is uncertainty of the time when the sufferings and financial stringencies may befall on the family. Moreover, every person is responsible to provide for the family. It would be a more pathetic sight in the world to see the wife and children of a man looking for some one more considerate and benevolent than the husband or the father, who left them unprovided. Therefore, the provision for children, till they reach earning period and for widow up to long life, should be made. Any other provision except life insurance will not adequately meet this financial requirement of the family. Whole life policies are the better means of meeting such requirements.

(b) Old-age needs

The provision for old age is required where the person is surviving more than his earning period. The reduction of income in old-age is serious to the person and his family. If no other family member starts earning, they will be left with nothing and if there is no property, it would be more pitiable state of affairs. The life insurance provides old-age funds along with the protection of the family by issuing various policies.

(c) Re-adjustment needs

At the time of reduction in income whether by loss of unemployment, disability, or death, adjustment in the standard of living of family is required. The family members will have to be satisfied with meager income and they have to settle down to lower income and social obligations. Before coming down to the lower standard and to be satisfied with that, they require certain adjustment income so that the primary obstacles may be reduced to minimum. The life insurance helps to accumulate adequate funds. Endowment policy anticipated endowment policy and guaranteed triple benefit policies are deemed to be a good substitute for old age needs.

(d) Special needs

There are certain special requirements of the family, which are fulfilled by the earning member of the family. If the member becomes disable to earn due to old-age or death, those needs may remain unfulfilled and the family will suffer.

(i) Need for Education

There are certain insurance policies, and annuities, which are useful for education of the children irrespective of the death or survival of the father or guardian.

(ii) Marriage

The daughter may remain unmarried in the case of father's death or in case of inadequate provision for meeting the expenses of marriage. The insurance can provide funds for the marriage if policy is taken for the purpose.

(iii) Insurance Needs for Settlement of Children

After education, settlement of children takes time, in absence of adequate funds, the children cannot be well placed, and all the education may go waste.

(e) Clean-up Funds

After death, ritual ceremonies, payment of wealth tax and income tax are certain requirements, which decrease the amount of funds of the family member. Insurance comes to help for meeting these requirements. Multipurpose policy, education, and marriage policies, capital redemption policies are the better policies for such special needs.

(B) Social Security to Business

The insurance has been useful to the business society also. Some of the uses are discussed below:

(i) Uncertainty of Business and Losses if Reduced

In world of business, commerce and industry a huge number of properties are employed. With a slight slackness or negligence, the property may be turned into ashes. The accident may be fatal not only to the individual or property but to the third party also. New construction and new establishment are possible only with the help of insurance. In absence of it, uncertainty will be to the maximum level and nobody would like to invest a huge amount in the business or industry. A person may not be sure of his life and health and cannot continue the business up to longer period to support his dependents. By purchasing policy, he can be sure of his earning because the insurer will pay a fixed amount at the time of death. Again, the owner of a business might foresee contingencies that would bring great loss. To meet such situations they might decide to set aside annually a reserve, but it can not be accumulated due to death. However, by making an annual payment, to secure immediately, insurance policy can be taken.

(ii) Business Efficiency is Increased with Insurance

When the owner of a business is free from the impact of losses, he will certainly devote much time to the business. The carefree owner can work, better for the maximization of the profit. The new as well as old businessmen are guaranteed payment of certain amount with the insurance policies at the death of the person; at the damage, destruction, or disappearance of the property or goods. The uncertainty of loss may affect the mind of the businessmen adversely. The insurance, removing the uncertainty, stimulates the businessmen to work hard.

(iii) Key Man Indemnification

Key man is that particular man whose capital, expertise, experience, energy, ability to control, goodwill and dutifulness make him the most valuable asset in the business and whose absence will reduce the income of the employer till the time such employee is not substituted. The death or disability of such valuable lives will, in many instances, prove a more serious loss than that by fire or any other hazard. The potential loss to be suffered and the compensation to the dependents of such employee require adequate provision, which is met by purchasing adequate life-policies. The amount of loss may be up to the amount of reduced profit, expenses involved in appointing and training of such persons and payment to the dependents of the key man. The term Insurance Policy or Convertible Term Insurance Policy is more suitable in this case.

(iv) Enhancement of Credit

The business can obtain loan by pledging the policy as collateral for the loan. The insured persons are getting more loans due to certainty of payment at their deaths. The amount of loan that can be obtained with such pledging a policy will not exceed the cash value of the policy. In case of death, this cash value can be utilized for settling the loan along with the interest. If the borrower is unwilling to repay the loan and interest, the lender can surrender the policy and get the amount of loan and interest thereon repaid. The redeemable debentures can be issued on the collateral of capital redemption policies. The insurance properties are the best collateral and the lenders grant adequate loans.

(v) Business Continuation

In a business, particularly partnership business may get discontinued at the death of any partner, although the surviving partners can restart the business. But in both the cases the business and the partners will suffer economically. The insurance policies provide adequate funds at the time of death. Each partner may be insured for the amount of his interest in the partnership and his dependents may get that amount at the death of the partner.

5.5 SUMMARY

The concept of insurance has passed through various stages. Initially, the insurance business was started for marine and later for fire. The life insurance concept was evolved little later and with slightly different meaning and purpose. In modern times, the insurance has become backbone for social security in different spheres of life of people around the globe. In India, the insurance business was taken over by the Government in 1956 and 1971 respectively for life and non-life insurance but the social expectations finally compelled the Government to re-think over it. Of late, the Government has started opening the insurance business for private sector but the social security is being put on the top agenda even in this case.

5.6 REVIEW QUESTIONS

1. Discuss the concept of social security and elaborate the evolution of insurance.
2. "The concept of social security is the backbone for insurance business." Comment.
3. Write short notes on:
   (a) Social Security for Individual; and
   (b) Social Security for Business.
4. Bring out the relevance of insurance in providing social security to individual and business. Is insurance a social compulsion? Support your answer with arguments.

6

CHAPTER

LIFE INSURANCE PRODUCTS

LEARNING OBJECTIVE

The main objective of this chapter is to make the students familiar with the important life insurance products available in India.

6.1 INTRODUCTION

Uncertainty is the only certainty in life. Yaksha asked Yudhisthira in the epic, 'Mahabharata' as to what is the most wonderful thing in the world? Yudhisthira's reply was that the most wonderful thing in the world is that men see everyday the dead being carried to the burial ground yet they believe they are eternal. Birth and death are the only definite and certain events of life, all other intervening events are uncertain. In mundane life wherever there is uncertainty there is an involvement of risk. The instinct and need for security against such risk is a motivating force for human behaviour and action.

If the breadwinner of a family dies, the income to the family ceases. If the breadwinner does not die, but retires from service, even then the regular income to the family ceases. Thus, life insurance has to cover both the contingencies of death or survival. They are mutually exclusive. The needs for life insurance are different. They vary according to contingency provided for according to age, according to family size, etc. Each plan of insurance provides for a kind of need. The needs of people for life insurance can be classified as under:

(i) *Family*: Protection of the interests of the family against loss of income due to death of the breadwinner.

(ii) *Children*: Provision for education, marriages, and start-in life.

(iii) *Old-age*: Post-retirement income for self and family/dependants.
(iv) *Special Needs*: Disability, accidents, expenses for treatment of diseases, loss of income due to sickness, etc.

Generally, all these needs exist simultaneously, but not in the same measure for all persons. The variations will depend on the age, size of families and dependants, nature of other properties and incomes. Insurance plans of various kinds are designed to meet these needs. Insurance plans are alike medicine. Each one is designed to meet certain needs depending upon the situation. No one plan will meet all the needs but all needs can be met through a judicious mix of different plans.

Basic Elements in a Life Insurance Product

A life insurance product has, essentially, two basic elements:

(i) *Risk cover*—i.e. benefit payable in the event of death.
(ii) *Saving*—i.e. the benefit payable in the event of survival.

Life insurance plans, which provide only risk cover during a specified period without any survival benefit, are called Term Insurance Plans. Life insurance plans, which provide for payment of policy monies only on survival of the period, are called pure endowment plans.

All plans of life insurance are combinations of both term insurance element and pure endowment element in different proportions. An endowment plan stipulates that a specified Sum Assured (SA) would be paid if the life assured dies within the term selected or survives that term. The death benefit is paid by term assurance and the survival benefit is paid by the pure endowment. An annuity plan is a pure endowment plan with the condition that the SA is payable in instalments over a specified period of time.

The life insurance policies may be without profit (non-participating) policies and with profit (participating) policies. The holders of without profit policies are not entitled to share the profits of the insurer. These policyholders get only the sum assured and no bonus is given to them. The holders of the with profit policies are entitled to share the profit of the insurer. Since the policyholders can share the profit and not the loss, they cannot be treated as co-owner of the insurance business. If there is loss, the policyholders cannot get bonus, i.e., the share in profit.

Having different elements in different policies, the policyholders are free to choose the best policies according to their requirements. It would be known that no one policy is the best policy for all the policyholders due to variance in cost, elements of investments and protection, requirements of the policyholders and availability of the policy. There are following types of plans available:

- Tern Life Insurance;

- Whole Life Insurance;
- Endowment Type Plans;
- Combination of Whole Life and Endowment Type Plans;
- Children's Assurance Plans; and
- Annuity and Pension Plans.

6.2 TERM LIFE INSURANCE

In the case of a Term Life Insurance contract, the sum assured is payable only in the event of death during the term. In case of survival, the contract comes to an end at the end of term. There is no refund of premium. These policies are usually non-participating. Since only death risk is covered, the premium is low and the contract is simple. Of late however, some companies do offer participating policies under term insurance plans.

Terms of life insurance contracts are usually long, even upto 40 years or more. The term may also be restricted to as short periods. They help to provide collateral security for loans. Some insurers offer term insurance policies for longer terms of 3, 5 or 6 years with fixed (level) premium payable each year. Such contracts can be renewed for further equal periods till the life assured reaches the age of 65 years.

The term insurance policies are useful to those:

(i) who need extra-protection for a short duration, or
(ii) who need protection for long duration but are unable to purchase for the time-being due to ill-health or lesser income,
(iii) a young businessman can take the policy to save the business-disaster during initial stage of the business,
(iv) key-men's insurances are generally on term insurance basis,
(v) a mortgagor of the property may be benefited by this scheme,
(vi) a father can take this policy during the period of education of his child, and
(vii) any such persons who are willing to provide insurance for a shorter period.

Term insurances are of the following types in India:

(i) Straight-Term (Temporary) Insurance

The Life Insurance Corporation of India issues term-insurance for two years, which is also called as two-years' temporary assurance policy. The sum assured will be payable only in the event of the life assured's death occurring within two years from the commencement of the policy. A single premium is required to be paid at the outset. The proposer is required to pay the medical examination fee. The policy is not entitled to any surrender value and no loan can be granted on the security thereof because, it is not of accumulative in nature and payment is not always certain. This plan cannot be converted into other plans.

This policy is beneficial to the dependents who are required to pay Estate Duty and to those persons who are given charity or donation of fixed property.

(ii) Renewable Term Policies

These policies are renewable at the expiry of term for an additional period without medical examination; but the premium rate will be altered according to the age attained at the time of renewal. This policy is beneficial to those whose health are deteriorating and will be uninsurable at an advanced age. With the help of this policy, they continue to enjoy the insurance benefit without going under fresh medical examination. However, the premium rate will be increasing according to the attained age.

(iii) Convertible Term Policy

Under this policy, option to convert it into whole life or endowment policy is available. The life assured under this plan has an option to convert the policy, provided it is in full force, into either a limited payment life policy or an endowment assurance policy, without having to undergo fresh medical examination, at any time during the specified term except the last two years. If the option of conversion is exercised, a new policy under the limited payment life plan or endowment assurance plan will be issued as the case may be subject to rates of premium and terms and conditions prevailing on the date of conversion. In other words, the premium rates will be increased according to the age attained.

Benefits of Term Insurance Plans

The benefits of Term Insurance Plans are as under:

(i) There is always a need for risk cover as protection against loss due to death.
(ii) Many insurance needs are of temporary or terminating nature (for example, mortgages) which can be protected with temporary or terminating insurance.
(iii) Few men can be adequately insured for even the minimum level of their real life values without the advantage of low premium term insurance.
(iv) Persons having low income can provide for meeting family obligations at low cost.
(v) Persons on the thresholds of new careers or business can avail of term insurance policies to save on costs, so that they can utilize their balance income or capital for developing their career or business.
(vi) Persons, who have invested substantially in new ventures by borrowing at heavy interest rates or mortgaging their property, can cover the risk of serious loss to the investment through term insurance at low premium.
(vii) Term insurance is also useful as supplement to endowment or

whole life policies with a view to get higher risk cover.

(viii) In modern business, indemnifying the loss to business, due to the death of the key person responsible for the running of the business, can be done through term insurance plan.

Insurers are careful while considering proposals for large amounts of term insurance. Some people who are not in good health may tend to take term insurance plans for large Sum Assured. That would be unfair advantage, contravening the principle of utmost good faith. As a result, there would be adverse selection against the interests of the insurance company and the community of policyholders.

The following products are available in the market:

Sl. No.	*Name of the Company*	*Type of Plan*
1.	Life Insurance Corporation of India	Two-year Term Assurance Convertible Term Assurance Mortgage Redemption Assurance Plan
2.	Allianze Bajaj Life Insurance Company	Risk Care, Term Care
3.	HDFC Standard Life Insurance	Regular Term Assurance, Single Company Premium Term Assurance, Loan Cover Assurance
4.	ICICI Prudential Life Insurance Company	ICICI Prulife guard
5.	TATA AIG Life Insurance Company	Yearly Renewal Term, 10-years Term, Term to age 60.
6.	Birla Sun Life Insurance Company	Birla Sun Life Flexi Term Plus
7.	SBI Cardiff Life Insurance Company	NIL
8.	Max New York Life Insurance Company	5-year Term Renewable and convertible policy

6.3 WHOLE LIFE INSURANCE

The risk is covered for the entire life of the policyholder, which is why they are known as Whole Life Policies. The policy monies and the bonus are payable only to the nominee or the beneficiary upon the death of the policyholder. The policyholder is not entitled to any money during his or her own lifetime, i.e. there is no survival benefit. This represents a serious drawback in the case of whole-life policies for they go on covering a policyholder's life even after his life has no further economic value for others. On the other hand, a policyholder would probably require the money for himself and his spouse during retired life but this would not be possible since the sum assured is payable only when the policyholder dies. In this sense, whole-life policies are fairly rigid and suitable only in a few very specific cases. The important whole life policies available in India are as follows:

(a) Whole-life Policy (with Profits)

This is a policy at lower rates of premium. The premiums are payable throughout the life time of the assured and the sum assured becomes payable on the death of the life assured or attaining of 80 years of age whichever earlier. Bonus addition is at a higher rate compared to endowment policies.

Minimum age at entry	:	15 years
Minimum sum assured	:	Rs. 30,000
Maximum sum assured	:	No limit (linked with income)
Maximum premium	:	35 years or till age 80 whichever is later paying term
Policy loan	:	After 3 years
Housing loan	:	Would depend upon the requirement and entitlement worked out on the basis of income, age of the assured and repayment capacity.

Benefits

On maturity	:	Sum assured + bonus payable on attainment of 85 years of age or on completion of 40 years from the date of commencement, whichever later.
Natural death	:	Sum assured + bonus accrued.
Accidental death	:	Double the amount of sum assured + bonus accrued.
Permanent disability	:	Treated as death and claim accordingly amounting to incapacitating the insured.

(b) Whole Life Limited Payment Plan

The payment of premium is limited to certain period, although the amount secured under this plan is payable on the death of the policyholder. Premium under this plan is higher than the premium payable under a whole life plan. The amount of premium depends upon the number of annual premiums stipulated since premiums are payable for a selected period of years or until death if it occurs within this period, the life assured is satisfied to know the amount of maximum premium payable. If the life assured survives the premium-paying period, the policy continues in full force, provided all premiums have been paid, but not further premiums are required to be paid.

This plan is suitable for persons in whose case the need for money would arise only on the happening of the death, but who either on account of personal and family history are not eligible for a whole life plan or do not want to extend the premium-paying period beyond their earning years. The plan is available both with and without profit. The plan with profit continues to participate in profits even after the completion of the premium paying term, until the death of the life assured.

Minimum age at entry	:	12 years
Maximum age at entry	:	60 years
Minimum sum assured	:	Rs. 30,000 for with profit plan and Rs. 50,000 for without profits plan
Minimum term	:	5 years
Maximum term	:	55 years
Maximum sum assured	:	No limit (linked with income)
Maximum age ceasing	:	70 years' premium
Policy loan	:	After 3 years
Housing loan	:	Would depend upon the requirement and entitlement worked out on the basis of income, age of the assured and repayment capacity.

Benefits

On maturity	:	Sum assured + bonus payable on attainment of 85 years of age or on completion of 40 years from the date of commencement, whichever later.
Natural death	:	Sum assured + bonus accrued.
Accidental death	:	Double the amount of sum assured + bonus accrued.
Permanent disability	:	Treated as death and claim accordingly amounting to incapacitating the insured

(c) Whole Life Single Premium Plan

Whole life single premium plan is not very common whereas the whole life limited payment plan is most popular because it is convenient to the policyholder to arrange the payment of premium during his income-earning period. Single premium is paid at the start of the policy. The policy is available both with and without profits.

Minimum age at entry	:	12 years
Maximum sum assured	:	60 years

Minimum sum assured	:	Rs. 30,000 for with profit plan and Rs. 50,000 for without profits plan
Maximum sum assured	:	No limit (linked with income)
Policy loan	:	After 3 years
Housing loan	:	Would depend upon the requirement and entitlement worked out on the basis of income, age of the assured and repayment capacity.

Benefits

On maturity	:	Sum assured + bonus payable on attainment of 85 years of age or on completion of 40 years from the date of commencement, whichever later.
Natural death	:	Sum assured + bonus accrued
Accidental death	:	Double of sum assured + bonus accrued

(d) Convertible whole Life Plan

The plan is useful to young persons who are at the start of their careers and their present income is low. The object of this is to provide maximum protection at minimum cost. It is a whole life without profit plan, premiums payable upto age of 70 year of the assured. The premium charged is that of whole life without profits and therefore sufficiently low. The risk is however covered for the full sum assured.

After 5 years, the life assured can convert it into an endowment with or without profits choosing the term without having to go in for a medical examination. If no option is exercised at the end of 5 years, the policy continues on original terms as whole life without profits with the premiums ceasing at the age 70 years.

Minimum age at entry	:	12 years
Maximum age at entry	:	45 years
Minimum sum assured	:	Rs. 50,000
Minimum term	:	10 years
Maximum term	:	55 years
Maximum sum assured	:	No limit (linked with income) Rs. 2 lacs for minors aged 12-17 years
Maximum age ceasing	:	70 years' premium
Policy loan	:	After 3 years

Benefits

On maturity	:	Sum assured + bonus when converted to endowment. If not converted, sum assured + bonus payable at age 5 or on completion of 40 years from the date of commencement,

		whichever later
Natural death	:	Sum assured + bonus accrued
Accidental death	:	Double of sum assured + bonus accrued
Permanent disability	:	Treated as death and claim accordingly amounting to incapacitating the insured

6.4 ENDOWMENT TYPE PLANS

Endowment policies cover the risk for a specified period, at the end of which the SA is paid back to the policyholder, along with all the bonus accumulated during the term of the policy. The endowment policies can be several, of which important endowment policies are discussed below:

(a) Pure Endowment Policy

The sum assured is payable on the life assured's surviving the endowment term. In the event of his death within the term (endowment), premiums may be returnable or not. In case of LIC all premiums paid, without any deduction, will be refunded to. Thus, the pure endowment policy is opposite of the term policy, because the insured is paid if he survives in pure endowment and if dies within the term in term policy. Actually, these two policies, i.e. pure endowment and term policies, are the base of all other policies. Pure endowment is for the benefit of the policyholder and term policy is for the benefit of others. So, the pure endowment policy has the element of investment and the term policy has the element of protection. Pure endowment grants protection against 'living too long' while the term policy grants protection against 'living too short'. The former is old-age protection while the latter is family protection.

This policy can be issued in the life of adult as well as in the life of child. In the case of a policy on the life of a child, payment of premiums does not cease on the death of the proposer, but must be continued during the whole currency of the policy. Paid-up and surrender values are allowed on this policy. The mode of payment of premium under this plan is only yearly or half-yearly.

This policy is useful to the person who does not care to present himself for medical examination. This is also beneficial to those who, for reasons of health, would be unacceptable for life insurance on standard premium. It is a sort of compulsory saving for old-age.

(b) Ordinary Endowment Assurance Policy

This is the most popular and sought after plan. The premiums under the plan are paid for a fixed term. In case the death takes place during the term, the sum assured along with accumulated bonus is paid to the policyholder. The plan offers the advantage of making a provision for the family of the life assured in case of his early death and also assures a lump sum amount at any desired age.

The plan is available with-profit and without-profit. The policy with-profit carries bonus on it, no bonus is attached to policies without-profit. Premium under with-profit policies is higher than that of the premium under without-profit policies. The premium paying term is restricted to 25 years for without-profit plan.

Minimum age at entry	:	12 years
Maximum age at entry	:	65 years
Maximum age at maturity	:	75 years
Minimum sum assured	:	Rs. 20,000 Rs. 25,000 if age between 61-65 years
Maximum sum assured	:	No limit (linked with income)
Minimum term	:	5 years
Maximum term	:	55 years
Policy loan	:	After 3 years Loan on policies on the lives of children is granted only when the policy vests in the name of the life assured.
Housing loan	:	Would depend upon the requirement and entitlement worked out on the basis of income, age of the assured and repayment capacity.

Benefits

On maturity	:	Sum Assured + bonus for full term.
Natural death	:	Sum assured + bonus accrued.
Accidental death	:	Double that amount of sum assured + bonus accrued.
Permanent disability	:	Treated as death and claim accordingly amounting to incapacitating the insured

(c) Double Endowment Policy

Under this policy, if the life assured dies during the endowment period, the basic sum assured is payable and if he survives to the end of the term, double of the sum assured is paid. Premiums are payable throughout the endowment terms or till the prior death of the life insured. The premiums are generally quoted according to the endowment period, irrespective of the age at entry subject to the provision that maturity age is not beyond 65. The term of policy is ranging from 10 years to 40 years but no policy is insured to mature at an age exceeding 65 years. This policy is combination of an endowment insurance and a pure endowment (without return of premiums) for the same period and for the same amount.

This plan is beneficial to the person who by reason of some physical disability is not eligible for acceptance at the tabular rates under any of the other classes of insurance. This is also to benefit to those who are confident of living long but would like to have some cover in the event of his early death. The investment element is higher than the protection element in this plan.

(d) Joint Life Endowment Plan

Under this plan, two lives can be insured under one contract. The sum assured is payable at the end of the endowment term on survival of both the lives insured, or on the earlier death of either of the two. Married couples can take such a policy covering the risk on both the lives, when both are having incomes of their own. Partners in business can also do the same.

(e) Marriage Endowment Plan

The marriage endowment plan has the specific condition that the sum assured is payable only after the expiry of the term even if death of the life assured takes place earlier. The term is fixed corresponding to the likely period when the daughter may get married. Premium ceases on the death of the life assured. This policy is designed to meet the needs of a family man who wants to make available a certain sum for marriage of a female dependents.

6.5 COMBINATION OF WHOLE LIFE AND ENDOWMENT TYPE PLANS

Some persons may need a lump sum amount even before the expiry of the term of the policy. If they take loans under the policies, the risk cover (amount payable on death) comes down and interest payable on the loan accumulates as a debt on the policy. To meet this need, insurers have devised plans wherein part of the S.A. is made payable periodically during the term of the policy. Notwithstanding the payments at periodic intervals, the S.A. at risk (payable at death), continues to be the same till the end of the term.

(a) Money Back (with Profits) Scheme

These are fixed term policies. The premium is paid till the end of the term or till the death of the policyholder whichever earlier. A part of the sum assured is returned to the policyholder once in 4 years or 5 years according to the plan. The risk cover continues for the full sum assured even after payment of instalments to the policyholder. The bonus also payable for the full term.

Scheme of Money Back Plan for a Policy for 20 Years

At the end to		
5 years	:	20% of sum assured
10 years	:	20% of sum assured
15 years	:	20% of sum assured
20 years	:	40% of sum assured + bonus
Minimum age at entry	:	13 years and 14 years where return of payment is after four years.

Maximum age at entry	:	50 years
Minimum sum assured	:	Rs. 40,000
Policy term	:	20 years fixed
Maximum sum assured	:	No limit (linked with income)
Maximum maturity age	:	70 years
Policy loan	:	Nil
Housing loan	:	Would depend upon the requirement and entitlement worked out on the basis of income, age of the assured and repayment capacity.

Benefits

On maturity	:	Balance survival benefit + bonus for 20 years.
Natural death	:	Sum assured + bonus accrued
Accidental death	:	Double of sum assured + bonus accrued
Permanent disability	:	Treated as death and claim accordingly amounting to incapacitating the insured

Scheme of Money Back Plan for a Policy of 25 Years

At the end of

5 years	:	15% of sum assured
10 years	:	15% of sum assured
15 years	:	15% of sum assured
20 years	:	15% of sum assured
25 years	:	40% of sum assured + bonus
Minimum age at entry	:	13 years and 14 years where return of payment is after four years.
Maximum age at entry	:	45 years
Minimum sum assured	:	Rs. 40,000
Policy term	:	25 years fixed
Maximum sum assured	:	No limit (linked with income)
Maximum maturity age	:	70 years
Policy loan	:	Nil
Housing loan	:	Would depend upon the requirement and entitlement worked out on the basis of income, age of the assured and repayment capacity.

Benefits

On maturity	:	Balance survival benefit + bonus for 25 years.
Natural death	:	Sum assured + bonus accrued
Accidental death	:	Sum assured + bonus accrued
Permanent disability	:	Treated as death and claim accordingly amounting to incapacitating the insured

The money back policy is useful for those who, besides desiring to provide for their own old-age and family, feel the need for lump sum benefits at periodical intervals. Under this scheme, the following benefits are payable:

(i) For a policy with a term of 12 years, 1/5th of the sum assured becomes payable on the life assured's surviving 4 years, a further 1/5th of the sum assured becomes payable on his surviving 8 years and the balance 3/5th of the sum assured on his surviving to the end of the term of 12 years.

(ii) For a policy with a term of 15 years, 1/4th of the sum assured becomes payable on the life assured's surviving 5 years, a further 1/4th of the sum assured becomes payable on his surviving 10 years and the balance 1/2 of the sum assured becomes payable on his surviving to the end of the term of 15 years.

(iii) For a policy with a term of 20 years, 1/5th of the sum assured becomes Payable on the life assured's surviving 5 years, a further 1/5th of the sum assured becomes payable on his surviving 10 years, a further 1/5th of the sum assured becomes payable on his surviving 15 years and the balance 2/5th of the sum assured becomes payable on his surviving to the end of the term of 20 years.

However in the event of death at any time within the selected term the full sum assured is payable without any deduction or adjustment for the amount that may have been paid earlier by way of survivance benefit. The bonus additions to the policy will be reckoned on the full sum assured and are payable at the end of the selected term of years or at the life assured's death, if previous.

The other Money Back Plans of LIC of India are as follows:

(a) Jeevan Samriddhi

This is a New Money Back Plan which assures periodic payment of basic sum assured in instalments on survival, with increasing benefits. 'Jeevan Samriddhi' gives you a wider choice of convenient terms—12,15,20,25 years, with added attractive features like Guaranteed and Loyalty Addition. It enables the assured to provide for future necessities, to ensure the timely availability of funds for marriages, education, illness and any unforeseen contingency.

(b) Jeevan Rekha Plan

Jeevan Rekha, a with-profit plan, is a novel combination of whole life and popular money back plans. This is a unique plan catering to the needs of insuring public who cherish to have inflow of income at regular intervals and at the same time provide their family a lump sum amount death.

(c) Jeevan Surabhi

This is a improved version of Money Back Plan where premiums are payable for limited period with—

(i) An added attraction of periodical increase in insurance cover.
(ii) Free risk coverage even during the non-premium paying period.
(iii) Available with premium payment periods of 12,15 and 18 years.
(iv) And policy terms of 15, 20 and 25 years.
(v) Money back at intervals of 4 or 5 years as per policy term.

6.6 CHILDREN'S ASSURANCE PLANS

Prior to nationalisation of life insurance business in 1956 and of a long period afterwards, children's assurance plans like the Children Deferred Assurance Plan, provided risk cover on life of the child after it had attained age of 18 years. The coverage of risk of the child was not immediate, primarily because of heavy mortality in childhood.

Insurance covering risk on the lives of children was also not encouraged because of lack of need for insurance at that stage. Death of a child, who is not earning, does not place the family at a financial loss. With the improvement of health services in our country, it is observed that the rate of mortality amongst children is reducing. More statistics about children mortality is now available and hence it is possible to grant risk cover plans to children at lower ages.

Since last few years L.I.C. had started offering risk cover plans like limited payment whole life, an endowment assurance plan from the age of 12 years and money back plan from the age of 13 years (completed). New plans have been specially designed for children where the risk of the child starts much earlier, say 7 years. Risk cover may not begin when the policy is issued. The date on which the risk may begin is called the "deferred date" and the period between the deferred date and the date of commencement of policy is called the "deferment period."

As children cannot enter into contract, policies on the lives of children are taken out by other elders. After some time, when the child becomes major and is competent to contract, the child may assume the ownership of the policy, either by a specific action of doing so or automatically by virtue of the provisions of the policy. The policy is then said to "vest" in the child. The date on which this happens is called the "testing date." On the testing date, the life insured must have completed 18 years of age.

(a) Children's Deferred Assurance Plan

This plan enables a parent or a legal guardian or a relative of the child to provide a sum for the child by way of a very low premium. It is an endowment assurance plan with profits the risk for which commences at a selected age.

The policy is in two stages, one covering the period from the date of commencement of the policy to the deferred date (the date of commencement of risk on the child's life) and the other covering the period from the deferred date to the date on which policy emerges as a claim either by death or on maturity of the policy. A combined policy is issued covering both the stages. The plans offer two options as regards the age of commencement of the risk which may be 18 or 21 of the child.

Age at entry	:	0-17 (when risk starting age 21)
		0-14 (when risk starting age 18)
Minimum deferment period	:	4 years
Sum assured		
Minimum	:	Rs. 20,000
Maximum	:	Twice the sum of the insurance of parents

The main advantage of this plan is that policy for a relatively large amount can be taken for a relatively low premium. This premium will continue even after the deferred date, irrespective of the state of health of the child then. The proposer has the option to say that the policy will not continue after the deferred date. In that case, the policy terminates on that date and cash payment is made to the proposer.

With a view to making the life assured, viz., the child, the absolute owner of the policy after the deferred date, a special provision is made by which the policy automatically vests in the life assured on the deferred date. Thereafter, the life assured becomes the absolute owner of the policy. The policy is deemed to be a contract between the insurance company and the life assured. That is why the testing age has to be at least 18 years. Otherwise, the assured would remain a minor and there cannot be a valid contract with the assured.

(b) Children's Deferred Assurance Plan (New)

While testing age cannot be earlier than 18, the deferred date (when risk on the life assured commences) can be earlier than 18. In such cases, deferred date will be different from the testing date. Under the New Children's Deferred Assurance plans, children between the ages of 5 and 11 years are insured, with the risk commencing at age 12.

Under Children's Assurance Plans, there are special provisions to cover contingencies before the deferred date. Premiums may be waived if proposer dies before testing date. The proposer, different from the life assured, can terminate the policy, in which case the premium will be refunded, subject to conditions. If the life assured dies before the deferred date, the benefits (return of premiums) follow different specifications. Participation in surplus normally will commence after the deferred date but can be effective retrospectively from an earlier date. There are variations in these matters between different policies.

The other LIC Plans for children are as follows:

(a) Child as a Policyholder

(i) Jeevan Kishore

Under the Jeevan Kishore Plan, children between the ages 1 and 12 years (age last birthday) are eligible to be insured. Risk commences either two years after the date of commencement or from the policy anniversary falling immediately after the completion of 7 years of age, whichever is later. If the child's age is 11 or 12 years when the policy is taken, the risk will commence at age 12.

(ii) Jeevan Sukanya

The Jeevan Sukanya is a limited premium-paying plan on the life of the female child. Deferment period in the policy is as in the case of Jeevan Kishore. When she gets married, the risk cover is extended to the life of her husband, risk on husband's life commencing three months after marriage, or one month after intimation of marriage or on attainment of age 20 by the life assured, whichever is the latest. Under this plan premiums will cease on attainment of age 20 by the life assured. Maturity is at age 50.

(iii) Jeevan Balya

This plan provides for a monthly income to the child up to the age 21 in case of the unfortunate death of the parent.

(b) Parent as a Policyholder and Child as Beneficiary

(i) Jeevan Chhaya

This is an ideal policy to make provision for a child's higher education.

- Money back paid in instalments starting three years proceeding the year of maturity.
- A with-profit plan.

(ii) Bal Vidya

Most parents, however may not be satisfied with what they provide to the child. They may aspire to give the child financial security, the best of education and support for the launch of a carrier. This is where LIC's Bal Vidya comes in handby:

- It provides not only life insurance for the breadwinner but also financial security to the child.
- Money in regular monthly instalments and in lump sums at specific points of time.
- These can take care of most of the expenses of the family—on school, college and professional education, health care, starting a career, etc.

(iii) Fixed Term (Marriage) Endowment/Educational Annuity

A plan suitable for making provision for start in life, marriage or education of children.

- Risk coverage for the breadwinner.
- A plan with-profits.

6.7 ANNUITIES AND PENSION PLANS

A contract providing for regular periodic payments during a specified period is an Annuity contract. If the specified period is fixed without regard to the duration of any life, it is called Annuity Certain. If it is related to life, it is called a Life Annuity.

The Annuity is a reverse of the life insurance principal. When a person purchases a life insurance contract he agrees to make a series of payments (premiums) to the insurer and in return the insurer agrees to pay a specified sum to the beneficiaries, in case of death of life assured or on maturity. If a person buys an Annuity Contract he pays the insurer a specified capital sum (Purchase Price), may be in instalments or lump sum and in return the insurer promises to make a series of payments to him as long as he lives.

A pension is also an annuity. When annuity is provided by an employer to the employees or their dependent in consideration of the service rendered, it is generally called pension. The necessity for pension has arisen mainly because of two reasons

(a) Improvement in Longevity

The average longevity of an individual is improving and at the same time the capacity to earn a living is limited beyond a certain age called superannuation age. The superannuation age is generally 58 to 60 years. However, income is necessary even after superannuation to pursue a normal life and at the same time provide for additional medical expenses at an old age.

(b) Break-up of Joint Family System

Joint family system in India is breaking up very fast and in big cities it has been eliminated to a great extent. As such the individual cannot expect much from the children or other relations and he has to depend on his own.

Employees of the State or private/public sector organisations may find that the pension provided by the employer is not sufficient. To supplement that they may like to have individual pension plans. Others who are not employees or whose employers do not have pension plans may also arrange for pensions on their own.

The various types of annuities are broadly available in the following two plans:

(i) Immediate Annuity
(ii) Deferred Annuity

Immediate Annuity

Here the purchaser of an annuity pays a lump sum, called purchase price, in return for a promise of monthly/quarterly/half-yearly/yearly annuity. The first instalment starts at the end of the month, quarter, half-year or the year as the case may be.

The annuity can be paid for 5, 10, 15, 20 or 25 years certain and thereafter during the life of the annuitant. If the annuitant dies during the selected term, the balance annuity instalments for the remaining part of the selected term will be paid to the nominee or legal heirs.

Deferred Annuity

Here the annuity is purchased by paying in instalments or by a single premium, and the annuity payment starts after a lapse of selected period, called deferment period. The deferred annuity contracts can also be had for a guaranteed certain period and life thereafter. If the annuitant dies before the date on which the annuity payments are due, i.e. during the deferment period the premiums paid are returned to the beneficiary.

The following products are available in the market:

Sl. No.	*Name of the Company*	*Type of Plan*
1.	Life Insurance Corporation of India	New Jeevan Suraksha
2.	Allianz Bajaj Life Insurance Company	NIL
3.	HDFC Standard Life Insurance Company	NIL
4.	ICICI Prudential Life Insurance Company	ICICI Pru for ever life
5.	TATA AIG Life Insurance Company	NIL
6.	Birla Sun Life Insurance Company	NIL
7.	SBI Cardiff Life Insurance Company	Sanjeevini, Sukhjeevan
8.	Max New York Life Insurance Company	NIL

Note: Any premium paid on the above-mentioned policies are eligible for tax benefits either under Section 80CCC or Section 88 of Income Tax Act, 1961.

Based on the above-mentioned broad categories, the life insurance products are formulated with some modification as per need of the society. As the need grows and more and more new players enter the insurance market, the life insurance product formulation will grow simultaneously.

6.8 SUMMARY

Life insurance is to mitigate the adverse consequences that may follow either on early death of a person or on his living too long. Every possible consequence that requires to be taken care of constitutes a need for insurance. The needs of people for life insurance can be family need, children need, old-age and special needs. To meet the needs of the people the insurers have developed different type of products such as Term Life Insurance, Whole Life Insurance, Endowment Type Plans, Combination of Whole Life and Endowment Type Plans, Children's Assurance Plans and Annuity Plans. These plans can be for an individual or for a group. These plans can also be with-profit or without-profit.

6.9 REVIEW QUESTIONS

1. Classify the needs of people for life insurance. Do these needs exist simultaneously and in same measure for all persons?
2. What are the various kinds of life insurance policies? Discuss.
3. What are the main benefits of Term Insurance Plans? Name any two Term Insurance Policies.
4. Describe the different types of endowment policies.
5. "Multi-purpose policy is fulfilling almost all types of human needs." Comment.
6. Who propose for insurance under children deferred assurance plan and on whose life? When does the risk start under this plan?
7. What are "annuities"? Of how many types broadly they are?

7

CHAPTER

GROWTH OF INSURANCE BUSINESS IN INDIA

LEARNING OBJECTIVE

The main objective of this chapter is to bring out the growth of life and non-life insurance in the country and to expose the learners to the major issues concerning the growth of insurance.

7.1 INTRODUCTION

It was in the 14th century in which the idea of insurance was first conceptualized. At that time it was used more as a tool for protection against financial loss of sea fearers involved in foreign trade. Since then this concept has undergone several changes. It is basically the unforeseen contingencies of human life that has given a very new look to the insurance industry. Gradually as competition increased the benefits given by the industry to its customers improved by leaps and bounds. It was the break-up of the traditional extended family system that provided a natural umbrella to each and every member of the family, which gave the insurance (life and non-life) institutions an impetus to excel.

With the growth of industry, trade and commerce the insurance also grew over a period of time and gained maturity. In terms of insurance premium collection, presently, India stands fifth in Asia with Japan having 40 times more premium collection than India. Despite a double digit growth in last two years, the ratio of insurance premium to GDP has remained low in China and India. Currently, only 70 millions people are insured in India out of the overall population of over one billion. On the other hand, the non-life insurance business has vital role to play to safeguard the properties of the nation. The gross domestic premium income of general insurance business in

India has increased to Rs. 9522 crores in 2000 from Rs. 184 crore in 1973. This speaks about the volume of growth in non-life insurance business in the country.

7.2 GROWTH OF LIFE INSURANCE

By 1956, 229 Indian insurers, provident insurance societies, and 16 non-Indian insurers were carrying on life insurance business in India. But since January 19, 1956, the Life business came under the control and ownership of government. In June 1956, a Bill was passed for establishing Life Insurance Corporation of India, which started functioning since September 1, 1956. The Corporation is a body corporate having perpetual succession and a common seal with powers to acquire, hold and dispose of property and may by its name sue and be sued. There will be not more than 15 members including a Chairman thereof. The Corporation is charged with the main duty to carry on life insurance business. It has one Central Office, 5 Zonal Offices and several Divisional and Branch Offices.

The growth of life insurance business has been analyzed under new business inclusive of group insurance business, new business individual insurance excluding annuities, growth in sum assured and number of policies, average amount per policy, rural new business, annuities, business in force, lapses, number of offices, productivity of assets, and process of new insurance plans.

Growth in New Business

Tables 7.1 and 7.2 give the detailed account regarding the growth of new business of life insurance in India and abroad.

TABLE 7.1

New Business (inclusive of Group Insurance Business)

(Amount in crores of Rs.)

	Business in India	*Business outside India*	*Total Business*
31st March, 1957	277.67	5.40	283.07
31st March, 1963	734.72	11.24	745.96
31st March, 1970	1025.80	10.28	1036.08
31st March, 1980	7998.16	11.22	8009.38
31st March, 1990	43490.34	100.00	43590.34
31st March, 1994	80560.88	199.07	80759.95
31st March, 2000	158110.37	340.00	158450.37

Source: Economic Surveys of Various Years.

TABLE 7.2

New Business Individual Insurance (Excluding Annuities)

(No. of policies in lakhs and sum assured in crores of Rs.)

Year	*In India*		*Out of India*		*Total*	
	No. of Policies	*Sum Assured*	*No. of Policies*	*Sum Assured*	*No. of Policies*	*Sum Assured*
1992-93	99.58	35956.82	0.10	158.98	99.68	36115.80
1993-94	107.26	41813.83	0.12	199.07	107.38	42012.90
1994-95	108.75	55228.50	0.13	240.32	108.88	55468.82
1995-96	110.21	51815.54	0.13	255.99	110.34	52071.53
1996-97	122.68	56740.50	0.123	253.44	122.81	56993.94
1998-99	148.43	75316.28	0.170	283.72	148.60	75600.00
1999-00	169.54	90872.02	0.230	342.23	169.77	91214.25

Source: Economic Surveys of Various Years.

Business in India

The new business in India has tremendously increased during the period of last 50 years. It has gone up from Rs. 277.67 crores in 1957, to Rs. 734.72 crores in 1963 and to Rs. 1025.80 crores in 1970 and again to Rs. 8787.26 crores in 1980-81 and Rs. 43490.34 crores in 1989-90 and Rs. 80560.88 crores in 1993-94 and Rs. 158450.37 crores in 1999-2000. Thus, it had shown a satisfactory progress so far new business was concerned up to 31 March 2000 from Rs. 43490.34 crores in 1989-90.

Business Outside India

The new business outside did not rise satisfactorily. It has gone up from Rs. 5.40 crores in 1957 to Rs. 11.73 crores in 1975 and to Rs. 14.41 crores in 1981, and Rs. 28.30 crores in 1984. The cause of the lesser rate of increase was that the Corporation has to compete with other concerns outside India whereas in India it is monopolistic concern. However, it improved in 1989-90 when it rose to Rs. 100.00 crores and 199.07 crores in 1993-94 and Rs. 340 crores in 1999-2000.

The new business of individual insurance (excluding annuities) has increased from 99.68 lakh policies in 1992-93 to Rs. 108.88 lakh policies in 1994-95 and 148.6 lakh policies in 1998-99; amounting to Rs. 36115.8 crores, Rs. 55468.82 crores and Rs. 75600 crores in the respective years. It indicate that the LIC is trying hard to increase its new business at a very rapid speed that is, more than 2 times during the period of five years. The business out of India increased to Rs. 283.72 crores in 1998-99 under 17 thousand policies.

The average amount per policy has also been rising constantly in India and outside India. The average amount has increased from Rs. 7,345 in 1970 and further to Rs. 9,807 in 1975, Rs. 13,041 in 1980, Rs. 19,913 in 1985 and Rs. 50,786 in 1995. Thus, the average sum assured has risen by about 12.3 times during the period of last 30 years in India.

TABLE 7.3

Average Sum Assured per Policy (New Business) Individual

Year	*India (Rs.)*	*Outside India (Rs.)*	*Total (Rs.)*
1963	4179	11834	4220
1970	7345	22055	7394
1975	9807	27985	9848
1980	13041	40129	13077
1985	19913	43256	19959
1990	31411	117523	31510
1995	50786	180637	50945
2000	53599	148795	53728

Source: Economic Surveys of Various Years.

The growth in average sum per policy was not as fast as the sum assured had risen. The rise in the average sum outside India was higher than the rise in India. The total average sum assured has also risen more than 12.4 times during this period.

Rural New Business

Rural LIC business has increased from Rs. 10,294.55 crores under 36.75 lakh policies in 1990-91 to Rs. 28,000 crore under 70 lakh policies in 1998-99. The percentage share of policies to total new policies increased from 42.5 to 49.2 during the period 1990-91 and 1996-97. Percentage share of rural new business in total new business of LIC has increased from 36.6 to 42.8 in the same duration. It is expected that the percentage share of rural business in the total business would not change in future. The LIC may not devote much time and energy for procuring new business in rural areas, as it has to compete with foreign insurers who would devote only in urban area. Profit motive is the basic object of foreign insurers. They would devote for enhancing business.

The role of LIC in enhancing rural business would socially be the essential but commercially, it would be loss-making endeavour because LIC's urban share would be snatched by foreign and domestic insurers. The inertia of large number applies in insurance. The mortality is comparatively lower in urban people than that of rural-people. Claim-people would be insured by private insurers, whereas the inferior stuff would be left to the LIC. It would cause deterioration in rural business.

Annuities

The amount of annuities has been declining with fluctuations. The deferred annuities in India have gone down from Rs. 12.68 crores in 1970 to Rs. 9.67 crores in 1975. However, there has been a slight improvement so far immediate annuities are concerned. It has gone up from Rs. 1.90 crores in

TABLE 7.4

Rural New Business

Year	*Rural New Business*		*Percentage share of Rural New Business in total new Business*	
	No. of Policies (in Lakhs)	*Sum Assured (Rs. in crore)*	*Policies*	*Sum Assured*
1990-91	36.75	10,294.55	42.50	36.60
1991-92	41.27	12,439.93	44.70	38.80
1992-93	44.39	14,084.03	44.60	39.20
1993-94	48.56	16,680.03	45.30	39.90
1994-95	49.02	21,571.00	45.10	39.10
1995-96	52.57	21,263.59	47.70	41.00
1996-97	60.33	24,278.73	49.20	42.80
1998-99	70.00	28,000.00	47.16	37.18

Source: Economic Surveys of Various Years.

1966 to Rs. 2.07 crores in 1975. Thus, the immediate annuities were gaining popularity. Moreover, the Group Super Annuation on Scheme has given a significant rise, it has gone up from Rs. 106.20 lakhs per annum, during 1979-80, 681 immediate Life Annuity amounted to Rs. 30.78 lakhs per annum and 141 Deferred Life Annuity amounted to Rs. 6.98 lakhs per annum. It declined in 1985 to the level of 28 Immediate Life Annuity Policies of Rs. 1.27 lakhs and 88 Dererred Life Annuity Policies of Rs. 4.10 lakhs per annum. Immediate annuities of Rs. 2.00 crores and Deferred Life Annuities of Rs. 7.11 crores were sold during 1994-95.

Business in Force

The life insurance business in force in case of individual and group business in India has been showing the upward trend as revealed by Tables 7.5 and 7.6.

(a) Individual Business

The life insurance business in force in India has been continuously rising from Rs. 6,425 crores in 1970 to Rs. 11,725 crores in 1975 and Rs. 19,114 crores in 1980 and Rs. 94,408 crores in 1990. Thus the business, in force, has increased by more than 4 times during the period of last 10 years. The total business in force has increased to Rs. 19,243 crores in 1980, Rs. 94,823 crores in 1990 and Rs. 254,572 crores in 1995. The individual business has risen to Rs. 452,200 crores in 2000.

(b) Group Insurance and Superannuation Schemes

Table 7.6 exhibits that the business-in-force of Group Insurance Schemes has rapidly been increasing from Rs. 39.0 crores in 1967 to Rs. 6137.46 crores in 1980 and Rs. 10218.56 crores in 1985, Rs. 23049.64 crores

TABLE 7.5

Individual Insurance Business in Force

(Rs. in crores)

	Indian	Non-Indian	Total Business
March 31st			
1955	1128	92	1220
1966	4282	112	3878
1975	11725	124	11852
1980	19114	129	19243
1985	33785	166	33951
1990	94408	415	94823
1995	253333	1239	254572
1996	294336	1422	295758
1997	343018	1601	344619
2000	450000	2200	452200

Source: Economic Surveys of Various Years.

in 1990, Rs. 51,034.71crores in 1995 and Rs. 81,000 crores in 2000. The business-in-force of Group Superannuation Schemes has increased from Rs. 1.79 crores of annuities in 1967 to Rs. 61.02 crores of annuities in 1980 and Rs. 146.51 crores in 1985 and further to Rs. 245.11 crores in 1990 and Rs. 422.66 crores in 1995 and Rs. 700 crores in 2000. This reveals that the Group Insurance has been constantly and rapidly rising in India. It is a very good indicator of the popular form of life insurance, which can be adopted to benefit the masses, individually, as well as a group.

TABLE 7.6

Group Insurance and Superannuation Scheme

(Business in crores)

As on March, 31	*Group Insurance Schemes*		*Group Superannuation Schemes*	
	Number of Schemes	*Sum assured (in Crores of Rupees)*	*Number of Schemes*	*Amount Annuities (in Crores Rs.)*
1967	259	39.00	—	1.79
1970	385	77.00	—	3.12
1975	2062	1457.07	366	6.59
1980	7442	6137.46	639	61.02
1985	14521	10218.56	1391	146.51
1990	37089	23049.64	2405	245.11
1995	71726	51034.71	3642	422.66
2000	270.00	81,000.00	7.00	700.00

Source: Economic Surveys of Various Years.

Policy Lapses

We know that the lapsation of policy is harmful for the insurers as well as insured because the goodwill and reputation of the former decline. whereas the benefits of insurance are not available to the latter one. Therefore, attempts should be made to reduce the lapse-percentage. It is a very encouraging sign that the percentage of net lapses to mean life insurance business-in-force has declined from the highest of 8.1 per cent in 1963 to 3.8 per cent in 1980 and 5.6 per cent in 1990. Even this percentage is very high and corporation should try to minimize the lapse-ratio. But it could not improve the problems of lapses as the lapse-ratio increased to 4.2 per cent in 1985 and again increased to 5.6 per cent in 1990 and 6.1 per cent in 1995 and 5.5 per cent in 2000.

TABLE 7.7

Percentage of Net Lapses to Mean Life Insurance Business-in-force

Year	*Percentage*
March 31, 1960	6.6
March 31, 1963	8.1
March 31, 1970	5.9
March 31, 1975	5.4
March 31, 1980	3.8
March 31, 1985	4.2
March 31, 1990	5.6
March 31, 1995	6.1
March 31, 1997	5.1
March 31, 2000	5.5

Source: Economic Surveys of Various Years.

Number of Offices

The number of offices has not increased satisfactorily. As compared to the bank-branches, the expansion in LIC offices has been almost negligible. The total offices of LIC have increased from 735 in 1963 to 888 in 1980 and 1160 in 1985 and 1603 in 1990. The number of branch offices has been growing from 340 in 1963 to 738 in 1980 and 1528 in 1990. The number of sub-offices increased to 179 in 1963 and declined to only 4 sub-offices in 1980. The number of development centres has also been decreasing from 175 in 1963 to 100 in 1980 and further to only 5 in 1985. The total number of LIC offices in 2000 was 2155, out of which 2048 were branch offices.

Productivity of Agents

Data shown in table 7.9 indicate that the Productivity of Active Agents has been constantly increasing from Rs. 31,000 in 1957 to Rs. 2,47,641 in 1980 by about 8 times and 3,63,772 in 1985 by 11 times. The productivity of agents has been Rs. 666,605 in 1990 and 1,063,101 in 1995 and Rs. 1,328,292 in 2000.

TABLE 7.8

Number of Offices

As on	*Zonal offices*	*Divisional offices*	*Branch offices*	*Sub-offices*	*Development centres*	*Total offices*
March 31, 1963	5	36	340	179	175	735
March 31, 1970	5	36	424	115	123	703
March 31, 1975	5	41	651	29	105	831
March 31, 1980	5	41	738	4	100	888
March 31, 1985	5	43	1107	—	5	1160
March 31, 1990	6	69	1528	—	—	1603
March 31, 1995	7	100	2021	—	—	2128
March 31, 2000	7	100	2048	—	—	2155

Source: Economic Surveys of Various Years and LIC Annual Reports of Various Years.

TABLE 7.9

Productivity of Agents

As on	*Number of Active Agents*	*Business Per Active Agent in (Rs.)*
December 31, 1957	8,900	31,000
March 31, 2000	6,83,190	13,28,292
March 31, 1963	1,41,000	52,070
March 31, 1970	1,32,790	77,241
March 31, 1975	1,46,103	1,20,518
March 31, 1976	1,44,385	1,45,722
March 31, 1980	1,10,366	2,47,641
March 31, 1984	1,32,947	3,29,980
March 31, 1985	1,47,783	3,63,772
March 31, 1989	2,96,713	5,80,455
March 31, 1990	3,48,325	6,66,605
March 31, 1994	5,24,427	7,97,324
March 31, 1995	5,19,504	10,63,101
March 31, 2000	6,83,190	13,28,292

Source: Economic Surveys of Various Years and LIC Annual Reports of Various Years.

7.3 PRODUCT DIVERSIFICATION BY LIC

Product diversification is essential to meet the varying needs, changing preferences and rising aspirations of the customers. Realizing the importance of product diversification LIC has introduced various insurance plans so as to increase its business multifold. The growth of LIC according to policies is given in Table 7.10. It is obvious from the table that the importance of whole life policies and endowment assurances are reducing gradually, that total sum assured under these policies are increasing although in relation to total individual business, they are not increasing.

Money back policies have increased to the level of Rs. 20,000 crore. It is prominent assurance policy because of its advantages of investment. The amount of children's anticipated endowment is reducing year after year. It has come down to nearly 10 crore.

Jeewan Raksha Policy has yielded insurance to the tune of Rs. 1600 crore in 1996-97. It is rapidly increasing. Similarly, Jeevan Mitra has crossed the level of Rs. 1927 crore. Jeevan Sathi is also becoming popular. The sum assured was Rs. 566.74 crore in 1996-97. The Marriage Endowment and Educational amenities have increased considerably to meet the requirements of marriage and education of children. Convertible whole life has gone down to the level of Rs. 165.74 crore in 1996-97. Jeevan Balya/Jeeven Kishore have been popular as they crossed the level of Rs. 800 crore. Similarly, Jeevan Chhaya has been gradually increasing although Bima Sandesh declined to Rs. 51.78 crore in 1996-97.

One may conclude from the foregoing details that those policies are becoming popular, which have features of investment and periodical payment along with coverage of risk.

TABLE 7.10

Progress of Insurance Plans in India

(Sum assured in crores of Rs.)

Name of Plan	*1985-86*	*1990-91*	*1995-96*	*1996-97*	*1999-2000*
Whole Life Policies	41.22	130.03	133.33	117.31	105.88
Endowment Assurance	2900.77	9538.92	10699.36	12314.79	22578.66
Money Back	2628.83	12979.08	16396.08	19426.77	20861.32
Children's Anticipated Endowment	87.33	82.08	9.96	9.80	13.13
Jeevan Raksha Policy (All)	35.11	525.22	1375.39	1666.05	2843.38
Jeevan Mitra	751.25	1885.55	1769.17	1927.46	2288.49
Jeevan Sathi	59.47	544.36	554.64	566.74	735.49
Marriage/Educational Endowment/Annuity	—	271.90	673.12	647.70	1736.26
Convertible Whole Life	273.92	473.62	198.16	165.74	—
Jeevan Balya Kiran	—	1090.65	834.96	865.67	—
Jeevan Chhaya	—	84.40	363.54	357.90	949.59
Bima Sandesh	—	205.01	64.69	51.78	—

Source: Economic Surveys of Various Years and LIC Annual Reports of Various Years.

As evident from the Table 7.11 that the LIC has diversified insurance products. Under this scheme, Asha Deep with some novel features was introduced in 1993-94. This plan besides providing death and maturity payment, provides benefits in case the life assured suffering from any of four

TABLE 7.11

Progress of New Insurance Plans (Policies)

(Sum assured in crores of Rs.)

	1991-92	1992-93	1993-94	1994-95	1995-96	1996-97	1999-2000
Bhavisya Jeevan	1.46	1.33	1.13	0.84	0.39	45.60	20.81
Jeevan Saathi	—	1157.07	1803.83	2084.62	3360.78	4858.71	735.49
Jeevan Sukanya	—	151.90	102.67	42.66	30.37	17.69	28.29
Asha Deep—I	—	—	4573.70	—	—	—	—
Asha Deep—II	—	—	—	—	1362.34	886.11	448.01
Jeevan Sarita	17.32	17.62	11.61	5.92	10.12	8.30	0.135*
Jeevan Griha	55.68	132.54	169.85	141.07	129.89	136.58	6.34*
Bima Kiran	—	—	—	19366.71	10944.84	9441.15	122.99*
Jeevan Shree	—	—	—	411.76	1320.34	1396.07	48.27*
Jeevan Aadhar	—	—	—	—	21.12	19.52	0.16*
Jeevan Sanchaya	—	—	—	—	—	287.39	44.70*
Jeevan Sneha	—	—	—	—	—	251.07	6.72*
Children's Money Back	—	—	935.31	1583.50	1253.88	—	19.07

Source: Economic Surveys of Various Years and LIC Annual Reports of Various Years. Information with star indicates the sum assured without profit.

major ailments, viz., cancer, paralytic stroke leading to permanent disability, renal failure of both kidneys and coronary artery diseases, where bypass surgery has been done.

1. Asha Deep-I

The total business under Asha Deep-I was Rs. 4573.70 crore under 6.42 lakh policies in 1993-94. Asha Deep-I did not continue later on.

2. Asha Deep-II

This plan was first introduced in September 1993 on an experimental basis for a period of 3 months. In response to public demand the plan was reintroduced as Asha Deep-II in the month of November, 1995. This plan besides death and maturity payment, provides for benefits in case the life assured is affiliated by any of four major ailments, viz., cancer, paralytic stroke leading to permanent disability, renal failure of both kidneys and coronary artery diseases where bypass surgery has been done. The amount of sum assured under this scheme was Rs. 1362.34 crore in 1995-96 and Rs. 886.11 crore in 1996-97.

3. Jeevan Aadhar

Jeeven Aadhar introduced in January 1996 is specially designed for the benefit of handicapped dependents. Contributions under this Plan are eligible for income tax relief under Section 88DDA of the Income Tax Act. This plan is basically a limited payment whole life assurance on the life of the proposer with provision for Guaranteed Additions and Terminal Addition to the basic sum assured. The claim amount will be payable partly in lump-sum and partly in the form of annuity to the handicapped dependents. The sum assured under Jeevan Aadhar was Rs. 21.12 crore in 1995-96 and Rs. 19.52 crore in 1996-97.

4. Jeevan Suraksha

This plan was introduced on 15th August, 1996. It enables individuals to provide for retirement income from a selected date. The policy is with life cover but can be taken without life cover under certain conditions. The policyholder taking policy with life cover provides minimum of 50% of the target pension to spouse on death during the deferment period. Spouse's pension is not provided under without life cover plan. On investing the policyholder has the option to receive 25 per cent of the notional case plan in lump sum and balance in annuity. The amount of Jeevan Suraksha was Rs. 102.65 crore in 1997-98.

5. Jeevan Sneha

It was introduced on 16th January, 1997 for women. It is a without profit money back type plan with the added features of guaranteed additions viz., encashment of survival benefit as and when required. Flexibility to pay premium in advance, inbuilt accident cover, for insurance cover for a period of 3 years from the date of first unpaid premium provided atleast 2 full years premium have been paid and option to receive pension in lieu of maturity benefits. The sum assured under this scheme was Rs. 251.07 crore in 1996-97.

6. Jeevan Sanchaya

This plan was introduced on 16th January, 1997. It is without profits money back type of plan with provision of loyalty addition and guaranteed addition. Accident benefit is also granted under this plan with an upper limit of Rs. 5 lakhs in addition to existing limit of Rs. 5 lakhs under other Plan.

7. Children's Money Back

Children's Money Back has assured Rs. 935.31 crore in 1994-95, Rs. 1583.50 crore in 1995-96 and Rs. 1253.88 crore in 1996-97. It is becoming popular because of inherent advantages to children. People want insurance for their children.

7.4 GROWTH OF GENERAL INSURANCE BUSINESS

In India, general insurance was brought by Britishers. Their operation was through agencies. The Triton Insurance Company Ltd. was the first general insurance company established in India in 1858 at Kolkata. It was British owned company and its share was held by them. The first general insurance company to be set-up by Indian was Indian Mercantile Insurance

Company Ltd. in Mumbai in 1907. It was to transact all types of general insurance business. Thereafter, a large number of both Indian and foreign insurance companies were set-up in the country. However, till independence as much as 40% of the insurance business was held by foreigners mainly Britishers.

With the setting up a large number of insurance companies, it was felt that there should be a code of conduct to be followed by these companies in order to ensure fair and sound business and prevent unethical practices. As a result, Insurance Association of India through its General Insurance Council framed a code of conduct, which was to be administered by the Controller of Insurance. Its head office was located at Delhi with branch offices at Mumbai, Kolkata and Chennai. Further, the need was also felt to retain maximum business in India. To achieve the above objective, Indian Reinsurance Corporation was established in 1956. All the insurance companies voluntarily decided to cede 10% of their gross direct premium to the Reinsurance Corporation. In 1961 the Government constituted Indian Guarantee and General Insurance Company Ltd. as a Government owned reinsurance Company, which coexisted along with Indian Reinsurance Corporation. The insurance companies were required to cede 10% of their premium to each of these two companies. In addition, insurers established two other organizations, namely, Fire Insurance Pool, the Marine Insurance Pool, and a percentage of companies of fire and hull insurance business was ceded to these pools respectively. The business ceded to these pools was retroceded to the ceding companies thereby ensuring the spread of risks amongst the members of pools.

In 1968, the Insurance Act, 1938 was amended which empowered the Controller of Insurance to regulate deployment of assets, provide for maximum solvency margin, issue licenses to surveyors, investigate, search and seize their books of accounts, etc. The amendment also facilitated setting up of Tariff Advisory Committee to be chaired by the Controller of Insurance. Its functions comprised of controlling and regulating rates, terms and advantages of General Insurance business in India.

After independence, under the planned development of the company, the Government came to the conclusion that a strong public sector under its direct control will be able to meet national objectives of growth, equity, resource mobilisation, employment generation, etc. In pursuance to the above objective, life insurance was nationalised in 1956, and banking sector in 1969.

The General Insurance business was nationalized with effect from January 1, 1973, through the General Insurance Business (Nationalization) Act, 1972. However, as a prelude to the above act, the Government took over the management of all the operating companies in 1971, through General Insurance (Emergency Provision) Act, 1971. The emergency act provided for the appointment of custodians who were empowered to exercise controls over these companies subject to the directions of the Central Government at the time of nationalization of these companies, there were a total of 107 companies underwriting general insurance business in India. All these companies were amalgamated and grouped into four, namely, the National Insurance Company Limited, the New India Assurance Company Limited, the Oriental Insurance Company Limited, and the United India Insurance Company Limited with head offices at Kolkata, Mumbai, Delhi and Chennai respectively. The General Insurance Company (GIC) was formed as a holding company in November 1972. The GIC was constituted for the purpose of superintending, controlling and carrying out the business of general insurance. The entire capital of GIC was subscribed by the Government and that of four companies by the GIC on behalf of the Government of India.

The main objectives of nationalization were to ensure the development of the general insurance business in sympathy with the best of interest and advantage to the community. Further, these companies were required to promote competition in the economy and to prevent the concentration of wealth and growth of monopoly. They were supposed to widely spread their activities over geographical area, innovate new products as per the requirements of different segments of population, and also meet social objective through formulating policies for weaker sections of society. The functions of GIC as laid down in the act were:

1. Carrying on of any part of general insurance business, if it thinks desirable to do so;
2. Aiding, assisting and advising the acquiring companies in the matter of setting up of standards of conduct and sound practice in general insurance business and in the matter of rendering efficient service to holders of policies of general insurance;
3. Advising the general insurance companies in the matter of controlling their expenses including the payment of commission and other expenses;
4. Advising the acquiring companies in the matter of investment of their funds; and
5. Issuing direction to acquiring companies in relation to the conduct of the general insurance business.

The progress of miscellaneous general insurances before nationalization has been analyzed in the following sections:

The gross premium of Indian Insurers has increased from Rs. 39.78 crores in 1969 to Rs. 45.90 crores in 1970 and further to Rs. 57.28 crores in 1972. The gross premium received by the Indian insurers has increased from 85.5 per cent of total gross premium in 1969 to 87.4 percent in 1971 and further to 88.5 per cent in 1972. This shows that the Indian insurers are getting increasing business. Consequently, the shares of non-Indian insurers were also declining from Rs. 14.5 crores in 1969 to Rs. 57.63 crores in 1971 and further to Rs. 64.70 crores in 1972.

As compared to total insurances, the share of Indian insurers to miscellaneous insurance had been higher. It was 82.6 per cent in case of total insurance and 88.5 per cent in case of miscellaneous insurance. Thus, the miscellaneous insurance of Indian insurers have been at higher level. Consequently the share of non-Indian insurer has been decreasing. The total gross premium has increased from Rs. 116.88 crores in 1969 to Rs. 131.62 crores in 1970 and further to Rs. 147.53 crores in 1971 and again to Rs. 195.83 crores in 1972. In both the cases, the share of Indian insurers to gross premium was rising.

The share of net claims payable to net premium has increased from 56.8 per cent in 1970 to 57.20 per cent in 1972. It means the amount of claim has been increasing in case of miscellaneous insurance. The net commission also increased from 11.4 percent of net premium in 1970 to 11.8 per cent in 1971 and further to 12.5 per cent in 1972. However, the percentage of management expenses has also been declining. The reserve has decreased but the balance of income has increased from 8.5 per cent of net premium in 1970 to 11.2 per cent in 1971 and declined to 10.3 percent in 1972.

The non-Indian Insurers have paid lesser amount in the shape of claims whereas the Indian insurers have paid more amount as compared to net premium. Expenses of management in case of non-Indian insurers are also increasing. It had increased from 32.7 per cent of net premium to 34.3 per cent in 1972. The balance of income has increased from 8.5 per cent in 1970 to 15.5 percent in 1971, but declined to 9.8 per cent in 1972. Thus, the non-Indian insurers were increasing their balances at higher speed.

The gross claims payable has been 40.7 per cent of gross premium in 1958, 64.9 per cent of gross premium in 1970 and again 51.8 per cent in 1972. Thus, the share of gross claims payable has been decreased in 1971. The percentage of direct commission has been constantly decreasing. The percentage of management expenses has been declining from 32.6 per cent in 1958 to 20.7 per cent in 1970 and further to 19.2 per cent in 1971 but increased to 20.1 per cent in 1972. The miscellaneous income has been increasing in both the cases. Similarly, the balance of income in case of Indian insurers has increased from 13.5 per cent of gross premium in 1958 to 22.0 per cent of gross premium in 1971 and declined to 21.2 per cent in 1972. The Non-Indian insurers have lesser balance of income than the Indian insurers had.

The Indian insurers have experienced increasing loss in case of miscellaneous insurance. The loss has gone up from 8.7 per cent in 1970 to 11.7 per cent in 1971. It was most probably due to increasing amount of claims payable and direct commission.

From the analysis of progress of different types of insurance it has been revealed that the Indian insurers were doing well more in marine insurance than in other types of general insurances.

Table 7.12 shows that the excess of income over outgo has been increasing from Rs. 2.66 crores in 1958 to Rs. 20.91 crores in 1970 and further to Rs. 32.88 crores in 1972. Thus, the reserve has also been increasing from Rs. 1.57 crores in 1958 to Rs. 7.31 crores in 1970 and further to Rs. 9.40 crores in 1972. The premium income in India has been constantly increasing from Rs. 12.96 crores in 1958 to Rs. 75.84 crores in 1970 and further to

TABLE 7.12

General Insurance: Income and Outgo in Respect of General Insurance

(Rs. in Crores)

		1958	1970	1971	1972
1. Premium less reinsurance	In India	12.96	75.84	86.45	103.13
	Out India	12.02	35.26	41.24	44.74
2. Net Interest Div. and Rents	..	0.37	3.21	4.18	5.16
3. Other Income	..	0.21	0.13	0.27	1.34
Total Income		25.56	114.44	132.14	154.37
1. Claims less reinsurance	..	12.56	57.04	62.80	73.58
2. Net Commission	..	3.33	12.51	14.89	18.72
3. Expenses of Management	..	6.77	23.38	24.45	28.78
4. Misc. Outgo	..	0.24	0.60	0.37	0.41
Total Outgo	..	22.90	93.53	102.51	121.49
Excess of Income over Outgo	..	2.66	20.91	29.63	32.88
Increase in Reserve	..	1.57	7.31	12.61	9.40

Source: Economic Surveys of Various Years.

Rs. 86.45 crores in 1971 and again to Rs. 103.13 crores in 1972. The total income has increased from Rs. 25.56 crores in 1958 to Rs. 132.14 crores in 1971 and again to Rs. 154.37 crores in 1973, but the increase in total outgo was lesser than this, so the excess of income over outgo and increase in reserve has been rapidly rising.

The general insurance could not increase rapidly as industrial production did up to 1967. The general insurance would have risen at least parallel to the development of industrial production does, it is a clear indication of satisfactory development of general insurance. The index of general insurance reveals that it had gone upto 137.5 in 1967 and 158.9 in 1968 whereas the index of industrial production has gone up 143.2 in 1967 and 152.9 in 1968. Thus, the general insurance started rising more rapidly after 1967. The index number of general insurance was 202.8 whereas the index number of industrial production was 182.6 in 1972. It reveals that the general insurance business was satisfactorily progressing.

7.5 GROWTH OF GENERAL INSURANCE AFTER NATIONALIZATION

The growth of general insurance over a period of time has been evaluated in terms of parameters such as growth of gross and net premium, geographical spread of the business, class-wise distribution of business, underwriting results, reinsurance operations, investment income, free and technical reserves, net worth, overall profitability, etc. The overall claim ratio expenses on management have also been examined. Based upon the data as given in Table 4.13, the following picture emerges:

1. The gross domestic premium income in India (GDPI), which was Rs. 184 crore in 1973, has increased to Rs. 9522 crore in 1999-2000, recording an average growth rate of about 16.90%. The premium income originating outside India went up over the level of Rs. 24 crore in 1973 to Rs. 460 crore in 1999-2000, registering annual growth rate of about 11.95%. The total gross premium income, which was Rs. 208 crore in 1973, stood at Rs. 9,982 crore in 1999-2000, recording average annual growth rate of about 16.50%. The total net premium income increased to Rs. 9364 crore in 1990-2000 from the level of Rs. 222 crore in 1973. It recorded average annual growth rate of about 15.75%. The net premium income as percentage to total premium income was 93.8% in 1999-2000, indicating that only about 7% of GDPI went outside the country through reinsurance. As compared to 1973, the GDPI in India has grown by about 47 times.
2. The net claim payable were at Rs. 7586 crore in 1999-2000 as against Rs. 1123 crore in 1973, accounting for 81% to net premium.
3. The expenses including management expenses, commission and other outgo which were Rs. 68 crore in 1973 increased to Rs. 2510 crore in 1999-2000. It constituted 31% and 27% of net premium income in 1973 and 1999-2000 respectively.
4. The expenses of the management increased from Rs. 43 crore in 1973 to Rs. 2264 crore in 1999-2000. It amounted to 22.7% of gross premium income and 24.1% of net premium.
5. The total investment increased from Rs. 355 crore in 1973 to Rs. 16659 crore in 1999-2000. It grew by about 47 times. The compound annual growth in investible funds was about 17%. The investment income increased from Rs. 21 crore in 1973 to Rs. 2392 crore in 1999-2000. The average annual gross yield on mean funds amounted to about 13%.
6. The paid up capital and free reserves increased from Rs. 37 crore and Rs. 62 crore in 1973 to Rs. 375 and Rs. 7745 crore in 1999-2000 respectively. The increase in reserve for unexpired risk which was Rs. 23 crore in 1973 increased to Rs. 485 crore in 1999-2000.
7. In so far the class-wise distribution of business is concerned, the fire, miscellaneous and marine accounted for 24%, 66% and 10% in 1999-2000 respectively. In miscellaneous portfolio, motor business, which is a loss-making business has steadily grown over a period of time and accounted for about 32% of the total business of the industry. However, this is in consonance with the

world-wide trend since in most of the countries of the world motor business was more than 30% of the total business. For instance, it was about 63, 56 and 54 per cent in Thailand, Malaysia and Taiwan respectively.

8. The geographical spread of the premium written in India indicates that the maximum, i.e. about 40% was generated from western region and minimum, i.e. about 9% from the eastern region. The northern and southern region contributed about 26% and 24% of gross premium in 1999-2000 respectively.
9. The underwriting profit of the industry was Rs. 18 crore (8.2% of the net premium) in 1973. However, over a period of time underwriting operations have resulted into losses and these losses amounted to Rs. 1215 crore in 1999-2000, accounting for 13% of net premium income.
10. The investment income amounting to Rs. 2392 crore was in excess of underwriting losses and produced profit for the industry. The level of profit was Rs. 1153 crore before tax payment and Rs. 874 crore after tax payment. In 1973 the profit before tax and after tax were Rs. 38 crore and Rs. 14 crore respectively.
11. Although the total number of insurance products in the general insurance industry are around 175, only a few, i.e. 40 to 50 products have dominated the market controlling about 75 to 80 per cent of the total market. Rest of the products have not been popular as they lack mass base, may be due to poor publicity and marketing, lack of awareness, higher premium rates, and might have been introduced without adequate database.
12. The rural and non-traditional business, which was practically nil in 1973, has gradually increased over a period of time. The premium collected through this business was only about Rs. 425 crore in 1999-2000, constituting only 4% of the total gross premium income. It calls for innovating new products for the rural population suiting to different income groups and marketing them aggressively. However, if the total policies issued by office in rural areas are taken into account, the premium from rural areas will account for about 30%.
13. According to the data shown in Table 7.14 the reinsurance operation of the industry indicates that the total reinsurance premium was Rs 1011 crore in 1997-98, accounting for about 13% of the gross premium. It indicates that about 87% of the premium was retained in the country. The operations between 1990-91 to 1997-98 reveal that the retention was about 85.5% of the gross premium. Further break-up of reinsurance premium indicates that about 45% is required for placement of large projects and specialised risk and another 45% is for the surplus treaties, which is necessary to create capacity. The cost of reinsurance reveals that in 1997-98 while the commission earned was Rs. 271 crore (3.5%

of GDP), the claim recoveries were Rs. 557 crore (7.2% of GDP), accounting for a total of Rs. 828 crore. It amounted to 10.7% of GDP against the reinsurance premium of Rs. 1011 crore. Thus, the net outflow of premium works out to be Rs. 183 crore which may be termed as net cost of reinsurance, accounting for 11.4% of GDP. For the years between 1990-91 to 1998-99, the average total reinsurance cost, commission earned, claim recovery and net cost of reinsurance as percentage of GDP works out to be 14.5%, 3.5%, 7.9% and 3.1% respectively.

In so far as the inward reinsurance business is concerned, in 1996-97, the total premium earned was Rs. 374 crore (5.3% of GDP), the commission paid was Rs. 124 crore (1.7% of GDP) and the balance resulted into net outflow of Rs. 81 crore (1.1% of GDP).

14. The general insurance industry has operations in 30 countries. Out of these in 16 countries it is operating directly and in 14 countries through subsidiary and associated companies. During 1999-2000, the total gross and net premium income from business operations in these countries were Rs. 488.76 crore and Rs. 440.36 crore respectively. The net claim during the year amounted to Rs. 288.19 crore amounting to 65.7% of the net premium.

Number of Employees

The total number of employees in general insurance industry has been increasing from 41582 in 1982 to 50559 in 1985 and again to 70940 in 1988-89 and 84561 in 1994-95. The number of employees has been maximum in New India followed by United India, Oriental and National. In the beginning National Insurance has the second lowest number of employees, which became the lowest in 1988-89.

Number of Offices

The number of offices of insurance industry has increased from 1550 in 1982 to 2731 in 1985, 3730 in 1988-89 and 4202 in 1994-95. It has also increased its branch offices from 1075, 2003, 2706, and 2997 in the respective years. The branch offices have been the main factors to procure business from the field. The productivity per branch office has been increasing constantly. The lowest number of offices has been in National whereas United India has the highest number of offices followed by New India. On the other hand, the business of New India has been the maximum. The productivity per office has been the highest in New India followed by United India, Oriental and National.

7.6 ISSUES CONCERNING GROWTH OF INSURANCE

Despite the fact that the industry has grown after nationalization in terms of premium income, introduction of new products, wide coverage of individuals and organizations, innovating new covers for weaker sections of

TABLE 7.13

Performance of the General Insurance Industry in India

(Rs. in crore)

	1973	1989-90	1990-91	1991-92	1992-93	1993-94	1994-95	1995-96	1996-97	1997-98	1998-99	1999-2000
Paid up Capital	37	168	268	268	375	375	375	375	375	375	375	375
Gross premium written direct in India	184	2175	2796	3287	3792	4449	4959	6047	7021	7736	8759	9522
Gross Premium Outside India	24	104	117	216	278	317	312	330	327	350	399	460
Total Gross Premium	208	2279	2913	3503	4070	4766	5271	6377	7348	8086	9158	9982
(% increase)	—	21.3%	27.8%	20.3%	16.2%	17.1%	10.6%	21.0%	15.2%	10.0%	13.3%	9.01%
Net Premium in India	—	1909	2419	2945	3284	3681	4102	5087	6041	6725	7732	8648
Net Premium Outside India	—	277	323	505	584	746	777	869	693	632	670	716
Total Net Premium	222	2186	2742	3450	3868	4427	4879	5956	6734	7357	8402	9364
Underwriting Profit	18	-119	-118	-77	-119	81	-705	-646	-628	-384	-687	-1215
Profit before Tax	38	371	482	669	779	1082	503	831	1084	1623	1467	1152
Income Tax paid	21	114	148	241	276	411	126	280	365	368	390	278
Net Profit	14	258	334	428	503	670	377	551	721	1255	1077	874
Investment Income	21	449	566	752	859	957	1150	1475	1697	1978	2220	2392

Source: Various Annual Reports of GIC.

TABLE 7.14

(a) General Insurance Industry: Reinsurance Business

(Rs. in crore)

Year	*Gross premium*	*Reinsurance cost*	*% to GDP*	*Commission as % of GDP*	*Claim recovery as % of GDP*	*Net cost as % of GDP*
(1)	*(2)*	*(3)*	*(4)*	*(5)*	*(6)*	*(7)*
1990-91	2796	376	13.5	3.0	12.9	2.4
1991-92	3287	342	10.4	2.8	10.0	
1992-93	3792	508	13.4	3.7	4.7	5.0
1993-94	4449	768	17.3	4.0	12.7	0.6
1994-95	4959	857	17.3	4.2	6.5	6.6
1995-96	6047	961	15.9	3.5	8.4	4.0
1996-97	7021	981	14.0	3.1	5.1	5.8
1997-98	7736	1011	13.1	3.5	7.2	2.4
Total	40087	5804	14.5	3.5	7.9	3.1

(b) Inward Insurance Programme

Year	*Premium*	*Commission*	*Claims*	*Balance*
(1)	*(2)*	*(3)*	*(4)*	*(5)*
1994-95	506	145	571	-210
1995-96	586	174	390	22
1996-97	374	124	331	-81

+ = Balance due from reinsurance.

– = Balance due to reinsurance.

Source: Compiled from various documents including Annual Reports of GIC.

TABLE 7.15

Number of Employees

	Employees in Each Category				*Total*
	Officers	*Development Officers*	*Supervisory & Clerical Staff*	*Subordinate Staff*	
1982-83	5849	10381	21481	3871	41582
1985-86	7845	12365	25345	5004	50559
1988-89	12737	14516	34973	8714	70940
1989-90	13694	14202	37431	10095	75422
1994-95	15327	13168	44845	11221	84561

Source: Various Annual Reports of GIC.

society, investment in social sectors, creating infrastructure at grass-roots level, etc., several weaknesses have also come to surface during these years of operation. These are:

1. Low level of insurance penetration.
2. Low level of insurance density.
3. Poor quality of insurance services.
4. Lack of qualitative and quantitative insurance products.
5. Low productivity.
6. Inadequate application of information technology.

Each of these issues has been discussed in the following section.

Insurance Penetration

Despite the growth of gross domestic premium increased by 47 times between 1973 to 1999-2000, the insurance penetration defined as insurance premium as share of gross domestic product was as low as 0.56% in non-life business in 1997. The life side accounted for 1.39% and the total penetration being 1.95%. It was as high as 4.64% and 4.53% for non-life side in USA and New Zealand respectively. The average for Asia was 1.90% while for the world it was 3.06%. Even amongst the developing economies and other East Asian Countries, the Indian insurance industry lagged far behind in this area. For instance, it was 3.79% for South Korea, 2.45% for Japan, 1.69% for Taiwan, 2.19% for Malaysia, 1.31% for Singapore, and 1.22% for Thailand. Low insurance penetration is pointer to the fact that spread of insurance business has relatively been poorer in the country and large section of insurable population is still isolated from the insurance coverage.

Insurance Density

Another parameter to measure the spread of insurance is the insurance density defined as premium per capita. The available data indicate that in 1997 for non-life side, it was US dollar 2.2. The total being US dollar 7.6, the life side accounting for US dollar 5.4. It was as high as US dollar 1403.7 in USA and US dollar 1296.6 in Switzerland. It was US dollar 176.8 for the world as a whole and 46.4 for Asia. Insurance density in the country was low even as compared to several developing countries. It was US dollar 338.3 in Singapore, US dollar 303 in South Korea, US dollar 299.2 in Hong Kong, US dollar 222.1 in Taiwan, US dollar 99.8 in Malaysia, US dollar 804 in Japan. Most of the African countries were also ahead of India in this respect. Although insurance density is positively correlated to the per capita income which is quite low in India, but what surprises is that the insurance density is lower even compared to several developing countries whose per capita income is even lower than India. The low insurance density and penetration are also partly due to lack of awareness on the part of general masses regarding the benefits flowing from the insurance in improving their standard of living and welfare.

TABLE 7.16

Insurance Penetration (Premiums as Percentage of Gross Domestic Product)

Country	*Total Business*	*Non-Life*	*Life*
USA	8.49	4.64	3.85
Canada	7.37	4.30	3.07
Argentina	1.77	1.21	0.56
Brazil	2.12	1.74	0.39
Mexico	1.29	0.79	0.50
Switzerland	11.94	3.61	8.33
United Kingdom	11.22	3.34	7.87
France	9.25	2.91	6.34
Germany	6.53	3.81	2.72
Italy	4.17	2.28	1.89
Spain	5.38	2.85	2.53
Poland	2.74	1.97	0.77
Yugoslavia	2.75	2.73	0.02
Russia	1.41	1.10	0.31
Romania	0.55	0.52	0.03
South Korea	15.42	3.79	11.63
Japan	11.87	2.45	9.42
Taiwan	6.09	1.69	4.40
Israel	5.89	3.02	2.86
Singapore	5.14	1.31	3.83
Malaysia	4.37	2.19	2.18
Hong Kong	3.55	1.12	2.43
Thailand	2.44	1.22	1.22
India	**1.95**	**0.56**	**1.39**
United Arab Emirates	1.44	1.17	0.27
Philippines	1.51	0.80	0.71
China	1.46	0.64	0.82
Indonesia	1.23	0.65	0.58
Pakistan	0.72	0.42	0.30
Kuwait	0.67	0.58	0.09
Saudi Arabia	0.53	0.52	0.02
South Africa	17.34	3.48	13.86
Mauritius	4.26	2.15	2.10
Zimbabwe	4.03	2.10	1.93
Kenya	3.19	2.57	0.62
Egypt	0.67	0.52	0.15
Australia	9.12	3.58	5.53
New Zealand	6.26	4.53	1.73
America	7.21	4.02	3.19
North America	8.41	4.61	3.80
Latin America	1.86	1.37	0.49
Europe	6.78	2.93	3.85
Western Europe	7.41	3.14	4.28
Eastern Europe	1.69	1.29	0.39
Asia	8.80	1.90	6.27
Africa	5.72	1.59	4.13
Oceanic	8.71	3.72	4.99
World Average	**7.32**	**3.06**	**4.26**

Source: World Insurance: Booming Life Insurance but Stagnating Non-life Insurance Business, *Sigma* (-Swiss) Re, No. 3/1999.

Share in the World Market

The total insurance business in India comprising both non-life and life business constituted only 0.42% of the total world insurance market in 1997. The relative figures for Japan, South Korea, UK and USA were 31.61%, 3.47%, 8.24% and 25.37%. The share of entire Asian insurance business in the total insurance business was 38.53%.

Availability of Insurance Products

Although on the general insurance side, there are a total of about 175 products covering most of the common insurance products in their portfolio, yet hardly 30 to 35 products are actively traded in the market. Today, customers desire to purchase package products instead of purchasing several multiple policies. There is very limited number of such package policies (such as Industrial All Risks Policy and Office Umbrella Policy). The policies catering to special needs of the public such as Advance Loss of Profit, Director's and Officer's Liability, etc. are quite limited in number. The products catering to rural sector where disposable income is increasing are limited in number and existing products have not been properly marketed. The policies in segments of Health covers, Household Risk covers, have not properly marketed and publicized. For instance, health insurance products roughly cover only 25 lakh population with premium income of about Rs. 20 crore. The entire thrust on health insurance has been on the products after the occurrence of illness while the preventive aspects have been ignored. The health care covering environmental and financial risks are non-existent. Another area, which has remained untapped, is the development of saving linked non-life policies in the country. The countries like Japan has innovated several saving linked non-life policies and the premium from these covers was as much as 40% of the total non-life business premium in 1986.

7.7 FUTURE POTENTIAL

The opening of the insurance sector offers ample opportunities to both existing as well as new players to penetrate into untapped areas, sectors and sub-sectors and unexploited segments of population as presently both insurance density and penetration are at a low level. As mentioned earlier, insurance penetration broadly measures the significance of insurance industry in relation to a country's entire economic productivity. It indicates importance of insurance industry in the national economy as a whole. On the other hand, insurance density reflects upon the country's insurance purchasing power. Both indices being at very low level in the country even compared to the countries with the same level of economic development and per capita income are indicative of the vast potential of the growth of this sector in future. Besides, as the economy grows at the rate of 6% in future, the scope for increasing insurance network in the country further grows up. The projected growth of premium is shown in Table 7.17.

In case the market grows at an average rate of 16% p.a. the total gross

TABLE 7.17

Projected Premium Growth Rate

(Rs. in Crore)

	16% GDPT	*17% GDPT*	*18% GDPT*	*19% GDPT*	*20% GDPT*
2001-02	13431.78	13664.36	13898.94	14135.51	14374.08
2002-03	15580.86	15987.30	16400.75	16821.26	17248.90
2003-04	18073.80	18705.14	19352.88	20017.30	20698.68
2004-05	20965.61	21885.02	22836.40	23820.58	24834.41

GDPT: Total Gross Direct Premium.

direct premium in India will be around Rs. 20,965 crore by 2004-5. In case the market grows at the rate of 20% p.a., the total gross direct premium income in India will be around Rs. 24,838 crore by 2004-05.

It is expected that the premium will grow in between these two limits but with the large number of firms operating in the market, it is likely to pickup starting from around 16% in 2001 and may touch 20% by 2004-5. Even the growth at that rate will be less as to touch the level of insurance penetration in the country to 1%. The total gross premium income was Rs. 9982 crore in 1999-2000. During the next five years, the scope for additional premium is in the range of Rs. 11,000 to Rs. 14,000 crore.

The shift from monopoly to competitive market besides being an opportunity, also poses challenge to both existing as well as to new firms. The challenge will be in terms of increasing sensitivity of the consumers to the quality of services offered by the firms, in terms of policy conditions, time consumed in the delivery of policy documents, pricing of products, expeditions settlement of claims, marketing channels etc. With the arrival of new firms in the industry, consumers will expect new product designs at lower prices, their professional selling, responsive services and the firms lagging being in these areas are likely to loose share of market in a very short time and may even be forced to leave the industry. Thus, the competition while offering ample opportunities to the firms to widen the horizon of the market are also subjected to serious challenges due to increased sensitiveness of consumers to the quality of customer's services. There will be change from sellers to the buyer's market in the insurance industry.

7.8 SUMMARY

By 1956, 229 Indian insurers, provident insurance societies, and 16 non-Indian insurers were carrying on life insurance business in India. But since January 19, 1956, the Life business came under the control and ownership of government. In June 1956, a Bill was passed for establishing

Life Insurance Corporation of India, which started functioning since September 1, 1956.

The Corporation is charged with the main duty to carry on life insurance business. It has one Central Office, 5 Zonal Offices and several Divisional and Branch Offices. The new business in India has tremendously increased during the period of last 50 years. The new business outside India did not rise satisfactorily. The average amount per policy has also been rising constantly in India and outside India. The average amount has increased from Rs. 7,345 in 1970 to Rs. 50945 in 1995.

Rural insurance business of LIC has increased from Rs. 10,294.55 crores under 36.75 lakh policies in 1990-91 to Rs. 21,263.59 crore under 52.57 lakh policies in 1995-96.

The life insurance business in Force in India has been continuously rising from Rs. 1,473 crores in 1957 to Rs. 450,000 crores in 2000. The business-in-force of Group Insurance Schemes has rapidly been increasing from Rs. 39.0 crores in 1967 Rs. 422.66 crores in 1995 and Rs. 700 crores in 2000. The number of offices has not increased satisfactorily. The total number of LIC offices in 1995 was 2128, out of which 2021 were branch offices.

The General Insurance business was nationalized with effect from January 1, 1973, through the General Insurance Business (Nationalization) Act, 1972. The main objectives of nationalization were to ensure the development of the general insurance business in sympathy with the best of interest and advantage to the community. The gross domestic premium income in India (GDPI), which was Rs. 184 crore in 1973, has increased to Rs. 9522 crore in 1999-2000.

The premium income originating outside India went up over the level of Rs. 24 crore in 1973 to Rs. 460 crore in 1999-2000, registering annual growth rate of about 11.95%. The net premium income as percentage to total premium income was 93.8% in 1999-2000. As compared to 1973, the GDPI in India has grown by about 47 times.

In so far the class-wise distribution of business is concerned, the fire, miscellaneous and marine accounted for 24%, 66% and 10% in 1999-2000 respectively. The geographical spread of the premium written in India indicates that the maximum, i.e. about 40% was generated from western region and minimum, i.e. about 9% from the eastern region. Although the total number of insurance products in the general insurance industry are around 175. The rural and non-traditional business, which was practically nil in 1973, has gradually increased over a period of time.

Despite the growth of gross domestic premium by 47 times between 1973 to 1999-2000, the insurance penetration defined as insurance premium as share of gross domestic product, was as low as 0.56% in non-life business in 1997. The total insurance business in India comprising both non-life and life business constituted only 0.42% of the total world insurance market in 1997.

In case the market grows at an average rate of 16% p.a. the total gross direct premium in India will be around Rs. 20,965 crore by 2004-5. In case the market grows at the rate of 20% p.a., the total gross direct premium income in India will be around Rs. 24,834 crore by 2004-05. The shift from monopoly to competitive market besides being an opportunity, also poses challenge to both existing as well as to new firms.

7.9 REVIEW QUESTIONS

1. Show with facts, the growth and development of life insurance business in India since the nationalization.
2. Discuss the growth of life insurance business in India in terms of the following:
   (a) New Business;
   (b) Rural New Business;
   (c) Policy Lapses; and
   (d) Production of Agents.
3. Present a detailed account about the growth of general insurance business in India since 1973.
4. Point out the main weaknesses related to the growth of insurance business in India.
5. Comment precisely on the future of insurance business in India.

8

CHAPTER

INSURANCE AND ECONOMIC DEVELOPMENT

LEARNING OBJECTIVE

The main objective of this chapter is to make the students familiar with the role of insurance in economic development and to expose them to the major issues concerning the role of insurance in developing countries.

8.1 INTRODUCTION

Most of the business activities carried out in an economy are expected to escalate the welfare of masses and placing them at higher levels of satisfaction on persistent basis. Pleasing to the eye consumers' liking is the definitive goal that all the sectors of economy cherish to achieve around the globe. Despite steady hard work made by developing countries to speed up the development process, more than 525 million people constitute about 40% of the total population still live below the poverty line in these countries. For reducing the level of poverty, there has to be continuous increase in productivity in all sectors of the economy, which will translate in generation income and productive employment to different sections of the society on a self-sustained basis. Although different sectors of the economy do not grow in isolation and contribute to each other's development, yet the development experience in both developed and developing economies disclose that as the economy progresses, the service sector assumes a prime role and its share in the national income rises.

The financial sector constitutes one of the foremost apparatus of the services sector, and within that sector, insurance services assume vital significance. The growth of insurance services in the world began about 300 years ago with Lloyds Insurance Association of London. In India, the growth of general insurance may be traced back to 1850 when the first general insurance company was set-up in Calcutta. From 1973 to 1999, the general insurance industry grew as a state monopoly under a sheltered environment, as was the case with most of the manufacturing and service sectors of the economy. The new economic policy pursued from mid-1980 onward focused attention on increasing productivity and efficiency of the economy through the instruments of competition and interplay of market forces. As a follow-up to the above policy, financial sector reforms were initiated in 1991 and insurance reforms in 1999 by the Government of India. During the pre-reform period, although there was a significant growth of the insurance industry, yet the deepening and widening of insurance services were not in tune with other developing economies of the world. The share of general insurance premium was as low as 0.23% of the world general insurance premium in 1999. The quality of consumer services was also poor. The new environment, ushering in competition, may generate immense benefits both to the consumer as well as to the economy taking case of existing shortcomings in the insurance industry.

8.2 ROLE OF INSURANCE IN ECONOMIC DEVELOPMENT

The role of insurance services in contributing to the course of economic development has not been properly valued in economic text. While a large number of studies and research material are available on the role played by other services such as banking, transport, communication, public administration, defense, etc. in accelerating the national income of an economy, there is a dearth of material on interlink ages between economic development on the one hand and insurance services on the other. One of the most lucid and exhaustive literatures on the subject is by Harold D. Skipper, Jr. who has comprehensively evaluated the contribution of insurance services to the economic growth process. The present chapter attempts to look at the relationship between the two.

In order to have clear awareness of interlinkage between the insurance and economic development, it would be worth expounding to understand the concepts first. As far as the concept of insurance is concerned, there is commonly accepted definition of the same without any vagueness and variation of view. Insurance may be defined as a contract between insurer and insured under which insurer indemnifies the loss of the insured against the identified perils for which mutually agreed upon premium has been paid by the insured. The contract lays down the time framework within which the insurer will meet the losses. The meaning of the concept of economic development is based upon the vast literature that has proliferated on the subject. Tracing the history of economic thought over a period of time right from classical economists, one discovers that the central theme and concern of these economists had been to identify the factors that contribute towards increasing the wealth, prosperity and welfare of the masses. The most authentic, lucid, and comprehensive literature in Economics by Adam Smith was itself titled as "Inquiry into the Nature and Causes of the 'Wealth of Nation' (1776)." He observed that 'capital is the main determinant of the number of useful and productive labourers who can be set to work'. He said that labour was put to motion by capital.

In the ancient economic literature, the prosperity of the nation was measured by the yardstick of the increase in the national income of the economy. The national income could be measured through its different variants such as gross domestic product (GDP) or net domestic product (NDP) at current or constant prices. Economic development was perceived as sustained increase in the gross domestic product (GDP) or per capita GDP over a period of time. Normally, in order to assess the real pace of development, the growth in GDP at constant prices was taken into account. These writings did not consider the qualitative changes such as structural and institutional transformation of the productive system within the ambit of the concept of economic development. The issues such as alleviation of poverty, reduction in inequalities of income and unemployment were assumed to be taken care of by the mere growth of GDP as it was conceived that the growth would automatically trickle down to the masses and to the grass-root levels on a self-sustained basis.

Modern writings on the subject questioned the above-mentioned concept of economic development as it failed to mirror upon the qualitative changes in the life of an individual and the nation. These qualitative changes can be measured through indices such as changes in the composition of production, technological and institutional organization of production, distributive pattern of income, reduction in poverty, unemployment, inequalities of income, etc. In relation to an individual and at the micro-level, the indices comprised of raising the level of education, health, nutrition, etc. are also equally significant in this context.

Economic development has to incorporate both sustained increase in the GDP per capita GDP as well as improvement in the basic indicators affecting the quality of life of the people. These economists distinguished the concept of growth from that of development. The concept of growth was defined as sustained increase in per capita GDP while development means both the rise in the national income as well as qualitative changes in the economic institutions and organizations of the country.

However, there was no unanimity of opinion amongst the economists regarding the indices to be taken into account for measuring qualitative changes and also the weightage to be assigned to them. One of the most popular approaches in this field had been that of Morris David. Morris used the indicators of infant mortality, life expectancy, and basic literacy to construct a simple composite index (PQLI).

In this section while snooping the relationship between economic development and insurance, the economic development has been taken up in the sense of growth implying sustained increase in the GDP/per capita GDP of the country. The qualitative concepts have by and large not been taken into consideration except in those areas where it is feasible to quantify.

The growth of GDP is a function of host of factors, both economic and non-economic in nature, which directly or indirectly contribute to it. From an economic angle, these factors could be grouped into the following four categories (Samuelson-Economics):

- Human resources (labour, education, discipline, motivation, etc).
- Natural resources (land, minerals, fuels, climate, etc.)
- Capital resources (machines, factories, roads, etc.)
- Technological resources (science, engineering, management, enterprise, etc.).

One of the most important factors contributing to the process of economic development particularly in developing or underdeveloped economies is the capital formation. The relationship between capital formation and insurance services in both developed and developing economics of the world has been quite prominent and noteworthy.

I. Savings and Insurance

The act of saving involves refraining from the present consumption and thereby placing a proportion of income for consumption at a later date. The act of investment can only take place only when there are savings. As a result, historically it has been established that economies with high rate of savings had also the high rate of growth of GNP. An IMF study has revealed that out of the 20 fastest growing economies over the last ten years, 14 had saving rates greater than 25 percent of GDP and none had saving rates less than 18 percent. As against above, out of 20 slowest growing countries, 14 had saving rates less than 15 percent (As quoted by Harold D. Skipper, Jr.). The relationship between saving/investment and the growth of GDP is quite simple and can be explained as follows:

$$g = s/k$$

where g = rate of growth of GDP,
s = saving ratio, and
k = capital-output ratio.

Capital-output ratio is defined as the number of units of capital required for producing one unit of output. For instance, if capital-output ratio is 4:1, it implies that 4 units of capital are required to produce 1 unit of output. Thus, with saving ratio of 20 percent and capital output ratio of 4:1, the resulting growth rate of GNP will be 5 percent.

It establishes a positive correlation between rate of saving and the rate of growth of GNP. Of course, at a constant rate of saving the rate of growth can also be increased by lowering capital-output ratio, which may be possible through new technologies or other methods resulting into increased productivity. At any given point of time, saving ratio has to be identical to the rate of investment in the economy.

The source of generation of savings could be both internal and external. The sources of internal savings could be voluntary cut in consumption, involuntary cut in consumption through taxation, forced lending to the government, inflation, etc. The internal savings flow from the following three sectors:

(a) Household sector;
(b) Private corporate sector; and
(c) Public sector.

The savings from the household sector constitute the major proportion of the total savings in the country. The household savings comprise of two components: physical and financial. The savings could be used to purchase physical assets such as land, buildings, gold, jewellery, etc. or these could be in the form of financial assets such as bank deposits, bonds, shares, mutual funds, small savings certificates, debentures, provident and pension funds and life insurance policies. As the economy progresses and attains maturity, progressively larger proportion of savings is invested in financial assets.

The life insurance premium takes the shape of contractual savings. The premium has basically two components, one going for risk coverage, and the other going towards savings. Life insurance funds constitute one of the important components in the financial savings of an economy. The non-life funds could not strictly be termed as savings as the premium paid is not returned back to the insured and it only covers the losses suffered by him. Of course, in the industry in general insurance and in particular, saving-linked policies could be designed, as has been the case in Japanese economy. These savings linked policies could become an important source of financial savings in an economy similar to life insurance funds.

Table 8.1 depicts the growth of domestic savings and contribution made by the above three sectors over a period of time. The rate of savings has fluctuated between 21 percent in 1980-81 to 25 percent in 1995-96. The contribution of household sector has throughout been maximum contributing more than 75 percent of the total saving during all these years. In 1999-2000, out of the total savings of 22.3 percent, household sector contributed 19.8 percent of the gross domestic product (GDP). It accounted for 88.8 percent of the total gross domestic savings (GDS). The private corporate sectors saving amounted to only 3.7 percent of GDP and 16.5 percent of GDS. For the last two years, public sector's contribution to savings rates was negative being –1.2 percent of GDP and –5.3 percent of GDS.

What is of relevance is that the bulk of domestic savings are generated from the household sector and within this category of saving, insurance funds are one of the major constituents. Although in Indian economy, the percentage of insurance funds in domestic savings is relatively at a low level, in developed economies it happens to be quite large and substantial.

TABLE 8.1

Composition of Gross Domestic Savings (%age to GDP)

Year	*Household Sector*	*Private Corporate Sector*	*Public Sector*	*Total*
1980-81	16.1	1.7	3.4	21.2
	(75.9)	(8.0)	(16.1)	
1990-91	2.5	2.8	1.0	24.3
	(84.3)	(11.5)	(4.2)	
1991-92	17.7	3.2	1.9	22.9
	(77.3)	(13.9)	(8.8)	
1992-93	17.7	2.8	1.5	22.0
	(80.4)	(12.7)	(6.9)	
1993-94	18.4	3.5	0.6	22.5
	(81.7)	(15.5)	(2.8)	
1994-95	19.8	3.5	1.7	25.0
	(79.2)	(14.0)	(6.8)	
1995-96	18.5	5.0	2.0	25.5
	(72.5)	(19.6)	(7.9)	
1996-97	17.1	4.5	1.7	23.3
	(73.4)	(19.3)	(7.3)	
1997-98	17.8	4.2	1.5	23.5
	(75.7)	(17.9)	(6.4)	
1998-99	19.1	3.7	-0.8	22.0
	(86.8)	(16.8)	(-3.6)	
1999-2000	19.8	3.7	-1.2	22.3
	(88.8)	(16.5)	(-5.3)	

Note: Figures in brackets indicate percentage to the gross domestic savings.
Source: Economic Survey (Various years), Government of India; Report on Currency and Finance (Various years), Reserve Bank of India.

Table 8.2 depicts the share of life insurance premium in the gross domestic savings (GDS) of different countries. In South Africa, life funds as percentage of GDP were as high as 80 percent. It was also quite high in UK (55.4 percent), Switzerland (28.2 percent), France (27.5 percent), Japan (27.1 percent), Australia (27.1 percent), South Korea (25.9 percent), USA (25.4 percent), Ireland (24.9 percent) and Netherlands (18.3 percent).

In so far as Indian economy is concerned, the percentage share of financial savings in household sector has gradually increased from 39.4 percent in 1980-81 to 53 percent in 1999-2000. The savings in the form of physical assets have declined from 60.6 percent of household savings in 1980-81 to 47 percent in 1999-2000. Life insurance funds comprised 3.9 percent of the household savings in 1980-81 and increased to 7.1 percent in 1999-2000. However, these funds remained by the large constant around 6 percent from 1990-91 onwards. The trend after 1990-91 indicates that as a percentage of household savings, these funds have remained static. Table 8.3 brings out these trends between 1980-81 to 1999-2000. Table 8.4 indicates the

TABLE 8.2

Life Premium as Percentage of Gross Domestic Savings

Country	*Life Fund as % of Gross Domestic Savings*
USA	25.40
Canada	15.70
Brazil	2.20
Argentina	3.20
Mexico	0.57
Columbia	3.20
Venezuela	0.12
Germany	4.05
UK	55.40
France	27.50
Italy	8.50
Spain	11.20
Netherlands	18.30
Switzerland	28.20
Sweden	10.80
Russia	1.30
Ireland	24.90
Poland	4.10
Greece	7.50
Japan	27.10
South Korea	25.90
China	1.70
Israel	24.50
Malaysia	9.20
India	6.20
Hongkong	8.20
Thailand	2.60
Indonesia	1.80
Singapore	7.10
Philippines	4.10
Pakistan	1.90
South Africa	80.90
Kenya	2.00
Australia	27.10
New Zealand	8.00

Source: Calculated from the *World Development Report, 1998-99, 1999-2000* and *World Insurance in 1997: Booming Life Insurance but Stagnating Non-Life Insurance Business, Sigma-Swiss*, No. 3/ 1999.

TABLE 8.3

Composition of Household Savings in India

	1980-81	*1990-91*	*1991-92*	*1992-93*	*1993-94*	*1994-95*	*1995-96*	*1996-97*	*1997-98*	*1998-99*	*1999-2000*
(A) Financial Savings of which:	39.4	45.3	56.9	52.4	63.1	55.6	45.5	52.6	55.6	57.0	53.0
(i) Currency	7.4	5.7	7.5	5.3	8.9	8.1	7.9	5.2	4.9	6.2	5.5
(ii) Net deposits	13.7	10.2	13.3	15.9	21.9	16.5	12.5	23.1	22.0	19,9	15.1
(iii) Shares and debentures	2.0	7.7	14.5	11.1	9.9	7.9	3.8	3.7	2.1	2.0	4.0
(iv) Net claims on Government	2.6	6.7	4.1	2.8	4.1	6.6	4.4	4.5	7.9	8.4	7.1
(v) Life insurance funds	3.9	4.9	6.1	5.4	6.1	5.6	6.3	6.0	6.8	6.8	7.1
(vi) Provident plus pension funds	9.7	10.2	11q.4	11.9	12.2	10.9	10.6	10.1	11.9	13.7	14.2
(B) Savings in physical assets	60.6	54.7	43.2	47.6	36.9	44.3	54.5	74.4	44.4	43.0	47.0

Source: Economic Survey (various years), Government of India; Report on Currency and Finance (various years), Reserve Bank of India; National Accounts Statistics, EPW Research Foundation (1998).

TABLE 8.4

Composition of Savings in India (As percentage of GDP at current market prices)

	1980-81	*1990-91*	*1991-92*	*1992-93*	*1993-94*	*1994-95*	*1995-96*	*1996-97*	*1997-98*	*1998-99*	*1999-2000*
1. Hosuehold Sector	—	20.5	17.7	17.7	18.4	19.7	18.1	17.0	17.8	19.1	19.8
I. Financial savings	—	—	—	—	11.0	11.9	8.9	10.3	9.9	10.9	10.5
(a) Currency	1.2	1.2	1.3	0.9	1.6	1.6	1.4	1.0	0.8	1.2	1.1
(b) Net deposits	—	—	—	—	3.9	4.2	2.9	4.4	3.9	3.8	3.0
(c) Shares and debentures	0.3	0.9	1.1	1.2	1.7	1.7	0.8	0.8	0.3	0.4	0.8
(d) Net claims on Government	0.5	1.5	0.8	0.6	0.7	1.3	0.8	0.8	1.4	1.6	1.4
(e) Life insurance funds	0.7	1.0	1.1	1.0	1.1	1.1	1.1	1.1	1.2	1.3	1.4
(f) Provident + pension funds	—	1.6	2.1	2.0	2.1	2.1	1.9	2.2	2.1	2.6	2.8
II. Savings in physical assets	—	—	—	—.	7.4	7.8	7.3	6.7	8.0	8.2	9.2
2. Private Corporate Sector	—	—	—	—	3.5	3.5	4.9	4.5	4.2	3.7	3.7
3. Public Sector	—	—	—	—	0.6	1.7	2.0	1.7	1.5	-0.8	-1.2
4. Gross Domestic Savings	21.2	24.3	22.9	22.0	22.5	24.8	25.8	23.2	23.5	22.0	22.3
5. % of Life Insurance Funds	9.9	10.7	10.6	10.3	9.7	10.1	13.9	11.4	10.	11.0	—

Source: As for Table 8.3.

TABLE 8.5

Non-Life Insurance Penetration in Industrialised Countries

	Non-Life Premium 1998 (US $ Billions)	GDP 1998 (US $ Billions)	GDP Breakup			Services Breakup As % of GDP			As % of GDP	
			Agriculture	Industry	Services	Agriculture	Industry	Services	Other Services	Insurance
USA	359.414	7746	154.92	1,781.58	5,809.50	2	23	75	70.36	4.64
Netherlands	14.832	360	10.80	97.20	252.00	3	27	70	65.88	4.12
Australia	14.037	391	15.64	109.48	265.88	4	28	68	64.41	3.59
UK	42.485	1272	25.44	356.16	890.40	2	28	70	66.66	3.34
France	40.653	1397	27.94	363.22	1,005.84	2	26	72	69.09	2.91
Croatia	0.494	19	2.28	4.75	11.97	12	25	63	60.40	2.60
Japan	102.949	4202	84.04	1,596.76	2,521.20	2	38	60	57.55	2.45
Denmark	3.912	161	6.44	49.91	104.65	4	31	65	62.57	2.43
Norway	3.534	153	3.06	45.90	104.04	2	30	68	65.69	2.31
Sweden	5.221	228	4.56	72.96	150.48	2	32	66	63.71	2.29
Italy	26.106	1145	34.35	332.05	778.60	3	29	68	65.72	2.28
Czech Rep.	1.166	55	3.85	34.65	16.50	7	63	30	27.88	2.12
Poland	2.679	136	8.16	53.04	74.80	6	39	55	53.03	1.97
Finland	2.204	116	6.96	46.40	62.64	6	40	54	52.10	1.90
Slovakia	0.374	20	1.00	6.20	12.80	5	31	64	62.13	1.87
Hungary	0.702	45	3.15	14.404	27.45	7	32	61	59.44	1.56
Bulgaria	0.132	9	0.90	2.97	5.13	10	33	57	55.53	1.47
Russia	4.851	441	30.87	171.99	238.14	7	39	54	52.90	1.10
Greece	1.035	119	19.04	33.32	66.64	16	28	56	55.13	0.87
Romania	0.182	35	7.35	14.00	13.65	21	40	39	38.48	0.52
Ukraine	0.132	44	5.72	17.16	21.12	13	39	48	47.70	0.30
Canada	25.929	603	0.00	0.00	0.00	0	0	0	0.00	4.20
Germany	80.010	2100	0.00	0.00	0.00	0	0	0	0.00	3.81
Switzerland	2.189	72	0.00	0.00	0.00	0	0	0	0.00	3.61
Ireland	2.189	72	0.00	0.00	0.00	0	0	0	0.00	3.04
Spain	15.134	531	0.00	0.00	0.00	0	0	0	0.00	2.85

Source: Calculated from the *World Development Report, 1998-99, 1999-2000* and *World Insurance in 1997: Booming Life Insurance but Stagnating Non-Life Insurance Business*, *Sigma-Swiss*, No. 3/1999.

TABLE 8.6

Non-Life Insurance Penetration in Developing Countries

	Non-Life Premium 1998 (US $ Billions)	*GDP 1998 (US $ Billions)*	*GDP Breakup*			*Services Breakup As % of GDP*			*As % of GDP*	
			Agriculture	*Industry*	*Services*	*Agriculture*	*Industry*	*Services*	*Other Services*	*Insurance*
South Korea	16.790	443	26.58	190.49	225.93	6	43	51	48.21	3.79
South Africa	4.489	129	6.45	50.31	72.24	5	39	56	52.52	3.48
Kenya	0.257	10	2.90	1.70	5.40	29	17	54	51.43	2.57
Malaysia	2.146	98	12.74	45.08	40.18	13	46	41	38.81	2.19
Zimbabwe	0.189	9	2.52	2.88	3.60	28	32	40	37.90	2.10
Morocco	0.617	33	6.60	10.23	16.17	20	31	49	47.13	1.87
Columbia	1.530	85	13.60	17.00	54.40	16	20	64	62.20	1.80
Brazil	13.676	786	110.04	282.96	393.00	14	36	50	48.26	1.74
Venezuela	1.072	67	2.68	31.49	32.83	4	47	49	47.40	1.60
Singapore	1.258	96	0.00	34.56	61.44	0	36	64	62.69	1.31
Thailand	1.915	157	17.27	62.80	76.93	11	40	49	47.78	1.22
Argentina	3.896	322	19.32	99.82	202.86	6	31	63	61.79	1.21
Ecuador	0.219	19	2.28	7.03	9.69	12	37	51	49.85	1.15
Hong Kong	1.915	171	0.00	25.65	145.35	0	15	85	83.88	1.12
Philippines	0.664	83	16.60	26.56	39.84	20	32	48	47.20	0.80
Mexico	2.647	335	16.75	87.10	231.15	5	26	69	68.21	0.79
Nigeria	0.281	37	16.65	8.88	11.47	45	24	31	30.24	0.76
Peru	0.409	62	4.34	22.94	34.72	7	37	56	45.34	0.66
Indonesia	1.398	215	34.40	90.30	99.30	16	42	42	41.35	0.65
China	5.280	825	165.00	420.75	239.25	20	51	29	28.36	0.64
Kuwait	0.203	35	0.00	14.70	20.30	0	42	58	57.42	0.58
India	**2.016**	**360**	**97.20**	**109.00**	**154.80**	**27**	**30**	**43**	**42.44**	**0.56**
Egypt	0.390	75	12.00	23.25	39.75	16	31	53	52.48	0.52
Pakistan	0.269	64	16.64	16.00	31.36	26	25	49	48.58	0.42

Source: Calculated from the *World Development Report, 1998-99, 1999-2000* and *World Insurance in 1997: Booming Life Insurance but Stagnating Non-Life Insurance Business, Sigma-Swiss*, No. 3/1999.

TABLE 8.7

Insurance Density and Per Capita GDP-1998 in US $ (Developing Countries)

	Per Capita GDP	*Per Capita Premium*
Singapore	32,000	1,645
Hong Kong	24,429	867
Kuwait	17,500	117
Zimbabwe	11,534	788
South Korea	9,630	1,485
Argentina	8,944	158
Brazil	4,793	102
Malaysia	4,667	204
Mexico	3,526	45
South Africa	.3,395	589
Venezuela	2,913	48
Thailand	2,574	63
Peru	2,480	21
Columbia	2,237	51
Ecuador	1,583	20
Egypt	1,250	8
Morocco	1,179	29
Philippines	1,137	17
Indonesia	1,075	13
China	672	10
Pakistan	467	3
India	375	7
Kenya	357	11
Nigeria	314	3
Average	5,793	26

Source: Calculated from the *World Development Report, 1998-99, 1999-2000* and *World Insurance in 1997: Booming Life Insurance but Stagnating Non-Life Insurance Business, Sigma-Swiss*, No. 3/ 1999.

share of life insurance funds in the gross domestic product (GDP) of the country. Household sector's savings as a percentage of GDP fluctuated between 17 to 20 percent during 1990-91 to 1999-2000. Financial savings as percentage of GDP were between 8 to 11 percent between 1993-94 to 1999-2000. Life insurance funds as percentage of GDP have also remained static and have oscillated around one percent. These funds remained unchanged at 1.1 percent between 1993-94 to 1996-97, but have gradually increased from 1.2 percent in 1997-98 to 1.4 percent in 1999-2000. Further life insurance funds as percentage of financial assets varied between 9 to 11 percent between the above years.

These trends are indicative of the fact that there is a vast scope and potential for insurance funds to be increased as these are quite low as

TABLE 8.8

Insurance Density and Per Capita GDP-1998 in US $ (Industrial Countries)

	Per Capita GDP	*Per Capita Premium*
Switzerland	41,857	4,998
Norway	38,250	1,744
Japan	33,349	3,959
Denmark	32,200	2,003
USA	28,903	2,454
Germany	25,610	1,672
Sweden	25,333	1,196
France	23,678	2,190
Finland	23,200	1,800
Netherlands	22,500	2,117
UK	21,559	2,419
Australia	20,579	1,877
Canada	20,100	1,481
Italy	20,088	838
Ireland	18,000	1,507
Spain	13,615	733
Greece	10,818	188
Czech Rep.	5,500	159
Croatia	4,750	140
Hungary	4,500	105
Slovakia	4,000	104
Poland	3,487	96
Russia	3,000	42
Romania	1,522	8
Bulgaria	1,125	18
Ukrania	880	4
Average	17,246	1,302

Source: Calculated from the *World Development Report, 1998-99, 1999-2000* and *World Insurance in 1997: Booming Life Insurance but Stagnating Non-Life Insurance Business, Sigma-Swiss*, No. 3/1999.

percentage to gross domestic savings, financial assets and gross domestic product and are capable of significantly contributing to the process of capital formation and economic development of the country.

2. Capital Formation and Insurance

Capital formation may be defined as an increase in the capital stock of country consisting of plant, equipment, machinery, tools, factory, buildings, raw material, semi-finished products, means of transport, communication, etc. Capital itself may be defined as a means of production. In economic literature, capital has always been regarded as a means of increasing specialisation, means of production, productivity in the economy and thereby contributing to the future stream of income to the economy as a whole. Capital performs the function of increasing both the total output as well as the output per worker in the society. For sustained growth of the economy, what is required is that the capital stock should grow not only at the rate adequate to replace the depreciated stock but should also contribute to the net addition to the same.

The process of capital formation envisages three essential steps. These are:

(a) Real savings,
(b) Mobilization and channelising of savings through financial and non-financial intermediaries to be placed at the disposal of investors; and
(c) The act of investment.

The contribution of insurance in the process of capital formation appears at all these stages. Insurance services act as a tool to mobilize savings, function as financial intermediary and at times, though rarely, also indulge in direct investment.

3. Insurance as a Financial Intermediary

As mentioned earlier, in the process of capital formation, one of the important steps involved is the mobilization of savings and placing them at the disposal of investors. The financial intermediaries carry out this function. In a market-oriented economy, while the act of savings is performed by a large number of units scattered across the country, the investment functions are carried out by different entities, which are also scattered. Financial intermediaries perform the function of channelising savings into domestic investment. These financial intermediaries with their specialized knowledge place the savings of these units into most productive investment channels. These intermediaries facilitate the efficient allocation of capital resources which in turn improve productivity and economic efficiency of them. It contributes in reducing the capital-output ratio in the economy. Insurance companies, both life and non-life, in their role as financial intermediaries perform extremely useful functions in the economy. Harold D. Skipper has pointed out that insurers promote financial system efficiency in the following three ways:

1. Reduction in Transaction Costs

Insurers, particularly life insurers, collect the premium from a very large number of policyholders and thereby command huge funds at their disposal. These insurers invest these funds in variety of projects scattered over different regions of the country. But for these companies, the policyholders would have to indulge in direct lending and investing which is both specialized job and is also time-consuming. Thus, insurers help in reducing the transaction costs in the economy.

2. Creating Liquidity

The funds at the disposal of insurers are being used for long-term projects and loans. The funds collected are out of the premium paid by the policyholders. In case of occurrence of loss, insurers immediately compensate for the losses and pay the requisite claim amount to the policyholders. Thus, the funds of policyholders are extremely liquid as there is no time lag between occurrence of loss and receipt of the claim. Besides, the borrowers of the funds are not required to repay the loans immediately. If the policyholders start direct lending of their funds, they may land up locking their funds in long-term illiquid assets. As pointed out by Skipper, "Insurers, thereby reduce illiquidity inherent in direct lending."

3. Facilitating Economies of Scale in Investment

Insurers in their role as financial intermediaries are in a position to invest in large projects requiring heavy investment. Insurance companies command huge funds at their discretion collected from large number of policyholders, which they can invest in huge projects requiring large investment such as national road projects, railways, ports, power projects, etc. These large projects create economies of scale, facilitate technological innovations and specializations, and thereby promote economic efficiency and productivity. With these funds the large investment become feasible.

8.3 ROLE OF INSURANCE IN DEVELOPING ECONOMIES

In fact, the role of financial intermediaries arises because of imperfection in the economic system. There exists an information gap between the suppliers of funds on the one hand and the investors on the other. They do not possess information about each other's location, volume of funds, nature of investment projects, etc. It necessitates the growth of financial intermediaries to perform these functions. It has, therefore, been contended that in a developed economy where the financial market is relatively more perfect, the role of intermediaries will diminish and their functions will increasingly be taken over by the financial market itself. However, in developing economies, financial intermediaries play relatively a greater role in supplying the funds and amongst these intermediaries insurers play an important role.

Insurers vs. *Other Financial Intermediaries*

In the economy, the functions of financial intermediaries are performed by several institutions, viz. insurers, co-operative banks, mutual fund, and asset management companies, etc. The advantage with insurance companies is that they are capable of deploying their funds in long-term projects compared to banks and other intermediaries who invest their funds mostly in short duration projects.

In addition to acting as mobiliser of savings and as financial intermediary, insurers also contribute to the third state of capital formation, i.e. the act of actual investment. Broadly, as pointed out by Skipper, insurers stimulate investment activities in the following manner:

1. Efficient Management of Risks

An investor while undertaking investment projects is subjected to several risks of varying intensity. These risks have been classified into different categories such as commercial risks, operational risks, supply and market risks, political risks, etc. Insurers play vital role in identifying, evaluating, and pricing these risks. It promotes healthy and congenial investment environment. In particular, insurers facilitate the investment activities through risk coverage in the following ways:

Risk Pricing

Insurers identify the risks to which the investment projects may be exposed to, and depending upon the severity of the risk, the price (premium) is fixed up. They also refuse to cover certain risks, if they find them as extremely hazardous, even at extremely high price. The information gained by the insurers, which is transparent and is transferred to investors, enables them to take preventive and precautionary measures to meet risk challenges. The above information also helps the investor to rationally calculate the rate of return on their projects. Further, the insurer thoroughly examines the credit-worthiness of the firm to whom it advances the loan and the knowledge so gained assists the potential investors and other interested parties to take appropriate decision on feasibility of the project.

Risk Transformation

Insurance companies enable the entrepreneurs and the individuals to transfer their risks to insurers at a price (premium) and thereby stimulate investment in the economy. The policyholders are in a position to convert their savings into insurance products, which are both safe and liquid.

2. Risk Pooling and Reduction

The insurance is primarily based upon the principle of risk pooling implying therein that the insurers transfer to themselves the risks of large number of units, whether individual or business enterprises, and this aggregation helps them in several ways. Larger the number of the risk aggregation, greater the precision in the prediction of losses that may occur in future. It reduces the fluctuations in the expected losses to the insurers. That enables insurers to charge lower premia and these premia are also stable over a long period of time.

Further, risk pooling places large number of funds at the discretion of the insurers enabling them to diversify their investment portfolios. The diversified nature of their investment helps them to compensate for the loss sustained from unsound borrowers through the profits generated from the sound borrowers. The experience gained therein, which is made possible through risk pooling, enables the insurers to charge lower rate of interest for their loans, which in turn induces investment in the economy.

As was mentioned earlier, the process of economic development involves sustained increase in the GDP and in this process besides the role played by capital formation, there are host of variables which facilitate the growth in GDP in one or the other way. Insurance services positively affect these variables, which in turn promote increase in GDP. Insurance services having positive impact on these variables have been examined below:

Loss Prevention Measures

Right from the construction stage of the investment project to the final stage of production of goods and services, the project is exposed to several risks and perils which the insurance companies insure. Over a period of time, based upon the underwriting experience, insurers gain knowledge and skills to prevent or minimize these losses. Even at the time of insuring a product, insurers insist on installing preventive devices to prevent and minimize these losses as a precondition to extend the cover. They also transfer their skill to the insured in loss prevention techniques. In India, Loss Prevention Association has been set-up by the insurance companies which is continuously engaged in innovating loss prevention techniques and passing it on to insured through publicity, advertising, awareness camps, etc. Insurance companies also continuously monitor the measures taken by the insured to minimise the occurrence of losses. Insurers, thus play an important role in the prevention of losses to the business enterprises and individuals, which is a tangible benefit to the economy and society.

3. Promoting Trade and Commerce

The increase in GDP is positively correlated to the growth of trade and commerce in the economy. Majority of products and services are produced only if liability insurance is available to them. For carrying out both domestic and international trade, insurance of traded products happens to be a pre-condition. Even the venture capitalists also insist for the comprehensive insurance cover for the products and services proposed to be produced through the borrowed capital. Financial specialization and flexibility in the economic system play important contributory role in the healthy and smooth growth of trade and commerce. Insurance covers promote such specialization and flexibility in the system.

Further, banks while advancing collateral or individual loans for purchase of assets normally demand insurance cover of the assets and the insurance premium constitutes a part of loan repayment schedule. For instance, in India, Integrated Rural Development Programme (IRDP), cattle insurance and other rural asset building programmes have in-built mechanism for coverage of assets through insurance. In this way, insurers promote trade and commerce in the society.

4. Facilitates Efficient Capital Allocation

Insurers provide cover to large number of firms, enterprises, and businesses and also deploy their funds in number of investment projects. The experience so gained builds up the vast pool of knowledge and expertise amongst the insurers enable them to distinguish between productive and high return projects on the one hand and unproductive and inefficient projects on the other. The knowledge so gained when shared with small savers and investors help them in identifying most productive projects. On their own, it would have not been possible for these savers and investors to evaluate these projects on merit owing to lack of time and resources at their disposal. The insurers continuously monitor the projects financed by them, act as a watchdog, and ensure that the management of these companies do not indulge in activities that may lead to increase in the risk profile of these companies. In this process, management of these companies function is in the best of interests of customers, creditors, employees, stockholders, etc. Insurers, therefore, promote efficient and productive allocation of capital resources, which in turn leads to improved productivity and efficiency in the system. It helps in reducing capital-output ratio in the economy.

5. Encouraging Financial Stability and Reducing Anxiety

Insurers promote financial stability in the economy. They insure the risks and losses of individuals, firms, organizations, etc. and in case for occurrence of loss, the insured are immediately compensated, and their losses are indemnified. In case, the loss occurs, in the absence of these covers, insured would be required to resort to borrowing from friends, relatives, private lenders, etc. and thus create financial instability in the market. In case of uninsured large losses, the firms may not be in a position to bear them, may become insolvent, and may even be forced to close down the business, which in turn may result into unemployment, loss to the firms supplying the raw materials and other inputs, loss to the customers in being deprived of these products and even loss of revenue (excise duty, sales tax, corporation tax) to the Government.

The individuals and business enterprises get mentally worried when they suffer losses to their life, property, and assets. The mental tension so caused often leads to delay or completely halting decision-making process in the firm. In so far as the insurable losses are concerned, the firms do not get panicky as these losses are transferred to the insurance companies. Insurers, therefore, help in reducing worries and anxieties of the individuals and firms.

6. Reducing the Burden on Government Exchequer

Insurance companies particularly life insurers provide a variety of insurance products covering the needs of children, women, aged, etc. These products serve as a social security network for a large segment of population and thereby reduce the burden on Government in providing these services. To that extent, Government saves expenditure on these items and the amount saved so can be utilized for development work in other sectors thereby accelerating growth of GDP. OECD has explicitly pointed out the role of insurers in this respect in a study. It states: "The fact that so many life insurance policies are purchased undoubtedly releases pressure on the social welfare systems in many states. To that extent, life insurance is an advantage in the context of public finance, and, as a result, is generally viewed with favour by governments.

Further, one of the studies conducted by Swiss Reinsurance Company (1987) has established that in 10 OECD countries there was a negative correlation between the spread of life insurance and the social security programmes funded by the government.

In the preceding sections, the role played by insurers in economic development has been examined and analyzed. The studies have also established that economic development itself promotes the insurance services in an economy. Insurance services from this angle become an effect of growth of GNP in the country. The effect of economic development on insurance spread has been examined below.

Composition of GDP and Insurance Penetration

The data from industrialized countries indicate that larger the share of service sector in the composition of the GDP, greater is the insurance penetration in these countries. In these countries, insurance penetration is inversely correlated to the share of agriculture and industry in the composition of GDP. This trend is clearly visible in Table 8.7.

In so far as the developing economies are concerned, it has been established that the higher the percentage of agriculture in GDP, lower the insurance penetration. Further, in these economies the visible trend is that larger the share of industry in the GDP, higher the insurance penetration. This is depicted in Table 8.7.

8.4 ECONOMIC DEVELOPMENT AND INSURANCE DENSITY

The insurance density has been defined as per capita expenditure on insurance premium. The insurance density has a direct correlation with per capita GDP income of the country. The lower per capita GDP translates itself into low insurance density in the country. The per capita of GDP is as high as US $ 17,246, on an average, for all industrial countries as against an average of US $ 5,793 for all developing countries (even this reduces by a third to US $ 3,755, if we ignore Singapore and Hongkong, which are developing in name only). The per capita GDP in India is US $ 375 as against average of US $ 5,793 for all developing countries. From the above data, it can be inferred that the higher per capita income translates itself into high insurance density and conversely the countries with low per capita GDP have low insurance density. Tables 8.7 and 8.8 portray the above trend.

8.5 SUMMARY

Insurance sector plays a vital role in the process of economic development of the country. The process of capital formation is encouraged by the insurance services. The sector acts as mobiliser of savings, as financial intermediary, as promoter of investment activities, as stabilizer of financial market, and as risk manager. Insurance services lead to efficient and productive allocation of capital resources, prevent the losses to the firms by encouraging loss preventive measures, facilitate growth of trade and commerce, complement government's social security programmes and assist the individuals and firms in efficient management of risks. In turn, economic development also facilitates swell of insurance both in terms of its dispersion and concentration. The larger share of services in the composition of GDP has resulted into higher insurance penetration in industrialized countries. However, in these countries there was an inverse correlation between share of industries in GDP and insurance penetration. In developing economies, the share of agriculture in GDP has been found to be negatively correlated with the insurance penetration. In so far as insurance density is concerned, countries with higher per capita GDP/income have higher insurance density and those with low GDP/income have lower insurance thickness.

8.6 REVIEW QUESTIONS

1. Discuss the role and importance of insurance in the economic development of a country like India.
2. Write short-notes on:
   (a) Capital Formation and Insurance.
   (b) Saving and insurance business in different countries.
3. Explain and illustrate the role of financial intermediaries in the economic development of a developing country.
4. "Household sector plays an important role in the gross domestic saving of a nation." Explain the statement in the light of modern trends in the insurance sector.

9

CHAPTER

ACTUARIAL INSURANCE

LEARNING OBJECTIVE

The present chapter is devoted to the discussion about the role of actuary in insurance industry.

9.1 INTRODUCTION

The opening of the insurance sector has also thrown a great challenge to the actuarial profession in India. The demand for actuarial skills and knowledge is growing up exponentially and the actuarial profession in India is gearing up its activities to meet this demand.

The actuary is a specialist who combines an understanding of risks and mathematical technique to develop financial products to manage these risks (insurance policies), price these product (calculate insurance premium rates) and compute reserves to be held for liabilities of companies undertaking these financial risks. An actuary may also be described as an applied mathematician responsible for the financial mathematics in insurance policies. In a broader sense, actuaries have been described as the professionals to call whenever money and probability interact.

The actuary helps in designing insurance plans and then evaluates the financial risk of the company which it takes while selling an insurance policy. The responsibilities as an actuary include making sure that the company properly defines and carefully evaluates the insurance risk; charge a fair price to suit the risk; and has an efficient system to pay claims and expenses as and when they occur. Actuaries must understand the entire operation of insurance field because their evaluations often influence organisation policies and practices. In fact, actuaries' calculations and judgement can commit organisations financially sound for future years. Because of many phases of organisation's business such as general management, marketing, research, investments, accounting, underwriting, administration and long-range planning, the actuaries have great role to play in the insurance industry.

Most actuaries working in insurance sector are mainly in life insurance. They are often found in high responsible management positions making decisions that are vital to the company's success. Insurance is a highly competitive business and actuaries are constantly making commercial decisions, which nevertheless must have a sound theoretical basis. The actuary's day-to-day tasks involve fixing premium rates and surrender values for policies and designing new types of policies. Actuaries have to make calculations also such as what funds will be needed to cover the company's long-term liabilities and advise on how profits should be distributed to policyholders and shareholders.

9.2 APPOINTED ACTUARY IN INDIA

An insurance company has to take the assistance of an actuary in conducting the business of insurance. The IRDA in consultation with the Insurance Advisory Committee has made regulations for appointment of actuary. Regulation 5 of the 'IRDA (Appointed Actuary) Regulations, 2000' provides that a life insurer shall not carry on business of insurance without an appointed actuary. The term 'appointed actuary' is a designation.

Eligibility

A person shall be eligible to be appointed as an appointed actuary for an insurer, if he or she shall be:

- ordinarily resident in India;
- fellow member of the actuarial society of India;
- an employee of the insurer or a consulting actuary in case of general insurance business;
- an employee of life insurer in case of life insurance business;
- a person who has not committed any breach of professional conduct;
- a person against whom no disciplinary action by the Actuarial Society of India or any disciplinary action pending with any other actuarial professional body;
- not an appointed actuary of another insurer;
- a person who possesses a certificate of practice issued by the Actuarial Society of India; and
- not over the age of seventy years.

Approval of IRDA

An insurer shall seek the approval of the Authority for the appointment of appointed actuary by submitting the application in prescribed Form IRDA-AA-1. The Authority shall, within thirty days of the receipt of such application either, accept or reject the same, however, before rejection of the application the authority (IRDA) shall give the insurer an opportunity of being heard. Where an insurer does not receive approval within thirty days of the receipt of such application by the Authority, the insurer shall deem that the approval has been granted by the Authority.

Relaxation of Qualification of Actuary

Where an insurer is unable to appoint an actuary in accordance with the regulations prescribed for qualifications of an appointed actuary [sub-regulation (2) of regulation 3 of IRDA (Appointed Actuary) Regulations, 2000] he may make an application to the Authority in writing for relaxation of one or more conditions mentioned therein. The Authority shall on receipt of the application communicate its decision to the insurer within 30 days of receipt. The appointment of an appointed actuary shall take effect from the date of approval by the Authority.

Cessation of Appointment of Appointed Actuary

An appointed actuary shall cease to be so, if he or she has been given notice of withdrawal of approval by the Authority on the following grounds:

- that he/she ceases to be eligible in accordance with the sub regulation (2) of regulation 3 of IRDA (Appointed Actuary) Regulations, 2000. [Sub-regulation (3) prescribes the qualifications for an appointed actuary]; or
- that he/she has in the opinion of the Authority, failed to perform adequately and properly the duties and obligations of an appointed actuary.

The Authority shall give an appointed actuary a reasonable opportunity of being heard, if given a notice of withdrawal of approval.

If a person ceases to be an appointed actuary otherwise than on grounds of ineligibility or failure to perform duties, the insurer and appointed actuary is required to inform the Authority the reasons thereof within fifteen days of such a cessation.

9.3 POWERS OF APPOINTED ACTUARY

The appointed actuary has been vested with substantial powers, the powers having enormous significance in insurance business are listed below:

1. An appointed actuary shall have access to all information or documents in possession, or under control of the insurer if such access is necessary for the proper and effective performance of functions and duties of the appointed actuary;
2. he may seek any information for the purpose of fulfilling his duties of an appointed actuary from any officer or employee of

the insurer;

3. he is entitled to attend all meeting of the management including that of the directors of the insurer;
4. he is empowered to speak and discuss matter. relating to the actuarial advice given to the directors, matters affecting solvency of the insurer, matters that may affect the ability of the insurer to meet the reasonable expectations of policyholders; and
5. he may attend any meeting of the shareholders or the policyholders of the insurer or any other meeting of members of the insurer at which the insurers annual accounts or financial statements are to be considered or at which any matter in connection with the appointed actuary's duties.

9.4 DUTIES AND OBLIGATIONS OF AN ACTUARY

The duties and obligations of an actuary shall include:

1. Rendering actuarial advice to the management of the insurer, in particular in the areas of product design and pricing, insurance contract wording, investments and reinsurance;
2. ensuring the solvency of the insurer at all times;
3. complying with the provisions of Section 64V of the Act, 1938 in regard to certification of assets, liabilities that have been valued accordingly.
4. complying with the provisions of Section 64VA of the Act, 1938 in regard to maintenance of required solvency margin in the manner required under that provision;
5. drawing the attention of management of the insurer, to any matter on which he/she thinks that action is required to be taken by the insurer to avoid any contravention of the Act, 1938 or prejudice to the interests of the policyholders;
6. complying with the Authority's directions from time to time:
7. ensuring in general insurance business:
   (a) that the rates are fair in respect of those contracts that are governed by the insurer's in-house tariff; and
   (b) that the actuarial principles, in the determination of liabilities have been used in the calculation or reserves for incurred but not reported (IBNR) and other reserves where actuarial advice is sought by the Authority;
8. informing the Authority in writing of opinion, within a reasonable time, whether:
   (a) the insurer has contravened the Insurance Act, 1938 or other related statutes;
   (b) the contravention is of such a nature that may affect significantly the interests of the owners or beneficiaries of policies issued by the insurer;

(c) the directors of the insurer have failed to take such action as is reasonable necessary to enable him to exercise his or her duties and obligations; or

(d) an officer or employee of the insurer has engaged in conduct calculated to prevent him/her exercising his/her duties and obligations.

Duties of an Actuary in Life Insurance Business

In case of the insurer carrying life insurance business the actuary shall perform the following duties:

1. certify the actuarial report, abstracts and other returns;
2. comply with provisions of Section 112 of the Act, 1938 in regard to further information required by the Authority;
3. comply with provisions of Section 40B of the Act, 1938 in regard to the bases of premium;
4. comply with the provisions of Section 112 of the Act, 1938 in regard to recommendation of interim bonus or bonuses payable by life insurer to policyholders whose policies mature for payment by reason of death or otherwise during the inter-valuation period;
5. ensure that premium rates of insurance products are fair;
6. certify that the mathematical reserves have been determined taking into account the guidance not issued by the Actuarial Society of India and any directions given by the Authority;
7. ensure that the policyholders reasonable expectations have been considered in the matter of valuation of liabilities and distribution of surplus to the participating policyholders who are entitled for a share of surplus; and
8. submit the actuarial advice in the interests of the insurance industry and the policyholders.

Absolute Privilege of Appointed Actuary

The appointed actuary shall enjoy absolute privilege to make any statement, oral or written for the purpose of performance of his functions as appointed actuary. This is, in addition, to any other privilege conferred upon an appointed actuary under any other regulations framed by the IRDA. Any provision in the letter of appointment of the appointed actuary which restricts or prevents his duties, obligations and privileges shall have no effect.

9.5 GLOBAL INSURANCE SCENARIO AND CHALLENGES FOR THE ACTUARY

An actuary is a financial-*cum*-mathematic expert who specializes in the statistical estimation of various risks and their financial consequences. He thus plays a key role not only in designing and pricing of risk covers, i.e.

insurance policies, but also in all aspects of insurance company management including reserving and distribution of surplus, investment of funds, corporate restructuring and mergers and also regulation of insurance sector.

The insurance industry in India till the year 2000 being a state monopoly, its history of the past few decades has been one of the stable and rather uneventful growth. However, one cannot ignore the fact that the insurance business is only one of the many interrelated financial services, and hence it can no longer remain unaffected by the vast changes sweeping the entire financial sector, both in India and abroad.

The most important and interesting development on the financial scene that we have been witnessing in recent times is a distinct trend towards integration or convergence of various financial services into a single business entity that may be referred to as "a financial super market." In our country this trend is signaled by gradual disappearance of the dividing line between long-term project finance and short term loans, as banks like SBI have entered in a big way into term lending business while long-term financial institutions like IDBI, ICICI and IFCI are making forays into working capital funds and commercial banking sector.

At the global level, this blurring of the distinctions among various financial business is even more prominent and radical, as evident from the emergence of concepts like Bancassurance, where banking giants have started acquiring life insurance companies so as to capitalize on their extensive branch network to sell protection-*cum*-saving products, while insurance companies are setting up their own banks and mutual funds. So much so that even retail chain stores that have always sold only tangible consumer goods so far, are embarking on insurance marketing, merely to cash on their competitive edge in marketing and special rapport with the consumer.

What are the implications of these financial upheavals for the future of insurance industry in India and for the actuarial profession, whose development is closely aligned with the prosperity of this industry?

As the Indian Government has permitted entry of private firms in insurance business, one thing is certain that all professionals including actuaries responsible for the blooming of this industry and its future growth will have to draw heavily upon the vast experience of insurance industries in developed countries of the US and Europe and also learn a few significant lessons from the fortunes and failures of those in other developing countries in South East Asia. It is quite appropriate and desirable, that for the Indian actuaries to take a hard look at some of the latest issues that are becoming centre-stage in the insurance debates and are exercising the minds of actuaries all over the world.

The most significant impact of this growing synergy among financial services on actuaries will be an inevitable move towards closer co-operation with other related professions such as Accountants, Engineers, Lawyers, Marketing Specialists, Bankers, Investment Analysis and so on.

As things stand today, a lack of understanding of what an actuary is and what he or she can do is not only confined to the so-called laymen but also pervades even "experts" engaged in these related professions.

The greatest challenge before an actuary today is how to reach out to those whose decisions will matter a lot to his own professional success, how to accept and incorporate their "non-actuarial" viewpoints into his actuarial principles, theories and models, and thus be accepted as a useful and pragmatic decision-maker in the overall management of financial services.

9.6 FUNCTIONS OF AN ACTUARY IN LIFE INSURANCE BUSINESS

While the main function of an actuary in life insurance has remained the same, viz. assessment and valuation of mortality risk apart from other risks, it is the extent of risk selection and methods of guarding against anti-selection which has become a subject of heated debate amongst life insurance actuaries in developed economies. What lies at the centre of this discussion is the vast advances in medical science and in particular in the field of genetics, which can throw much more light on human vulnerability to certain fatal diseases than traditional medical tests. This progress opens up tremendous possibilities in the medical selection of lives for the purpose of insurance.

This certainly about the life span will obviously threaten the very existence of life insurance which thrives on the uncertainty regarding the exact time of death and which motivates a voluntary sharing of losses among people with different life spans, or rather compels the many fortunate people who happen to live long to pay for those unfortunate few who happen to die early. However, it is unlikely that the productive capacity of genetics will reach this limit of certainty. Nevertheless the progress in this direction can have far-reaching consequences for the future of life insurance.

The advances in genetic research have enabled detection of potential diseases or disorders. This gives rise to two questions in life insurance context:

(a) Should an insurer conduct a genetic test on a life proposed, to obtain additional information relating to probable future mortality and also to guard against anti-selection by those who already possess this information?

(b) Should any genetic information, even that which is already available, be used at all by the insurance industry to charge higher premiums for those who possess some genetic disorders?

On the first question, which is merely an extension of the basic arguments for and against insurance selection, one has to weigh two opposite considerations, viz. need to guard against anti-selection and benefit of such expensive tests relative to their cost.

Medical selection by the insurer is necessary and desirable both on grounds of 'actuarial fairness', i.e. charging premiums to different lives on the basis of their different levels of risk and for financial viability of the insurance company.

The second question of whether genetic information should be used as a basis for insurance rating of impaired lives, however, is much more controversial, for it raises not only financial or actuarial issues, but also wider ethical and moral considerations.

9.7 FUNCTIONS OF AN ACTUARY IN GENERAL INSURANCE BUSINESS

With the growing complexity of business operations and increasing technological development, individuals and companies are coming face to face with newer and greater risks, e.g. risks of computer breakdowns, satellite communication failures, financial losses suffered by professionals from client litigation, etc. These risks provide increased opportunities of profitable business for insurance companies and thus open up additional career avenues for actuaries.

Risk management has become an important managerial function in large business houses, where a professional risk manager assesses the nature and extent of the company's exposure to a specific mix of risks and decides whether to retain the risk in house or to transfer it to an insurance company. Nevertheless, even in case of risk retention, companies do seek other services such as underwriting, actuarial and risk management advice from insurers. It is here that the general insurance actuary has to demonstrate his competence not only in accurate risk appraisal, but also in understanding the needs of the business manager, so as to build up a mutually beneficial and long lasting relationship between the insurers and the business community.

Health Insurance

Health Insurance sector offers the most exciting opportunities and yet poses the biggest problems for the actuaries in India. This is because:

- the country has very little experience of his own in this field to rely upon, except in the case of Medical Insurance sold by GIC subsidiaries; and
- the types of covers provided under this generic term in western countries is quite large, viz. Private Medical Insurance (PMI), Critical Illness Cover (CIC), Long Term Care Insurance (LTCI) and Permanent Health Insurance (PHI). Even within each type the variety of terms and benefits can be large, leading to different rating methods, valuation assumptions, solvency margins, investment strategy, etc.

So, where do the actuaries look for the designing health covers suitable for Indian conditions?

As far as medical insurance and Public Health Insurance (PHI) are concerned, the experience of GIC and Employee State Insurance Scheme (ESIS) respectively can provide useful initial guide. We can draw on the long experience of the US health business in general. The US economy spends 15 per cent of its GDP on health care.

With the persistent weakening of joint family system in urban areas and growing proportion of aged population, the need for insurance for the elderly is likely to grow. Hence, the insurers and the actuaries must prepare themselves well in advance to exploit this potential demand. The first challenge to actuaries in this field will be designing of different types of health covers, keeping in view the objectives of:

- a need-based approach;
- simplicity of benefits and administration, and
- avoidance of fraud and anti-selection.

Their role would also include collection and analysis of morality data and advising the Government on an effective regulatory mechanism, so as to protect the interests of the policyholders.

9.8 ROLE OF AN ACTUARY IN INVESTMENT POLICIES

Actuaries need to be closely associated with framing of investment policies of insurance companies, since better than average investment return is often the biggest source of surplus, particularly in life insurance. It is also the unique selling proposition in unit-linked business, which is growing in popularity worldwide, in relation to the traditional life insurance policies.

The basic objective of investment policy in an insurance company remains unchanged, viz. to match the cash flows (both in terms of timing and amount from assets to those from liabilities, i.e. insurance contracts, so as to minimize the "actuarial risk", i.e. the probability of not being able to meet the liabilities when due, and subject to the above goal, to maximize the return on assets, especially in the long-term.

However, it is the balance between these two objectives of risk and return and the precise methods of achieving the goal that is undergoing a radical change, with the evolution of ever-new investment products.

9.9 ACTUARIAL SOCIETY OF INDIA

The Actuarial Society of India was established in 1944 to provide a Central Organisation for Members of the actuarial profession in India for the purpose of elevating the attainment and status as also promoting the general efficiency of all who are engaged in the pursuits of an Actuary. It is the Indian counterpart of the Institute of Actuaries, London. Any person with a high degree of aptitude for Mathematics and Statistics can become an Actuary. Generally, first class graduates or post-graduates in Mathematics or Statistics or those who had Actuarial Science as an optional subject at the degree level will be in a better position to qualify as Actuaries. To become a full-fledged Actuary, one has to clear, through self-study, a series of

Examinations conducted by the Actuarial Society of India, Mumbai.

Since almost all actuaries in India qualified from Institute of Actuaries, London, the bond between the London Institute and Indian Society became stronger day-by-day. The Institute of Actuaries, London always lends full support to the Actuarial Society of India.

The traditional field for actuaries was life insurance. But actuaries gradually entered into wider fields like Pension, General Insurance, Health Insurance and Investment. The basic subjects taught in the actuarial courses are Mathematics, Statistics and Finance. At the higher level, particularly at fellowship level, a student has to learn and master application of the basic actuarial techniques. The method of training helps an actuarial student to acquire skill for analyzing any type of complex problems.

To become an actuary one must obtain a fellowship by completing the examinations through one of the following professional bodies:

1. Institute of Actuaries of England and Wales.
2. Institute of Actuaries of Australia.
3. Actuarial Society of India.
4. Societies of Actuaries of North America.
5. Faculty of Actuaries of Scotland.

9.10 SUMMARY

Actuaries are the backbone of the insurance companies. They apply mathematical, statistical and economic analysis to a wide range of practical problems in insurance, investment, financial planning and management. In short, they are disciplined problem-solvers. A creative aspect of the work of actuaries is forecasting of future contingent events.

9.11 REVIEW QUESTIONS

1. Define an Actuary. What are necessary requirements for a person to be appointed as an actuary?
2. List out the powers, duties and obligations of an Actuary.
3. What are the functions of an Actuary in Life Insurance Business and General Insurance Business?
4. "Actuaries are the backbone of the insurance companies." Comment.

10 CHAPTER

CONTEMPORARY ISSUES IN INSURANCE

LEARNING OBJECTIVE

The main objective of this chapter is to enrich the knowledge of the students with current developments in insurance.

10.1 INTRODUCTION

In the era of Nationalized Insurance Sector, there have been significant developments. The geographical coverage of insurance companies has been tremendous with a large net work of its branches all over India next only to the network of the branches of State Bank of India. A large number of Surveyors and Agents act as selling agents, and loss settlement agencies of the insured public. But the fact is that, the presence of all of them, has not enabled the growth of the market to the extent, it is felt desirable nor has it encouraged the spread of insurance education. For a country like India, which is the fifth largest economy in the world, the cover that its population has in regard to property and life is next to nothing. The figures only 18% of the population is covered with insurance and around 2% of GDP is total premium income from insurance business, which clearly shows the position that the insurance penetration of this country is the largest in South-East Asian region.

In the last so many years, the industry has been under the State Control. It has grown to about Rs. 19274 crores on the Life side and Rs. 7647 crores on the General Insurance side in 1998. The present situation is that insurance products are not available to all, although the need for them may be genuine.

The barriers distinguishing the various Financial Services and products have also been removed. There is now a single regulator governing the financial services in the country. Banks have Life Insurance Covers across the counter. The trade unions have become an important challenge for protecting the need for the unorganized sector to purchase insurance products. Looking back to 2001, it is fortunate that the new entrants into Indian Insurance Sector were able to press upon the need for individuals to buy insurance. Facilitating the customer has become their motto and this has been reflected in the products futures, service and means of collection of premiums.

As far as Contemporary Issues are concerned, it is well known fact that in the Life Insurance Segment it was entirely the monopoly of LIC of India for which there were no competitors. Non Life Business was controlled by the four Subsidiary Companies of the General Insurance Corporation of India Ltd. which acted as a holding company and regulating the business of reinsurance. It is only the year 2000 when Private Sector players have also come to play their role in the Life and Non-Life segments in this field. Keeping this fact in view some important contemporary issues of the Insurance Industry are discussed in the subsequent pages.

10.2 LIFE INSURANCE IN INDIA

Life Insurance in its existing form came to India from the United Kingdom with the establishment of a British firm Oriental Life Insurance Company in Calcutta in 1818 followed by Bombay Life Assurance Company in 1823.

The Indian Life Assurance Companies Act, 1912 was the first Statutory measure to regulate life insurance business. Later in 1928 the Indian insurance companies Act was enacted to enable the government to collect statistical information about both life and non-life insurance business including provident insurance societies. In 1938 with a view to protecting the interest of insuring public earlier legislation was consolidated and amended by the Insurance Act, 1938 with comprehensive provisions detailed and effective control over the activities of insurers.

The Act was amended in 1950 resulting in far reaching changes in the insurance sector. These included a statutory requirement of equity capital for companies carrying on life insurance business, ceiling on share holding in such companies, stricter control on investments, submission of periodical returns relating to investments and such other information to the controller. The controller could also call for appointment of administrators and put a ceiling on expenses of management and agency commission for mismanaged companies. By 1956, 154 Indian insurers, 16 foreign insurers and 75 provident societies were carrying on life insurance business in India. Life insurance business was concentrated in urban areas and confined to the higher strata of the society. On January 19, 1956, the management of life insurance business of 245 Indian and foreign insurers and provident societies then operating in India was taken over by the Central Government. Life Insurance Corporation was formed in September 1956 by an Act of Parliament, viz. LIC Act, 1956 with a capital contribution of Rs. 50 million.

The then Finance Minister Mr. C.D. Deshmukh while piloting the bill for nationalization outlined the objectives of LIC thus:

> "To conduct the business with utmost economy with the spirit of trusteeship, to charge premium not higher than warranted by strict actuarial considerations, to invest the funds for obtaining maximum yield for the policyholders consistent with safety of capital, to render prompt and efficient service to policyholders thereby making Insurance widely popular."

Sector-wise Break-up of Investments in India

Sector		*Book value of Investment & Loans Outstanding as at 31.3.99 (Rs. in crores)*	*% to Total*
(a) Public Sector		96,410.45	84.49
(b) Co-operative sector		2,094.53	1.84
(c) Private Sector			
(i) Joint Sector	549.26		
(ii) Others	15048.42	15,597.70	13.67
Total		1,14,102.68	100.00

10.3 GIC AND ITS SUBSIDIARY

In 1973, the business of 107 private general insurers was taken over by the government and amalgamated and distributed among General Insurance Corporation and its four subsidiaries, viz. New India Insurance, Oriental Insurance, National Insurance and United India Insurance. GIC is the holding company and today undertakes mainly re-insurance business apart from a bit of aviation insurance. The bulk of the general insurance of Fire, Marine, Motor and Miscellaneous Insurance business is undertaken by the four subsidiaries. The industry has been growing at the rate of 17% p.a. In 1998 the premium income of GIC stood at Rs. 80.85 billion with an investment portfolio of Rs. 166.91 billion. 30 million documents are issued every year and 2.2 million claims are settled annually. With the increase in social awareness and the taking up of large risks, the premium levels are expected to touch Rs. 140 billion by the year 2001. There are about 150 products on offer in the industry. Only 30 of them contribute about 80% of premium income. The four subsidiaries are not really competing with each other as there is inflexibility in fixing of tariffs and co-insurance requirements.

10.4 PRIVATE PLAYERS IN THE INSURANCE SECTOR AND IRDA

General Perspective

Insurance is seen as "an essential characteristic of economic

Organizational Set-up as on March 31, 1999

Company	*Regional Offices*	*Divisional Offices*	*Branch Offices*
National	20 (19)	263 (254)	673 (681)
New India	23 (21)	366 (352)	738 (788)
Oriental	18 (18)	278 (274)	675 (680)
United India	22 (22)	334 (322)	756 (777)
Total	83 (80)	1241 (1202)	2842 (2926)

Figures in brackets indicate the number as on March 31, 1998.

Gross Direct Premium Income In India

Name of the Company	*Fire*		*Miscellaneous*		*Marine*		*Total*	
	1998-99	*1997-98*	*1998-99*	*1997-98*	*1998-99*	*1997-98*	*1998-99*	*1997-98*
National	423.05	390.58	1199.10	1004.48	199.17	209.76	1821.32	1604.82
New India	681.78	624.17	1749.96	1496.92	297.74	312.64	2729.48	2433.73
Oriental	434.77	401.13	1287.12	1059.68	208.91	217.14	1930.80	1677.95
United India	548.17	500.22	1381.22	1144.29	291.89	286.13	2221.28	1930.64
Total	2087.77	1916.10	5617.40	4705.37	997.71	1025.67	8702.88	7647.14

Source: BSE Official Directory, July 2000.

development of a country." It promotes financial stability and reduces anxiety, acts as a lubricant for trade and commerce, mobilizes national savings, enables risks to be managed more efficiently, helps the Insured to reduce losses, and facilitates efficient allocation of a country's capital.

Insurance sector reforms became imperative in the wake of economic liberalization initiated in the early nineties. Malhotra Committee was set-up to recommend insurance sector reforms. Allow private sector entry in Life and General business. Permit entry of foreign players in partnership with Indian Companies. Gradual relaxation of investment norms.

Insurance Regulatory and Development Authority (IRDA) Act was passed by parliament and as a result IRDA was established which promulgated various regulations. The regulations provides for compulsory registration of new private sector companies.

Consumer's Perspective

The emerging scenario provides the consumers with choice of insurance, wider range of new and innovative products, competitive pricing of products and services, access to information about companies and products, continuous consumer education, a well trained and highly professional sales force, prompt and courteous front office response, greater focus on customers' services, world class pre and post-sales services and efficient and customer-friendly claim administration systems.

Society's Perspective

It provides for the followings:

(A) Direct Employment Opportunities

As Agents, Brokers and Back office operations staff, Surveyors and Assessors. Managers for functions like Sales and Marketing, I.T Training, HR, Finance and Accounts, Actuarial and Understanding, Board and Secretariat, Asset Management, etc.

(B) Indirect Employment Opportunities

IT Industry, Higher demand for insurance related hardware as well as software solutions, Greater demand for computer engineers and software developers, Expertise to develop application software systems like premium accounting system, Claim administration and payment systems, Sales Activity Management (SAM) systems, Customer Relationship Management (CRM) systems.

(C) Miscellaneous Service Providers

Greater demand for outsourced services like HR, Accounting, Actuarial, Consultancies, etc., Real Estate Advisory Services, Postal and Courier Services, Cleaning and Pantry Services, and Security Services.

(D) Training and Education Services

Need for expansion of existing facilities to meet the rising demand for trained—sales and marketing personnel, Technical support staff to manage back office operations, Emphasis on insurance related research anddevelopment activities, Opportunities for universities and management institutes to offer insurance-related education and training courses, Greater demand for qualified people certified by the Insurance Institute of India (III) and Actuarial Society of India (ASI), Insurance Intermediaries, Brokers, Loss Assessors and Surveyors, Need for adequately qualified to be certified by appropriate statutory professional bodies which may be set-up in due course. Premium on appropriate training facilities, etc.

(E) Market Research Agencies

These agencies will Stand to gain as competition will force insurance companies to undertake periodic market researches to establish a more objective relationship between the buyers and the products on offer. Product development will assume great significance and market research will be an essential input. Greater demand for professional market research companies.

Advertising, PR and Event Management services. Professionals will also have a booming business to meet the progressively rising demand for their services in the emerging scenario in the insurance industry.

(F) Support to Infrastructure

Another significant benefit which society should look forward to is the tremendous support that competitive insurance industry is likely to provide, a few years down the line though, to infrastructure rate. Greater mobilization of people's savings towards insurance premia will have the effect of diverting more investments of insurance funds into long-term infrastructure projects, consistent with prudent ALM norms and also the IRDA Guidelines. Higher investment in infrastructure projects will have the effect of pushing up the industrial growth rate of related industries.

Job/Professional Opportunities

The insurance sector offers the following job opportunities:

1. The Actuary;
2. Professional Underwriters;
3. Marketing of Insurance Policies;
4. Software Professionals;
5. Investment Professionals;
6. Administrative Officers;
7. Development Officers;
8. Insurance Brokers;
9. Insurance Surveyors; and
10. Insurance Agents.

Therefore, the new set-up will have entry of more players in the insurance sector, rapid growth of Insurance business and massive mobilization of savings. It will also provide substantial support to infrastructure projects involving long-term investments and scope of Insurance business in rural or social sector. The new scenario offers bonanza of opportunities for well trained and highly motivated professionals in the Insurance Sector.

The Insurance Regulatory Development Authority has given licenses to a total of 24 players which exists in the insurance sector today. 17 are private players who are new to the market. Two of the 17 are 100% Subsidiaries of Reliance Group—the only company to set-off without a foreign partner. The rest 15 are all Joint Ventures where the Foreign Partner's stake has been limited to 26%.

10.5 IMPORTANT CONTEMPORARY ISSUES

The following are some of the important Contemporary Issues in Insurance Business which requires a detailed study.

The New Entrants in Insurance

Indian Partner	*Foreign Insurer*	*Specialization*
HDFC	Standard Life UK	Life
Reliance	No Partner	Non-Life
Sundram	Royal & Sun Alliance	Non-Life
Max India	New York Life, USA	Life
HDFC	Finalising	Partner
Bajaj Auto	Allianz	Life, Non-Life
Kotak Mahindra	Old Mutual, South	Life
ICICI	Prudential, UK	Life
ICICI	Lombard	Non-Life
IFFCO	Tokio Marine, Japan	Non-Life
Reliance	No Partner	Life
Tata Group	AIG, USA	Life, Non-Life
Aditya Birla Group	Sun Life, Canada	Life
State Bank of India	Cardif	France
Vysya Bank	ING	Life
Dabur	CGNU, UK	Life
Hero Group	Zurich, Switzerland	Life, Non-life

I. Increased Pension Coverage

A few years back FICCI conducted a study on Pension as a social security scheme. It concluded that the lack of comprehensive social security system in the country, coupled with willingness to save, means that Indian demand for pension products would be very large. However, unfortunately the present penetration of pension coverage is poor. By March 1988, the Life Insurance Corporation of India's (LIC) pension premium was only Rs. 100 crore. The study further concluded that making pension products into attractive saving instruments would require only simple innovations which is already common in some other markets.

The fact is that in the Indian context, building of retirement benefits in a structured manner remained confined to only the employed sector, and the social security benefit in a small measure is available only to the destitute above 65 years of age. Currently, pension benefits are available to employees in organised sectors like the government and private. At present, there is no pension benefit for self-employed and Agricultural workers in the unorganised sector.

In India at present about 89% of population, that is, the informal sector workers have been kept out of the pension schemes so far. The Social Security measures till now are state controlled by and large in this country and Insurance has very less role to play bearing a few schemes.

THE BRITISH GOVERNMENT, states that the State takes care of its citizen from cradle to the grave. They have the National Health Scheme which underwrites the health of the members of the public and they have also got pension scheme which takes care of the widows, orphans and the old.

In India, there is no such system of social security exists. The following table clearly indicates the insufficiency of Indian Pension Funds to act as a cushion for social security of the old. India has the highest number of people above 60 years of age among the 14 countries in the World Development Indicators table appended below but its pension assets per rank lasts in the study. The main reason being the coverage of pension plan in India covers only 8% of the working population.

International Comparison of Pension Funds

Country	*Population of aged 60 and above (mn.)*	*Assets of Pension Funds (sbn)*	*Pension Fund per an old individual ($ 'ooo)*
USA	42.08	2915	69.27
UK	9.44	643	68.11
Germany	16.40	59	3.59
Japan	25.00	182	7.28
Canada	4.80	187	38.96
Netherlands	2.70	145	53.7
Sweden	1.98	87	43.94
Denmark	0.95	22	23.16
Switzerland	1.40	173	123.57
Australia	2.70	62	22.96
France	11.60	22	1.89
Chile	12.60	15	1.19
Singapore	2.70	60	22.22
India	74.32	35	0.47

Source: BSE Official Directory, 2001.

The Insurance Regulatory and Development Authority (IRDA) has recently recommended a new, voluntary pension regime for every one, including the unorganised sector, according to the Dave Committee implementation report. The report submitted now by IRDA to the Finance Ministry, suggests wide-ranging reforms for this sector. The report, however, does not mandate any minimum annual contribution or the spacing of contribution across time. In short, an individual will be able to access the collection points at any time and will have complete freedom to transfer a part or the full asset from one scheme to another with the same or different provider company.

The Scheme's basic purpose is to bring this class under the purview of pensions. There are four areas under the present system:

(a) Contribution collection;
(b) Record-keeping;
(c) Assets Management; and
(d) Annuity Payment.

A trust-based entity will be set-up that will provide integrated services. Anybody can do it including the MF's having a capital of Rs. 50-75 crores.

As per the report multiple providers of the Pension Services will bring competition into system. Sound companies with good track record in the Asset Management area will be favoured. It will be a regime of defined contribution, fully funded individual retirement plan on voluntary bases. At present, it is the government which pays from its current revenue. Now the contribution would be defined and accumulated, and the fund would be buying the annuity for you.

HDFC Standard Life Insurance Co. Ltd. will launch shortly its Pension Product, becoming the first Private Sector Insurance Company to launch such a scheme.

Therefore, in view of the above, it is a step in the right direction. There has been a pressing need for a funded retirement plan defined contribution to be implemented in India. It will address the long pending need for a strong pension system for the country. The private sector players in the insurance sector are now in the process of studying the potential of the pension market. The scope of pension funds if enlarged by the Government, will definitely provide a real competition in the Insurance Sector.

Present Position

The Insurance Regulatory Development Authority in its pension report has projected an exponential growth in the post-reforms pension sector with the aggregate market size estimated to touch Rs. 4,06,500 crore in year 2025. The market, currently, stands at Rs. 56,100 crore. The IRDA had said that the aggregate pension market would grow to Rs. 1,16,600 crore in 2005, Rs. 1,56,900 crore (2010), Rs. 2,15,400 crore (2015) and Rs. 2,98,600 crore (2020). The pension market includes the Employees' Provident Fund (EPF), Employees' Pension Scheme (EPS), Government Provident Fund (GPF), Public Provident Fund (PPF) and the Voluntary Contributions through the future schemes in the individual and group pension categories. The regulator also suggested setting up a single integrated domestic pension system by October 2001. While suggesting stripping of regulatory powers of the existing Employees' Provident Fund Office, it recommended that IRDA monitor this sector as well.

The report had also not laid any restrictions on the number of players and said that foreign equity should be allowed in the sector. It had also suggested that minimum returns must be linked in the bank rate initially and payouts should be exclusive preserve of Life Insurance Companies.

2. Convergence of Insurance and Banking Industry

It was the evolution of banks entering into the Insurance Sector and Selling Products across the counter that saw an increasing reach into the rural areas. Many new players were hesitant of such possibilities, stating that the rural India reflected huge numbers in terms of lives to be insured, business volumes would be negligible. It was not until some insurers decided to tap Micro-Insurance possibilities and came out with special products for the rural masses, that insurance penetration to rural India actually took.

Bancassurance is equally a major factor and plus point for spreading insurance to rural areas. Even state or public sector entities, which till then had depended solely on the tied agents, capitalised on the branch network of public sector banks. Insurance spread across the country as banks offered to cross sell products. The concept of Universal Banking is now taking a shape in Indian Financial Sector and the very scope of Insurance business will be widened. For example, SBI Life Insurance Company Ltd. and other Banks with their Joint Venturers have started making a dent into rural business. This was not much possible earlier and is the result of entry of private players into the Insurance Sector.

Thus, the State owned Insurance Sector could not earlier make much use of bank branch network in the country for insurance business, which has now become possible. This contemporary issue of participation of banks in marketing/selling of insurance products in the country is of much significance. The Insurance business had the less number of insured due to the above reasons which is going to be increased now manifold and that too with qualitative products and services,. Many of the banks are now entering into MOU with Insurance Companies to sell their insurance products through network of their bank branches.

Bancassurance

Public Sector banks in India can emerge as leading players in the distribution of Insurance products across all parts of the country. With their net work of 60000 branches two-thirds of which are in rural areas and their 117 million customer accounts, insurance companies would be well advised to use them as a channel for their products.

Bancassurance in India has a great future. Funds generated through the Bancassurance model will play a pivotal role in mobilising savings particularly in rural areas and short and long-term funds mobilised could, in turn, be used for developmental activities. PSU banks, will however, have to gear themselves adequately to undertake this task as it would entail adequate training in well designed products. With the emergence of Private banks, PSU banks have realised that customers' expectations have risen dramatically in the past few years.

3. Alternate Channels of Distribution

Nowadays there is a thinking in the Insurance Sector about alternative channels of distribution like Internet and Bancassurance. Many insurers are willing to take advantage of these changes. As far as the Internet is concerned, most people are using the net for information, to see whether the number quoted by the agent are accurate. For the purchase they turn to the agent as there is no price difference for the buyer. It is a fact now that all companies are looking at the Internet and banks. But Life Insurance is a personal decision. In banks, staff is changed occasionally and when you visit the bank branch again, the earlier person is not there and the new person has no idea why one has purchased the policy in the first instance.

Multiple distribution channels help insurers reach out to different sectors of society, with Trade Unions or post offices being focal points of sale. Many companies in the private sector have now tied up with the trade unions of railways, and have provided them with customized products to suit the needs of the employees.

Thus, new channels of distribution and marketing have seen the emergence of customisation of Insurance covers tailored out to meet the various needs of specific groups. Even nowadays sugar co-operatives have also become a high selling point of products especially among the farmers and farm labourers. The distribution channels have, therefore, to play a vital role in increasing the quantum of Insurance business. It is one of the important factor of internal environment for any Insurance Company as more and innovative channels of distributions will always have an edge over others.

Intermediaries and Distribution Channels

In the light of one of the important contemporary issues of Insurance Sector, the modern set-up of Intermediaries and distribution channel now comprises the following.

(i) *Direct Response*: includes telephone, off the page, mail and T.V., etc.

(ii) *High Street*: includes bank branches, finance houses, kisoks, retail stores, etc.

(iii) *Electronic*: includes Internet, interactive T.V., etc.

(iv) *Agency*: includes Issues, conduct, quality, demand for exclusivity, cost, etc.

(v) *Financial Advisors*: includes among others, independent financial advisors, stock and securities brokers.

Prior to entry of private players in the insurance sector, there were no alternative channels of distribution. It is the result of information technology which provided new channels of distribution and liberalisation provided new intermediaries to Insurance.

4. Uniform Tax Concessions

There are certain sections of the Income Tax Act, 1961 which provide some concessions to Life Insurance Corporation of India, viz. Sections 80 CC(I), 88, 193, 194A and Section 36(V) of the Income Tax Rules, which are not available to recently joined private sector Insurance Companies. At present, tax rebate is granted on repayment of Loans taken from L.I.C. for the purchase and construction of residential houses under Section 88 of the

Income Tax Act. L.I.C. interest earnings are also exempted from withholding of tax under section 193 and 194A of the Income Tax Act. Currently, the Gratuity and Super-annuation policies purchased from LIC are eligible for deduction under Section 36(V) of the Income Tax Rules. At present investment upto Rs. 10,000 P.A. in LIC's Pension Product gets a rebate of 20% under section 80CC(1) of the Income Tax Act.

The Private Life Insurers have also demanded a "Level Playing Field" with the Life Insurance Corporation of India on the above tax concessions. Thus, there are three areas which require changes in the Income Tax Act, 1961 and these are:

(a) Tax rebate on re-payment of loans.
(b) Exemption from withholding tax on interest earned.
(c) Deduction of employer's contribution to gratuity and super-annuation policies.

Many companies in the Private Sector such as Prudential ICICI Life, HDFC Standard Life, SBI Life, Om Kotak Life, Tata AIR, Birla Sun Life, Bajaj Allianz Life, Ing-Vysya Life have already started Life Insurance business in a big way. These companies are awaiting the necessary changes in the Income Tax Act and Rules that grants certain benefits to L.I.C. They are now referring to the Budget statement of Finance Minister for ensuring "Level Playing field for Private Companies."

Tax concessions on uniform basis in the Insurance Sector has become a very important issue. Unless it is settled and made uniform, the private sector companies can not compete for a longer period with the Life Insurance Corporation of India. This issue therefore, requires urgent action on the part of the Government of India so that the insured may take the maximum benefit of various Insurance Products being offered by the Insurers.

5. Cost and Competitiveness

Life Insurance Corporation's monopoly has been broken with new players entering the Life Insurance Sector. Almost for three decades the L.I.C. was the unchallenged master. But now it is facing a challenge from Private Sector players who may cut on the business of L.I.C. For the customers who now want to have life covers for which there are many providers. All the new players offer endowment schemes and money back schemes which are based on the model of LIC, at different premiums.

Different Companies follow a different system of calculating the bonus. There are other special deals offered by several companies. For example, some companies offer a special premium in cases of accidental deaths. Some others also offer a waiver of premium if a person is unemployed. There is a different set of documentation which is followed by these companies. The claim settlement period also differs with all these different rules of their administration cost of life covers also differs. A comparative Table showing cost of Life Cover to various Insurers is given here below.

Cost of Life Cover

Policy	*Company*	*Age of Assured (P.A.)*	*Premium (Rs.)*	*Total sum at maturity (Rs.)*
1. Endowment Policy (20 yrs.)	L.I.C.	27	4852	2,75,000
	TATA—AIG	27	7144	3,16,663
	HDFC—Standard Life	27	4805	N.A.
	ICICI Prudential Life	27	4450	2,41,171
	Max New York Life	27	N.A.	N.A.
2. Endowment Policy (30 yrs.)	L.I.C.	39	3702	3,51,000
	TATA AIG	39	4973	5,25,243
	HDFC Standard Life	39	3586	N.A.
	ICICI Prudential Life	39	3079	3,74,531
	Max New York Life	39	N.A.	N.A.

From the above table, it is clear that there are different cost for different Insurance Providers, which has a bearing on their profitability. The cost factor is equally important for creating competition in between the various insurers. More people would be looking to the insurer who provides Insurance at less premium. This cost and competition factor will ultimately affect the quantum of business of different Insurers besides increasing the total Insurance business in the country. The rate of premium, service and incentives also have a bearing on the non-life business in the country.

Therefore, various components of cost of Public Sector Insurance providers and those of the Private Sector would be different, making it one of the major issues, which have to be kept in view always. This provides an insight into the opportunities which will now be available to the new Insurers *vis-a-vis* the old one.

State Owned Insurers

The public sector insurance companies are geared up to face competition, with the Life Insurance Corporation (LIC) buying about 14 per cent stake in Corporation Bank. LIC had also planned alliances with IIMs for training, increase off shore activity by entering Canada, Australia and New Zealand, give a thrust on mass and group business, introduce innovative products and set-up new cells for high-end customers.

The Government passed a bill to amend the General Insurance Business (Nationalisation) Act which delinked the four nationalised general insurance companies from the General Insurance Corporation of India (GIC). GIC's holding in the four companies—New India Assurance Co. Ltd., United India Insurance Co. Ltd., National Insurance Co. Ltd. and Oriental Insurance Co. Ltd.—would be transferred to the Government. GIC will now be the Indian Reinsurer.

6. Exposure Norms for Public and Private Sector

The Insurance Regulatory Development Authority came up with the stiff exposure norms for the private sector companies. It stipulated that investments by any insurance company could not exceed 10 per cent of the total subscribed share capital, free reserves, debentures and bonds of the investee company or 10 per cent of the insurer's total assets in the case of non-life insurance companies and 10 per cent of the controlled funds in the case of life insurers, whichever was lower.

The IRDA's revised investment regulations also said that for the public sector insurance companies, the investment exposure can not at any point exceed 20 per cent of the subscribed share capital, debentures and bonds of the investee company or 5 per cent of controlled funds of the life insurer or 10 per cent of the general insurers total assets.

Within the above exposure limit, the Authority has said that the investment in equity instruments including preference shares, investment in equity convertible part of debentures should not exceed 50 per cent of the overall exposure ceiling. A similar 50 per cent exposure norm limit would also apply to investments in immovable property.

The regulators has also barred life insurance companies from entering into reinsurance treaty arrangements with its promoter company or any other associate or group companies without prior approval. The regulations direct companies to draw up an independent programme of reinsurance of their own. It also said that the efforts of each company while making the reinsurance programme should be to maximise retention of premium earned within the country.

7. Entry of Financial Institutions into the Insurance Business

In view of the interest evinced by some of the All-India Financial Institutions (FIs), falling within the regularity and supervisory domain of RBI, in entering the Insurance business, the guidelines for entry of the financial institutions into insurance business have since been formulated. The FIs desirous of entering into insurance business, and meeting the following criteria may make an application to the IRDA along with the necessary particulars duly certified by their statutory auditors.

A. *Insurance Business without Risk Participation*

1. FI having net owned fund of Rs. 2 crore would be permitted to undertake Insurance Business as agent of Insurance Companies of fee basis, without any risk participation.

B. *Insurance Business with Risk Participation*

2. The FIs which satisfy the eligibility criteria given below, will be permitted to set-up a joint venture company for undertaking insurance business with risk participation, subject to safeguards.

The maximum equity contribution that the FI can hold in the joint venture company will normally be 50 per cent of the paid-up capital of the Insurance company. On a selective basis, the Reserve Bank of India may permit a higher equity contribution by a promoter FI initially, pending divestment of equity within the prescribed period (See Note (1) below). The eligibility criteria for joint venture participant will be as under, as per the latest available audited balance sheet.

(i) The owned fund of the FI should not be less than Rs. 500 crore. The owned fund for the purpose should be computed as per the definition of 'net owned fund' under section 45-1A of the RBI Act, 1934,

(ii) The CRAR of the FI should be not less than 15%;

(iii) The level of net non-performing assets should be not more than 55 of the total outstanding loans and advances;

(iv) The FI should have earned net profit for the last three continuous years;

(v) The track record of the performance of the subsidiaries, if any, of the concerned FI should be satisfactory; and

(vi) Regulatory compliance with the RBI guidelines for raising of resources by the FIs should be demonstrated.

3. In case where a foreign partner contributes 26 per cent of the equity with the approval of Insurance Regulatory Development Authority/Foreign Investment Promotion Board, more than one FI may be allowed to participate in the equity of the insurance joint venture. Since such participants will also assume insurance risk, only those FIs which satisfy the criteria given in paragraph 2 above, would be eligible.

4. No FI would be allowed to conduct insurance business with risk participation, departmentally. A subsidiary or a company in the same group of the FI or of another FI engaged in non-banking or banking business, will not normally be allowed to join the insurance company on risk participation basis.

5. FIs, falling within the regulatory and supervisory domain of RBI, which are not eligible as joint venture participant, as per the foregoing criteria, can make investments upto 10 per cent of the owned fund of the FI or Rs. 50 crore, whichever is lower, in the insurance company. Such participation shall be treated as an investment and should be without any contingent liability for the FI. The eligibility criteria for these FIs will be as under:

(i) The CRAR of the FI should not be less than 15 per cent;

(ii) The level of net NPA should be not more than 5 per cent of total outstanding loans and advances; and

(iii) The FI should have earned net profit for the last three continuous years.

6. All FIs entering into insurance business as agents or investors or

on risk participation basis will be required to obtain prior approval of the Reserve Bank. The Reserve Bank will give permission to the FIs on a case to case basis keeping in view all relevant factors. It should be ensured that risks involved in Insurance Business do not get transferred to the FI and that is business does not get contaminated by any risk which may arise from insurance business.

Note: Holding of equity by a promoter FI in an Insurance Company or participation in any form in insurance business will be subject to compliance with any rules and regulations laid down by the IRDA/Central Government. This will include compliance with section 6AA of the Insurance Act as amended by the IRDA Act, 1999, for divestment of equity in excess of 26 per cent of the paid up capital within a prescribed period of time.

10.6 SUMMARY

At the end of next 7 to 8 years, there will be an upsurge in awareness of consumers, an increase in his expectations that his hopes and inspiration be delivered by the industry. This will however, put immense pressure on the insurance industry and the industry will have to respond to it. Technology will also decide, if present players will be able to hold out or not. The companies will have to deliver the desired goods quickly. Shri N. Rangachary, Chairman, I.R.D.A. says, "that classification of business will change from general and life to time-bound and insurance cover will then be either short-term or long-term risk coverage. The regulator will also have to change his approach to guiding the business and a more holistic approach to the financial sector will have to be considered. He has however, cautioned that the insurance is a global phenomenon and international events such as the recent terrorist attacks will have a significant impact on the Indian Insurance Sector. Thus, the fact remains that to succeed, the players in the insurance sector need to treat the consumer as the master and satisfy his every need. There are plans to incorporate the participation of brokers in the market system in the near future.

Therefore, it is concluded that the environment will become more competitive and sensitive to the demands of the market and there will be shift from manufacturing to services. The customers will become the driving force and the companies will have to recognise the central role of the customers in their business planning and decision-making.

10.7 REVIEW QUESTIONS

1. Discuss three major contemporary issues of Insurance Business in India.
2. Private Life Insurers have demanded a "Level Playing Field" with the Life Insurance Corporation on certain tax concessions. What are those? Please explain.

3. Discuss the scope of Pension Funds in the Insurance Sector.
4. How Banking Industry can help for the growth of Insurance Business in India.
5. Explain in brief the exposure norms fixed by IRDA for Public and Private Sector Insurers.

PART B

ENVIRONMENT AND INSURANCE

11

CHAPTER

BUSINESS ENVIRONMENT AND INSURANCE

LEARNING OBJECTIVE

The main objective of this chapter is to make the students proverbial with kind of internal and external environment that directly impinge on the insurance business.

11.1 INTRODUCTION

Insurance has come up as a very important financial service in most of the part of the world. The Insurance is considered as one of the important segment in an economy for its growth and development. This industry provides long-term funds that are essential for the development of basic infrastructure. The insurance industry also provides depth to the debt and capital market including market for the Government Bonds. The Indian insurance industry is more than 150 years old. This industry has witnessed many phases of the working from the days when there were many private sector companies initially and then moved to Nationalization and again to the Private Sector. Being one of the segments of financial sector, it has in the recent past gone through a transformation and change including the passing of IRDA (Insurance Regulatory and Development Authority) Act, 1999. There have been many reforms in the past in the Banking and Capital Market segments, which for the first time are being witnessed after the passage of IRDA Act in the Insurance Segment.

Insurance is basically defined as a financial agreement that redistributes cost of unexpected losses; today stands both as a service and the industry in its own right. The tremendous enthusiasm by the prospective new players across the globe as well as domestic industry is well understood after the privatisation of insurance industry and passage of IRDA Act. There exists a ready-made market for about 20-25 crores population of the country in the immediate future and may grow at 15-17 per cent per annum.

Following an entry of new players back in the early 21st Century, virtually every men, women and child in the country know the importance of the Insurance and total risk protection. They have brought a new meaning to the word "Insurance" and since then the market has simply grown manifold. Selecting an Insurance Policy is very important. Say in case of Life Insurance, one can chose Term Plan, Whole Life, Money back, Endowment and Annuity Policies. The need for Life Insurance with change is as one grows older. One has to be also particular and careful about choosing an Insurer because a policy will perhaps, lock you into one of the most Long Term relationships you will ever have with a company. Insurance needs differs for different individuals depending on their age, family obligations and financial goals.

11.2 INTERNAL ENVIRONMENT

The Insurance business in a country is affected by a large number of factors for its healthy development and growth. A congenial environment is a pre-requisite, which is governed by various factors such as the economic state of a country, political stability, awareness amongst the public, awareness of Investment for surplus generated, and good steady and reasonable returns, and better corporate governance. There are certain other internal factors which have a direct or indirect effect on the insurance environment. These internal factors are explained below:

1. Risk Management

Risk Management is an integral part of Insurance Business. The Derivative Market in India is gaining importance. Today, Financial Engineering offers sophisticated tools and techniques to hedge, interest rate, Foreign Exchange and Commodity risks. It is now well known in the Financial World, as to how risk can destroy corporate value and how value addition can be achieved through Risk Management.

At present, risk assessment and risk hedging models are being increasingly used in the Corporate Sector. Financial Engineers are now well equipped with latest tools and techniques and products of risk management. A number of insurers are selling financial risk management products, and insurance multiples are being placed directly in the Capital Markets and the Corporate Sector. The value creation approach through integrated risk management has been gaining importance, particularly in companies with huge multiple and diversified investments.

Integrated risk management involves both insurance and financial risks. It generally uses the technology available in both these areas including operational and business. This technique is called comprehensive and its utility is visible from the fact that insurable and financial risks can disrupt earnings, create problems of funding new investments, or even push terms into bankruptcy. It is a fact that contribution of each source of risk cannot be very easily isolated.

In finance, a firm's capacity to absorb risk is determined by its current exposure to other risks. Therefore, an integrated strategy to eliminate the risk is required. But the introduction of new products in financial markets, the increased volatility in prices of both financial assets and goods due to globalisation may result in great risks. The capital adequacy for the new Insurers has been fixed only at Rs. 100 crores which is not sufficient to take care of certain unexpected risks. The IRDA recently decided to impose a 10 per cent surcharge on future fire and engineering policies to create a 'CATASTROPHE RESERVE FUND'. Given the prolonged history of terrorism within our borders, ironically it took a terrorist attach on another nation for to run for cover. Therefore, better risk management system will affect the environment of generation of more Insurance business in the country.

2. Transport Rules and Regulations

Now there are large number of Insurers in the Life and Non-Life business. These companies have their own set of rules and regulations for different type of insurance business and policies. These require proper control while formulating and implementing their respective rules and regulations. In case there is no such a check or control then it may create difficulties for the Insured. The Insurance Regulatory and Development Authority (IRDA) have come a long way, since its inception in November 1999. It has made lot of efforts to put in place, a much-needed regulatory framework for commencing of smooth Insurance business operations both by the new Insurers and existing one in the Domestic Insurance Sector.

The following regulations have already been notified and the others are in process:

(i) Appointed Actuary;
(ii) Actuarial Report and the Abstract;
(iii) Assets Liabilities and Solvency Margin of Insurers;
(iv) Licensing of Insurance Agents;
(v) General Insurance—Reinsurance;
(vi) Registration of Indian Insurance Companies;
(vii) Insurance advertisement and disclosures;
(viii) Obligation of Insurers to rural social sectors;
(ix) Regulations on Investment—Life and Non-Life;
(x) Regulations on Accounts; and
(xi) Surveyor's Regulations.

Thus, the transparent and better the regulations in place, better would be environment for generation and growth of Insurance business in the country.

3. Role of Technology

Technology plays a strategic role in providing a competitive edge, be it in aiding design and administering of products and building life long customer relationships. In fact, technology will help to enhance service, ensure effective and efficient service, delivery and lead to greater customization of products and greater transparency. Most of the Insurers have to set-up national call centres, interactive voice response systems and web sites, etc. to grab the maximum business. It will facilitate and help create brand positioning. It may commit to bring millions of dollars worth of business and savings. Before the emergence of information technology, no insurer could ever think of such advantages.

The technology has also helped in providing value-added services such as Email, Calculators and a virtual office for the users. It is a great facilitator for the agents and customers residing in far off places. In addition, it will also help the Insurance Sector to conduct approved training programmes at different centres across the country. I.T. is a new kind of pressure on the consumer profile, customerised products and customerised services. Use of Internet is for purchase of products, catering to one's servicing needs, payment of premium, etc. The others may include the following:

(a) Provide for Tele-services offerings
(b) Advising on right kind of Insurance Covers
(c) Advising on extent of Life Cover required
(d) Advising on right Investment decisions
(e) Advising on matter of taxation, purchase assistance by directing the sales persons.

4. Scope for Rural Insurance

There has been confusion as to what constitutes rural insurance business. The IRDA has now defined it and has made compulsory to do a certain percentage of rural business by the private sector players. The rural insurance business has a vast scope as it remained untapped to the extent it provides opportunities. While competition in rural areas is often cut throat and unhealthy. The rural areas are characterised by milder competition. In the rural areas, the policies will be relatively smaller amounts, but this will be compensated by a large number than in urban areas.

It is necessary to identify the right agents to harness the full potential of the vibrant and dynamic rural markets. Thus, the rural insurance should be looked upon as an opportunity and not an obligation. It is very important to take advantage of the immense potential that resides in the rural sector. In fact, marketing to the poor is all about understanding the requirements of the customers and satisfying them profitably. A number of innovative products and an efficient delivery system are the two aspects that have to be developed in order to penetrate the rural markets.

Now the new entrants in the insurance sector will definitely form their efforts on rural sector. Although this sector presents a number of challenges, it will also provide great opportunities. It is also necessary to tap into the immense knowledge base that exists with public sector banks and insurance players that have been operating in the rural areas. It is one of the very important internal factors of insurance business environment in the country and therefore, must be harnessed fully

5. The Business of Retailing Risk

The extent of risk that an insurance company can bear is determined by its net worth. The minimum capital prescribed by IRDA for insurance companies is Rs. 100 crores. Now all private non-life insurance companies are looking at the corporate market to gain market share, as they do not have the infrastructure to sell to the retail segment. Going by the solvency norms, insurance companies will not be in a position to issue a policy covering a single middle size of industrial unit on their own. This is where re-insurance comes in. Reinsurance is the back bone on which non-life insurance companies operate world-wide. But the weak side of re-insurance is that if companies are allowed to freely re-insure their entire risks overseas, they will end up merely fronting for the international companies. This means that there will not be any build up of domestic insurance capacity and there will be large out flows of foreign exchange.

To build up domestic reinsurance capacity, the Government has designated the General Insurance Corporation of India as the national reinsurer. All non-life insurers have to compulsorily part with 20 per cent of their premium to the GIC. In return the GIC shares their claims in the same ratio. In addition to receiving premium from the domestic insurance companies, GIC is aiming at increasing its business from African, East European, Chinese, Russian and the Gulf countries. At the same time, GIC expects higher penetration of insurance to increase the concentration of risks in the Indian market.

In addition to the compulsory cessation of premium to GIC, non-life insurers have to finalise their excess of loss treaties with re-insurers. These treaties protect the balance by reimbursing them in case a claim in any particular year due to extra ordinary events such as earth quakes, cyclones or riots exceeds a certain level. In case of large units, insurers have to obtain project specific or facultative covers as well. Therefore, it is evident that better the business of retailing risk, the better will be considered the internal environment for insurance business.

6. Specified Training and Customised Programmes

The insurance business environment in any country is reflected with the kind and quality of training is available for the agents and intermediaries. The IRDA has stipulated that all insurance sales agents have to undergo a 100 hours of training and clear an examination conducted by the Insurance Institute of India. The reason is that all the players entering the insurance market need to have sales agents trained by the IRDA accredited institution.

The IRDA training is the basic training which an agent needs to clear the examination and get a licence. Thus, all insurers particularly the private players are concentrating on this aspect. The syllabus of 100 hours is split in to 60% technical and rest on sales motivation and teamwork. Now there are many institutions in the country which are providing such training to the agents. Many institutions have introduced in their training system, a lot of user friendly tools and features in portals like e-mail facility, calculators, information on policies and schemes, down loadable forms and virtual office.

On line and distance learning are proving to be a boon in training of insurance agents in rural areas and far flung towns and cities. There is now classroom training to ensure quality through the integrity of the testing system. Developing sound database is the essence for the efficient functioning of the insurance sector. Now there are many companies which are offering customerised training for specific clients and upgrading their courses beyond the mandatory 100 hours.

The more the trained personnel, the better it will be for the insurance business of a country.

7. The Pricing of Products

The pricing of products in insurance sector has a definite bearing on insurance business. The pricing of products will undergo changes and the regulator will have to monitor it in order to create a healthy competition and insurance market in the country in view, entry of private players. The tariff system for certain risks is bound to continue for some time more. However, there would be more pressure on the market flexibility and the players. The providers and receivers, both will have to interact very closely to secure a fair deal on the pricing of the deal, as the Good State Insurance Sector will no longer be in a monopolised position.

It has always be kept in mind that the insurance is after all a fund of money to take care of calamities of few and there should be a meaningful and viable price for any product to be marketed and sustained. There will be a definite pressure to move away from tariff rating and the market will only determine the price particularly for personal life insurance.

However, responsible companies can only afford to cut prices to a certain point, if they are to preserve their own financial stability and ability to meet their obligations. The insurance reforms have allowed private insurers to co-exist with LIC and GIC, alongwith setting up of IRDA. It ensures financial soundness of industry. It enables risk to be managed more efficiently through risk pricing and risk transfers and this is an area which provides unlimited opportunities in the Indian context for consultancy, broking and education in the post-privatisation phase with new employment opportunities

8. Growing Consumerism

The Indian Economy, with its growth of around 6 per cent, is now moving towards raising the standards of living of the people. The very base of the middle class population is broadening to around 300 million. It is a known fact today that China and India are attracting the maximum attention of the world, as they are not only most populated countries, but also the most closely viewed developing economies in the world.

The shift in the Indian Economy from controlled one to that of openness and the competition has lead to an era of well-defined consumerism. The emerging society is throwing unprecedented opportunities and at the same time growing in a very sophisticated manner. The society is having multifarious choices. Then there is a new kind of pressure on the consumer profile aspiring for quality, effectiveness and adaptability. These parameters would now determine the survival of the market operators. With the competitiveness, the emphasis would be in innovative of new products, and the value-added customer service. Thus, aggressive market approach would be significantly required to encash the opportunity.

The new century, would present a different market from the traditional in the area of consumer choice. The newly opened insurance sector has been evincing the maximum interest only in one direction, i.e. THE CUSTOMER, by way of devising new methods to reach him with the kind of products and services which he expects today. The option of having a choice and that too varied has certainly raised customers' expectations. Today, the reality is that the customer is more aware not only of his rights but also about the alternatives available to him for better products and services as well as new avenues for redressal of grievances.

To achieve the above goals, it calls for continued focus on the customers which calls for total quality performance (TQP) with continued growth. The new players shall have to be committed to TQP in products and services so as to provide total customer satisfaction.

9. Consumer's Perspective

The emerging scenario will provide the consumer with:

(i) Choice of insurance, wide range of new and innovative products.
(ii) Competitive pricing of products and services.
(iii) Access to information about the companies and products.
(iv) Continuous consumer education.
(v) A well trained and highly professional sales force.
(vi) Prompt and courteous front office response.
(vii) Greater focus on customer service.
(viii) World class Pre and Post-Sales Service.
(ix) Efficient and Customer friendly claim administration systems.

10. Long-term Savings and Investment

The long-term savings generated will be a big boon for the Indian Economy catalysing additional funds for the infrastructure investments. Insurance companies will also bring long-term capital to the market, which will add to the depth and breadth of our financial sector. It is hoped that it will bring in long-term investors in the Primary and Secondary Markets and will also add to the market stability.

It is a fact that in a capital starved country like ours, long-term capital is the urgent requirement and an important issue. The new insurance companies are capitalised at Rs. 100 crores. As the business grows, these companies will have to bring additional capital to comply with the solvency requirements. Therefore, all the new entrants do not have any option but to bring additional funds for the first five years of their operations.

The LIC and GIC both have invested huge capital in housing and other infrastructural projects. If the additional funds are to be generated for the economic development of the country, such capital investment has to come necessarily from the insurance sector. The point is that the insurance players require investment in such projects which will give them steady rate of return. If this avenue is provided by the Government then it will certainly be useful in generating more insurance business in the country.

11. Organisational Control and Efforts

The business of insurance may be classified broadly into three significant areas. The first and the foremost is the Business General Mode, where the companies engage themselves in the selling of policies and collection of premiums. The second or the Intermediate stage would be that of Maintenance Efforts to see that the companies retain the business that has been developed and service the clients. The third, and the final stage is where the companies pay out the claims. If one is particular to look into the organisation efforts that go into each of these areas, one can easily find out the effectiveness of the organisation. From any intelligent measurement, the middle sector, namely, the maintenance mode must be very clean and efficient.

However, the experience world over has been that the insurance companies do take care of selling aspect of policies here they deploy their best personnel and keep their maintenance organisation clean to care for the claim settlement process to such an extent that the entire goodwill is built on the management practices that are put to use in that area. In the Indian situation, the impression one might get is that it is the middle mode which is fairly large. In the present set-up, i.e. before IRDA and entry of private players in the insurance sector, too many people look after the maintenance and not many doing either the sales or the claim settlement portion to the desired extent. The perception of the general public is that Indian Insurance Industry does not offer utmost care for the insured public. The fact is that the insurance is a service industry and exists for the welfare and needs of the customers. Therefore, the concern for the customer should be reflected in the industry's performance. This has not been achieved in India. In India, the customer may not get a cover which he needs. Even if he is extended coverage, the small print could be utilised to contest the claim that arose from payment.

The insurance business will now be very competitive with the entry of new players. The products are pretty, and of much standard and can very easily be replicated. With everyone offering 'better service', how clear will be difference is not known. Certainly this aspect will affect the insurance business in India. Price competition is not a viable option for new comers, when LIC will compete on 'positioning' themselves in the minds of consumers. In this endeavour each country will use its 'parentage' or 'pedigree' as strength. As far break even new players may take 5 to 6 years. This is due to the cost dynamics of the 'agency model' of selling. In the same better management control will be a key factor in generating more insurance business.

12. Social Family Set-up of Indian Society

It is now a known fact that the Indian Society which had been totally sheltered and protected is breaking up. Many of our generation are members of joint families which have been kept together and which have shown tendencies of living together. Many of the present generation may not be aware of inherent advantages of joint family system. The joint family not only acted as a Socialist Society in which every member of the family was treated equally irrespective of his earning capacity, where the family acted as a health provider. Nursing services were available besides resources to provide an old-age protection and a security. With the breaking of this system, the responsibility has to be found outside the family set-up for these obligations to be performed. In India, these obligations are not met by the Government. However, in many western countries, the state has taken up the liability and the responsibility of keeping its citizens fed, protected and care for. In Britian, the State takes care of its citizens from cradle to grave. The insurance and pension products are long-term investments and would play a dominant role in future. The opening of insurance sector to encourage long-term savings had resulted in the opening of the pension business also. The changes in the society like the breaking of joint family system and the increasing life expectancy have necessitated planning for post-retirement life. Pensions would now play a crucial role in protecting Life in post-retirement years. People now aspire for a better life even post-retirement for which they would need to save for a longer period. People would have to plan their post-retirement life even in their mid-30s. In the developed countries, pension had become the largest component of the Insurance Industry and there are no reasons as to why it should not happen in India.

13. Challenges and Strategies

The Insurance Sector is not free from challenges thrown open by its privatization and entry of more and more players to operate within The regulatory framework of IRDA. Some important challenges to be faced by this Sector of Economy in the coming years may included:

(i) Insurance and Growth.
(ii) Regulatory Framework.

(iii) Integrated Risk Management

Risk Management is too important an issue to treat highly. There are no two ways about it. We need risk management even when insurance is inexpensive. One is not against low-cost insurer *per se*. The problem arises when one relies solely on Insurance, no matter what the prices to protect one's company.

(iv) Disaster Management and Re-Insurance.
(v) Comprehensive Risk covers for Mega Project.
(vi) Squeeze in the Global Insurance Market.
(vii) Minimising Transaction Costs.
(viii) Introduction of Innovative Risk Hedging Models.
(ix) Scope for Reckless Profiteers.
(x) Massive Retrenchment and Job Losses.

The above challenges can be met with and mitigated in many ways:

(1) In Indian Context too, there is a huge employment opportunity and potential. For instance, the U.K. equivalent to M.P. in size and with a population of 55 million provides six lakh Insurance jobs whereas India, with a population of over a billion employs only close to five lakhs.
(2) The fear of job loss is also unfounded. This can be seen by the experience of Insurance Liberalisation in South Korea, the Philippines and other countries. The Insurance Sector provides opportunities to qualified persons from the tradition field of Engineering, I.T., Health, Finance, Accountancy and Marketing.
(3) The Insurance reforms have allowed Private Insurers to Co-exist with LIC and GIC, along with setting up of IRDA. Its role comprises:
    (a) Protecting consumers' interest;
    (b) Ensuring financial soundness of the Industry; and
    (c) Making sure the market growth healthy.
(4) It enables risk to be managed more efficiently through risk pricing and risk transfers and this is an area which provides unlimited opportunities in the Indian context for consultancy, broking and education in the post-privatisation phase with new employment opportunities.
(5) Competition brings in more products with more complex and extensive risk categorisation, better technology and better consumer service, including faster settlements. Moreover, the opening up of the Insurance Sector would immensely benefit the consumer who will have a choice of cheaper and newer products, better service, and quicker settlement claims.

14. New Millennium

It is in context with the above scenario that opening up the market has arrived and customer expectations are as never before. Competition will improve service dramatically. What is likely to be different for customers particularly those who have been neglected so far. The following will be the areas in which positive changes are expected to be seen:

(1) Generating awareness.
(2) Choice of products and price.
(3) Better qualified/trained and knowledgeable agents and brokers.
(4) Clear explanation of scope of cover—what can he get and what he cannot get.
(5) Statement of rights.
(6) Faster Claim service based more on the spirit of contract than on the cold Letter of Insurance Contract.
(7) Re-establishment of the concept of utmost good faith.
(8) When a claim is not admissible, the fact is conveyed with reasons.
(9) Frequent contact with communications from the Insurer and the Intermediary.
(10) Increased use of Technology.
(11) Many financial services through the same window.

The costs may come down eventually. Speed, efficiency, accuracy, are hallmarks of good service. We are about to see these manifest in our midst soon. Claims scene will see important changes. In short, basic principles will be re-established. Most claims will be processed on good faith and settled quickly.

11.3 EXTERNAL ENVIRONMENT

The external environment of insurance business has been classified in four parts, namely, legal, economic, financial, and commercial. Let us discuss them in detail by taking one by one:

A. Legal

The insurance sector cannot function in isolation. It's operations, growth and development is always conditioned by various factors of which external business environment is one of the significant factor. The external business environment is the result of legal and economic conditions prevailing in the country from time to time. For some legal and economic base, it is the political environment of a country that provides the climate for effective legislative and regulatory measures for any sector of the economy.

There are various Laws and Acts which have direct or indirect application in the insurance sector, the knowledge of which is a pre-requisite for all those who are concerned with the business of insurance in any capacity. Some of the important Acts which are applicable in insurance are as under:

(i) Insurance Act, 1938;
(ii) Life Insurance Act, 1956;
(iii) General Insurance Business (Nationalisation) Act, 1972;
(iv) The IRDA Act, 1999;
(v) General Insurance Business (Nationalisation) Amendment Act, 2001;
(vi) Main Provisions of Indian Contract Act, 1872;
(vii) Main Provisions of Indian Companies Act, 1956; and
(viii) Service Tax.

B. Economic

Similarly, the economic conditions prevailing in a country are related to the following that again have a direct bearing on the insurance sector:

(i) The State of Insurance Business;
(ii) Industrial Policy of the Country;
(iii) System of Economic Planning;
(iv) Liberalisation, Privatisation and Globalisation; and
(v) Comparative World-wide Insurance Environment.

In the following discussion, we will throw some light on the impact of legal and economic environment on the insurance sector, i.e. its working development and growth.

11.4 LEGAL AND ECONOMIC ENVIRONMENT

Extensive regulation of insurance business in India was brought into effect with the enactment of the Insurance Act, 1938. It tried to create a strong and powerful supervisory and regulatory authority in the Controller of Insurance with powers to direct, advise, caution, investigate, inspect, search, seize, amalgamate, authorise, register and liquidate insurance companies. However, consequent upon the nationalization of insurance business (Life in 1956 and General in 1972) application of the Insurance Act was greatly modified by the nationalizing enactments and Government notifications issued thereunder. Most of the regulatory functions were taken away from the Controller of Insurance and vested in the insurers themselves.

The Government of India in 1993 had set-up a high powered committee headed by Sh. R.N. Malhotra, former Governor, Reserve Bank of India, to examine the structure of the insurance industry and recommend changes to make it more efficient and competitive keeping in view the structural changes in other parts of the financial system of the economy. This Committee submitted its report in January 1994 and recommended that an independent insurance regulatory apparatus should be activated and proposed the establishment of a strong and effective Insurance Regulatory Authority in the form of a Statutory Autonomous board quite akin to the Securities and Exchange Board of India.

The recommendations of this committee were debated at various forums including managements of General Insurance Corporation, Life Insurance Corporation, trade unions, chambers of commerce and consumer interest groups. These recommendations found wide support. In view of this, the Government decided to bring in an insurance legislation to establish an independent insurance regulatory authority. Since enacting legislation was to take time, the then Government constituted through a Government resolution an interim insurance regulatory authority on 23rd January 1996. The Insurance Regulatory Authority Bill was introduced in the Parliament in 1996. The Bill has since been referred twice to the Standing Committee on Finance. The Bill was retitled Insurance Regulatory and Development Authority and introduced again in 1999 along with three schedules containing amendments to the Insurance Act, 1938, Life Insurance Corporation Act, 1956 and General Insurance Business (Nationalisation) Act, 1972.

IRDA Act, 1999

The preamble to the Insurance Regulatory and Development Authority Act, 1999 reads: An Act, to provide for the establishment of an authority to protect the interests of holders of insurance policies, to regulate, promote and ensure orderly growth of the Insurance Industry and for matters connected therewith or incidental thereto. Section 3 of the Act provides for the establishment and incorporation of Authority. The Authority established shall be a body corporate having perpetual succession, and common seal with a power to acquire, hold and dispose of property, both movable and immovable and shall sue and be sued by the said name. Section 4 lays composition of the Authority. It shall have a chairperson and other members not exceeding nine in number, of whom not more than five shall be whole-time members appointed by the Central Government from amongst persons having knowledge of general insurance, life insurance, actuarial science, finance, economics, law, administration.

Section 14 of the Insurance Regulatory and Development Authority Act, 1999, lays the duties, powers and functions of the Authority. The Authority shall have the duty to regulate, promote and ensure orderly growth of the insurance business and reinsurance business.

11.5 FINANCIAL ENVIRONMENT

The Indian Financial Sector is dominated by Public Sector whether it is in the segment of Insurance, Banking or development finance. But the scene is fast changing. With the passing of Insurance Development and Regulatory Act in January 2000, the Insurance Industry has opened the way for participation by private sector entities. It is hoped that the new entrants will bring with them experience of financial and commercial business environment that will enrich the Insurance Sector. Most of the Private Sector players who have entered the Insurance Sector so far have rich experience of working in the Financial Sector with vast commercial acumen and scope of handling the varied type of activities. The fact is that no business entity can grow unless it has proper systems and mechanism relating to its financial and commercial activities. The Insurance Sector, therefore, is no exception to the above corporate business principle.

Financial institutions play a key role in the growth process. They help mobilise large savings. They also help to allocate resources more efficiently among competing demands. Financial Institutions are called financial intermediaries because they act as a conduit for the transfer of financial resources from net savers to net borrowers. This basic function of intermediation is performed through transformation mechanism which are:

(1) Liability—assets transformation,
(2) Size transformation,
(3) Maturity transformation,
(4) Risk transformation, and
(5) Commercial and Marketing Transformation.

The gain to the real sector of the economy depends on how effectively or efficiently the financial sector performs this basic function of intermediation. However, institutions, like Insurance Companies perform additional function over and above being financial intermediaries. They provide a service such as risk coverage. The risk to be insured must result in a loss which is measurable in financial terms. Insurance applies to situations where a loss may or may not occur. It cannot apply to situations where loss is expected to happen. Insurance is based on the operation of the law of large members. There must be a sufficient number of risks of a similar class being insured so that the probability of loss can be estimated. Pure risks are those which have an element of losses break even but not gain. Examples are fire, flood, accident, etc., all such cases involve the probability of loss without any chance of gain. It is in this sense, pure risk has to be distinguished from speculative risk. For managing such risks the insurance sector has to be careful in.

Insurance and Integrated Risk Management

Risk Management is an integral part of Insurance Business. The Derivative Market in India is gaining importance. Today, Financial Engineering offers sophisticated tools and techniques to hedge interest rate, Foreign Exchange and Commodity risks. It is now well known in the Financial World, as to how risk can destroy corporate value and how value addition can be achieved through Risk Management.

At present, risk assessment and risk hedging models are being increasingly used in the Corporate Sector. Financial Engineers are now well equipped with latest tools, techniques and products of risk management. A number of insurers are selling financial risk management products, and insurance multiples are being placed directly in the Capital Markets and the

Corporate Sector. The value creation approach through integrated risk management has been gaining importance, particularly in companies with huge multiple and diversified investments.

Integrated risk management involves both insurance and financial risks. It generally uses the technology available in both these areas including operational and business. This technique is called comprehensive and its utility is visible from the fact that insurable and financial risks can disrupt earnings, create problems of funding new investments, or even push terms into bankruptcy. It is a fact that contribution of each source of risk cannot be very easily isolated.

In finance, a firm's capacity to absorb risk is determined by its current exposure to other risks. Therefore, an integrated strategy to eliminate the risk is required. But the introduction of new products in financial markets, the increased volatility in prices of both financial assets and goods due to globalisation may result in great risks.

Keeping the above in view, the Corporate Sector, Banks and Financial Institutions should first indentify the sources of risk and the resulting loss of value from such risks. After the sources are identified, a number of risk management strategies can be worked out and applied. The wider the range of alternative strategies better the risk handling and management.

The major benefit of an integrated approach is that it will help both Corporate and the FI's make optional investment decision. Through this integrated approach the Corporate Entities can minimise transaction costs. Any financial crisis, may be in the Foreign Exchange Credit or Stock Markets, effects the FI's Banks, Investment Institutions, Mutual Funds and Corporates also.

Risk Management Strategies can also cover and solve many problems of risk-related costs. The Insurance covers are not cost specific. For example, when there is a need to reduce one of these risks, the agency/bankruptcy costs and other losses can be reduced with the strategy of lowering leverage. The Insurance Sector is always keen in minimising the loss. It's expertise, enables it to control losses at different levels.

To conclude in the present economic scenario when the domestic markets are increasingly integrated with the international, and the pricing of the products and services reflect International trends, integrated risk management becomes all the more crucial. Thus, co-ordination and diversification are also important in risk management decisions. The decision to purchase an integrated insurance policy extends relief and provides cover to all such risk costs. Though there are many risk management strategies, many of them overlap, and that is why an integrated approach is required to be adopted.

New Risk Insurance Issues

On September 11, 2001, four places went on a suicide mission and changed the world, when Twin Towers in New York (U.S.A.) were destroyed by the Terrorists alongwith the places and passengers aboard on them. On the business side nobody was more deeply and immediately effected than the world's Insurance and Airline Companies. Never in their worst situations (Realistic Disaster Scenario's, as Lioyd's of London terms it) could insurers have calculated of such an even occurring.

Immediately after the above happening in U.S.A., President George Bush called the horrific deed of terrorism as an "Act of War." There were reactions of the Insurance Industry that Insurance providers may try to involve an "Act of War exclusion" and thereby escape liability. This speculation was short lived. It was felt that any attempt to evade coverage obligations by either Primary Insurers or Reinsurers would tear at the faith of the American population in the Insurance Industry.

Finally, the world's leading Insurers agreed not to apply war risk exclusions and to paying all the claims related to terrorists attacks—estimated at more than $ 5 billion only in property damage. However, in view of war clouds Insurers put the aviation world on notice that w.e.f. 24th September 2001, they would not provide liability coverage for war perils, especially they cancelled the write back clause in their Airlines policies that includes war risk perils upto the limit of policy.

Action by Insurers and Airliners

The Insurers and Airliners all over the world took immediate steps to meet with the situations like above. From 1st October 2001, a surcharge of $ 1.25 per passenger to cover war risk perils was imposed, topped up by a 0.05 per cent surcharge levied by war risk underwriters. The Insurers put a $ 50 million cap per Airline to cover property damage and third party liability. Many Airlines, such as Lufthansa, Emirates, and Singapore Air Lines, faced with the situation of rising of Insurance costs and falling passenger loads were quick in raising fares ranging from $ 5 to $ 8 per passenger. Indian Airlines has also levied a Rs. 100 Surcharge whereas Air India is yet to announce.

In consequence of the above, the Joint War Committee of Underwriters in London has revised War Risk Premium on vessels calling on 19 sensitive ports. The India, Pakistan, Bangladesh, Cyclone, Shipping Conferences, a consortium of 13 shipping companies hiked the freight rates across the board by $ 150 per container this month to cover this increased war risk premium.

Who should Bear the Additional Costs

It is very pertinent question as to who should bear the additional costs arising out of such abnormal situations. All the businesses do not have the capacity to absorb the extra burden or ability to pass it on to their customers.

When war breaks out, companies find themselves in a situation that is not of their own and is beyond their control. Thus, why should business or consumers be asked to foot the bill for a situation which is the direct result of the political situation of their Government. Therefore, it is only fair if at such times, the Governments should play the role of Insurer of Last resort and make or bear the additional cost. The USA Government moved quickly to provide for a $ 15 billion bail out package to its beleaguered airlines, which goes much beyond just insurance support.

Action by Indian Government

In our Country, the Government has offered a Letter of Support (valid for a month) for the two-state-owned Air-lines. The Private Carriers, i.e. Jet Airways and Sahara Airlines have to manage themselves. The Indian Ships are however, covered by a Government War Risk Fund, which was used in part during Gulf War.

Creation of Catastro Reserve Fund: The Indian Insurers, in consultation with the Ministry of Finance and IRDA, decided to impose a 10% surcharge on future fire and engineering policies to create a CRF. Thus, in view of prolonged history of terrorism within our borders, the Indian Government has to run for sufficient cover even in the situation that the present terrorist attack was on some other country.

Capital Adequacy Requirement

The Insurance Regulatory and Development Authority has prescribed the following scale of capital Adequacy requirement in the shape of paid up equity capital for the entities doing Insurance Business.

(i) Companies engaged in the business of Life Insurance—Rs. 100 Crores.
(ii) Companies engaged in the business of General Insurance—Rs. 100 Crores.
(iii) Companies doing the business of Reinsurance—Rs. 200 Crores.

No company or other entity can do/or will be allowed to do Insurance Business unless it comply with the minimum Capital Adequacy Requirement as mentioned above.

Investment of Assets—New Norms

Every Insurance Company includes investment of its funds from time to time. It is not open to a company to make investments as it may like. There are prescribed yardsticks for making investment in different forms. The following percentages have been prescribed by the IRDA for making investments by the Insurance Companies:

(1) 50% of Funds in Government Securities.
(2) 20% of Funds in Corporate Debts.
(3) 15% of Funds in Market Investments.
(4) 15% of Funds in Social Sector.

The Social Sector includes Infrastructure, viz. roads, highways, bridges, airports, ports, railways, water irrigation projects, telecommunications, housing, generation, distribution and transmission of power. Investment in Government Securities tends to be highly liquid, particularly in the following interest.

Consortium Financing by Insurance Companies

The four companies in the general insurance business used to participate in the consortium finance, with the consortium leaders, usually financial institutions or banks. Due to increasing non-performing assets, the four major general Insurance Companies have now decided to withdraw from all consortium financial arrangements with Financial Institutions and Banks. The reason for this decision is that consortium financing is no longer viable due to the reason as interest rates have dropped to record low. At present, the yield on assets of the four insurance companies, Oriental Insurance Company Ltd., New India Assurance Company Ltd., National Insurance Company Ltd. and United India Insurance Company Ltd. was now under nine per cent.

All the Insurance Companies currently follow the mercantile system of accounting. In the event of their switching over to accounting on realised basis, the yield on assets could drop further. Moreover the mercantile system of accounting treatment of assets classified as NPAs by the consortium leaders as either sub-standard or loss assets.

Method of Measuring Underwriting Losses

NPA build ups also point to the un-sustainability of high underwriting losses. The normal method of measuring such underwriting losses is through assessment of claim ratios. Claim ratios of Insurance Companies have historically been above 100 per cent by high asset yields and consequently high income from Investments which will cease to exist. Therefore, the insurance companies have to be more careful in underwriting losses. The only risk to be avoided is that the losses may not increase in any case the yield by way of underwriting.

Foreign Equity in Insurance Sector

The Insurance Act, 1938 allows only Indian Insurance Companies registered under the Companies Act, 1956 to transact insurance business in India after registration with the Insurance Regulatory and Development Authority. Several representations were made to include and allow the Co-operative Sector into Insurance Sector. The Act is, therefore, being amended accordingly.

The Government has decided to put foreign equity in the Insurance Sector on the list of items on automatic route, but will not be increasing the invest cap beyond 26 per cent level. The Companies entering the Insurance Sector will not be required to seek an approval from the Foreign Investment Promotion Board (FIPB) and have now only to comply with R.B.I. formalities. The Associating Joint Venturers can invest only up to 26% of the equity in the Insured Sector. There is now a demand that this limit requires upward revision in view of the requirement of more capital for Insurance Business managing two important activities/functions, i.e. financial and commercial.

11.6 COMMERCIAL ENVIRONMENT

The insurance industry and business have to be made itself fully aware of the breadth and depth of the:

(a) knowledge,
(b) experience, and
(c) expertise of its officers and other intermediaries.

It should make constant efforts in assessing problems, and finding out their solutions in the most scientific professional and cost effective manner. It should have a clear vision and be ready to implement advanced management systems, procedures and controls whereever required in its working. It should have a clear goal to achieve high levels of efficiency productivity and competitiveness. We should not forget about the competition which is likely to be faced in between the large number of operators in the public and private insurance sector. Therefore, to have effective commercial viability the players in the insurance sector should update themselves and acquire new levels of knowledge and expertise with clear dimensions.

Product Development and Innovations

There has been lot of efforts for the development of various products and these innovations both in the life and non-life insurance in the country. With the entry of private sector players and the demand of the prospective customers in view of mounting competition, more and more products are likely to be developed to cater to the requirement of the customers at different levels. The insurance sector has to provide to its customers wide choice of products and price. The competition will ensure innovation and constant improvement of service. The non-life sector will face much competition. In the case of existing players, they are already in the process of connecting their distribution channels. Their managements have realised that if they do not come up with new products and better services they may stand to lose in the face of stiff competition.

Thus, innovative products should be made available as per the developments of technology particularly in service industry, viz. telecommunication, satellite, computers, and entertainment, etc. Product development and research will attract greater attention of players and they have to update themselves as far as their products are concerned. The marketing concept of general insurance will undergo a major change by infusion of research and design of the products and the innovation of new products.

Customer Service

The insurance sector is operating in the service providers' sector, where the customer service is very important. Customer service is an organisational approach to delight a customer and not merely satisfy him by simply fulfilling all his expectations. A very positive approach, tone of speech and appearance are attitudes that creates a first and last impression on customers. Feedback is the best way of delivering quality services. Therefore, the moment license is issued to a new player in the market, there could be competition of a very high quality new products and services. New thinking and new perceptions will arise to make excellence sustainable in a liberalised insurance market in india.

Customer Expectations

In the present day competitive insurance environment, the role of insurer has expanded tremendously. Beyond issuing traditional insurance policies, they have to act as a consultant, advisor and advocate to meet with the requirements of the prospective customers. At different stages, an insured may expect:

1. value-added service from the insurance,
2. development of new products,
3. excellence in pricing and services,
4. financial security,
5. technological development,
6. quality training to its staff,
7. after sales services, and
8. customer satisfaction.

Thus, the customer's expectations have to be studied, reviewed from time to time so as to get better business in the prevailing competitive environment in the insurance sector.

Marketing Insurance

In the process of marketing of various insurance products we cannot ignore two vital constituents of it, i.e. demand and supply. The supply side of insurance and the demand of the need will now undergo a major shake up with the advent of new players in the market. The general insurance market, which consisted of 107 companies in the 1970's produced a market premium of Rs. 105 crores, whereas at the end of 2000, the premium figure of the state insurers stood at around Rs. 10,000 crores. The focus of the marketing by the state insurance during all these years was on laying the foundation of infrastructure, creating need-based cover and also caters to the social insurance requirements of the Indian population.

Therefore, with the emergence of new players there will be emphasis on the marketing of general insurance products both by Government owned as well as the private sector players. It is expected that the penetration of players will enhance the growth of general insurance premium. Thus, marketing will be a focus item if change in the coming days due to competition in the insurance sector, there is going to be a drastic change in the distribution channel for marketing of general insurance products. Reinsurance concept will also play a major role in the marketing of general insurance products.

Technology is changing very fast, and Information Technology is one which will revolutionise the marketing of insurance products. E-commerce and internet will enable the direct purchase without intermediaries and thus, this is a major change which the marketing field in insurance is going to face. Customer relationship management and culture of insurance players as a quality service provider will have its own role to play in marketing of various types of innovative insurance products.

Pricing of the Product, i.e. Tariff

The pricing of the insurance product will also undergo changes and the regulator will have to monitor it in order to create a healthy insurance market. However, the tariff system for certain risk is bound to continue. This is due to the reason that there would be more presence on the market for flexibility and the players; both the providers and receivers will have to interact closely to secure a fair deal on the pricing of the product.

It is a fact that insurance is after all a fund of many to take care of the calamities of few and there should be a meaningful and viable price for any product to be marketed and sustainable. There will thus be a definite pressure to move away from the tariff rating and the market will determine the price specially for personal insurance.

In Indian insurance sector a lot is waiting to be done to have viable and fair external environment for its financial and commercial activities. It should have a lock and insight in the areas of reforms in the market environment, the legal/tax/accounting complexities. The process can continue towards new insurance legislations and it may be allowed in the areas where it is possible under the current scenario. The new baby of financial engineering like that of securitisation for making investment in infrastructure projects and for health care receivables, air craft leases, air fare, insurance could be few potential products which should be made used of by the insurance sector for commercial viability and risk management.

11.7 SUMMARY

There are some expectations from the new players—ensuring credibility and not adopting unethical practices, educating the consumers, raising awareness through marketing and sales practices and developing a strong sales force of consultants and agents to improve services to the consumers. Now with the entry of competition, the rules of the game are set to change. The market is already witnessing a rise in number of players and is making more products. The new companies will have to adopt systems to observe which factor is all potential risks. In such a scenario, it will difficult to visualise the scope of different players—products, pricing or service. The profile of the Indian customer is also very fast changing.

The boundaries between various financial products are now getting blurred, people are looking for not just at the products but also at integrated financial solution that can offer them stability of returns alongwith total protection. Insurance products will be required to be customerised to satisfy varied needs of the customers.. Many new Indian private insurance players need to cope with the challenges of managing a joint venture partner, competing with large and well established government insurance players, overcoming regulatory hurdles, changing the attitude of new recruits and satisfying some very high customer expectations. In the present day insurance business environment the players will have to consider the Indian market as a long-term investment and have clear-cut objectives and constant monitoring at all levels.

11.8 REVIEW QUESTIONS

1. "Reinsurance is the back bone of the non-life business but it has a flip side as well." Explain.
2. "Risk management is an integral part of insurance business environment." Explain.
3. Pricing of insurance products has a definite bearing on insurance business. Discuss
4. What is the effect of growing consumerism on the development of insurance business? Discuss.
5. "Long-term savings and investments are the pillars of success of insurance business in the country." Elaborate.
6. How far social family system in India has affected the environment of insurance business? Explain.
7. What is the role of financial and commercial environment in the indian insurance sector?
8. "Integrated risk management involves both insurance and financial risks." Explain?
9. Explain the scale of capital adequacy requirement prescribed for the insurance companies. What is the prescribed yardstick for making investment in different forms by the insurance companies in india?
10. How far it is desirable for the insurance companies to participate in the consortium finance with other financial institutions and banks?
11. To achieve high levels of efficiency, productivity, and competitiveness in the insurance sector, a very favourable commercial environment is essential. Explain.

12

CHAPTER

SOCIAL RESPONSIBILITY OF INSURANCE

LEARNING OBJECTIVE

The main objective of this chapter is to make the students aware of the concept and importance of social responsibilities of a business in general and that of the insurance business in particular. The chapter also discusses the emerging needs in India with respect to social responsibilities of insurance business.

12.1 INTRODUCTION

In the present day, the organisms of business enterprises affect a broad continuum. The resources, they put together for investment in business activities, are not limited to those of the proprietors, therefore, the impact of their operations is experienced by many other people who are, perhaps, candidly not associated with these enterprises. The shareholders, the suppliers of resources, the consumers, the employees, the local community, and society at large are affected by the manner an enterprise functions. For this reason, business enterprises have to be in general quick to respond toward the expectations of many stakeholders and have to ensure a public sense of balance between the divergent interests of these stakeholders.

While delivering the C.C. Desai Memorial Lecture in 1978, George Goyder argued that if the corporation has to function effectively, it has to be accountable to the public at large; and he further sought to equate the suggestion of a responsible company with the trusteeship concept advocated by Gandhiji, the aim of which was to ensure that private property was used for the common good. The declaration issued by the international seminar on social responsibility of business held in India in 1965 also co-related the Gandhian concept of trusteeship with the social responsibility of business as "responsibility to customers, workers, shareholders and the the public."

There has been a growing recognition of the plea that business should be socially responsible in the sense that the bushiness enterprise, which makes use of the resources of society and depends on society for its functioning, should discharge its duties and responsibilities in enhancing the welfare of the society of which it is an integral part. The High-Powered Expert Committee on Companies and MRTP Acts (Sachar Committee), in development of corporate ethics, we have reached a state where the question of in its report submitted to Government in 1978, observed that, in the "Development the social responsibility of business to the community can no longer be scoffed at or taken lightly." The committee further points out that, "In the environment of modern economic development, the corporate sector no longer functions in isolation." If the plea of the companies that they are performing a social purpose in the development of the country is to be accepted, it can only be judged by the test of social responsiveness shown to the needs of the community by the companies. The company must behave and function as a responsible member of society, like any other individual. It cannot shun moral values, nor can it ignore actual compulsions. The real need is for some focus of accountability on the part of the management that is not limited to shareholders alone. In modern times, the objective of business has to be the proper utilization of resources for the benefit of others. A profit is still a necessary part of the total picture, but it is not the primary purpose. This implies that the claims of various interests will have to be balanced, not on the narrow ground of what is best for the shareholders alone but from the point of view of what is best for the community at large. The company must accept its obligation to be socially responsible and to work for the larger benefit of the community.

12.2 THE CONCEPT OF SOCIAL RESPONSIBILITY

The term "social responsibility" is not simple to describe. We use in the perspective of a firm as "willingness to sacrifice short-term profits in order to promote the public interest." Under this definition, the motives of the firm need not to be thoroughly splendid because the definition does not rule out sacrifice of short-term profits in the hope of even larger long-term profits. According to this view, the concept of social responsibility does not discard the behaviour of the firm motivated by long-term self-interest.

12.3 WHY SOCIAL RESPONSIBILITY?

Social responsibility can also be viewed as consideration of impact of the firm's action on society. Business and society interact with each other. Business exists in the context of a society. Business wishes society as much as society wishes business. Therefore, business have to be socially responsible.

From the standpoint of business, the various elements, which would constitute the public, are: owners/shareholders, managers, workers, suppliers, distributors, consumers, government officials, and similar social groups. All these have a stake in business and are called as stakeholders. Corporations are now being called upon to respond to the needs of stakeholders also, other than the stockholders.

A company not only has the responsibility to maximize the value of the shares of those who have invested in it but also in fulfilling their responsibilities to their investors. According to this view, Boards and Executives also have to fulfil their core responsibility to the rest of society "to other stakeholders such as their employees, members of their community and fellow citizens because they help assure that society's productive assets are allocated to their most efficient use.

Some of the advocates of corporate social responsibility argue that what is good for the company's stakeholders in the long-run is also good for its stockholders. That is, if one looks ahead to the future, all interests converge. All stakeholders are ultimately the same. All have interest in strong economy, well paid employees, a clean and healthy environment and a socially tranquil society.

There is this important aspect of managing a company that cannot be measured in Rupees and Paise which is an idea of building a better community and which is aimed at adding richness to the lives of the people.

The government regulations are shaped "at least indirectly" by the concept of social responsibility. Many people think that private firms, particularly large ones, should shoulder social responsibility that leads to 'self-regulation'. The idea seems to be that these firms are expected to be guided by a body of social ethics that may impose higher standards of conduct than imposed by the law itself. The clear implication behind this expectation is that if the firm does not measure up to socially responsible standards, the laws are likely to be altered to reflect the desired standards. Thus, the socially responsible standards are more than an empty wish on the part of the public.

In this background it would be worthwhile to study the development of Life Insurance Industry in India. As you all are aware, Insurance Industry in India was nationalized at the behest of devoted and honest leaders. In 1956, the then Union Finance Minister, Shri C.D. Deshmukh had said, the misuse of power, position and privilege that we have reason to believe, occurs under existing conditions is one of the most compelling reasons that have influenced us in deciding to nationalize life insurance.

While putting arguments for liberalization, one should see whether the objectives of nationalization have been fulfilled. If they are not fulfilled, then arguments for liberalization may be accepted with the assumption that the liberalization would remedy all the problems and help the nation to succeed in achieving its socio-economic development.

One should not forget that insurance, and more particularly life insurance, is not purely a commercial industry. It is a social institution, too.

The Government should provide social security, safety and welfare to the people of India. It is not possible for the government to achieve all these objectives at the same time while carrying the responsibility of governance. Hence, it is desirable that an institution or industry of national character takes over this social responsibility. Life Insurance industry thus has a major role in discharging various social responsibilities in the ever changing scenario. Over two decades ago, Peter Drucker stated in the context of American business, "if there is one development during the last ten years that stands out above all others, it is the eagerness with which business has embraced social responsibilities."

12.4 ARGUMENTS FOR SOCIAL RESPONSIBILITY

The arguments presented in favour of business assuming social responsibilities are as follows:

(i) Business is a Creation of the Society and so it should Respond to the Demands of the Society

Since business uses the resources, which belong to the society, it is necessary that every business enterprise should fulfil its social obligations. Business managers are obliged to use the social resources for the common good of society.

(ii) The Long-term Self-Interests of the Business are Best Served when Business Assumes Social Responsibilities

There is a growing realization on the part of the enlightened businessmen that it is in their self-interest to fulfil the demands and aspirations of the society. People who have good environment, education, and opportunity make better employees, customers, and neighbours for business than those who are poor, ignorant, or oppressed.

(iii) It is the Moral and Right thing to Do

It is widely agreed that businessmen today have considerable social power. This power is virtually granted to them by the society, which must have a general relationship with social responsibilities. The social responsibilities of businessmen must be proportionate to their social power. If the businessmen do not assume social responsibilities, their social power must be taken away by the society through Government controls and regulations and other measures.

(iv) Public Image of Business would be Improved

The business will retain the needed credibility with the public if it performs its social obligations. It will also avoid conflict with the society in its own interest. Good relation with the workers, consumers, and suppliers will lead to success of business.

(v) The Consumers are Well Informed

They expect higher quality products at reasonable price. If they don't get fair treatment from business, they will organize themselves and compel the business to perform its social responsibilities.

12.5 SOCIAL RESPONSIBILITIES OF BUSINESS

While there is no denying the fact that business is an economic activity (as judged against the objectives listed in the foregoing sections), it is also true that business is an organ of society and as such it must justify its continuance by fulfilling its role and responsibilities to society. One may even go to the extent of asserting that a business enterprise is a trust of the community that must discharge its obligations towards the various sections of the community. Some of the specific responsibilities of business may be outlined as under:

The Enterprise and the Shareholders

In the first place, corporate business must provide a fair return on capital to shareholders and must provide them with regular, accurate and full information about the working of the enterprise. The shareholders should also meet their obligations by evincing keen interest in company.

The Enterprise and the Workers

It is the responsibility of the management to provide opportunities to the workers for meaningful work. Also, the management of a business should try to win the cooperation of the workers by creating the right conditions in the enterprise. The business enterprise owes it to the workers to provide recognition to the workers' unions, accept the workers' right to associate and to help them to develop their own leadership 'in the unions through education. Social security, profit sharing, fair promotions, proper grievance settlement and employee welfare are some of the other well recognized responsibilities of business firms to their employees.

The Enterprise and the Consumers

A business enterprise has the responsibility of providing the goods and other services needed by the community at the most reasonable possible prices. It must guard against adulteration, poor quality, lack of service and courtesy to customers, misleading and dishonest advertising, etc. The consumers also need protection against monopoly and restrictive trade practices. Such protection can be provided best if bushiness learns to play its part with fairness and liberalism.

The Enterprise and the Community

An enterprise must respect the law and pay taxes regularly and honestly. It must behave as a good citizen and take care to avoid bad effluents, smoky chimneys, ugly buildings and devote attention to housing and workers' living conditions. It has the responsibility of maintaining proper relations with the community through the press and its meetings.

12.6 SOCIAL RESPONSIBILITY FOR LIFE INSURANCE

Make an effort now for getting yourself attentive of the areas where life insurance owes social responsibilities. There are basically two categories wherein life insurer's responsibilities could broadly be divided. These are:

(1) Business areas; and
(2) Non-Business areas.

The Business areas would cover various social security schemes to be managed and monitored by a life insurer. In this, the insurer is expected to respond by offering its products and services to the selected segments of the population. Whereas Non-Business areas of social responsibility for a life insurer shall cover his contribution to the development in the fields of education, health care, environment, employment, infrastructure, poverty alleviation and thus national economy. Insurance is directly related to the status of an individual in society. Improving the standard of living would affect the values of the society, which in turn would affect the Insurance Industry in qualitative terms.

Every economist will say that sensible social security schemes should be good for individual life insurance, because they increase the demand for goods and services from old people, widows and orphans. (Table 12.1).

TABLE 12.1

Social Protection and Private Insurance in Europe

	Per Capita GDP	*Private Insurance (%GDP)*	*Social Protection (GDP)*
Luxemburg	125.6	3.95	25.2
Germany	112.8	5.81	27.5
France	108.6	5.99	27.6
Denmark	108.2	4.45	29.8
United Kingdom	105.1	9.38	21.9
Italy	103.1	2.50	23.1
Netherlands	103.1	7.67	31.0
Belgium	102.6	4.06	26.7
Spain	77.8	3.22	20.1
Ireland	69.0	10.42	20.2
Portugal	55.7	3.09	16.6
Greece	52.6	1.40	20.7
EUR 12	100.0	5.56	25.2

Source: *Yogakshema*, Vol. 43, No. 6, June 1999.

The Insurance Industry is responsible to the objectives in the following areas:

⊡ Profit	viability
⊡ Employees	productivity
⊡ Agents/Distributors	performance
⊡ Policyholders	satisfaction
⊡ Regulators	compliance
⊡ Civil authorities	interaction
⊡ Auditors	transparency
⊡ Community	social responsibility

12.7 SOCIAL SECURITY PROGRAMMES IN DEVELOPED COUNTRIES

Let us now look around the world in developed economies to understand the social security programmes being implemented there.

The Old Age Survivors Disability and Health Insurance (OASDH) programme, commonly known as social security programme, protects eligible workers and their dependents against the financial losses associated with death, disability, superannuation, and sickness in old-age.

The old-age benefits provide a life time pension beginning at a stipulated age to reach eligible worker and certain eligible dependents. The amount of pension is based on the worker's average earning during some period in the working years.

Although the social security legislation in advanced countries originally provided only retirement benefits, complaints that the existing system was unfair to workers who died before retirement led to extending the benefits to the dependents of a deceased worker or retire. The survivor's portion of the programme provides covered workers with a form of life insurance, the proceeds of which are payable to their dependent children and surviving spouses.

Disability benefits were extended to an insured worker who became disabled and such a person is treated as if he or she has reached the retirement age. The workers and dependents become eligible for the benefits that would otherwise be payable on retirement.

Medicare Benefits offer protection against the high cost of hospitalization, skilled nursing, and other kinds of medical care. In addition, it provided an option by which those eligible for basic benefits under the medical programme may purchase subsidized medical insurance to help pay for doctor's services and other expenses not covered by the basic plan.

These social security programmes basically operate on 'Pay-as-you-go' system. Under the pay-as-you-go system, those who are eligible, receive benefits out of social security taxes paid by those who are working. In turn, today's worker will receive his benefits upon retirement from funds that are paid by labour force at that time.

In addition to the perils of death and disability, the individual faces loss of income due to another factor, unemployment. This has been one of the major problems in some of the advanced economies in the recent past. It promises to become even more critical in future. The commercial insurance companies cannot deal with the risk of unemployment. US Government has therefore, undertaken a system of unemployment compensation to protect society against the loss from this ever present threat.

A few private insurers offer private unemployment insurance in connection with consumers' instalment debt. The insurance covers the payments on an instalment debt when the insured debtor becomes involuntarily unemployed. The amounts of insurance are small, and the coverage is generally overpriced.

12.8 SOCIAL SECURITY SCHEMES IN INDIA IMPLEMENTED THROUGH LIC OF INDIA

LIC's group insurance schemes provide security to weaker sections of the society, identified in 24 occupation groups, by offering insurance protection through its various schemes.

The maximum amount of insurance cover at present is Rs. 5000 whereas the amount of cover due to accident is Rs. 25000, which also in clause permanent and partial disability benefit, at no extra cost. Under these schemes 50% of the premium is paid out of social security fund and the balance 50% is paid by the beneficiaries or the Nodal Agencies. (Table 12.2).

LIC's crusade received due recognition when on 15th August, 1987 the world's largest group insurance scheme covering about 1.20 crore families of landless agricultural labourers throughout the country was announced. Under this scheme at present, heads of the families, who are landless agricultural labourers between ages 18-60 years, stand insured for a sum of Rs. 2000 No premium is being charged from the beneficiaries. The claims under the scheme are paid out of the Social Security Fund set-up by the Central Government. (Table 12.3).

To offer greater security to the families and mitigate the hardship in the event of sudden death of the head of the family, a group insurance scheme was launched for the beneficiaries under the Integrated Rural Development Programme (IRDP), which provides cover of Rs. 5000, in case of death by accident the amount payable is Rs. 10000. The claims are paid out of the fund set-up by the Government for the purpose and no premium is charged from the beneficiaries. (Table 12.4). So far, about 2.30 crore people have availed the benefits under this scheme.

With the objective to provide life insurance protection to the rural masses, a Rural Group Life Insurance Scheme (RGLIS) was launched for the persons between age group of 20 years to 50 years. A subsidiary of 50% is offered to persons belonging to the household below the poverty line. The subsidy is being administered through elected Panchayats. (Table 12.5)

The LIC has been investigating its funds in various socially oriented sectors like:

(1) Housing Sector.
(2) Power generation in Industrial and Rural areas for Industrial and

TABLE 12.2

Social Security Schemes in India Implemented Through LIC of India

Persons covered during 1993-94 and 1997-98 are as under:

1993-94	1994-95	1995-96	1996-97	1997-98
3705494	4330575	4246621	4935027	5019941

The claims paid under the above 24 groups during the 5 years are as under:

	1993-94	1994-95	1995-96	1996-97	1997-98
No. of claims paid	14251	16516	18580	24876	21309
Amount of claims paid (in crores)	486	652	854	902	930

Source: Annual reports of LIC.

TABLE 12.3

Landless Agricultural Labourers' Group Insurance

About 1.20 crore families of landless agricultural labourers are getting the benefit under the scheme. During the last 10 years 495093 claims for Rs. 85.97 crore have beeen paid. The details of 5 years are as under:

	1993-94	1994-95	1995-96	1996-97	1997-98
No. of claims paid	70524	58403	55149	58324	52593
Amount of claims paid (in crores)	1343	1317	1216	1223	1166

TABLE 12.4

Integrated Rural Development Programme

About 2.30 crore people have availed the benefits of this scheme. During the last 10 years 74276 claims of Rs. 30.66 crore have been paid to the beneficiaries. Lives assured as at 31.3.1998 are about 1.22 crores. The details of 5 years are as under:

	1993-94	1994-95	1995-96	1996-97	1997-98
No. of claims paid	11698	9803	11251	9231	814
Amount of claims paid (in crores)	337	448	512	527	490

agricultural use.

(3) Piped water supply and sewerage schemes in Urban as well as Rural areas.

(4) Development of Road Transport.

(5) Assistance to Small Scale Industries through Co-operative Industrial Societies.

TABLE 12.5

Progress of Rural Group Life Insurance Schemes

States and U.T.	*In the First Year 15.8.95 to 14.8.96*				*In the Second Year 15.8.96 to 14.8.97*	
	New	*Renewed*			*New*	*Renewed*
	GEN	*SUB*	*GEN*	*SUB*	*GEN*	*SUB*
M.P.	73	5074	453	462	0	0
U.P.	8159	180145	5115	192216	58	2678
Assam	956	33671	547	0	0	0
Manipur	17	71	1	1370	1	65
Orissa	0	0	209	1732	0	0
Punjab	805	51	93	0	0	0
Rajasthan	2843	3853	298	641	67	0
Haryana	186	0	231	0	0	0
J & K	14	0	41	1192	0	0
Chandigarh	83	0	0	0	0	0
A.P.	671	484	1766	18720	0	20
Karnataka	548	6343	1866	354750	87	1855
Maharashtra	199	4095	2455	28511	5	638
Goa	489	0	20	187	29	0
Gujarat	0	20	1748	4777	0	0
Total	15043	233807	31643	604568	247	5256

States and U.Ts.	*In the First Year 15.8.97 to 14.8.98*				*In the Fourth Year 15.8.98 to 30.11.98*			
	New		*Renewed*		*New*		*Renewed*	
	GEN	*SUB*	*GEN*	*SUB*	*GEN*	*SUB*	*GEN*	*SUB*
M.P.	0	0	0	0	0	0	0	0
U.P.	1215	71044	61	1216	1	3258	0	181
Assam	0	0	0	0	0	0	0	0
Manipur	0	0	0	0	0	0	0	0
Orissa	349	1885	0	0	0	0	0	0
Punjab	116	40	0	0	0	0	0	0
Rajasthan	1227	2053	58	0	0	42	61	0
Haryana	110	0	0	0	0	0	0	0
J&K	0	0	0	0	0	0	0	0
Chandigarh	0	0	0	0	0	0	0	0
A.P.	76	7381	72	1975	13	430	0	101
Karnataka	5123	186202	2341	61425	908	33280	254	15535
Maharashtra	752	28243	1099	5081	3	422	10	240
Goa	22	44	54	93	0	0	0	22
Gujarat	1345	2025	57	393	0	0	0	0
Total	10335	298917	3742	70183	925	37432	325	16079
Grand Total		383177				54761		

Source: ***Yogakshema*, Vol. 43, No. 6, June 1999.**

TABLE 12.6

Such Investments are Aimed at Building Better Infrastructure Facilities in the Country

Authorities	*Amount Advanced during 1997-98 (Rs. in crores)*	*Cumulative Amount advanced upto 31.3.1998 (Rs. in crores)*
1. Electricity:		
State Electricity Boards/Electric Power Corporations	96510	841291
2. Housing:		
(a) State Governments for Housing Schemes	30015	241506
(b) Apex Co-operative Housing Finance Societies, LIC Housing Finance Ltd., HUDCO, HDFC, NHB, etc.	88000	7666235
3. Water Supply & Sewerage:		
(a) Municipal Committees/Water Supply and Sewerage Boards and to State Govts. for Urban Water Supply Schemes	13640	156567
(b) Zilla Parishad for Rural Piped Water Supply Schemes	9960	69729
4. Transport:		
State Road Transport Corporations	1175	55142
5. Industrial Development:		
Joint Stock Companies (including Loans to Public Sector Corpns.)	62562	650396
Total	301862	2780866

Source: *Yogakshema*, Vol. 43, No. 6, June 1999.

12.9 EMERGING NEEDS IN INDIA

Life Insurance cannot afford to lose the sight of its social relevance and shy away from its social responsibilities. It has to constantly study the emerging needs of the market, arising due to the change in the values of social life. Demographic changes also produce the different needs amongst the population. It will be the duty of the life insurer to satisfy the demands so arising. The concept of family in undergoing metamorphosis—a Joint family has given way to the small families which now face the threat of further changes like single parenting, live-in-relationship, double income no child units, etc. The product design has to be oriented to this changing family scenario.

With the liberalization and globalization, the days are not far when labour laws would be brought in tune with those of the other developed economies. These economies are already facing a threat of involuntary unemployment of an earning member of a family. The contingency, which may arise due to such an event resulting in stoppage of earning, needs to be provided for by a life insurer.

With the decline in the birth rate as well as mortality rate, the composition of population will be showing the tendency of increase in the proportion of aged people. The longevity over and above the earning span of an individual will further open the huge pension market in India.

The population is also being affected by other factors like growing terrorism, increase in number of accidents and calamities as also the spread of disease like 'AIDS' at exponential rate. The insurer needs to identify his role to address those issues that are adversely affecting the social fabric of our country.

The contribution to the nation-building through strengthening the economy of a country, improvement of the health care facilities, education as well as employment shall go long way to ultimately improve the quality of life individual members of society. Investment in infrastructure projects shall set the country on a road to the progress on one hand and create goodwill and favourable Organizational Image in the minds of public on the other hand.

Life Insurer will also have to play a role for encouraging development of technology and make its effective use by enhancing the matching skills of inside public. The employees are also needed to be developed to interact with the associate at large for harmonious existence. Poverty alleviation programmes and schemes for unorganized sector of the society, are some more areas, where life insurer can make a favourable impact.

Summing up, it may be said that it is the responsibility of a Life Insurer to completely integrate itself with the society by offering peace of mind to each constituent of the society. Insurer has to build up the economic confidence of the society members by providing for financial contingencies. It has to build up confidence by providing instruments to face the uncertainties and thus create a conductive environment. It has to make this world a better place for living.

12.10 SUMMARY

Social responsibility can be viewed as consideration of impact of the firm's action on society. Business and society interact with each other. Business exists in the context of a society. Business determines society as much as society determines business. Therefore, business must be socially responsible.

A company not only has the responsibility to maximize the value of the shares of those who have invested in it but also in fulfilling their responsibilities to their investors. According to this view, Boards and Executives also have to fulfil their core responsibility to the rest of society "to other stakeholders such as their employees, members of their community and fellow citizens because they help assure that society's productive assets are allocated to their most efficient use." There are basically two categories wherein life insurer's responsibilities could broadly be divided. These are: (1) Business areas, and (2) Non-Business areas. In business areas, the insurer is expected to respond by offering its products and services to the selected segments of the population. Whereas Non-Business areas of social responsibility for a life insurer shall cover his contribution to the development in the fields of education, health care, environment, employment, infrastructure, poverty alleviation and thus national economy.

LIC's group insurance schemes provide security to weaker sections of the society, identified in 24 occupation groups, by offering insurance protection through its various schemes. Here, it may be said that it is the responsibility of a Life Insurer to completely integrate itself with the society by offering peace of mind to each constituent of the society. Insurer has to build up the economic confidence of the society members by providing for financial contingencies.

12.11 REVIEW QUESTIONS

1. What do you mean by social responsibility of business? Give arguments in favour of social responsibilities of a business concern.
2. Thrash out the areas of social responsibilities for Life Insurance.
3. Furnish a brief account of social security programmes in advanced countries.
4. Discuss the social security schemes implemented through LIC of India.

13

CHAPTER

INSURANCE AND INDUSTRIAL POLICY

LEARNING OBJECTIVE

The main objective of this chapter is to make the students' understand about the impact of industrial policies on insurance business in India.

13.1 INTRODUCTION

Insurance is an industry and risk is prime factor in this industry. No risk in the history of modern civilization had affected the fortunes of corporate world so adversely as the Black Tuesday of September 11, 2002. The business all over the world was left in a state of shock and confusion. Financial analyst and policymaker are busy calculating the losses consequent to terrorist attacks on WTC and Pentagon in USA, insurance companies are likely to face claim arising out of life, accident, health, property and liability insurance covers as a fall out of the attacks.

In view of above, it may be worthwhile to state that insurance being an important service industry must invite special attention of the Government through its industrial policy. Although, in India, the Government has taken numerous steps through its various industrial policies both in life and non-life insurances but still we have miles to go to treat insurance industry as an integral part of our industrial policy. Some of the glimpses of various industrial policies framed so far have been discussed in this chapter right since independence.

13.2 INDUSTRIAL POLICY RESOLUTION, 1948

The resolution emphasized expansion of production in the short-run, along with need and importance of public enterprises (PE) to grow. In the words of the resolution: "Any improvement in the economic conditions in the country postulates an increase in national wealth; a mere redistribution of existing wealth would make no difference to the people and would merely mean the distribution of poverty . . . when the masses of the people are below the subsistence level, the emphasis should be on the expansion of production . . . the problem of State participation in industry and the conditions in which private enterprise should be allowed to operate must be judged in this context. There can be no doubt that the State must play a progressively active role in the development of industries but ability to achieve the main objectives should determine the immediate extent of State's responsibility and the limits to private enterprise." The decision therefore, was "that for some time to come, the State could contribute more quickly to the increase of national wealth by expanding present activities wherever it is already operating and by concentration on new units of production in other fields, rather than on acquiring and running existing units." Meanwhile, "private enterprise, properly directed and regulated, has a valuable role to play."

According to this resolution, industries were divided into three broad categories. The first category comprised:

(i) manufacture of arms and ammunition,
(ii) production and control of atomic energy, and
(iii) the ownership and management of railway transport.

These were to be "the exclusive monopoly of the Central Government."

For the second category, the State including the Central and State Government and public authorities like Municipal Corporations, were to be exclusively responsible for the establishment of new undertakings except when the private cooperation was needed in the national interest. This category covered six industries, namely:

(i) Coal;
(ii) Iron and Steel;
(iii) Aircraft manufacturing;
(iv) Ship building;
(v) Manufacture of telephone, telegraph and wireless apparatus (excluding radio receiving sets), and
(vi) Mineral oils.

The rest of the industries were "normally" to be left to private enterprise subject to the provision that the State will also progressively participate in this field, and will not "hesitate to intervene whenever the progress of an industry under private enterprise is unsatisfactory."

The resolution also referred to the steps to be taken by the Government to remedy the hurdles in the way of State management and ownership of industry "in particular by creating a body of men trained in business methods and management."

13.3 ARTICLE 39(B) AND (C) OF THE CONSTITUTION OF INDIA

The Constitution of India directs the State to secure "that the ownership and control of the material resources of the community are so distributed as best to sub-serve the common good" and "that the operation of the economic system does not result in the concentration of wealth and means of production to the common detriment." Attainment of these objectives is fundamental to the growth of public enterprises (PEs), as the presumption is that PEs alone would help achieve these objectives.

Decision for a Socialist Pattern of Society

On 21st December 1954, the Lok Sabha after a debate on the economic situation resolved, among others, that "the objective of our economic policy should be a socialist pattern of society."

The Second Plan document commenting on this concept stated: "Essentially, this means that the basic criterion for determining the lines of advance must not be private profit but social gain, and that the pattern of development and the structure of socio-economic relations should be so planned that they result not only in appreciable increase in national income and employment but also in greater equality in incomes and wealth. Major decisions regarding production, distribution, consumption and investment and in fact all significant socio-economic relationships must be made by agencies informed by social purpose. The benefits of economic development must accrue more and more to the relatively less privileged classes of society, and there should be a progressive reduction of the concentration of the incomes, wealth and economic power, for creating the appropriate conditions the State has to take on heavy responsibilities as the principal agency speaking for and acting on behalf of the community as a whole. The public sector has to expand rapidly."

13.4 INDUSTRIAL POLICY RESOLUTION, 1956

The second Industrial Policy Resolution of 1956 referred to Article 39 (b) and (c) of the Constitution, to the socialist pattern of society, and to the need for a planned and rapid development, and declared that "all industries of basic and strategic importance, or in the nature of public utility services, should be in the public sector." Other industries "which are essential and require investment on a scale which only the State could provide have also to be in the public sector." The Government was therefore " to assume direct responsibility for the future development of industries over a wider area."

Industries were classified into three categories. The first, where the future development was to be exclusive responsibility of the State was to cover 17 industries, listed in Schedule "A" to the resolution. In addition to the nine industries covered in the first and second categories of the 1948 resolution, eight others were:

(i) Air transport;
(ii) Heavy casting and forgings of iron and steel;
(iii) Heavy plant and machinery required for production of iron and steel for mining and machine tools;
(iv) Heavy electrical plant;
(v) Mining of iron and manganese ore, etc.;
(vi) Mining and processing of copper, lead, zinc, tin, etc.;
(vii) Minerals used for producing atomic energy; and
(viii) Generation and distribution of electricity.

Further, "lignite" was added to "coal", as given in the 1948 list.

In the second category were 12 industries to be progressively State-owned and where State was to take initiative to establish new undertakings, along with private enterprise to supplement the efforts of the State. These were:

(i) Aluminum and other non-ferrous metals;
(ii) Fertilizers;
(iii) Machine tools;
(iv) Antibiotic and other essential drugs;
(v) Road transport;
(vi) Sea transport;
(vii) Chemical pulp;
(viii) Carbonisation of coal;
(ix) Ferro-alloys and tool steels;
(x) Basic and intermediate chemical produce;
(xi) Synthetic rubber; and
(xii) All minerals except "minor minerals."

The third category comprised the remaining industries, the further development of which was generally to be left to the initiative and enterprise of the private sector, but "it will be open to the State to start any industry even in this category."

The division of industries with reference to State ownership and control was not intended to be rigid. For example, even for the first category, the expansion of the existing privately owned units or the possibility of the State securing cooperation of private enterprise in the establishment of new units, if in the national interest, was not excluded. But this was to be secured either through majority equity participation by the State or in such other way as the State retained the requisite powers to guide the policy and control of the operations of the undertaking. The resolution observed that "inevitable there will not only be an area of overlapping but also great deal of dovetailing between industries in the private and the public sector." The Government not only allowed the existing iron and steel and power units under the control of Tata's to stay but also provided promotional finance to them. That in a way exemplified the above spirits.

The State was to facilitate and encourage the development of private enterprise which develops as part of five year plans by ensuring the development of transport, power and other services and by other appropriate measures. Further, private units were allowed "to produce an item falling within Schedule A, for meeting their own requirements or as be products." The resolution added that where both privately and publicly owned units existed in an industry, "it would continue to be the policy of the State to give fair and non-discriminatory treatment to both of them." Thus, while recognizing the role which private enterprise was to play in the economy, the commitment to have a large and expanding public sector was unequivocal.

Regarding steps to improve PE management, the resolution stated that "proper managerial and technical cadre in the public services are being established". It was recognized that "speedy decisions and a willingness to assume responsibility are essential if these enterprises are to succeed. For this, wherever possible, there should be decentralization of authority and the management should be on business lines. Public enterprises have to be judged by their total results and in their working they should have the largest possible measure of freedom." Unfortunately, these valuable ideas were never taken up seriously and sincerely for implementation.

13.5 INDUSTRIAL POLICY STATEMENT, 1977

The industrial policy announced by the Janata Party Government on December 23, 1977 envisaged PE as a means of socializing the means of production in strategic areas and for providing a countervailing force to the growth of large houses and large-scale enterprises in the private sector. It also envisaged a greater role for PE in several fields, e.g., producing of important and strategic goods of basic nature, acting as a stabilizing force for maintaining essential supplies for the consumer; and encouraging a wide range of ancillary industries in the small-scale and cottage industry sectors.

The Government was also expected to operate PEs on profitable and efficient lines in order to ensure adequate returns on investment made in them.

13.6 INDUSTRIAL POLICY STATEMENT, 1980

The policy statement of the Congress Government made in the Lok Sabha on 23rd July, 1980 fully endorsed the 1956 resolution, which according to it "reflects the value system of our country and has shown conclusively the merit of constructive flexibility." The statement referred to the "gigantic task" of rehabilitating "faith in the public sector" and of evolving "effective operational systems of management" in PE.

In the statement, the Government emphasized the desirability of allowing private sector undertakings "to develop in consonance with targets and objectives of national plans and policies", but it did not want "the growth of monopolistic tendencies or concentration of economic power and wealth in a few hands."

The statement added that "the Government has decided to launch a drive to revive the efficiency of public sector undertakings. Industrial undertakings in this sector will be closely examined on a unit-by-unit basis and corrective action would be taken in terms of a time-bound programme wherever necessary. Priority will be accorded to convert losing concerns into viable ones through broad restructuring of the system and providing dynamic and competent management." But nothing substantial or effective in this regard was done.

13.7 POST-INDIRA GANDHI GOVERNMENT POLICIES

The Rajiv Gandhi Government which was in power from 1984-89 never made any formal statement of its PE policy, but continued to show faith in PE. In his address to the National Development Council (1985), Mr. Gandhi said, "there was no question of reducing the role of the public sector. The key role assigned to public sector was intact."

The National Front Government which followed, through its industrial policy announced on 31st May, 1990 opened large areas for the private sector and the multinationals. The new policy permitted foreign investment up to 40 per cent of equity, both for new and expansion of existing units.

The Narasimha Rao Government which came to power in 1991, gave a totally new direction to PE policy, which is considered in the following paragraphs:

13.8 POLICY AS STATED IN THE COMMON MINIMUM PROGRAMME (CMP) OF THE UNITED FRONT GOVERNMENT

The CMP announced on 5th June 1996 envisaged the public sector to be strong and competitive. It contemplated PEs as essentially commercial enterprise, expected them to conduct their business on commercial lines and show a healthy return on the capital employed. The Government promised to identify public sector companies that have comparative advantages and support them in their drive to become global giants. Other profit-making and efficient PEs were to be strengthened and their managements were to be professionalised. Sick or potentially sick PEs will be rehabilitated "through a menu of options that may include handling over the management to professional groups or workers' cooperatives."

A Disinvestment Commission was proposed to be established to advise the Government on withdrawing the public sector from non-core and non-strategic areas. The CMP promised that decisions to disinvest will be taken and implemented in a transparent manner, and revenues generated from the disinvestments were to be utilized in the areas of health and education, particularly in the poorer and backward districts of the country. A part of such revenues were to be earmarked to create an investment fund to be used to strengthen other PEs.

13.9 RAJIV GANDHI GOVERNMENT AND AFTER

The Rajiv Government (1984-89) had a marked thrust towards liberalization, *inter alia*, through large-scale delicensing, broad banding of industries which remained within the ambit of licensing, and the higher endorsement of capacity. Some fields like telecommunication, oil exploration, oil refining and civil aviation, exclusively reserved for PEs were also thrown open to the private sector. The Government never came out with any formal policy statement but it was repeatedly stated that there was no change in the industrial policy and "there was no deviation from the pursuit of a socialist pattern of society." Mr Rajiv Gandhi told the Lok Sabha on 18th December 1985 that the public sector would continue to be "the key to our development and a path finder to take the country to the 21st century."

The Seventh Five Year Plan (1985-90) justified private enterprise growth by stating that "the industrial economy visualized in the Industrial Policy Resolution, 1956 is characterized by a symbiotic and complementary relationship between the public and private sector." This, however, hides the important fact that the 1956 Resolution aimed at PE operating as a dominant and pervasive force and the private sector was only to complement and supplement it.

The Seventh Plan document de-emphasised PE when it observed that the stress "should be on consolidation, improvement and modernisation rather than on large expansion of capacity except when it is imperative."

However, till the Narasimha Rao Government came to power in 1991, basic commitment to PE philosophy continued. For example, Mr. V.P. Singh as Prime Minister told the National Development Council on 18th June, 1990 that "we are not and will not be *laissez faire* economy. The Government must retain strategic control over the broad directions of industrial development."

13.10 CHANGE IN POLICY: JULY 1991 POLICY STATEMENT

The Industrial Policy Statement of the Narasimha Rao Government totally reversed the PE policy. Though the statement began with a reverential reference to Pandit Nehru and his contribution and philosophy, it was a clean break from the policy of the socialist pattern. In the words of the VIII Plan (1992-97) document, the policy now was of "managing the transition from centrally planned economy to market led economy." The policy's aim has been to "roll back" the public sector investment from those sectors of the economy where the private sector could move in.

Ridiculing the hypocrisy of the Congress leadership that the Nehruvian model of the economy was intact, Mr. Yaswant Singh, a former Finance Minister remarked: "Having turned down the Nehruvian model upside down the Congress party is now trying to stand on its head to prove that it has not departed from the model." The fact is that the Congress leadership has clinged to Nehru's name as it did not have adequate courage to have a break from the traditional Congress idiom. In this regard, it would be of interest to refer to the first para of the policy statement of 1991, which is reproduced below:

> "Pandit Jawaharlal Nehru laid the foundations of modern India. His determination have left a lasting impression on ever facet of national endeavour since Independence. It is due to his initiative that India now has a strong and diversified industrial base and is a major industrial nation of the World. The goals and objectives set out for the nation by Pandit Nehru on the eve of Independence, namely, the rapid agriculture and industrial development of our country, rapid expansion of opportunities for gainful employment, progressive self-reliance remain as valid today as the time Pandit Nehru first set them out before the nation. Any industrial policy must contribute to the realization of these goals and objectives at an accelerated pace. The present statement of industrial policy is inspired by these very concerns, and represents a renewed initiative towards consolidating the gains of national reconstruction at this crucial stage."

13.11 REASONS FOR MAJOR CHANGE IN POLICY

As noted in the policy statement, the Government felt that "after the initial exuberance of the public sector entering new areas of industrial and technical competence, a number of problems have begun to manifest themselves." Six of these listed in the statement were:

(i) insufficient growth in productivity,
(ii) poor project management,
(iii) over managing (which means employing more persons than necessary for performing a job),
(iv) lack of continuous technological upgradation,
(v) inadequate attention to R & D and human resource development, and
(vi) a very low rate of return on the capital employed.

According to the policy statement, all these resulted in many PEs becoming "a burden rather than asset to the Government."

The fact of the matter is that government itself has been responsible for poor management of PEs. Most PEs were never provided adequate autonomy to perform, and an effective and professional board of directors. PEs also lacked a sense of direction in the absence of an unambiguous set of mission and objective. Decisions were taken to serve a vague and varying 'public interest', ignoring the impact on commercial performance and morals of PE manager.

Changes Envisaged by the Policy Statement

1. Priority areas for growth will be PEs in:
   (i) essential infrastructure goods and services,
   (ii) exploration and exploitation of oil and mineral resources,
   (iii) areas crucial in the long-term development of the economy where private sector investment is inadequate, and
   (iv) defence equipment.
2. PEs essential for the operation of the industrial economy will be made more growth-oriented and dynamic.
3. There will be a greater thrust on performance improvement through the memorandum of understanding (MoU) system through which management would be granted greater autonomy and will be held accountable.
4. PEs faltering at present but are potentially viable will be restructured and given a new lease of life.
5. The government ownership in areas:
   (i) where the private sector has developed sufficient expertise and resources,
   (ii) are non-strategic,
   (iii) are based on low technology,
   (iv) are inefficient and unproductive, and
   (v) have low or nil social consideration or public purpose, will be reviewed with gather realism.
6. Government will ensure that PEs are "run on business lines as envisaged in the Industrial Policy Resolution of 1956 and would continue to innovate and lead in strategic areas of national importance."
7. The public sector will not be barred from entering areas not specifically reserved for it.
8. The monopoly of any sector or any individual enterprise in field of manufacture, except on strategic consideration, will be abolished. All manufacturing activity will be open to competition.
9. Chronically sick PEs which are unlikely to be turned around will be referred to the Board for Industrial and Financial Reconstruction (BIFR).
10. Boards of PEs would be made more professional and given greater powers.
11. Technical expertise on the part of the Government would be upgraded to make the MoU negotiations and implementation more effective.
12. In selected PEs, a part of government equity holdings will be disinvested:
    (i) to provide further market discipline to their performance,
    (ii) to encourage wider public participation, and
    (iii) to raise resource.

The disinvested equity would be offered to mutual funds, financial institutions, general public and workers.

13. PEs:
    (i) in the reserved areas of operation,
    (ii) in high priority areas, and
    (iii) which are generating good or reasonable profits, would be strengthened.

    This will be done by providing a much greater degree of management autonomy through the system of MoU, and through competition by inviting private sector participation.
14. To facilitate a fuller discussion on performance, the MoU would be placed in Parliament. While focusing on major management issues, this would also help place matters on day-to-day operation of PEs in their correct perspective.

13.12 INSURANCE AND INDUSTRIAL POLICY

Before the era of Payment of Wages Act, 1936, the workers were exploited to the extend possible. The worker was working day and night without rest. He was giving his best to the organization but in-turn no wages no payments for the kind of job he performed. At the most, the employer will give the employee few kilograms of food so that his family barely survives in the name of compensation for the job, what to talk of regular wages or salary. Making both ends meet was a vicarious task. In nut shell the worker was badly exploited by the employer. This gave momentum to enactment by the Government of India. This is one part of the life of the Industrial worker in both organized sector and the unorganized sector. The other part is the compensation in event of death of bread earner for the family. The Government of India through Insurance Companies devised various covers like Workmen's Compensation Act, 1923, ESI, Personal Accident Policy, Janta Personal Accident Policy (in Industrial and Single), Mediclaim (Individual and Group), Long-Term Hospitalization Policy.

The industrial policies of India have helped the Indian insurance sector to grow manifold during the last 50 years. It is the industrial and economic policies of our country, which helped the insurance sector to occupy a vital position in the financial sector of our economy. The insurance sector has helped the economy of our country to grow along with the banking and capital markets, as insurance sector cannot function and grow in isolation.

13.13 SUMMARY

The resolution emphasized expansion of production in the short-run, along with need and importance of public enterprises (PE) to grow. In the words of the resolution: "Any improvement in the economic conditions in the country postulates an increase in national wealth; a mere redistribution of existing wealth would make no difference to the people and would merely mean the distribution of poverty . . . when the mass of the people are below the subsistence level, the emphasis should be on the expansion of production . . . the problem of State participation in industry and the conditions in which private enterprise should be allowed to operate must be judged in this context. There can be no doubt that the State must play a progressively active role in the development of industries but ability to achieve the main objectives should determine the immediate extent of State's responsibility and the limits to private enterprise." The decision therefore, was "that for some time to come, the State could contribute more quickly to the increase of national wealth by expanding present activities wherever it is already operating and by concentration on new units of production in other fields, rather than on acquiring and running existing units." Meanwhile, "private enterprise, properly directed and regulated, has a valuable role to play."

According to this resolution, industries were divided into three broad categories. The first category comprised:

(i) manufacture of arms and ammunition,
(ii) production and control of atomic energy, and
(iii) the ownership and management of railway transport.

These were to be "the exclusive monopoly of the Central Government."

The Constitution of India directs the State to secure "that the ownership and control of the material resources of the community are so distributed as best to subserve the common good" and "that the operation of the economic system does not result in the concentration of wealth and means of production to the common detriment." Attainment of these objectives is fundamental to the growth of PE, as the presumption is that PEs alone would help achieve these objectives.

The second Industrial Policy Resolution of 1956 referred to Article 39 (b) and (c) of the Constitution, to the socialist pattern of society, and to the need for a planned and rapid development, and declared that "all industries of basic and strategic importance, or in the nature of public utility services, should be in the public sector." Other industries "which are essential and require investment on a scale which only the State could provide have also to be in the public sector." The Government was therefore "to assume direct responsibility for the future development of industries over a wider area."

Industries were classified into three categories. The first, where the future development was to be exclusive responsibility of the State was to cover 17 industries, listed in schedule "A" to the resolution. In addition to the nine industries covered in the first and second categories of the 1948 resolution, eight others were:

(i) Air transport;
(ii) Heavy casting and forgings of iron and steel;
(iii) Heavy plant and machinery required for production of iron and steel for mining and machine tools;

(iv) Heavy electrical plant;
(v) Mining of iron and manganese ore, etc.;
(vi) Mining and processing of copper, lead, zinc, tin, etc.;
(vii) Minerals used for producing atomic energy; and
(viii) Generation and distribution of electricity.

Further, "lignite" was added to "coal", as given in the 1948 list.

The industrial policy announced by the Janata Party Government on December 23, 1977, envisaged PE as a means of socializing the means of production in strategic areas and for providing a countervailing force to the growth of large houses and large-scale enterprises in the private sector. It also envisaged a greater role for PE in several fields, e.g, producing of important and strategic goods of basic nature, acting as a stabilizing force for maintaining essential supplies for the consumer; and encouraging a wide range of ancillary industries in the small-scale and cottage industry sectors.

The Government was also expected to operate PEs on profitable and efficient lines in order to ensure adequate returns on investment made in them. The policy statement of the Congress Government made in the Lok Sabha on 23rd July, 1980 fully endorsed the 1956 resolution, which according to it "reflects the value system of our country and has shown conclusively the merit of constructive flexibility." The statement referred to the "gigantic task" of rehabilitating "faith in the public sector" and of evolving "effective operational systems of management" in PE.

In the statement, the Government emphasized the desirability of allowing private sector undertakings "to develop in consonance with targets and objectives of national plans and policies", but it did not want "the growth of monopolistic tendencies or concentration of economic power and wealth in a few hands."

The Rajiv Government (1984-89) had a marked thrust towards liberalization, *inter alia,* through large-scale delicensing, broad banding of industries which remained within the ambit of licensing, and the higher endorsement of capacity. Some fields like telecommunication, oil exploration, oil refining and civil aviation, exclusively reserved for PEs were also thrown open to the private sector. The government never came out with any formal policy statement but it was repeatedly stated that there was no change in the industrial policy and "there was no deviation from the pursuit of a socialist pattern of society." Mr Rajiv Gandhi told the Lok Sabha on 18th December 1985 that the public sector would continue to be "the key to our development and a path finder to take the country to the 21st century."

The Industrial Policy Statement of the Narasimha Rao Government totally reversed the PE policy. Though the statement began with a reverential reference to Pandit Nehru and his contribution and philosophy, it was a clean break from the policy of the socialist pattern. In the words of the VIII Plan (1992-97) document, the policy now was of "managing the transition from centrally planned economy to market led economy." The policy's aim has been to "roll back" the public sector investment from those sectors of the economy where the private sector could move in.

Ridiculing the hypocrisy of the Congress leadership that the Nehruvian model of the economy was intact, Mr. Yaswant Singh, a former Finance Minister remarked: "Having turned down the Nehruvian model upside down the Congress party is now trying to stand on its head to prove that it has not departed from the model." The fact is that the Congress leadership has clinged to Nehru's name as it did not have adequate courage to have a break from the traditional Congress idiom. As noted in the policy statement, the Government felt that "after the initial exuberance of the public sector entering new areas of industrial and technical competence, a number of problems have begun to manifest themselves." Six of these listed in the statement were:

(i) insufficient growth in productivity,
(ii) poor project management,
(iii) over managing (which means employing more persons than necessary for performing a job),
(iv) lack of continuous technological upgradation,
(v) inadequate attention to R & D and human resource development, and
(vi) a very low rate of return on the capital employed.

According to the policy statement, all these resulted in many PEs becoming "a burden rather than asset to the Government."

Before the era of Payment of Wages Act, 1936, the Workers were exploited to the extend possible. The worker was working day and night without rest. He was giving his best to the organization but in-turn no wages no payments for the kind of job he performed. At the most, the employer will give the employee few kilograms of food so that his family barely survives in the name of compensation for the job, what to talk of regular wages or salary. Making both ends meet was a vicarious task. In nut shell the worker was badly exploited by the employer. This gave momentum to enactment by the Government of India. This is one part of the life of the Industrial worker in both organized sector and the unorganized sector. The other part is the compensation in event of death of bread earner for the family. The Government of India through Insurance Companies devised various covers like Workmen's Compensation Act, 1923 ESI, Personal Accident Policy, Janta Personal Accident Policy (in Industrial and Single), Mediclaim (Individual and Group), Long-Term Hospitalization Policy.

The industrial policies of India have helped the Indian insurance sector to grow manifold during the last 50 years. It is the industrial and economic policies of our country, which helped the insurance sector to occupy a vital position in the financial sector of our economy. The insurance sector has helped the economy of our country to grow along with the banking and capital markets, as insurance sector cannot function and grow in isolation.

13.14 REVIEW QUESTIONS

1. Explain and elucidate the main features of Industrial Policy Resolution of 1948. How far this resolution was different from the present policy.
2. Bring out the role of the government in the development of insurance business through its industrial policies. Do you think that the insurance needs some more emphasis in industrial policies? If yes, give suggestions in this connection.
3. "In the pre-liberalization era industrial policies did not perfectly recognize the role of insurance in an economy like India." Comment.

14
CHAPTER

LPG AND INSURANCE BUSINESS

LEARNING OBJECTIVE

The foremost objective of this chapter is to make the students comprehend with reference to the liberalization, privatization, and globalization of insurance business in India and their impact on our insurance industry.

14.1 INTRODUCTION

In our experienced life, it is a proved fact that wherever there is uncertainty, there is an involvement of risk. The instant for security against such risk is one of the basic motivating forces for determining human attitudes. As a sequel to this quest for security, the concept of insurance has been born. The urge to provide insurance or protection against the loss of life and property must have prompted people to make some sort of sacrifice willingly in order to achieve security through collective co-operation. In this sense, the story of insurance is probably as old as the story of mankind. Thus, the urge of security and protection against risk in a man lead to the concept of insurance.

Initially, the idea of insurance was first conceptualized. At that time it was used more as a tool for protection against financial loss of sea hazards involved in foreign trade. Since then this concept has undergone several changes. It is basically the unforeseen contingencies of human life that has given a totally new look to the insurance industry. Gradually as competition increased the benefits given by the industry to its customers improved by leaps and bounds. It was the breakup of the traditional extended family system that provided a natural umbrella to each and every member of the family, which gave the insurance (life and non-life) institutions an impetus to excel.

14.2 INSURANCE BUSINESS IN PRE-NATIONALIZATION ERA

Keeping into account the long life of insurance business in India, let us analyze the performance of insurance industry under various time periods.

In India, the history of insurance, in its present form, can be traced with the establishment of a British Firm, Oriental Life Insurance Company in Calcutta in 1818. This was followed by the formation of Bombay Life Insurance Company in 1823, the Madras Equitable Life Insurance Company in 1829 and the Oriental Government Security Life Insurance Company in 1874. The first general insurance limited company was established in 1850. The Indian Mercantile Insurance Company Limited, which was set-up in Bombay in 1907, was the first Indian Company to transact all classes of general insurance business. Even though the first life insurance company was established as early as 1818, there was no exclusive legislation to govern the activities of insurance companies during the nineteenth century. The Indian Companies Act passed in 1866 regulated all companies, including insurance companies.

To control the operations of life insurance business in India, the Indian Life Insurance Companies Act was enacted in 1912. This act was based on Assurance Companies Act, 1909 of U.K. In 1938, the Indian Insurance Companies Act was passed. This act amended the 1912 Act and provided for collection of statistics concerning insurance business other than life business. It also covered the foreign companies operating in India. The Act made provisions for required equity capital to carry out insurance business, ceilings on share holding pattern, stricter controls on investments, ceilings on management expenses and agency commission, etc. Subsequently, a separate wing was established in the Ministry of Finance to administer the provisions under the Act.

After the Indian Insurance Companies Act, 1938 was passed, there was mushroom growth of insurance companies in India. In spite of mushrooming of many insurance companies per capita insurance in India was merely Rs. 8 in 1944 as against Rs. 2000 and Rs. 600 in US and UK respectively. Even this limited growth is marked by many malpractices, deficiencies, and frequent liquidations of insurance companies shaking public confidence and depriving policyholders of their savings and security. It is reported that in those days insurance and banking was in the control of big industry houses resulting in interlocking of funds between banks and insurance companies. These irregularities were mainly of two types. Firstly, malpractices that had crept into management of insurance companies especially during 1940s such as acquisition of insurance companies by financiers and use of life insurance funds to serve other enterprises in which the financier was interested or for speculation, payment of large emoluments to nominees of the controlling interests and interlocking of funds between banks and insurance companies. Secondly, factors which have operated for years towards disruption of Indian insurance such as excessive costs, rebating and unsatisfactory standards of management of business.

These dark deeds of dishonest insurance men helped to intensify the public chauvinism and invited public demand for nationalization. As a consequence Government of India nationalized life insurance by amalgamating all the private companies under one corporation, i.e. Life Insurance Corporation of India. At the time of nationalization of life insurance in 1956, one hundred and fifty four Indian insurers, sixteen Non-Indian insurers, and seventy-five provident societies were carrying on the life insurance business in India. Despite of this broad-based organization of life insurance, the insurance business was mainly restricted to cities and towns at that time.

14.3 INSURANCE BUSINESS IN POST-NATIONALIZATION ERA

Life Insurance Corporation of India set-up by Government of India in the year 1956 dominated life insurance sector. General Insurance Sector still was in private hands. It was mainly confined to small entrepreneurs and ancillary units attached to big industrial plants. With the growth in the process of industrialization in India, number of companies in the general insurance sector increased steadily and by 1972 their number had gone to 107. But many of these companies did not have a strong financial base as they were mainly dependent upon premiums received from industrial units to run their operations. Because of three wars in a decade (1962, 1965 and 1971) focus of Central Government shifted from industrial sector to defence sector. This shift caused economic slowdown, which resulted in fund shortage faced by industrial units. All these developments had a bad effect on the general insurance sector. Of the 107 companies in existence at the end of 1972, more than 50% were in financially bad shape.

Taking into account the bad health of private operators and vast fund mobilization potential in this sector, Government of India nationalized the general insurance sector with effect from Ist January 1973. It formed four subsidiaries (The New India Assurance Company Ltd., the Oriental Insurance Company Ltd., the United India Insurance Company Ltd. and the National Insurance Company Ltd.) with a holding company (General Insurance Corporation of India). Presently, all these subsidiaries are working independently.

Since 1973, the insurance sector has been totally under the control of Government of India through LIC and GIC and its subsidiaries. As a result, revenue of both of them increased significantly in the later years. The amount of savings pooled by LIC increased from Rs. 2704 crores in 1974 to Rs. 57670 crores in 1994 showing an annual growth rate of 16.53% which is quite high rate. Similarly, premium underwritten by GIC rose from 280 crores in 1973 to Rs. 7647 crores in 1998 showing an annual growth rate of 25.18%. Factors contributing to the growth were:

(i) Monopoly

The insurance sector till now enjoyed monopoly so it has total control over the business.

(ii) Social Factors

Collapse of joint family system and advent of nuclear family system because of better career opportunities at places far away from native places as a result of increasing industrialisation caused greater social security. So more and more people were motivated towards insurance.

(iii) Economic Factors

More jobs and better job opportunities, because of industrialisation improved the standard of living. New products and services changed the life style of people. So they opted for insurance for covering the risk of theft, fire and other mishappening.

Besides other factors like more tension in challenging jobs, tax benefits associated with insurance instruments, greater life expectancy, increased risk to the life of a person because of rapid changes in the environment also resulted in more persons going for insurance.

Trends and Progress in the Business of LIC

LIC has been growing at an annual rate of 15 to 20% consistently for the last several years. The claim settlement ratio of LIC is at the order of 97%. The Malhotra Committee Report, which looked into the performance of this sector, found a fairly high degree of consumer satisfaction. Government of India invested by way of equity Rs. 5 crore in LIC in 1972. Without additional need for investment in equity LIC has generated enormous surpluses and has been paying large dividends and corporate taxes to the government year after year. The dividend for the year 1997-98 paid by LIC to the government was of the order of Rs. 197.97 crore after paying corporate taxes of Rs. 563.03 crores. Policyholders have in general received good returns on their investment. This is confirmed by increase in bonus rates, which has gone up from Rs. 12.80 per thousand to Rs. 85 per thousand for endowment policies and from Rs. 16 per thousand to Rs. 102 per thousand for whole life policies in the period 1997-98.

Table 14.1 shows the growth of LIC. Different parameters shown reflects the progress of LIC. If further analyzed it revealed that a growth of 11.5 per cent in number of new policies issued, 21 per cent in first premium income and 18.5 per cent in total premium income. During 1999-2000 increase in the number of new policies issued was 14.4 per cent, first year premium income was 24.3 per cent, total premium income was 20.4 per cent and life fund was 20.9 per cent.

Data available concerning to LIC clearly shows the excellent growth rate of LIC. Today, LIC has become the leading investment institution of India. In order to reach to people in every part of the country it has developed a vast service network, comprising of 7 Zonal offices, 100 divisional offices and 2048 branch offices which together employ 1,24,000 persons and 6,51,000 agents. Besides LIC contributed in social welfare

TABLE 14.1

Progress of LIC

	1974-75	*1998-99*	*Annual Growth Rate*
First premium (Rs. in crores)	85.67	4071.73	31.76%
Renewal Premium	411.70	17710.22	30.82%
No. of claims settled (In lacs)	4.68	59.84	19.96%
Life fund	3033.79	127389.06	30.60%
No. of policies in force (In lacs)	188.20	917.26	11.98%
Investments (Rs. in lacs)	2798.43	120445.00	30.83%

Source: Annual reports of LIC of different years.

projects, like water supply, electricity, sewerage facilities, housing and transport, etc. mainly through life funds. Book value of socially oriented investment increased from Rs. 1218.52 crores in 1974-75 to Rs. 88,831 crores in 1998-99 showing an annual growth rate of 35.82%.

Trends and Progress in the Business of GIC

Based upon the data as given in Table 14.2 the following picture emerges:

1. The gross domestic premium income in India (GDPI), which was Rs. 184 crore in 1973, has increased to Rs. 9522 crore in 1999-2000, recording an average growth rate of about 16.90%. The premium income originating outside India went up over the level of Rs. 24 crore in 1973 to Rs. 460 crore in 1999-2000, registering annual growth rate of about 11.95%. The total gross premium income, which was Rs. 208 crore in 1973, stood at Rs. 9,982 crore in 1999-2000, recording average annual growth rate of about 16.50%. The total net premium income increased to Rs. 9364 crore from the level of Rs. 222 crore in 1973. It recorded average annual growth rate of about 15.75%. The net premium income as percentage to total premium income was 93.8% in 1999-2000 indicating that only about 7% of GDPI went outside the country through reinsurance. As compared to 1973, the GDPI in India has grown by about 47 times.
2. The net claim payable were at Rs. 7,586 crore in 1999-2000 as against Rs. 1,123 crore in 1973, accounting for 81% to net premium.
3. The total investment increased from Rs. 355 crore in 1973 to Rs. 16,659 crore in 1999-2000. It grew by about 47 times. The

TABLE 14.2

Trends and Progress in the Business of GIC

(Rs. in crores)

Year	*1973*	*1991-92*	*1994-94*	*1998-99*	*1999-2000*
Paid-up Capital	37	268	375	375	375
Gross Premium in India	184	3287	4959	8759	9522
Gross Premium outside India	24	216	312	399	460
Total Gross Premium	208	3503	5271	9158	9982
% Increase over previous year	—	20.3	10.6	13.3	9.01
Net Premium in India	222	2945	4102	7732	8648
Net Premium outside India	—	505	777	670	716
Total Net Premium	222	3450	4879	8402	9364
Underwriting Profit	18	-77	-705	-687	-1215
Profit Before Tax	38	669	503	1467	1152
Income Tax Paid	21	241	126	390	278
Net Profit	14	428	377	1077	874
Investment Income	21	752	1150	2220	2392

Source: Various Annual Reports of GIC.

compound annual growth in investible funds was about 17%. The investment income increased from Rs. 21 crore in 1973 to Rs. 2,392 crore in 1999-2000. The average annual gross yield on mean funds amounted to about 13%.

4. The paid up capital and free reserves increased from Rs. 34 crore and 62 crore in 1973 to Rs. 375 and Rs. 7,745 crore in 1999-2000 respectively. The increase in reserve for unexpired risk which was Rs. 23 crore in 1973 increased to Rs. 485 crore in 1999-2000.
5. In so for the class-wise distribution of business is concerned, the fire, miscellaneous and marine accounted for 24%, 66% and 10% in 1999-2000 respectively. The net income claim ratios were 41%, 99% and 70% in fire, miscellaneous and marine business in 1999-2000 respectively. In miscellaneous portfolio, motor business, which is a loss-making business has steadily grown over a period of time and accounted for about 32% of the total business of the industry. However, this is in consonance with the world-wide trend since in most of the countries of the world motor business was more than 30% of the total business. For instance, it was about 63, 56 and 54 per cent in Thailand, Malaysia and Taiwan respectively.
6. The geographical spread of the premium underwritten in India indicates that the maximum, i.e. about 40% was generated from western region and minimum, i.e. about 9% from the eastern region. The northern and southern region contributed about 26%

and 24% of gross premium in 1999-2000 respectively.

7. The underwriting profit of the industry was Rs. 18 crore (8.2% of the net premium) in 1973. However, over a period of time underwriting operations have resulted into losses and these losses amounted to Rs. 1,215 crore in 1999-2000, accounting for 13% of net premium income.
8. Interestingly, the investment income amounting to Rs. 2,392 crore was in excess of underwriting losses and produced profit for the industry. The level of profit was Rs. 1,153 crore before tax payment and Rs. 874 crore after tax payment. In 1973 the profit before tax and after tax were Rs. 38 crore and Rs. 14 crore respectively.
9. Although the total number of insurance products in the general insurance industry are around 175, only a few, i.e. 40 to 50 products have dominated the market controlling about 75 to 80% of the total market. Rest of the products have not been popular as they lack mass base, may be due to poor publicity and marketing, lack of awareness, higher premium rates, and might have been introduced without adequate database.
10. The rural and non-traditional business, which was practically nil in 1973, has gradually increased over a period of time. The premium collected through this business was only about Rs. 425 crore in 1999-2000, constituting only 4% of the total gross premium income. It calls for innovating new products for the rural population suiting to different income groups and marketing them aggressively. However, if the total policies issued by office in rural areas are taken into account, the premium from rural areas will account for about 30%.
11. Regarding the reinsurance operations of the industry, data indicate that the total reinsurance premium was Rs. 1,011 crore in 1997-98, accounting for about 13% of the gross premium. It indicates that about 87% of the premium was retained in the country. The operations between 1990-91 to 1997-98 reveal that the retention was about 85.5% of the gross premium. Further break-up of reinsurance premium indicates that about 45% is required for placement of large projects and specialised risk on facultative basis and another 45% is for the surplus treaties, which is necessary to create capacity. The cost of reinsurance reveals that in 1997-98 while the commission earned was Rs. 271 crore (3.5% of GDP), the claim recoveries were Rs. 557 crore (7.2% of GDP), accounting for a total of Rs. 828 crore. It amounted to 10.7% of GDP against the reinsurance premium of Rs. 1011 crore. Thus, the net outflow of premium works out to be Rs. 183 crore which may be termed as net cost of reinsurance, accounting for 2.4% of GDP. For the years between 1990-91 to 1998-99, the average total reinsurance cost, commission earned, claim recovery and net cost

of reinsurance as percentage of GDP works out to be 14.5%, 3.5%, 7.9% and 3.1% respectively (Table 14.2).

In so far as the inward reinsurance business is concerned, in 1996-97, the total premium earned was Rs. 374 crore (5.3% of GDP), the commission paid was Rs. 124 crore (1.7% of GDP) and the balance resulted into net outflow of Rs. 81 crore (1.1% of GDP).

12. The general insurance industry has operations in 30 countries. Out of these in 16 countries it is operating directly and in 14 countries through subsidiary and associated companies. During 1999-2000, the total gross and nèt premium income from business operations in these countries were Rs. 488.76 crore and Rs. 440.36 crore respectively. The net claim during the year amounted to Rs. 288.19 crore amounting to 65.7% of the net premium.

14.4 WEAKNESSES IN INSURANCE SECTOR

Notwithstanding of the fact that the insurance industry has grown-up after nationalization in terms of premium income, introduction of new products, wide coverage of individuals and organizations, innovating new covers for weaker sections of society, investment in social sectors, creating infrastructure at grass-roots level, etc., it suffers from several weaknesses which have come to the face for discussion nowadays. These are as follows:

1. Insurance Penetration

Despite the growth of gross domestic premium by 47 times between 1973 to 1999-2000, the insurance penetration defined as insurance premium as share of gross domestic product, was as low as 0.56% in non-life business in 1997. The life side accounted for 1.39% and the total penetration being 1.95%. It was as high as 4.64% and 4.53% for non-life side in USA and Newzealand respectively. The average for Asia was 1.90% while for the world it was 3.06%. Even amongst the developing economies and other East Asian Countries, the Indian insurance industry lagged far behind in this area. For instance, it was 3.79% for South Korea, 2.45% for Japan, 1.69% for Taiwan, 2.19% for Malaysia, 1.31% for Singapore, and 1.22% for Thailand. Low insurance penetration is pointer to the fact that spread of insurance business has relatively been poorer in the country and large section of insurable population is still isolated from the insurance coverage.

2. Insurance Density

Another parameter to measure the progress of insurance is the insurance density defined as premium per capita. The available data indicate that in 1997 for non-life side, it was US dollar 2.2 in India. The total being US dollar 7.6, the life side accounting for US dollar 5.4. It was as high as US dollar 1403.7 in USA and US dollar 1296.6 in Switzerland. It was US dollar 176.8 for the world as a whole and 46.4 for Asia. Insurance density in the country was low even as compared to several developing countries. It was

US dollar 338.3 in Singapore, US dollar 303 in South Korea, US dollar 299.2 in Hong Kong, US dollar 222 in Taiwan, US dollar 99.8 in Malaysia, US dollar 26.3 in Thailand, and US dollar 6.91 in Indonesia. It was as high as US dollar 804 in Japan. Most of the African countries were also ahead of India in this respect. Although insurance density is positively correlated to the per capita income which is quite low in India, but what surprises is that the insurance density is lower even compared to several developing countries whose per capita income is even lower than India. The low insurance density and penetration are also partly due to lack of awareness on the part of general masses regarding the benefits flowing from the insurance in improving their standard of living and welfare.

3. Relatively Poor Quality of Insurance Services

In general the quality of insurance services has been at a low key. The quality of insurance services may primarily be evaluated in terms of expeditious settlement of claims, delivery of policy documents and after sales services. At the end of March 2000, a total number of 10,09,542 claims were outstanding, of which about 55% were suit claims. Of the total suit claims, motor suit claims accounted for about 75%. Time-wise analysis of pending claims indicate that about 45% claims were pending for more than one year and out of these about 23% were pending for more than three years. Although a total number of documents issued during 1999-2000 were quite large amounting to 3,39,70,855, yet as many as 10,12,908 documents were still outstanding as on March 2000. The delivery of these documents was still outstanding as on March 2000. The delivery of these documents also takes a long time. Although the cost of the insurance services measured in terms of the price of insurance products for the non-tariff products has been by and large, fair and competitive but there is still ample scope for lowering the rates with proper control on management expenses, optimal utilization of investible resources and through wider coverage of insurable population.

4. Availability of Insurance Products

Although on the general insurance side, there are a total of about 175 products covering most of the common insurance products in their portfolio, yet hardly 30 to 35 products are actively traded in the market. On life side out of 52 products two products dominate with majority share. Today, customers desire to purchase package products instead of purchasing several multiple policies. There are very limited number of such package policies (such as Industrial All Risks Policy and Office Umbrella Policy). The policies catering to special needs of the public such as Advance Loss of Profit, Director's and Officer's Liability, etc. are quite limited in number. The products catering to rural sector where disposable income is increasing are limited in number and existing products have not been properly marketed. The policies in segments of Health covers, Household Risk covers, have not been properly marketed and publicised. For instance, health insurance products roughly cover only 25 lakh population with premium income of about Rs. 20 crore. The entire thrust on health insurance has been on the products after the occurrence of illness while the preventive aspects have been ignored. The health care aspect in health insurance has yet to gain in importance. The products covering environmental and financial risks are non-existent. Another area, which has remained untapped, is the development of saving linked non-life policies in the country. The countries like Japan has innovated several saving linked non-life policies and the premium from these covers was as much as 40% of the total non-life business premium in 1986.

5. Productivity

There could be several parameters to measure the productivity in the insurance sector. These could be in terms of collection of premium per development officer, issuance of documents per employee, claim settlement per employee, underwriting results, yield on investment income, etc. However, measuring productivity in terms of collection of premium per development officer, issuance of policy documentation and claim settlement by Class III employees indicate that it was quite on a low scale and needs to be enhanced. For instance, collection of premium per development officer is about 600 and the claim settlement per Class III employees is 50 on an annual basis.

6. Lower Spread of Information Technology

The spread of information technology in the industry has not been to the desired extent. The upgradation of technology does not necessarily restrict itself to the process of computerization, which is already taking place in the industry, but through it a wide database has to be built up for being utilized by the insurance companies, agents and consumers. There is a need to create technology infrastructure such as electronic fund transfer, internet, automatic teller machines, interactive voice response, electronic data interchange, local network services, etc. The use of internet and e-commerce for selling the insurance products has yet not commenced in the industry. Presently about 0.2% of premium in USA and 0.02% in Europe is generated through internet.

However, the increasing importance of internet in marketing of insurance products is revealed by the fact that out of the total customers with internet access 45% in USA and 7% in Europe used internet for on-line search even though the policies were sold through conventional methods. Further, as per the estimates of the Swiss Re Economic Research and Consultancy by 2005 out of the total of personal lives business, the on-line sale will rise by 8% in USA and 4% in Europe.

7. India's Share in the World

The total insurance business in India comprising both non-life and life business constituted only 0.42% of the total world insurance market in 1997. The relative figures for Japan, South Korea, UK and USA were 31.61%,

3.47%, 8.24% and 25.37%. The share of entire Asian insurance business in the total insurance business was 38.53%.

14.5 LIBERALIZATION OF INSURANCE INDUSTRY IN INDIA

The Government of India in 1993 had set-up a high powered committee by R.N. Malhotra, former Governor, Reserve Bank of India, to examine the structure of the insurance industry and recommend changes to make it more efficient and competitive keeping in view structural changes in other parts of the financial system of the economy.

Major Recommendations of Malhotra Committee

The committee submitted its report in January 1994 recommending that private insurers be allowed to coexist along with government companies like LIC and GIC companies. This recommendation had been prompted by several factors such as need for greater and deeper insurance coverage in the economy and a much greater scale of insurance sector is at least partly driven by fiscal necessity of tapping the big reserves of savings in the economy. Committee's recommendations were as follows:

(i) Raising the capital base of LIC and GIC upto Rs. 200 crores, half retained by the government and rest sold to the public at large with suitable reservations for employees.

(ii) Private sector be granted permission to enter insurance industry with a minimum paid up capital of Rs. 100 crores.

(iii) Foreign insurance companies be allowed to enter by floating an Indian company preferably joint venture with Indian partners.

(iv) Steps to be initiated to set-up a strong and effective insurance regulatory in the form of statutory autonomous board on the lines of SEBI.

(v) Limited number of private companies to be allowed in the sector. But no firm be allowed to operate in both lines of insurance (life or non-life).

(vi) Tariff Advisory Committee (TAC) is delinked from GIC to function as a seperate statutory body under necessary supervision by the insurance regulatory authority.

(vii) All insurance companies be treated on equal footing and governed by the provisions of the insurance act. No special dispensation is given to government companies.

(viii) Setting up of a strong and effective regulatory body with independent source for financing before allowing private companies into sector.

14.6 INTRODUCTION OF INSURANCE REGULATORY AND DEVELOPMENT AUTHORITY (IRDA) ACT, 1999

On the basis of the recommendations of Malhotra Committee the government constituted through an interim Insurance Regulator Authority on 23rd January, 1996. IRA bill was introduced in Parliament in 1996. The Bill was retitled as Insurance Regulatory and Development Authority and introduced again in 1999 along with three schedules containing amendments to the Insurance Act, 1938, LIC Act, 1956 and GIC Act, 1922 and was passed.

Main Provisions of IRDA Act

Preamble of IRDA Act, 1999 reads "An Act to provide for the establishment of an authority to protect the interests of holders of insurance policies, to regulate, promote and insure orderly growth of the insurance industry and for matters connected therewith and incidental thereto." Section 14 of IRDA Act, lays the duties, powers and functions of the authority. The power and function of the authority shall include the following:

(i) Issue to the applicant a certificate of registration, to review, modify, withdraw, suspend or cancel such registration.
(ii) To protect the interest of policyholders in all matters concerning nomination of policy, surrender value of policy, insurable interest, settlement of insurance claims, other terms and conditions of contract of insurance.
(iii) Specifying requisite qualification and practical training for insurance intermediary and agents.
(iv) Specifying code of conduct for surveyors and loss assessors.
(v) Promoting efficiency in the conduct of insurance businesses.
(vi) Promoting and regulating professional regulation connected with the insurance and reinsurance business.
(vii) Specifying the form and manner in which books of accounts will be maintained and statement of accounts rendered by insurer and insurance intermediaries.
(viii) Adjudication of disputes between insurers and intermediaries.
(ix) Specifying the percentage of life insurance and general business to be undertaken by the insurers in rural or social sectors, etc.
(x) Section 25 provides that Insurance Advisory Committee will be constituted and shall consist of not more than 25 members.
(xi) Section 26 provides that authority may in consultation with insurance advisory committee make regulation consistent with this Act and the rules made thereunder to carry out the purpose of this Act.
(xii) Section 29 seeks amendment in certain provisions of Insurance Act, 1938 in the manner as set out in First Schedule. The amendments to the Insurance Act are consequential in order to empower IRDA to effectively regulate, promote, and insure

orderly growth of the insurance industry.

(xiii) Sections 30 and 31 seek to amend LIC Act, 1956 and GIC Act 1972.

14.7 IMPACT OF LIBERALIZATION ON INSURANCE INDUSTRY

The opening-up of insurance sector for competition offers ample opportunities to both existing as well as new players to penetrate into untapped areas, sectors and sub-sectors and unexploited segments of population as presently both insurance density and penetration are at low level. Both indices being at very low level in the country even compared to the countries with the same level of economic development and per capita income are indicative of the vast potential of the growth of this sector in future.

I. Opportunities

1. Untapped Market

New comers will get the benefit of untapped market. While nationalized general insurance companies and LIC of India have done a commendable job in extending their services throughout the country but the choices available to the insuring public are inadequate in terms of services, products and prices the untapped potential is quite large. The Malhotra Committee, which went into various aspects of India's insurance industry, estimated that in life insurance, 22% of the insurable population has been tapped so far. In India, premium per capita is only 2 and premium as percentage of GDP is 0.55%, which is very less in comparison of USA where premium per capita is 1381 and premium as percentage of GDP is 4.80. This huge gap from the global bench mark is itself lucrative.

2. Mandatory Insurance

In disaster prone areas, Government of India is going to make insurance mandatory. The interim report of the high powered committee set-up by the centre on disaster management, has proposed mandatory insurance of life and property by people residing in disaster prone area such as coastal belts, flood prone areas, site near nuclear, chemical and hazardous industries and thickly populated areas.

3. More Products Offered

A state monopoly has little incentive to offer a wide range of products. It can be seen by a lack of certain products from LIC's portfolio and lack of extensive categorization in several GIC products such as health insurance. More competition in this business will spur firms to offer several new products and more complex and extensive risk categorization.

4. Growth of Economy

With allowing of holding of equity shares by foreign company either itself or through its subsidiary company or nominee not exceeding 26% of paid up capital of Indian Insurance Company, various joint ventures between foreign investors and Indian partners will be operated resulting into supplementing domestic savings and economic progress of the nations.

5. Opportunity for Banks

Banks with their wide area network with branches in all the parts of the country will have very good opportunity to enter the insurance business. They will succeed in this sector because they have data base of customers, trained staff, a good network of branches besides synergy benefits.

6. Better Customer Services

It would result in better customers services and help improve the variety and price of insurance products. Competition will compel the players to bring new and innovative product, wider choice of prices and quality service to consumers.

2. Challenges

Whether the insurer is old or new, private or public, expansion of market will present multitude of challenges.

1. New Insurers

New insurers will have to invest a minimum capital of Rs. 100 crore. The normal gestation period is of five years. Hence, the new insurers will have to lock up their capital for at least five years before earning any profits. Besides they will face problems of shortage of trained manpower for the insurance industry. The setting up of various offices and distribution network is a time consuming process. Further, the new insurers will have to compete with the established insurance companies like LIC and GIC which have a corporate image and market presence for several years.

2. Expectations of the Consumers

Today, LIC has more than 60 products and GIC has more than 180 products to offer in market. But most of them are outdated, as they are not suitable to the needs of the consumers. Hence, all the insurers will have to offer innovative products to the consumers. The consumers are particularly expecting good pension plans, health insurance, term insurance, and investment products like unit linked insurance from the life insurers. Similarly, the consumers expect innovative products from the general insurers for managing health care, property insurance, accident insurance and other products at an attractive terms and premium. The consumers also expect reduction in the premium of the insurance products as the mortality rate in India has come down by three times in the last five years.

3. Premium on Customer Service

The days of giving fixed insurance products are over. Now customers need insurance solutions that match their wants. The large scale of operation, public sector bureaucracies and cumbersome procedures hampers nationalised insurers. Therefore, potential private entrants expect to score in the areas of customer service, speed and flexibility. It may mean better products and choice for the consumer. For giving better services insurance companies will have to build call centres to provide call free telephone-based sales and service. The call centres will provide product-related information, customer account information, query and complaint handling. These call centres can also be used for outbound sales and marketing campaigns.

4. *Distribution Channel*

In the liberalized insurance market, there will be multiple distribution channels, which will include agents, brokers, corporate intermediaries, bank branches, affinity groups and direct marketing through telesales and internet. There will be competition among the channels. Intense competition will grow among the old and new insurers in the market to win consumers. This will pose a great challenge to the insurers in the liberalised insurance market.

There would be substantial shift in the distribution of insurance in India. Many of these changes will echo international trends. World-wide, insurance products move along a continuum from pure service products to pure commodity products then they could be sold through the medical shops, groceries, novelty stores, etc. Once the products gain awareness and popularity then they can move to remote channels such as telephone or direct mail.

5. *Consumer Education*

The existing level of awareness of the consumers for insurance products is very low, it is so because 62% of the population is literate and less than 10% well educated. Even the educated consumers are ignorant about the various products of insurance. Hence, it is necessary that all the insurers should undertake the extensive plan for education of consumers. The consumer organisations and media also can play very important role in education of the consumers. This will result in expansion of the insurance market and will also enable the needy consumer to purchase appropriate products. In fact, the private entrants have already started putting a lot more emphasis on advertising and using creative tricks to educate the consumers.

6. *Consumer Grievance Redressal*

The insurers will have to face an acute problem of the redressal of consumers' grievances for deficiency in products and services. The IRDA has already appointed ombudsman for looking into the grievances of the policyholders, its judgement will be binding on insurers. In the competitive market, awareness level of consumers will increase and it will help consumers to fight for their legal right for deficiency in services. Hence, the number of legal cases filed by the consumers against insurers is likely to increase substantially in future. This will be a challenge to the insurers.

7. New Product Innovations

One researcher shows that two products of LIC dominate with majority share out of 52 products. With more competition good products will become an important differentiator among the various competiting insurance products. A lot will depend on the kind of products that these outfits launch. Initially after launching simple products multinationals will shift to specialised products. Royal Sundaram Alliance for example will launch a mix of personal and commercial insurance policies. This will cover fire, marine, motor, personal accident and health insurance. HDFC-Standard Life will launch two core life insurance products and then another dozen of the same type.

8. Positioning of Insurance Products

On the ground, the biggest challenge for the insurance companies will be to change the mindset of people, specially in life insurance. In India, life insurance is seen more as a tax saving mechanism rather than safety net in case of death. ICICI Prudential Life Insurance chief marketing officer Sangata Gupta also says that "working on consumer attitude will be the greatest challenge." New types of products should be futuristic in outlook. To start with, low premium high cover policies should be introduced and better savings products at a latter stage.

9. Rural Area Exploitations

It is said that the life insurance business suffers from high premium and low returns. A normally competitive industry should be able to increase coverage, mobilize large savings, and provide high returns. India is ranked at 27th in the world in terms of mobilizing savings in the form of insurance. In countries like U.K. and South Africa, life insurance premiums account for over 50 per cent of gross domestic savings (GDS). Insurance in India has been a priority of the urban few. Now with numerous companies set to enter, the rural areas are expected to be tapped as well. IRDA has made it mandatory for life insurers to sell 5 per cent of their aggregate policies in the rural areas during the first year of operation that will be progressively increased to 15 per cent by the fifth year. But with gestation period long and investments large new entrants will feel very difficult to do it.

10. Information Technology

Information technology (IT) has become an intrinsic part of the insurance industry world-wide from general accounting to customer service, reinsurance, underwriting, and risk management. Further, these have integrated application and are decision-oriented. In the Indian insurance industry, IT is used as a reporting tool whereas overseas it is used more as a decision-making instrument. Once on line customers with net connectivity would be able to check policy details from their balance to nominee schemes, the type of loans available and the amount in their investment accounts. Similarly, insurance advisors can check their customer's accounts as well as their own account.

3. Strategies

To be more competitive and responsive to the needs of the societies, the insurance players would be required to concentrate on the following major strategies:

1. Environmental Analysis

The companies should concentrate on environmental change, its direction, magnitude and its short-term and long-term impact, formulating strategies to meet the challenges of high competition, preparing contingency plans and then designing action plans for effective implementations of formulated strategies.

2. Restructuring Organisations

The traditional hierachy system is very slow in making decisions due to several levels of management, due to its procedural inflexibility and slow communication. A manager in the privatised scenario is required to be an organisational specialist, country specialist and a global specialist.

3. Speed, Cost Effectiveness and Innovations

The insurance companies will have to make substantial investments in customer relationship management technologies. They will be required to have wide area networks (WAN) connecting branches spread across wide geographical locations and workout modalities facilitating premium payment through the internet. LIC is setting up an interactive response systems in more cities so that a policyholder need not to travel to company's office for information. After all, the customer should have the choice of getting work done in the shortest possible time without having to visit insurer's office.

4. Human Resource Development

Human capital is important for any organisation especially for organisations whose activities revolve around special human interactions. Alongwith products and services the new insurers need people with the right set of knowledge, skills and aptitude for insurance. The persons who are involved in selling the product and those who are doing the back office work need to equip themselves with newer skills and insights into every aspect of company's functioning. They have a daunting task of exploiting potential in the industry and at the same time bring good risks to the company for providing insurance coverage. They have to retain the existing customers for which they need to have better understanding of products and services by creating healthy internal environment with group harmony. Existing companies will have to frame their human resource policies to retain the competent and motivated staff since new entrants will be eying them by offering lucrative salaries.

5. Efficiency in Distribution

It is very important factor and may prove bottleneck to the new players. Insurance companies are making the products available through the ready distribution channels of banks, non-banking finance companies and housing companies. One has to be careful doing this, since creating distribution and distances doesn't automatically mean controlling them. With the starting of corporate agencies, there will be more places from where customer can buy insurance besides the consultants and agents currently selling these policies. Taking this aspect into consideration 'Bancassurance' has emerged which is defined as a service that the insurance companies use to offer their products through the distribution channels of banking industry. A need to augment sources of revenues for survival has prompted two big classes of financial institutions to combine their strengths and create a new means of marketing and servicing their products. Convergence of banking sector traditionally considered being more competitive and insurance sector having a vast untapped potential of growth has resulted into bancassurance.

6. Risk Management

Like all intermediaries in financial markets, insurance companies will have to bring sophistication in market research techniques future portfolio expansion.

7. Efficient Marketing Strategies

Marketing strategies for insurance products in the emerging scenario could be understood in following steps:

$$R \rightarrow STP \rightarrow MM \rightarrow I \rightarrow C$$

where R = Market research,
STP = Segmentation, Targeting, Positioning,
MM = Marketing Mix,
I = Implementation, and
C = Control.

The focus of emerging strategies would centre on the prepositions like reduce costs, increase profitability, reduce time to market, improve customer intimacy, retain customers for life, establish strong partnerships. Formulation of a marketing strategy is more a process than an event. Environmental factors like macro-economic parameters, regulatory norms and themes, technology, infrastructure, legal set-up, competition by way of new entry, degree of globalisation need be scanned and considered in framing the likely scenarios. The competitive advantage of a company may stem from the many discrete activities in value chains. Each of these activities can contribute to a company's relative cost position or create a basis for a differentiation.

8. Ethical Issues

The governance problems in service industry like insurance have been raised time and again and they have created as well as risk management techniques. Companies will need to leverage this sophistication backed by information technology to select good risks and rate them. On the other hand, insurance companies invest the policyholder's funds as well as owned capital and accumulated surpluses and reserves. Companies tries to earn highest rate of return possible on investments consistent with risk objectives, because premiums are related to investment performance. As the rate of return on investment increases, the company can lower the premiums it charges on new policies. Higher rate of return provide higher earning on cash values and lesser the need for premium revenues. Premium rates are a competitive factor and high investment returns are crucial in maintaining and improving an insurance company's sales position. Strong investment performance supports growth in policy sales and sense of helplessness among the employees and customers alike. Companies must realise this particularly in the emerging scenario of intense competition wherein customers will have a range of options. At the same time regulators and companies will have to be cautious of customers who indulge in unethical practices by manipulating or hiding vital information in their dealings with companies and inflict losses resulting in increase in cost of insurance. Ethics will have to be insured in every activity of the company.

14.8 CURRENT SCENARIO OF INSURANCE INDUSTRY

After opening up of insurance to private sector, seventeen new players have entered in the field of insurance both life and non-life business. Some of these are Tata-AIG, Birla Sunlife, HDFC Standard Life Insurance, Kotak Mahindra Old Mutual Life Insurance, Reliance General Insurance, ICICI Prudential Life Insurance, Royal Sundaram Alliance Insurance, Bajaj Auto Alliance, IFFCO Tokyo General Insurance, INA Vysya Life Insurance, SBI Life Insurance, Dabur CJU Life Insurance, Max New York Life.

SBI Life Insurance has launched three products—Sanjeevan, Sukhjeevan and Young Sanjeevan and so far it has sold more than 300 policies under its plan. Various insurance companies have tied up with banks to market their products. For example, HDFC Standard life has tied up with Indian Bank and UCO Bank in the eastern region. It has also entered into MOU with Peerless Bank as the corporate branches will help a rural reach for insurance company. Proposed joint venture Dabur CJU Life Insurance where Dabur group holds 74 per cent and U.K.-based CJU life's 26 per cent stake would be started with an equity capital of Rs. 110 crores. CGNU group being U.K's largest insurer and world's sixth larger insurer with assets worth $ 300 bn under its management and Dabur being India's leading FMCG Company, this venture may emerge as a leading player in insurance indsutry. Kotak Mahindra is likely to get approval for two more products which include term insurance and equity link policy in a bid to offer wider range of products.

14.9 SUMMARY

In India till now only 20% of the insurable population is covered under insurance while the remaining population is yet to be insured. As the insurance sector has been opened up, the monopoly of government companies has broken and many new private players have entered into the insurance sector and thus the sector has become highly competitive with full of challenges. The insurance and the economic growth of the country mutually influence each other. As the economy grows, the standard of living people also improves. In fact as the economy widens, the demand for insurance product emerges. A well developed insurance sector promotes economic growth by encouraging risk taking. The average annual rate of growth of the economy in the first three decades after independence was 3.5%. In the nineties, the average annual rate of growth of income has been 5.8% per annum. Life expectency has also increased from 32 years in fifties to 61 years now. As life expectancy increases there will be a need to take care of long retired life. Hence, the Indian life insurance market alongwith general insurance market is full of potential. Only the need is to frame strategies to tap the whole market in more efficient and effective manner.

14.10 REVIEW QUESTIONS

1. Evaluate the performance of insurance industry in pre-liberalization era?
2. Why there was a need to liberalize the insurance business?
3. What are the challenges before the players in liberalization era and how can they effectively manage them?

15

CHAPTER

COMPARATIVE ENVIRONMENT OF INSURANCE

LEARNING OBJECTIVE

The main objective of this chapter is to make the students familiar with the comparative understanding of insurance environment in India and abroad.

15.1 INTRODUCTION

The development of insurance industry is linked with the broad-spectrum escalation of industry, trade and commerce. The derivation of insurance services may be traced back to 14th century in Italy when ships carrying goods were covered under poles apart. The logical and orderly beginning of insurance industry took place in UK at Lloyds coffee house at Tower Street in London. The insurance industry assisted the growth process of the UK economy in several ways. This prompted the rapid imitation of institutionalization of insurance industry in other developed countries. The primary functions of insurance business being drinking of unforeseen contingent financial losses from business operations helped the smooth progress of trade and commerce in these countries. Later on, insurance industry also became an additional tool for mobilization of savings, promoter of investment activity, stabilizer of financial market and an agent to allocate capital resources efficiently. Although the insurance industry has grown rapidly in the insurance developed economies, its growth in developing countries has neither been satisfactory nor in tandem with the growth of other sectors of the economy. The 12 most industrialized countries in the world still account for 88% of global premium volume. The share of developing countries is extremely low. Regrettably, the Indian insurance industry has been lagging behind even amongst the developing countries of the world.

Table 15.1 depicts the share of life insurance premium in Gross Domestic Savings (GDS) of different countries of the world. In South Africa, life fund as a percentage of GDS was as high as 80 percent. It was also quite high in UK (55.4%), Switzerland (28.2%), France (27.5%), Japan (27.1%), South Korea (25.9%) and USA (25.4%). This share is perceptibly low in case of most of the developing countries including India (6.2%), Malaysia (9.2%), China (1.2%), Brazil (2.2%). It indicates that sophistication of financial markets is reflected generally in the high ratio of life premium to GDS. In other words, development of financial market requires strengthen of insurance industry to a large extent. The point of clarification in this context is that the non-life funds are usually not termed as savings as the premium paid is not returned to the insured and it only covers the losses suffered by him. Of course, in the general insurance also, there could be savings linked polices as has been the case in Japanese economy.

Composition of Gross Domestic Product (GDP) and Insurance Penetration has close relationship. Invariably, larger the share of service sector in the composition of GDP, higher the insurance penetration in these countries. Since, it is the developed countries, that are having higher share in service sector and developing countries have relatively lower proportion of their GDP originating from services, same trend can be found in insurance penetration in these countries. Table 15.2 shows this trend quite clearly.

TABLE 15.1

Life Premium as Percentage of Gross Domestic Savings (GDS)

Country	*Life Fund as % of GDS*
USA	25.40
Canada	15.70
Brazil	2.20
Germany	4.05
UK	55.40
France	27.50
Switzerland	28.20
Japan	27.10
South Korea	25.90
China	1.19
Malaysia	9.20
India	6.20
Philippines	4.10
South Africa	80.90

Source: Calculated from the *World Development Report, 1998-99, 1999-2000* and *World Insurance in 1997: Booming Life Insurance but Stagnating Non-Life Insurance Business, Sigma-Swiss*, No. 3/ 1999.

TABLE 15.2

Life Insurance Penetration in Various Countries

Country	*GDP Break up (as % of GDP)*			*Services Break up (as % of GDP)*	
	Agri.	*Ind.*	*Services*	*Other services*	*Insurance*
USA	2	23	75	70.36	4.46
UK	2	28	70	66.66	3.34
France	2	26	72	69.09	2.91
Japan	2	38	60	57.55	2.45
Russia	7	39	54	52.90	1.10
South Korea	6	43	51	47.21	3.9
South Africa	5	39	56	52.52	3.48
Malysia	13	46	41	38.81	2.19
Brazil	14	36	50	48.26	1.74
Philippines	20	32	48	47.20	0.80
China	20	51	29	28.36	0.64
India	27	30	43	42.44	0.56
Egypt	16	31	53	52.48	0.52
Pakistan	26	25	49	48.58	0.42

Source: Calculated from the *World Development Report, 1998-99, 1999-2000* and *World Insurance in 1997: Booming Life Insurance but Stagnating Non-Life Insurance Business, Sigma-Swiss,* No. 3/1999.

TABLE 15.3

Insurance Density and Per Capita GDP in 1998 (US $)

Country	*Per capita GDP*	*Per Capita Premium*
Switzerland	41,857	4998
Japan	33,349	3959
USA	28,903	24,54
Germany	25,610	1672
UK	21,559	2419
Russia	3,000	42
South Korea	9630	1485
Brazil	4,793	102
Malaysia	4667	204
China	672	10
India	375	7
Indonesia	1075	13

Source: Calculated from the *World Development Report, 1998-99, 1999-2000* and *World Insurance in 1997: Booming Life Insurance but Stagnating Non-Life Insurance Business, Sigma-Swiss,* No. 3/1999.

The insurance density has been defined as per capita expenditure on insurance premium. The insurance density has a direct correlation to per capita GDP income of the country. The lower per capita GDP translates itself into low insurance density in the country. The per capita of GDP is as high US $ 17,250, on an average for all developed countries as against an average of US $ 5800 for all developing countries. The insurance density in developed countries is US $ 1302 against the insurance density in developing countries of US $ 26.3. Table 15.3 gives the details related to insurance density and per-capita GDP during the year 1998 (in US $).

15.2 GROWTH AND REGULATION OF INSURANCE INDUSTRY

Insurance constitutes as one of the major segments of financial market. Insurance services play predominant role in the process of capital formation of the country as mobiliser of savings and also financial intermediary. The insurance industry commands massive funds through sale of insurance products to a large number of individuals and organizations. During the process of conducting insurance business, insurers also create liabilities and commit themselves to compensate for the losses occurring to the policyholders on a future date. The insurance business is unique in the sense that it is rewarded for managing the risk of other parties. And management of risk has inherent problem of asymmetry of information leading to adverse selection and moral hazard. Obviously, insurance business is more risky in comparison to other financial services. The long-term nature of funds management also aggravates the riskiness of this industry. The issue of regulation of insurance industry becomes more pertinent in the wake of policy of encouragement to private competition in the insurance sector. In view of the problems and risks involved in the insurance services the governments have regulated the growth and practice of insurance the world over. The forms of controls and regulations exercised over insurance industry have differed from country to country. The nature and pattern of controls in a country are shaped by its political and economic philosophy, economic and social compulsions, and pressure from invested groups and past experience, etc. Based upon these factors, different countries have evolved their own regulatory mechanism being applicable to insurance industry. Some of the countries have imposed controls over the activities of insurers to promote free and healthy competition amongst them, while others have encouraged self-control system to greater role being assigned to actuaries, auditors, professionals, etc.

In the present chapter, the endeavour is to highlight the growth and regulation-related issues of UK, USA, Japan, and its comparison with the overall environment of Indian insurance industry.

15.3 INSURANCE INDUSTRY IN UK

Insurance services in UK, grew as early as in 16th century, the sector was practically without government control and intervention till 1870, when Life Insurance Act was passed. The Act as such did not impose any restriction on the sector but simply made it obligatory on the companies engaged in insurance business to disclose their financial and other details to the public and get their finances evaluated by an actuary. The companies were required to be transparent in their dealings and make their accounts and evaluation reports available to the Board of Trade. It may be pertinent to mention here that no powers were delegated to the board to initiate any action against any company. Basically it reflected the policy political philosophy of UK, which believed in the policy of *laissez-faire*.

The economic basis of the insurance contract, which was started in inceptive marine insurance contract form in 14th century by Italian traders as an add-on feature for commercial contract for export of goods was fully developed by Lloyds' Marine Underwriters and later on by British Fire Insurance Company Underwriters in 19th century to stabilize the instability in the operation of fire insurance companies. Early approach of fire and marine underwriters to the issue of pricing of risks was appreciated and supported by Adam Smith in 1776 in the following words: "That the chance of loss is frequently undervalued and scarce ever valued more than its worth, we may learn from a very moderate profit of insurers. In order to make insurance, either from fire or sea risk, a trade at all, the common premium must be sufficient to compensate the common losses to pay the expense of management and to afford such profit as might have been drawn from an equal capital employed in any common trade."

Underwriting of fire insurance business by British progressed on the basic principle of generating surplus after payment of agency commissions and claims and by incurring of administrative expenses. Monopoly pricing of fire insurance was, however, challenged by British policyholders after the historical event of Tooley Street Fire in June 1861 which led to the amendment of London Mercantile Tariff and establishment of Fire Office's Committee to monitor changes in premium rates of various types of industrial risks developing during the phase of industrial revolution. The same approach of pricing insurance risk was adopted by underwriters of miscellaneous accident business, which developed to meet socio-economic technological needs of new economy emerging in UK and Europe.

Modularization of insurance sector also emerged from the same approach of sharing of surplus generated by charging right type of price for risk and sharing of the losses or surplus amidst the policyholders and insurers who had direct stake in the ownership and management of mutual as compared to the shareholders of stock companies whose interest was only in terms of security of their capital and adequate return thereon. By the end of the 19th century insurance industry in UK was subject to widening statutory control through insurance legislation. Price control of insurance products, particularly, pertaining to covers for social insurance risks like employer's liability and medical insurance remained under vigilance of the Government. The basic financial equation of the operation of general insurance market in the 19th century in Britain was: Premium—[(Claims + Expenses + Commission) + Reserve Strain)] = Underwriting surplus.

Pricing of the insurance product was expected to generate underwriting surplus by all insurers irrespective of whether they were members of tariff association or operated as non-tariff insurers. Investment income generated from insurance funds was treated as welcome add-on to the pricing of general insurance products.

It is worth mentioning that global recession of 1930s did not affect the financial health of general insurance sector of UK. Interestingly, as per UK Government Committee's reports, from 1925 insurers for workmen's compensation insurance charged onwards excessive price and that became an important factor behind the take-over of this scheme by post-war labour government in 1945. The labour government also started National Health Insurance Scheme keeping private general insurance companies, again out of this scheme for the same reason.

Some of the important developments in the insurance sector, after the post-war period in UK are mentioned as under:

- Excessive competition for business led to decline of premium rates (price for insurance products) to inadequate level creating underwriting losses on long-term basis.
- Return on investment in stocks/security market promoted cash flow basis for development of general insurance business. Investment income became the primary source of profit compensating underwriting losses arising from inadequate pricing.
- Formation of captives, pools, self-insurance schemes, supported by global reinsures promoted shift from conventional to non-conventional insurance systems.
- Concentration of business in limited number of mega-size companies. Medium· size and small companies could not withstand the practice of competition and had to survive on limited volumes of business from their niche market sectors.

In UK, as many as 96% of the bank and the building societies deal with insurance.

15.4 INSURANCE INDUSTRY IN USA

USA is the most developed and refined economy of the world and so is state of development of its insurance industry. But even in USA the industry is substantially regulated by the Controllers of Insurance Office. In the US, 3500 general insurance companies are in operation, but only 15 (0.4 percent) of them control 50 percent of the market. Six percent of the companies together control ninety-five percent of the market. Similarly, there are more than 1500 active life insurance companies of which top 10 account for 50 percent of the total assets in the Sector (Bedi, 2001). Other indicators related to insurance sector also support the highly developed nature of US insurance business. For instance, in USA insurance density or per capita premium in 1997 was US $ 2570.6 (Non-Life US $ 1167.0 + Life US $ 1167.0). Insurance penetration or premium as percent of GDP in USA in 1997 was 8.49 (Non-Life 4.64 + Life 3.85). While Life Premium as percent of Gross Domestic Saving (GDS) in USA was 25.40. USA has been known for its innovations in product development and coverage of new sectors into insurance sector. Health insurance, insurance of agricultural produce, reinsurance, insurance through Internet are some of the features of the innovative nature of US insurance sector.

USA depends primarily upon the private players in insurance business with a regulatory framework encouraging and ensuring free competition amongst the participants. Since 1982, above 370 general insurance companies have become insolvent while, one life insurance company goes into liquidation every month because of risky investments.

In health insurance sector in US, all the players are private companies covering around 70 percent of population. However, coverage is highly unequal as premium charged for health coverage depends on age, sex, and disease. Obviously premium differ from case to case basis and sometimes even refusal is also possible on the part of insurers. The important point to note in this connection is that there is minimal government regulation with the obvious implications on medical costs that are unusually high. In agriculture sector, US companies have gone ahead and introduced the concept of covering loss to revenue arising out of fall in agricultural prices. In most of the other countries, the common perils to which agriculture is exposed to are covered under crop insurance. These include perils caused by fire, flood, hailstorm, earthquakes, landslides, damage by birds and animals, pests, insects, diseases, etc. Normally, losses sustained due to price fluctuations are not covered. But USA insurance sector has made provision for this also, in sense assuring farmers' minimum support price of their produce for payment of a risk premium. In this unique way farmers get security of revenue without depending upon the government budgetary support. The schemes with different features are optional for the farmers. And premium ranges between 5 percent and 7 percent of the value of insured crop. The point to note here is that in most of the schemes, government acts as a reinsurer. The scheme is managed by "Federal Crop Insurance Corporation, Commercial and Mutual Insurance Companies, and Managing General Agencies."

Bancassurance (Synergising the strength of bank with insurance company) was initially developed and popularized in France. But over the last 10 years the US insurance industry has gone for Bancassurnace in a big way to tap the America's mass market. In 1998, two financial giants City Bank and the Travelers, engineered a $ 37 billion merger to form Citigroup with the goal of integrating banking and insurance operations. In fact in USA, commonly bankassurance policy is tilted towards leasing space to insurance company and retail products of multiple insurers. This has led to an increase in buyer's confidence in the products. In addition to bancassurance in the US 53 percent of the total media spend is on direct marketing.

The need for reinsurance follows the same business and financial considerations as an original insured would require insuring with any insurance company. The US insurance companies being in the hands of private owners have focused to manage their risk in a more professional manner. To cover the unforeseen and unique risk like terrorist attack on WTC on Sept. 11, 2001 and earthquake in Jan. 26 in Kutch, Gujarat most of the smart insurance companies go for reinsurance cover to compensate for losses beyond pre determined magnitude. Insurance companies in the USA have found alternative ways to combat default risks through introduction of innovative financial instruments or non-conventional insurance techniques. The coverage of such schemes is designed tailor-made to suit the insurance company's requirement and achieve the broader objectives. Priorities have shifted to Solutions, which protect the entire balance sheet. Whether clients refer to them as funding, financial, finite, blended or non-traditional reinsurance, they are but the same by going beyond conventional reinsurance. In this system, practically the ceding company pays most of its losses, but the reinsurer ensures that such burden on the ceding company's liquidity is evenly spread over a period of time.

15.5 INSURANCE INDUSTRY IN JAPAN

Japan has one of the most developed insurance sectors in the world. The insurance density was as high as US $ 3896 (Non-Life US $ 3092 + Life US $ 804). The insurance penetration is 11.87 percent (Non-Life 9.42 percent + Life 2.45 percent). The growth rate in real terms for entire industry was 0.8 percent in 1990s, while in non-life business it was –4.0 percent and in life business at 2.1 percent. The share of the total insurance premium to world premium was 23.05 percent reflecting a disproportionately large share in world insurance business. In non-life business, share of Japan in world premium as 11.29 percent while it was 31.61 percent in case of life business. The entire insurance business is regulated under Insurance Business Law, 1995. Insurance Division of the Ministry of Finance supervises the insurance business. For obtaining a license to conduct insurance business, the minimum capital requirement is Japanese yen Y 30 million. Under the new business act, both foreign and domestic companies receive same treatment.

The new regulatory framework put in place in Japan in 1995 has encouraged the competition in insurance sector. The analyses of the performance of the insurance industry indicate that the deepening and widening of the insurance services are positively correlated to the degree of competition and the number of firms in the market. The Japanese general insurance market has growth from US $ 0.15 billion in 1950 to US $ 80 billion in 1990. Thereafter it has shown fluctuating trend. The basis of sound growth of insurance sector in post-war has been the policy of maintaining the level of tariff ensuring underwriting surplus in the region of 0.5 percent to 2.0 percent

Another notable feature of Japanese insurance industry is the concentration of business with limited number of large-size companies. This was the outcome of Japanese corporate structure that tied corporate portfolios to their group insurance companies. Even though personal insurance sector developed through new products like Saving Linked Insurance Schemes which contributed 70 percent of total non-life insurance premium in 1980, yet stiff competition at economic price resulted in concentration of business in large size companies with huge financial reserves ensuring higher investment returns on saving linked part of premium. Since 1990s the tariff controlled Japanese general insurance business started its transformation into free market-based system. This transformation was forced by the intense pressure exerted by the wave of globalization in Japanese markets in the 1990s. The market forces pushed the premium rates down eliminating the traditionally enjoyed underwriting surplus in Japanese market. The impact of the disappearance on insurance surplus in Japan is more than substantial. Since the 1990s premium growth rate has declined sharply affecting the financial viability of the industry. According to an estimate, Japanese market is not in a position to recover underwriting surplus in the region of 2 percent and generate underwriting loss at the level of 5 percent like western developed markets, it will be necessary for Japanese insurers to increase their traditional investment returns in the region of 4 percent to the adequate level to absorb underwriting loss and produce cumulative surplus which will give satisfactory returns to shareholders of insurance companies. In this difficult environment there will be further concentration of business in top 4-5 giant insurance companies and possibility of elimination of medium companies through closure or take-over is real. The recent trends indicate the growing importance of foreign companies in Japanese market. Particularly big insurance companies from USA and Western Europe are making their presence felt.

15.6 INSURANCE INDUSTRY IN INDIA

In India, Manusmriti (200 BC) provides Indian version of primitive marine insurance stipulating that "The trader should be made to pay (taxes or duties) to the state for providing Yogakshema (risk and safety) taking into consideration the terms of purchase, sale, the length of journey, expenses and incidentals. But the Britishers introduced the modern concept of insurance in India. Their operation was through agencies. The Triton Insurance Company Ltd. was the first insurance company established in India in 1858 at Kolkata. It was fully owned by the Britishers. The first Indian insurance company was Indian Mercantile Insurance Company Ltd. in Mumbai in 1907. However, till independence around 40 percent of the insurance business was controlled by the foreigners. In order to ensure fair and sound business and prevent unethical practices, Insurance Council framed a code of conduct that was administered by the Controller of Insurance. In 1956, to retain the reinsurance business within India, Indian Reinsurance Corporation was established. In 1961, Government constituted Indian Guarantee and General Insurance Company Ltd. as a government owned Reinsurance Corporation. The insurance companies were required to cede 10 percent of their premium to each of these two companies. In 1968, the Insurance Act, 1938 was amended in order to empower the Controller of Insurance to regulate deployment of assets, provided for maximum solvency margin, issue license to surveyors, investigate, search and seize their books of accounts, etc.

The general insurance business was nationalized w.e.f. Jan. 1, 1973, through the General Insurance business (Nationalization) Act, 1972. After nationalization in total 107 companies in business at that time were merged to form four companies, namely, the National Insurance Company Limited, the New India Assurance Company Ltd., the Oriental Insurance Company Ltd. and the United Insurance Company Ltd. with head offices at Kolkata, Mumbai, Delhi and Chennai respectively. In addition, the General Insurance Company was formed as a holding company in Nov. 1972. The main objectives of nationalization were to ensure the development of general insurance business in sympathy with the best interest and advantage to the country.

Initially, life insurance in India did not receive much attention. Therefore, Government of India in 1956 set-up Life-Insurance Corporation to promote life insurance in the country.

Since 1973, the insurance sector was totally under the control of Government of India. As a result of nationalization, revenue of both LIC and GIC, increased significantly over the years. The amount of savings pooled by LIC increased from Rs. 2704 crores in 1974 to Rs. 57,670 crores in 1994, showing an annual growth rate of 16.53 percent. Similarly, premium underwritten by GIC rose from Rs. 280 crores in 1973 to Rs. 6500 crores in 1997 showing an annual growth rate of 25.18 percent. Today, LIC has become the leading investment institution of India. In order to reach to people in every part of the country, it has developed a vast service network, comprising 7 zonal offices, 100 divisional offices and 2048 branch offices which together employ 1,24,000 persons and 6,61,000 agents. Besides, LIC contributed in social welfare projects like water supply, electricity, sewerage facilities, housing and transport, etc. mainly through life funds. Book value of socially oriented investment increased from Rs. 1218.52 crores in 1974-75 to Rs. 88,831 crores in 1998-99, showing an annual growth rate of 35.82 percent.

The growth in general insurance sector of its nationalization has equally been impressive. The Gross Domestic Premium Income (GDPI) in India, which was Rs. 184 crore in 1973, increased to Rs. 9522 crore in 1999-2000, recording an average growth rate of about 16.90 percent. Presently, although the total number of insurance products in general insurance industry are around 175, only 40 to 50 products have dominated the market controlling about 75 to 80 percent of total market. The rural and non-traditional business, which was practically nil in 1973, has gradually increased over a period of time. The premium collected through this business was about Rs. 425 core in 1999-2000, constituting only 4 percent of the total gross premium income.

The reinsurance operation of the industry indicate that the total reinsurance premium was Rs. 1011 crore in 1997-98 accounting for about 123 percent of the gross premium. It indicate that about 87 percent premium is retained in the country. Indian general insurance industry has spread its wings beyond the border to India. Presently it has operations in 30 countries. Out of these, in 16 countries it is operating directly and in 14 countries though subsidiary and associated companies. During the year 1999-2000 the total gross premium income from operations in these countries were Rs. 488.76 crore.

Despite the fact that the industry has grown after nationalization in terms of premium income, introduction of new products wide coverage of individuals and organization, creation of infrastructure at grass-root level, etc. several weaknesses have also been noticeable, particularly after the liberalization of economy since 1990s and changing requirement of the industry in its wake. Some of the problem areas are as follows:

Low Level of Insurance Penetration

Despite the growth of gross domestic premium by 47 times between 1973 to 1999-2000, the insurance penetration (insurance premium as share of gross domestic product) was only 0.56 percent in case of non-life business and 1.39 percent in the case of life insurance. This is much lower not only comparison to developed countries but even developing countries.

Low Level of Insurance Density

The available data shows that in India insurance density for non-life business was US $ 2.2 per capita, while for life business it was US $ 5.4. This is incredibly low in comparison to most of the developed and developing country.

Share in World Market is also pathetic to say the least. Presently it is only 0.42 percent of total world insurance market. One of the feature as well as the cause behind number of other problems in insurance sector in India is the lack of innovation in terms of product design, services, capturing of new sectors/markets, etc. As already mentioned only around 175 products are on office while really in demand product are barely 40 to 50. This needs immediate improvement.

15.7 RECENT DEVELOPMENTS IN INDIAN INSURANCE

The basic factor behind most of the shortcomings pointed out in Indian insurance sector, has been supposed to be lack of competition in Indian insurance market. The nationalized insurance companies perceive themselves to be extension of government and accordingly function in bureaucratic manner without giving regard to emerging requirement of the economy. This is reflected in their lack of innovation with regard to designing of products. Appreciating these concerns and realizing the utmost need of vibrant insurance industry Government of India decided to liberalize the industry. Accordingly, Insurance Regulatory and Development Authority Act, 1999 (IRDA, 1999) was enacted. The IRDA has been assigned basically three functions:

- The protection of consumer's interests;
- To ensure financial soundness of the insurance industry; and
- To ensure healthy growth of the insurance market.

In pursuance of its mandate, the IRDA acted with enthusiasm and announced draft guidelines for insurance brokers and agents for the first time differentiating the role of an insurance agent from that of a broker. In July 2000, the IRDA announced guidelines outlining the investment norms for private insurance companies, besides segregating the holding of foreign institutional investors (FIIs) from the purview of the 26 percent equally cap in insurance joint venture. IRDA has also started issuing licenses to private players in insurance sector. The IRDA guidelines for private players have stipulated specific norms regarding rural coverage, foreign investment, and reinsurance.

For instance, in the life insurance segment, as much as 5 percent of the policies would have to sold in rural sector, while for the general insurance sector this limit has been kept at 2 percent. Subsequently these limits will go up to 15 percent and 6 percent in case of life and non-life respectively.

Foreign investment has been limited to 26 percent of equity of the insurance firm. However, Foreign Institutional Insurers (FIIs) are kept outside this limit of 26 percent. On reinsurance, IRDA has been rather strict towards new entrants. It has ensured that the role of GIC will remain unhindered as national reinsurer.

The guidelines of IRDA have started showing results with the entry of number of new private insurance companies in the field. Their true impact will take some time to show an impact and it is too early to pass remark at this point of time.

15.8 SUMMARY

The growth of insurance industry is connected with the general growth of industry, trade and commerce. The most developed countries accounts for a lion's share in world premium volume. The share of developing countries in extremely low. The Indian insurance industry has lagged behind even amongst the developing countries of the world.

Most of the indicators for the development of insurance sector reflect the mature stage of insurance development in developed countries. For instance, Life insurance premium as percentage of Gross Domestic Savings in developed countries is around 30 percent, while it is around 8 percent in developing countries. Similarly, per capita insurance density in developed countries is US $ 1302 and it is only US $ 26.3 in developing countries.

Insurance industry in UK evolved in 16th century without any government central till 1870. But with the evolution of industry government also started regulatory the industry. Of late, excessive competitions by insurance industry has led to decline in premium rates causing loss to most of companies in business. New developments also indicate towards better fund management on the past of insurance companies.

US insurance industry primarily depends upon the private players, with a regulatory framework encouraging and ensuring free competition amongst the participants. The US insurance industry is known for its innovations in product development and coverage of new sectors. Health insurance, insurance of agricultural produce, reinsurance, insurance through internet are some of the features of the innovative.

Insurance business in Japan is also highly developed. Only 4-5 giant insurance companies dominate Japanese insurance sector. Since 1990s, the tariff controlled Japanese insurance business has started transforming itself into free market-based system.

Britishers in India started the modern insurance business in 1858. Life insurance sector was neglected by the private players, which prompted the government to establish Life Insurance Corporation in 1956. In 1972, the Government of India also nationalized general insurance business. Despite all these efforts, Indian insurance industry is far behind in comparison to most of the countries. The Government of India took new initiatives and decided to liberalize Indian insurance sector. Accordingly, Insurance Regulatory and Development Authority Act, 1999 was enacted. The IRDA has allowed entry of private players into insurance section in the country. Foreign participation up to the extent of 26 percent of total equity of the company has also been permitted. The new private players have started operations in the country. The effect of these private players will be known in future, as their operations are hardly 7-8 months old.

15.9 REVIEW QUESTIONS

1. Why development of insurance sector is dependent on the development of industry trade and commerce? Explain.
2. Discuss the evolution and statement feature of insurance sector in UK.
3. USA is known for its innovations in insurance sector. Discuss with suitable examples.
4. Why in Japan, insurance business is concentrated amongst 4-5 mega-size companies?
5. In India, nationalization failed to achieve the stated objectives. Comment.

16 CHAPTER

GOVERNMENT AND INSURANCE BUSINESS

LEARNING OBJECTIVE

The main objective of this chapter is to make the students familiar with the government schemes for motivating insurance business in India.

16.1 INTRODUCTION

The Union Government introduced the Insurance (Amendment) Bill, 2001 during the recently concluded monsoon session of Parliament. The draft bill proposes entry of cooperatives in the insurance sector, appointment of brokers as intermediaries, and payments for insurance through credit cards. The bill seeks to permit co-operative societies to enter the underwriting business by setting up a separate society. It also seeks to permit cooperative societies to enter the distribution business. It recognizes brokers as intermediaries in the insurance business and enables them to receive brokerage fee. At present, cooperative societies can only enter the insurance sector by floating an entity under the Companies Act. Once the bill is cleared by Parliament they can set-up an underwriting company under the Cooperatives Act.

Insurance in India: Some Burning Issues

The liberalization of the Indian insurance sector has been the subject of much heated debate for some years. The policy-makers wanted competition, development, and growth of this insurance sector, which is extremely essential for channeling the investments into the infrastructure sector. At the other end the policy-makers had the fears that the insurance premia, which are substantial, would seep out of the country; and wanted to have a cautious approach of opening for foreign participation in the sector.

As one of the rare occurrences the entire debate was put on the back burner and the IRDA saw the day of the light thanks to the maturing polity emerging consensus among factions of different political parties. Though some changes and some restrictive clauses as regards to the foreign participation were included, the IRDA has opened the doors for the private entry into insurance.

Whether the insurer is old or new, private or public, expanding the market will present multitude of challenges and opportunities. But the key issues, possible trends, opportunities and challenges that insurance sector will have still remains under the realms of the possibilities and speculation. What is the likely impact of opening up India's insurance sector?

Broadening of Benefits

The large scale of operations, public sector bureaucracies, and cumbersome procedures hampers nationalized insurers. Therefore, potential private entrants expect to score in the areas of customer service, speed, and flexibility. They point out that their entry will mean better products and choice for the consumer. The critics counter that the benefit will be slim, because new players will concentrate on affluent, urban customers as foreign banks did until recently. This seems to be a logical strategy. Start-up costs such as those of setting up a conventional distribution network are large and high-end niches offer better returns. However, the middle-market segment too has great potential. Since insurance is a volumes game, therefore, private insurers would be best served by a middle-market approach, targeting customer segments that are currently untapped.

Unrealistic—Fears

An often-voiced concern is that private players, especially foreign ones, will swamp the market, grabbing a large share. A similar threat was overplayed in the case of basic telephone services and when the private players started their operations the dominance and might of DoT has remain unaltered. This hypothesis that the private players would swamp the market has been disproved in many emerging markets world-wide not only in case of the insurance but also in numerous different sectors (Power, Energy, Telecom, Insurance, etc.).

Yet, multinational insurers are keenly interested in emerging insurance because their home markets are saturated while emerging countries have low insurance penetrations and high growth rates. International insurers often derive a significant part of their business from multinational operations. As early as 1994, many of the UK's largest life and general insurers derived 40% to 60% of their total premia from outside their home markets. Though the global operations of the multinational insurers have an immense impact on the business of this sector but foreign insurers take only a small share of an individual country's market. For example, in Taiwan the foreign companies took only a 3% share even seven years after opening up while in Korea, their share was barely 1% after 20 years. Moreover, India is a large, quite diverse and complex market thus private insurers will have to learn and unlearn quite a few things before they can make any headway to grab the market share. Yet for the new entrants this small share of a large and growing market can be profitable.

Untapped Opportunities

There is no doubt that the potential market for the buyers of insurance is significant in India and offers a great scope of growth. First, while estimating the potential of the Indian insurance market we often tempt to look at it from the perspective of macro-economic variables such as the ratio of premium to GDP, which is indeed comparatively low in India. For example, India's life insurance premium as a percentage of GDP is 1.3% against 5.2% in the US, 6.5% in the UK or 8% in South Korea. But the fact is that the large part of the India's (the number of potential buyers of insurance) is certainly attractive. However, this ignores the difficulties of approaching this population. New entrants in other mass industries such as consumer products or retail banking have discovered this after burning their fingers. Much of the demand may not be accessible because of poor distribution, large distances or high costs relative to returns.

Secondly, most new entrants have a tendency to target the business of existing companies rather than expanding the market, this is myopic. This not only leads to intense competition for the new players and much of their efforts is spent on trying to capture existing customers by offering better service or other advantages. Yet, the benefits of this strategy are likely to be limited. For example, 50% of the current demand for general insurance comes from the corporate segment. The corporates are likely to shop around for the best rates, products, and service. Nevertheless, the corporate segment, as a whole will not be a big growth area for new entrants. This is because penetration is already good, companies receive good service because of their size, and rates are tariff-governed. In both volumes and profitability, therefore, the scope for expansion is modest. A better approach may be to examine specific niches where demand can be met or stimulated.

Key—Innovation and Variety of Products

The new entrants would be best served by micro-level two pronged strategies. First, is to introduce innovative products offering a right mix of flexibility/risk/return depending which will suit the appetite of the customers and the secondly they would target specific niches, which are poorly served or are not served at all

The first prong of a new insurer's strategy could be to stimulate demand in areas that are currently not served at all. For example, Indian general insurance focuses on the manufacturing segment. However, the services sector is taking a large and growing share of India's GDP. This offers immense opportunities for expansion opportunities. For example, revenue from remote processing activities in information technology is estimated at USD 50 billion in the next ten years. Insurers could respond with various liability covers.

Being the agrarian economy again there are immense opportunities for the new entrants to provide the liability and risks associated in this sector like weather insurance, rainfall insurance, cyclone insurance, crop insurance, etc.

Next, the financial sector is aggressively targeting retail investors. Housing finance, auto finance, credit cards and consumer loans all offer an opportunity for insurance companies to introduce new products like creditor insurance, etc. Similarly, organized sector sales of TVs, refrigerators, washing machines, and audio systems in 1998 were around Rs. 110 billion. Only a negligible portion of these purchases was insured. Potential buyers for most of this insurance lie in the middle class. Existing players can also profitably exploit these areas.

In case there are products, which are not serving adequately new products many of them, which are already prevalent in different markets can be customized to the Indian markets and used to expand the markets. For example, life insurance products provide a good example. Life Insurance products have to compete with savings and mutual funds hence should offer various dimensions of risk/return/flexibility so they can be linked to stock market indices, inflation, etc. making them more competitive and appropriate risk/return appetite for different investors at present there are no such products. Similar problems apply to pensions. For instance, pure protection products like term assurance account for up to 20% of policies sold in developed countries. In India, the figure is less than one percent because policies are inflexible. They compete with investment and savings options like mutual funds. It is imperative that they should offer comparable returns and flexibility and there is immense scope of developing pure insurance products with flexibility.

The lack of a comprehensive social security system combined with a willingness to save means that Indian demand for pension products will be large. However, current penetration is poor. Making pension products into attractive saving instruments would require only simple innovations already prevalent in other markets. For example, their returns might be tied to index-linked funds or a specific basket of equities. Buyers could be allowed to switch funds before the annuities begin and to invest different amounts at different times

Health insurance is another segment with great potential because existing Indian products are insufficient. By the end of March, 2001, the GIC's Mediclaim scheme covered only 2.5 million people. Indian products do not cover disability arising out of illness or disability for over 100 weeks due to accident. Neither do they cover a potential loss of earnings through disability

Distribution—A Paradigm Shift

Since distribution will be a key determinant of success for all insurance companies regardless of age or ownership. The nationalized insurers currently have a large reach and presence. New entrants cannot and does not expect to supplant or duplicate such a network. Building a distribution network is expensive and time consuming. Yet, if insurers are to take advantage of India's large population and reach a profitable mass of customers, new distribution avenues and alliances will be imperative. This is also true for the nationalized corporations, which must find fresh avenues to reach existing and new customers. There would be substantial shifts in the distribution of insurance in India. Many of these changes will echo international trends. World-wide, insurance products move along a continuum from pure service products to pure commodity products then they could be sold through the medical shops, groceries, novelty stores, etc. Once communization, popularity, and awareness of the products are attained then the products can move to remote channels such as the telephone or direct mail. In the UK for example, retailer Marks and Spencer now sells insurance products. At this point, buyers look for low price. Brand loyalty could shift from the insurer to the seller. Recognizing this trend, the financial services industry world-wide has successfully used remote distribution channels such as the telephone or the Internet to reach more customers, cut out intermediaries, brings down overheads and increase profitability.

The Trinity of IT—Distribution—Training

Most of the opportunities and challenges that we have discussed apply equally to existing and new insurers. It must be emphasized that the opening of the insurance market is far from a bad thing for nationalized insurers. With a strong presence, a wide network, and considerable brand equity, they are in a good position to tap the very same segments profitably, while improving their product and service offerings. All insurers in a liberalized Indian market will have to address a host of other issues. They will have to:

Leverage information technology to service large number of customers efficiently and bring down overheads. Technology can complement or supplement distribution channels cost-effectively. It can also help improve customer service levels considerably.

Use data warehousing, management and mining to gauge the profitability and potential of various customer and product segments and ensure effective cross selling. Understanding the customer better will allow insurance companies to design appropriate products, determine pricing correctly, and increase profitability.

Ensure high levels of training and development not just for staff but also for agents and distribution organizations. Existing organizations will have to train staff for better service and flexibility, while all companies will have to train employees to cope with new products and an intensive use of information technology.

The importance of alliances and tie-ups means that companies will have to integrate related but separate providers into their systems to ensure seamless delivery.

Build strong relationships with intermediaries such as agents.

Regulation—The Catalyst

Indian insurance is on the threshold of deep and fundamental changes. The life insurance industry was nationalized in 1956 and the general insurance industry in 1972. Before that India had a thriving and competitive insurance industry with hundreds of private and foreign operators. Indian companies held a 60% market share even then. Yet, insufficient regulation also meant that there were a number of abuses. In a reopened Indian insurance market, regulators must formulate strong, fair and transparent guidelines and make sure that old and new players are subject to the same rules. Companies meanwhile must be prepared to set and meet high standards for themselves. The big challenge for both companies and regulators is to ensure that they replicate the benefits of the past while eliminating its ills.

What Government is doing for Insurance Business

The social sector has been defined to incorporate both the unorganized and organized sector equally in the urban and rural areas. There is no immense dilemma in defining the organized sector but unorganized sector includes self-employed workers such as agricultural labourers, bidi workers, brick kiln workers, carpenters, cobblers, construction workers, fishermen, hamals, handicraft artisans, handloom and khadi workers, lady tailors, leathers and tannery workers, papad makers, power loom workers, physically handicapped self-employed persons, primary milk producers, rickshaw pullers, safai karmacharis, salt growers, sericulture workers, sugarcane cutters tendu leaf collertors, toddy tappers, vegetable vendors, washerwomen, working women in hills, or such other categories of persons. Within this sector economically vulnerable or backward classes mean people who are below the poverty line and other categories of person include persons with disability as defined in the Persons with Disabilities (Equal Opportunities, Protection of Rights and full Participation) Act, 1995 and who may not be gainfully employed and also includes guardians who need insurance to protect spastic persons or persons with disability. The Government tries to discharge its responsibility through insurance sector by providing some insurance cover to different categories of people. Some or such linkages between Government and insurance policies have been discussed in this chapter.

16.2 NATIONAL AGRICULTURAL INSURANCE SCHEME (NAIS)

This scheme, known as Rashtriya Krishi Bima Yojana (RKBY), was brought into force from 22nd June 1999 and has its primary objective of providing insurance coverage and financial support to the farmers in the event of failure of crops as a result of natural calamities, pests and diseases. The scheme extends to all States and Union Territories.

Crops Covered

Food crops (cereals, millets and pulses) and oilseeds, cotton, sugarcane, and potato in the first years and other annual commercial/ horticultural crops in a period of three years.

Risks Covered

(a) Natural fire and lightning.
(b) Storm, Hailstorm, Cyclone, Typhoon, Tempest, Hurricane, Tornado, etc.
(c) Flood, Inundation and Landslide.
(d) Drought, Dry spells.
(e) Pests, Diseases, etc.

The policy cover operates from the stage of sowing to harvesting

Sum Insured

The sum insured is fixed with reference to: The Threshold Yield (TY) for a crop based on past three years' average yield in case of Rice and Wheat and five years in case of other crops. This is multiplied by the level of indemnity viz., 90%, 80%, and 60% corresponding to Low Risk, Medium Risk, and High Risk.

Premium Rates

(a) Kharif season: Bajra and Oil seeds—3.5% on S.I., or
Other food crops—2.5% on S.I. actuarial rates.
Rabi season—Wheat—1.5% on S.I.
Other food crops—2.5% on S.I.
(b) Annual Commercial/Horticultural Crops: Actuarial rates.

Premium Subsidy

The 50% subsidy in premium is allowed to small and marginal farmers. The Government of India and State/UT Government equally share this. This applies in the first year of the scheme and the subsidy will be phased out on sunset basis.

Farmers Covered

(a) Loanee farmers, i.e. farmers growing insurable crops and availing Seasonal Agricultural Operation (SAO) loans from Financial Institutions. Insurance is compulsory.
The amount of crop loan is the minimum amount of sum insured.
- Sum insured upto the value of threshold yield at normal rates at the option of the farmer.
- Higher sum insured upto 150% of the value of the average yield—at commercial rates of premium.

(b) Other farmers i.e. 'non-loanee' farmers growing insurable crops. Insurance is voluntary.
- Up to the value of threshold yield—normal rates.
- Up to 150% of value of threshold yield—commercial rates.

Scheme Approach

(a) Widespread Calamities: The scheme would operate on the basis of 'Area Approach'. The defined area, e.g. Gram Panchayat, block, Taluka is to be decided by the State/UT Government.

(b) Localized Calamities: Such as hailstorm, landslide, cyclone and flood. The scheme would operate on individual basis.

Implementing Agency (IA)

Until such time an exclusive organization is set-up, the G.I.C. of India will be the implementing agency for the scheme. The Government of India/ States reimburses G.I.C. with 100% expenses in the 1st year which will be reduced on sunset basis.

How to Buy Insurance

Loanee farmers automatically get covered under the insurance scheme as and when crop loans for insured crops are disbursed to them. Non-loanee farmers are required to contact designated bank branches or the GIC's local offices with a proposal. They should have a Bank A/c with the bank and pay requisite premium to obtain insurance coverage.

Loss Settlement

Widespread Calamities

In case of Area Approach the farmers need not intimate crop losses to bank/GIC. The crop losses/reduction in yield as compared to guaranteed (threshold) yield should be reflected in Crop Estimation Surveys of the State government, and the shortfall in yield. If any, shall be paid to the farmers as claim through the Bank.

Localized Calamities

Loss assessment will be done on individual basis initially on experimental basis for few select areas as per procedure laid down. The farmers need to intimate the crop loss within 48 hours. The claim amounts are paid by way of cheques or through designated bank branches so that amount gets credited to their accounts.

Corpus Fund

To meet catastrophic losses, a corpus fund shall be created with contributions from the Government of India and State/UT on 50:50 bases. The role and responsibilities of the State Government/UT and financial institutions are specified in the scheme.

State Government/UT administration will, among other things:

- Provide Unit—Area-wise immediate past 10 years yield data for all notified crops in advance to the GIC.
- Notify crop-wise areas and premium rates well in advance of the season.
- Maintain communications with financial institutions regarding notified crops, areas, premium rates, etc.
- Strengthen Crop Estimation Survey machinery in order to furnish accurate yield estimates.
- Assist G.I.C in assessing crop losses of individual farmers in case of localized calamities.

Financial Institutions

These are scheduled institutions falling within the norms fixed by RBI/NABARD for disbursing Seasonal Agricultural Operations (SAO) Loans.

Their responsibilities are, among other things:

- Follow the RBI/NABARD guidelines while disbursing crop loans and ensure end use of the loans.
- Advance additional loan to loanee farmers to meet premium requirement as applicable to the extent of crop loan.
- Educate the farmers on the scheme and guide them in filling proposals.
- Submit month-wise, crop-wise and defined area-wise statistics of insurance charges for loans farmers and other farmers to the GIC.

16.3 PERSONAL ACCIDENT SOCIAL SECURITY SCHEME (PASS)

The Central government introduced in the year 1985, the Personal Accident Social Security Scheme for the benefit of poor families. 'Poor families' are defined in the policy and include landless labour households, families of traditional craftsman, etc. whose total annual income does not exceed Rs. 7200. The scheme provides for payment of Rs. 3000 in the event of accident death of any person in the age group of 18 to 60 who is an earning member of poor family. Accident deaths include such deaths due to snakebite, drowning, food poisoning, lighting, fall from a tree, and killing by armed criminals or wild animals. The cases specified are illustrative in nature and not exhaustive.

The beneficiaries are:

(1) Surviving spouse, or
(2) If there is no surviving spouse, the payment be made to all dependent children jointly who will share equally. Where the payment is to be made to minor children, the same may be made

by way of Post Office deposits, or

(3) If there are no surviving children, the payment can be made to dependent surviving parents.

Compensation is Not Payable

- For Death arising or resulting from breach of any law with criminal intent.
- When compensation higher than Rs. 3,000 is receivable by virtue of any other law/statute e.g. Motor Vehicles Act, Solatium Fund, Employees' State Insurance Scheme, Workmen's Compensation Act, etc. If compensation/relief available under (b) is less than Rs. 3000 compensation under the Scheme will be limited to the amount, which would bring the total compensation/relief from all sources to Rs. 3000.

Procedure

(a) Application for compensation in the prescribed form is to be made to the Claims Enquiry-*cum*-Settlement Officer of the Sub-District or Taluka notified by the State Government as early as possible but not later than 45 days from the date of death for claims arising within the districts and 90 days where the deceased belonged to another district/State U.T.

(b) The Claims Enquiry-*cum*-Settlement Officer shall consider and settle the claims and his duties shall be:

1. To receive application in the prescribed form from the claimants.
2. To hold enquiries in respect of the claims.
3. To call for reports from the Police and media authorities including post-mortem reports where available in respect of accidents.
4. To hold enquiries and be satisfied that the applicant belongs to "poor families" and the claim is payable under the terms and conditions of the Scheme.
5. Where there is more than one claimant, to decide as to who are the rightful claimants and the amount payable to each.
6. To prepare report in the prescribed form and authorize payment to the rightful claimant(s).

(c) After the payment is authorized by the Claims Enquiry-*cum*-Settlement Officer, the State Government may direct immediate payment to be made to the beneficiaries from its own fund and obtain reimbursement from the concerned office. If however, any State Government would not desire to make payment from its own funds, arrangement will be made for payment by the concerned office of the designated insurance company by cheque or money order less money order commission on receipt of the Claims Enquiry-*cum*-Settlement Officers' report which should include the claim form, document certifying death by accident, and the discharge voucher.

(d) The designated insurance company for the district shall prepare and submit to GIC and the District Consultative Committee a quarterly report on the working of the scheme.

For overseeing the claims settlement procedure and implementing the scheme, District Consultative Committees have been constituted. The District Consultative Committee consists of a representative of the concerned office of the designated insurance company who would act as the Member Secretary and in this capacity function as Convener of the Committee, the District Magistrate, the District Superintendent of Police and such other officials as the State Government may nominate. The State Government decides the Chairman of the District Consultative Committee.

To oversee the operations of the Scheme in the districts, State level Consultative Committees are constituted. The State Level Consultative Committees consists of representative of the designated insurance companies one of whom shall be the Convener, and State Government representative who could be Home Secretary, Revenue Secretary and Secretary, Social Welfare.

The State Government has the overall responsibility to scrutinize and settle the claims and will notify claims. For deaths of persons occurring in the selected districts who belong to other districts, the State Government will take such special measures as are found necessary for speedy disbursement of the accident benefit to the affected family. The State Government will also nominate their representatives to the State Level and District Level Consultative Committee. While the premium for the scheme will be paid entirely by the Central Government, the administrative costs incurred by the State Governments for implementing the scheme in their territories will be borne by them.

The G.I.C and its subsidiaries will notify the designated insurance companies and their concerned Officer for each of the districts and also their representatives for all District and State Level Consultative Committees. G.I.C will have the overall responsibility for the administration of the Scheme. The operation of the Scheme will be monitored closely and reviewed annually by GIC. Annual appraisal reports of the Scheme would be prepared by the GIC and submitted to the Government of India. Modification would be introduced as may be required in the light of the annual review.

16.4 HUT INSURANCE SCHEME

Hut Insurance Scheme was introduced by the Central Government with effect from 1st May 1988. The Scheme provides for payment compensation to very poor families in rural areas when their huts and/or belongings are destroyed by fire (Rs. 1000 for huts and Rs. 500 for belongings). 'Very Poor Families' are defined in the scheme and include landless labourers, small farmers etc., whose annual family income does not exceed Rs. 4800.

The scheme operates along the lines of Personal Accident Social Security Scheme as mentioned above.

16.5 SOLATIUM INSURANCE SCHEME

The Solatium Insurance Scheme, 1989 under the Motor Vehicles Act, 1988 has been made by the Central Government for the payment of compensation to the victims of hit and run motor accident. The scheme came into force from 1st July, 1989. Hit and run accident is "an accident arising out of the use of a motor vehicle or motor vehicles the identify whereof cannot be ascertained in spite of reasonable efforts for the purpose."

The compensation payable for death claims is fixed at Rs. 25,000 and in respect of 'grievous hurt' Rs. 12,500 after the amendment to Motor Vehicles Act, 1988. (Earlier to amendment, it was Rs. 8,500 for death and Rs. 2,000 for grievous hurt). The payment of compensation for Hit and Run accident is subject to the condition that if any compensation is awarded for such death or grievous hurt under any other provisions of the Motor Vehicles Act or any other law the amount paid under Hit and Run accident has to be deducted from such compensation.

The Solatium Fund consists of contributions from the General Insurance Industry, the Central Government, and the State Government as decided by the Central Government. The scheme provides that the G.I.C. shall nominate offices of the Companies in each district for settlement of Claims within six months from the date of accident. A person seeking compensation has to make an application to the Claims Enquiry Officer designated for each district.

The Claims Enquiry Officer will hold an enquiry and submit a report to the Claims Settlement Commissioner nominated for the district by the State Government, for sanction. The sanction order supported by claim papers is communicated to the nominated office of the insurance company, which makes payment to the claimant by Cheques/Demand Draft. The payment shall be made within 15 days from the date of receipt of the sanction order. The nominated office has to submit a monthly return of claims paid and pending and other details to the Claims Settlement Commissioner with a copy to Claims Enquiry Officer and G.I.C.

The G.I.C. has to prepare an annual report on the working of the scheme and submit to the Standing Committee and to the Central Government. The Standing Committee is constituted to oversee and review the working of the Scheme. The members of the Committee are nominees of the Government, G.I.C and its four subsidiaries companies, etc. The District Level Committee is constituted to perform functions connected with the implementation of the Scheme at the district level. The Divisional Manager of the insurance company is the Member Secretary of the Committee.

16.6 TAX BENEFITS UNDER INSURANCE POLICIES

Tax Benefits: The basic objective of taxation is to provide sufficient revenue to the state. But at the same time to encourage long-term saving, income tax act has provided some concessions on tax with the help of different clauses under it.

A LIC policy can be taken out by an individual or by Hindu undivided family. Life Insurance Policy is eligible for Income Tax benefits. Rebate can be claim on insurance premium paid by an individual on his/her own life, on spouse life, on children life may be adult children. Rebate of 20% is allowed on premiums paid for life insurance under section 88 to an individual/Hindu undivided family.

Jeevan Suraksha Plan

A deduction to an individual for any amount paid or deposited by him in Jeevan Suraksha annuity plan for receiving premium (from a fund set-up by LIC of India) is allowed, the deductions will be restricted to Rs. 10,000 under Section 80 CCC.

Special Note:—As in Income Tax Act it is categorically stated in section 80 DD and Section 80 CCC about Life Insurance Corporation of India's scheme and U.T.I.'s schemes. No other pension scheme will get this advantage till further amendment in I.T. Act

The above deductions are allowed from the Gross Income before Calculations of Income Tax.

Insurance on Joint Lives

Premium paid under joint life policy are eligible to get tax rebate under Section 88. Joint life means husband and wife or in case of a Hindu Undivided family, jointly on the lives of two or more members of the family is eligible for the stated deduction under Section 88. However, such rebate will not be allowed on single premium policies or jointly on the lives of other relatives.

Handicapped Dependants

At present, deductions are allowed up to Rs. 15,000 u/s 80 DD in respect of medical treatment of handicapped dependents and another amount upto Rs. 20,000 u/s 80 DDA in respect of Deposit made for maintenance of handicapped dependent under any scheme framed in this behalf by LIC, i.e. "Jeevan Adhar" or by U.T.I.

As per new amendments in this regard the existing Sections 80 DD and 80 DDA will be merged together to form a new Section 80 DD with increased limit from Rs. 35,000 to Rs. 40,000.

Rebate in Respect of Contribution to GILS

According to Section 88 the amount of contribution made towards the group insurance linked scheme is allowed as rebate. It is important to note that this kind of contribution is found mandatory in many organizations.

Rebate of Income Tax under Section 88 [Special Reference to Insurance Policies]

- Premiums paid to effect or to keep in force an insurance policy on the life of the assessee or on the life of the wife or husband or any child (whether minor or major) of the assessee irrespective of the status of the child.
- Premiums paid to effect or to keep in force a policy for a deferred annuity on the life of the assessee or on the life of the wife or husband or any child (whether minor or major) of the assessee provided that such a contract does not contain a provision for the exercise, by the assured, of an option to receive a cash payment in lieu of the payment of the annuity.
- If the assessee is an employee participating in an approved insurance superannuation fund, his contribution to such fund in the previous year.
- As a contribution for participation by the individual in the Unit Linked Insurance Plan, 1971 of the Unit Trust of India.
- If the assessee is an employee participating in a recognized mutual insurance fund, his own contribution to such fund in the previous year.
- Any amounts deposited in a ten-year account or a fifteen-year account under the insurance scheme (Cumulative Time Deposits) Rules, 1959, as amended from time to time.
- Contribution for participation in the Unit Linked Insurance Plan of the LIC Mutual Fund (Dhanraksha Plan).
- Payment made towards Pension schemes of LIC like Jeevan Dhara, Jeevan Akshay.
- Contribution to pension fund set-up by UTI (Retirement Benefit Unit Scheme) and Kothari Pioneer Mutual Fund (Kothari Pioneer Pension Plan).
- Subscription not exceeding Rs. 10,000 to any units of any mutual fund or UTI, notified under insurance clause (23D) of Section 10 of the Income Tax Act, 1961.

Amounts Exempted from Income Tax

Under the provisions of Sub-section 10D of Section 10 of Income-tax Act, 1961, any sum received under a life insurance policy, including the sum allocated by way of bonus on such policy other than any sum received under Sub-section (3) of Section 80 DD (i.e. amount to be refunded under Jeevan Adhar Insurance Plan in case the handicapped dependent predeceases the individual or under a Keyman Insurance Policy) at the time of maturity or on death is exempted from the tax.

Key Notes for Income Tax Exemption

- Policies of insurance include Children's Deferred Endowment Assurance Policies, i.e. policies of insurance effected by a person for the benefit of a minor.
- In the case of a Hindu Undivided Family, no deduction is permissible in respect of sums paid to affect a contract of Deferred Annuity.
- In the case of contribution to the Unit Linked Insurance Plan, it is provided that where the member withdraws from the plan before contributions have been made for five years, no deduction shall be allowed to the assessee in respect of the contributions made in the year of withdrawal and further an amount equal to the aggregate of the amounts, allowed as deductions on account of the contribution made in the earlier year(s) will be included in the total income of the previous year in which the member withdraws from the Trust.
- Where the tax payer discontinues a Life Insurance Policy before two years and the premiums for two years have been paid, no deduction will be allowed in respect of the premium, if any, paid during the previous year in which the policy is terminated and the deduction allowed in respect of the premiums paid in the year preceding the previous year shall be deemed to be the income of the Assessee for the previous year and chargeable to tax accordingly.
- The condition that the premium paid in excess of 10% of the Sum Assured does not qualify for deduction is withdrawn w.e.f. 1996-97.
- If any equity shares or debentures with reference to the cost of which a deduction is allowed, are sold or otherwise transferred by the assessee to any person at any time within a period of three years from the date of their acquisition, the aggregate amount of the deduction of Income tax so allowed in respect of such equity shares or debentures in the previous year or years preceding the previous year in which such sale or transfer has taken place shall be deemed to be tax payable by the assessee for the assessment year relevant to such previous year and shall be added to the amount of income tax on the total income of the assessee with which he is chargeable for such assessment year.

The Mediclaim Policy

The Mediclaim policy of GIC provides the Policyholder cover against unforeseen illness, injuries, and diseases requiring hospitalization treatment.

Policy compensates expenses for specified ailments covered under the policy. Under this scheme an exemption of Rs. 15,000 or actual premium paid whichever is less can be claimed as exempt from the taxable income u/s 80D of the IT Act, 1961.

16.7 SUMMARY

The liberalization of Indian economy is, now, convincingly mature conception. However, within this conception, the liberalization of insurance sector is relatively new notion. With the opening of this sector for private players in India, some un-realistic fears like swamping the market and grabbing a large share are still being hotly debated amongst the experts and professionals in the country.

The Government of India nationalized the life insurance and general insurance in 1956 and 1971 respectively and tried to make the schemes of insurance, particularly life insurance schemes, popular by providing tax benefit covers to almost all policies. By providing the tax exemptions/ deductions, the Government has been able to mobilize sizable investments in insurance policies. Though, the exemptions are still available but no body knows how long these would last and what would happen with insurance business if there is no exemption.

16.8 REVIEW QUESTIONS

1. Discuss the provisions relating to tax benefits available to insurance policies. Comment over the existing provisions.
2. "Insurance business will be tested when tax incentives will go." Explain the statement.
3. Discuss the salient features of National Agricultural Insurance Scheme.
4. Explain in detail Personal Accident Social Security Scheme.
5. Explain and illustrate the latest developments in the field of insurance business in India.

17

CHAPTER

LEGAL DIMENSIONS OF INSURANCE

LEARNING OBJECTIVE

The main objective of this chapter is to make the students aware about the legal dimensions of insurance particularly to those, which are more commonly in practice.

17.1 INTRODUCTION

Up to the end of nineteenth century, the insurance was in its inceptional stage in India. Therefore, no legislation was required till that time. Usually the Indian Companies Act, 1883 was applicable in business concerns, banking and insurance companies. New Indian Insurance companies and Provident Societies started at the time of national movement; but most of them were financially unsound. It was asserted that the Indian Companies Act, 1883 was inadequate for the purpose. Therefore, two Acts were passed in 1912, namely, Provident Insurance Societies Act V of 1912 and Indian Life Insurance Companies Act VI of 1912. These two Acts were in pursuit of the English Insurance Companies Act of 1909 with the difference that the Indian Life Insurance Companies related to life insurance only and excluded the non-life business from its fold. The Act put the life insurance business in India on sounder footing and resulted in creating a healthier atmosphere than before. It was also instrumental in the dissolution of some unsound Indian as well as non-Indian life offices or in the merging of some of them with the others. The legislation in India was confining to life business because there were very few general insurance companies and did not call for any legislation. To prevent financial weakness the insurers were required to keep certain stated deposits. The Indian insurers were required to submit returns giving particulars of their business. The foreign insurers were exempted from submitting separate particulars regarding the business done in India. Some English companies ceased to underwrite further business with a view to avoid submission of reports to the Government of India. Some Indian Companies, which conducted business on assessmentism or on actuarially unsound basis, either dropped or mortgaged them to conform to actuarial requirements. The policies issued by these companies were not less than Rs. 1,000. The aim of the Provident Insurance Societies Act, 1912 was to govern Provident Insurance Societies which were engaged in issuing life policies worth Rs. 1,000 or less and marriage and disease policies, of every nominal amount. This act was purely based on the Friendly Societies Act.

These two enactments were governing only life insurance. There was no control on general insurance since such businesses were not so developed. Besides, there were the following defects of these Acts:

1. The control and enquiry was slight. Non-compliance of rules and regulations was not strictly penalised.
2. The foreign companies were to submit report of their total business both in India and outside India. But separate particulars regarding business done in India were not demanded and the absence of these made it impossible to get any idea of the cost of procuring business in India for foreign companies and comparing them with similar data of the Indian companies.
3. The Government Actuary was not vested with the power to order investigation into the conduct of a company even when it appeared that the company was insolvent under the power of exemption.
4. Any one can start life insurance business only with the sum of Rs. 25,000. It was too low to prevent the mushroom growth of companies. Foreign insurer was not bound to deposit a certain sum of life policy issued in India.

These defects were compelling the above Acts to be replaced. Public was aware of the fact that the Indian companies in foreign countries or in England were directed to have a certain sum in the shape of reserve as contrary to above regulation. The law in India was not in line with the law in force in other countries. Persistent demands were made by various important public bodies in the country for statutory provisions which would provide for disclosure and publication of the business carried on in India by foreign companies. After a few years it was realised that there should be another efficient and adequate act.

So, the Government placed a bill for essential amendment of the Act, in 1924. The bill was containing a wide scope of insurance business. The bill came to the legislative assembly after thorough comments by different bodies.

During the time, an important thing happened miraculously about the enactments of insurance business in England. The Government of India thought it fit to watch the course of new legislation on Insurance Law in England. Great Britain appointed Clauson (under the chairmanship of Mr. A.C. Clauson) Committee to report the possible and required changes in the Legislation. Therefore, the Government of India thought it wise to postpone the bill to include the reports of Clauson Committee. The Clauson Committee submitted its report in February 1927, but the Government of England took no action on its recommendations. The Government of India in 1928 passed stopgap legislation with the main object of collecting statistics regarding insurance matters so that the information collected would be of value when the time would come to pass a comprehensive Act. This act was not very comprehensive. The Government of India wanted to wait the English Legislation, which was expected to be passed in 1929 or so and base the law for India on the British model, but the legislation was not passed in Britain. The slow progress of events in Britain again reviewed the agitation for amendment of the law of Insurance in India.

Since the Act of 1928 was not very comprehensive, demand for another act was made. The Government accepted the genuine demand and appointed one special officer for investigations the special and required reform of legislation in 1935. He was a well-known Calcutta Solicitor and was placed on special duty to report on the amendments necessary to modernise insurance legislation in India. His report was considered by the Advisory Committee (comprising representatives of all branches of insurance) appointed by the Government of India. The committee made several changes and the Government of India introduced the bill in the Legislative Assembly in 1937 and after much debate and several changes, it emerged as the Insurance Act of 1938.

17.2 INSURANCE ACT, 1938

The Act does not follow the principle of minimum interference with maximum publicity and direct control. It was well balanced and was the first comprehensive piece of insurance legislation in this country governing both life and non-life branches of insurance. This Act provided to prevent the growth of mushroom companies, to enforce working on sound principles, to prevent misappropriation of funds and to protect the assets.

This Act of 1938 was wide and more comprehensive. There was strict control over the insurance business. This Act was amended from time to time. Since 1938, there were six amendments up to 1945. In 1945, it was deemed necessary to protect the interest of Insured Companies. Therefore, in the Chairmanship of Sri Kavas Ji Jahangir, a Committee was appointed which was to investigate all the misconduct of the insurance business. The committee gave its reports after a thorough inquiry on which recommendation was made for amending many important sections and to introduce new sections. On this basis one amendment bill was made and was sent to different select committees and at last it was enacted on 18th April, 1950 by the Parliament. According to this Amended Act, there are provisions pertaining to administration. The total right of control is with the Central Government. The Central Government controls the insurance business by appointing Controller of Insurance. The insurance companies must follow the rules and regulations, otherwise they will be penalised under this Act. The life insurance business was nationalised in 1956 and certain provisions of this Act apply to the Life Insurance Corporation of India. General Insurance Corporation of India act was passed in 1972 to govern the business of general insurance which were nationalised in 1972.

Salient Features of The Insurance Act, 1938

The Salient Features of Insurance Act, 1938 have been discussed under the following headings:

1. Wide Scope
2. Requirements as to Capital
3. Deposits
4. Registration
5. Submission of Returns
6. Prohibition of Rebates, Restriction of Commission
7. Licensing of Insurance Agents
8. Investment
9. Prohibition of loan
10. Investigation
11. Duties and Power of Controller of Insurance

Wide Scope

The Act applies to all types of insurance business—life, fire, marine, etc.—done by companies incorporated in India or elsewhere. It also governs the provident companies, mutual offices and cooperative societies.

According to Sec. 2(c) of the Act, there is prohibition of transaction of insurance business by certain persons.

Save as hereinafter provided, no person shall, after the commencement of the Insurance Act, begin to carry on any class of insurance business in India and no insurer carrying on any class of insurance business in India shall after the expiry of one year, from such commencement, continue to carry on any such business unless he is—

(a) a public company, or
(b) a society registered under the Cooperative Societies Act, 1912 or under any other law for the time being in force in any State relating to co-operative societies, or
(c) a body corporate incorporated under the law of any country outside India not being of the nature of a private company.

Requirement as to Capital

No insurer carrying on the business of life insurance, general insurance or re-insurance in India on or after the commencement of the Insurance Regulatory and Development Authority Act, 1999, shall be registered unless he has:

(i) a paid-up equity capital or rupees one hundred crores, in case of a person carrying on the business of life insurance or general insurance; or
(ii) a paid-up equity capital of rupees two hundred crores, in case of a person carrying on exclusively the business as a reinsurer:

Provided that in determining the paid-up equity capital specified under clause (i) or clause (ii), the deposit to be made under Section 7 and any preliminary expenses incurred in the formation and registration of the company shall be excluded:

Provided further that an insurer carrying on business of life insurance, general insurance or re-insurance in India before the commencement of the Insurance Regulatory and Development Authority Act, 1999 and who is required to be registered under this Act, shall have a paid-up equity capital in accordance with clause (i) and clause (ii), as the case may be, within six months of the commencement of that Act. (Section 6)

Deposits

To prevent the growth of insurers of small financial resources or speculative concerns, the Act provided for registration of all insurers and a substantial deposit with the Reserve Bank.

According to Section 7, every insurer shall, in respect of the insurance business carried on by him in India, deposit and keep deposited with the Reserve Bank of India in one of the offices in India of the bank for and on behalf of the Central Government, the amount hereafter specified, either in cash or in approved securities, estimated at the market value of the Securities on the day of deposit or partly in cash and partly in approved securities so estimated—

(a) in the case of life insurance business, a sum equivalent to one per cent of his total gross premium written in India in any financial year commencing after the 31st day of March 2000, not exceeding rupees ten crores;
(b) in the case of general insurance business, a sum equivalent to three per cent of his total gross premium written in India, in any financial year commencement after the 31st day of March 2000, not exceeding rupees ten crores;
(c) in the case of re-insurance business, a sum of rupees twenty crores:

Provided that, where the business done or to be done is marine insurance only and relates exclusively to country craft or its cargo or both, the amount to be deposited under this sub-section shall be one hundred thousand rupees only.

Registration

Section 3 states that, no person shall, after the commencement of this Act, begin to carry on any class of insurance business in India and no insurer carrying on any class of insurance business in India shall after the expiry of three months from the commencement of this Act, continue of carry on any such business, unless he has obtained from the Authority a certificate of registration for the particular class of insurance business:

Provided that in the case of an insurer who was carrying on any class of insurance business in India at the commencement of this Act, failure to obtain a certificate of registration in accordance with the requirements of this sub-clause shall not operate to invalidate any contract of insurance entered into by him if before such date as may be fixed in this behalf by the Central Government by notification in the Official Gazette, he has obtained that certificate.

Every application for registration shall be accompanied by:

(a) A certified copy of the memorandum and articles of association.
(b) Name, address and occupation of directors.
(c) A statement of the class or classes of insurance business done or to be done.
(d) Principal place of business or domicile outside India.
(e) A certified copy of the published prospectus.
(f) The receipt showing payment of fee as may be determined by the regulations which shall not exceed fifty thousand rupees for each class of business as may be specified by the regulations made by the Authority.
(g) Such other documents as may be specified by the regulations made by the Authority.

If, on receipt of an application for registration and after making such inquiry as he deems fit, the Authority is satisfied that—

(a) the financial condition and the general character of management of the applicant are sound;
(b) the volume of business likely to be available to, and the capital structure and earning prospects of, the applicant will be adequate;
(c) the interests of the general public will be served.

The Authority may register the applicant as an insurer and grant him a certificate of registration. The Authority shall withhold registration or shall cancel a registration already made if any requirement is not satisfied.

The Authority shall cancer the registration of an insurer either wholly or in so far as it relates to a particular class of insurance business as the case may be:

(a) If the insurer fails to comply with the provisions of Section 7 or 8 of deposits; or

(b) If the insurer is in liquidation or is adjudged an insolvent; or
(c) If the business has been transferred to any other insured; or
(d) If the whole of the deposit made in respect of insurance business has been returned to the insurer under Section 9; or
(e) When clause 9 of Section 2 related to insurer's definition ceased or cancelled or suspended;
(f) Defaults in complying with any rules; and
(g) Carry any business other than insurance business or any prescribed business.

Submission of Returns

The audited accounts and balance sheet and actuarial report and abstract and four copies thereof shall be furnished as returns to the Authority in the case of the accounts and balance sheet and the actuarial report within six months and in the case of the abstract within nine months from the end of the period to which they refer. If the principal place is outside India, the period of submission may be extended by three months.

Of the four copies so furnished one shall be signed in the case of a company by the Chairman and two directors and by the principal officer of the Company and, if the company has a managing director or managing agent, by that director or managing agent, in the case of a firm, by two partners of the firm, and, in the case of an insurer being an individual, by the insurer himself and one shall be signed by the auditor who made the audit or the actuary who made the valuation, as the case may be.

Where the insurer's principal place of business or domicile is outside India, he shall forward to the Authority, along with the documents, a certified statement showing the total assets and liabilities of the insurer at the close of the period covered by the said documents.

The insurer shall, within the time specified in sub-section (1) of Section 15, furnish to the Authority four certified copies in the English language of every balance-sheet, account abstract, report and statement supplied to the public authority and in addition thereto four certified copies in the English language of each of the following statement:

(a) a statement audited by an auditor or by a person duly qualified under the law of the insurer's country showing the assets held by the insurer in India at the date of any balance sheet so furnished;
(b) a separate account of receipts and payments and a revenue account for the period covered by any account to furnished;
(c) a separate abstract of the valuation report in respect of all business transacted in India in each class or sub-class of insurance business; and
(d) a declaration in the prescribed form stating that all amounts received by the insurer directly or indirectly whether from his head office or from any other source outside and have been shown in the revenue account.

Restriction of Commission and Prohibition of Rebating

Prohibition of Payment by Way of Commission or Otherwise for Procuring Business

No person shall, after the expiry of six months from the commencement of this Act, pay or contract to pay any remuneration or reward whether by way of commission or otherwise for soliciting or procuring insurance business in India to any person except an insurance agent or a principal, chief or special agent. [Section 40(1)]

No Insurance agent shall be paid or contract to be paid by way of commission or as remuneration in any form an amount exceeding, in the case of life Insurance business, 40% of the first year's premium payable on any policy or policies effected through him and 5% of a renewal premium, payable on such a policy, or, in the case of business of any other class, 15% of the premium:

Provided that insurers, in respect of life insurance business only, may pay, during the first ten years of their business, to their insurance agents 55% of the first year's premium payable on any policy or policies effected through them and 6% of the renewal premium payable on such policies. [Section 40(2)]

Limitations of Expenditure on Commission (Section 40A)

1. No person shall pay or contract to pay to an insurance agent, and no insurance agent shall receive or contract to receive by way of commission or remuneration in any form in respect of any policy of life insurance issued in India by an insurer after the 31st day of December 1950, and effected through an insurance agent, an amount exceeding:
   (a) where the policy grants an immediate annuity or a deferred annuity in consideration of a single premium, or where only one premium is payable on the policy, 2% of that premium,
   (b) where the policy grants a deferred annuity in consideration of more than one premium, 7½% of the first year's premium, and 2% of the each renewal premium, payable on the policy, and
   (c) in any other case, 35% of the first year's premium, 7½% of the second and third year's renewal premium, and thereafter 5% of each renewal premium payable on the policy:

   Provided that in a case referred to in clause (c), an insurer, during the first 10 years of his business, may pay to an insurance agent, and an insurance agent may receive from such an insurer, 40% of the first year's premium payable on the policy.
2. No person shall pay or contract to pay to a special agent, and no special agent shall receive or contract to receive, by way of commission or as remuneration in any form, in respect of any policy of life insurance issued in India by an insurer after the 31st

day of December 1950 and effected through a special agent, an amount exceeding:

(a) in a case referred to in clause (a) of Sub-section (1) one-half per cent of the premium;

(b) in a case referred to in clause (b) of Sub-section (1) two per cent of the first year's premium payable on the policies; and

(c) in a case referred to in clause (c) of Sub-section (1) fifteen per cent of the first year's premium payable on the policies.

Prohibition of Rebates (Section 41)

1. No person shall allow or offer to allow either directly or indirectly as an inducement to any person to take out or renew or continue an insurance in respect of any kind of risk, relating to lives or property in India, any rebate of the whole or part of the commission payable or any rebate of the premium shown on the policy, nor shall any person taking out or renewing or continuing a policy accept any rebate, except such rebate as may be allowed in accordance with the published prospectuses or tables of the insurer:

   Provided that acceptance by an insurance agent of commission in connection with a policy of the insurance taken out by himself on his own life shall not be deemed to be acceptance of a rebate of premium within the meaning of this sub-section if at the time of such acceptance the insurance agent satisfies the prescribed conditions establishing that he is *bonafide* insurance agent employed by the insurer.

2. Any person making default in complying with the provisions of this section shall be punishable with fine which may extend to Rs. 5000.

Licensing of Insurance Agents (Section 42)

1. The Authority or an officer authorised by him in this behalf shall, in the prescribed manner and on payment of the fee determined by the regulations, which shall not be more than two hundred and fifty rupees, issue to any person making an application in the prescribed manner determined by the regulations, a licence to act as an insurance agent for the purpose of soliciting or procuring insurance business provided that:

   (a) in the case of an individual, he does not suffer from any of the disqualification:

      (i) that the person is a minor;

      (ii) that he is found to be of unsound mind by a court of competent jurisdiction;

      (iii) that he has been found guilty of criminal

misappropriation or criminal breach of trust or cheating or forgery or an abetment of or attempt to commit any such offence by a court of competent jurisdiction:

Provided that, where at least five years have elapsed since the completion of sentence imposed on any person in respect of any such offence, the Authority shall ordinarily declare in respect of such person that his conviction shall cease to operate as a disqualification under this clause;

(iv) that in the course of any judicial proceedings relating to any policy of insurance or the winding up of an insurance company or in the course of an investigation of the affairs of an insurer it has been found that he has been guilty of or has knowingly participated in or connived at any fraud, dishonestly or misrepresentation against an insurer or an insured;

(v) that he does not possess the requisite qualifications and practical training for a period not exceeding twelve months, as may be specified by the regulations made by the Authority in this behalf;

(vi) that he had not passed such examination as may be specified by the regulations made by the Authority in this behalf:

Provided that a person who had been issued a licence under sub-section (1) of this Section or sub-section (1) of Section 64UM shall not be required to possess the requisite qualifications, practical training and pass such examination as required by clauses (e) and (f); and

(vii) that he violates the code of conduct as may be specified by the regulations made by the Authority.

(b) in the case of a company or firm, any of its directors or partners does not suffer from any of the said disqualifications:

Provided further that any licence issued immediately before the commencement of the Insurance Regulatory and Development Authority Act, 1999 shall be deemed to have been issued in accordance with the regulations which provide for such licence.

2. A licence issued under this section shall entitle the holder to act as an insurance agent for any insurer.

3. A licence issued under this section, after the commencement of the Insurance Regulatory and Development Authority Act, 1999, shall remain in force for a period of three years only from the date of issue, but shall, if the applicant, does not suffer from any of the disqualification mentioned above and the application for renewal of the licence reaches the issuing authority at least thirty

days before the date on which the licence ceases to remain in force, be renewed for a period of three years at any one time on payment of the prescribed fee which shall not be more than two hundred and fifty rupees, and an additional fee of a prescribed amount, not exceeding one hundred rupees by way of penalty if the application for renewal of the licence does not reach the issuing authority at least thirty days before the date on which the licence ceases to remain in force.

Investments

Every insurer shall invest and at all times keep invested assets equivalent to not less than the sum of:

(a) the amount of his liabilities to holders of life insurance policies in India on account of matured claims, and

(b) the amount required to meet the liability on policies of life insurance maturing for payment in India, less:

(i) the amount of premiums which have fallen due to the insurer on such policies but have not been paid and the days of grace for payment of which have not expired, and

(ii) any amount due to the insurer for loans granted on and within the surrender values of policies of life insurance maturing for payment in India issued by him or by an insurer whose business he has acquired and in respect of which he has assumed liability.

In the manner following, namely, twenty-five per cent of the said sum in Government securities, a further sum equal to not less than twenty-five per cent of the said sum in Government securities or other approved securities and the balance in any of the approved investments specified in sub-section (1) of Section 27A or, subject to the limitations, conditions and restrictions specified in sub-section (2) of that Section, in any other investment.

Section 27-A

1. No insurer shall invest or keep invested any part of his controlled fund otherwise than in any of the following approved investment, namely:
   (a) Approved securities;
   (b) Securities of, or guaranteed by Government of U.K.;
   (c) Debentures or other securities of Municipality in a State;
   (d) Debentures or other securities issued by a body constituted by any Central Act or Act of State Legislature;
   (e) First Mortgage on immovable property under any housing or building scheme;

(f) Debentures secured on first charge on immovable property;
(g) First debentures secured by a floating charge on all its assets;
(h) Preference shares of any company;
(i) Shares of any company which have been guaranteed by any company;
(j) First Mortgage on immovable property;
(k) Immovable property situated in India or in any other country;
(l) Loans on life interests, or on policies of life insurance within their surrender values;
(m) Life interests;
(n) Fixed deposits with banks;
(o) Debentures of, or shares in cooperative societies;
(p) Such other investments as the Authority may declare to be approved investments.

Prohibition of Loan

No insurer shall grant loans or temporary advances either on hypothecation of property or on personal security or otherwise, except loans on life policies issued by him within their surrender value, to any director, manager, managing agent, actuary, auditor, or officer of the insurer if the company or where the insurer is a firm, to any partner therein, or to any other company or firm in which any such director, manager, managing agent, actuary, officer or partner holds such position. [Section 29(1)]

Investigation

The Authority may, at any time, by order in writing, direct any person (Investigating Authority) specified in the order to investigate the affairs of any insurer and to report to the Authority on any investigation made by him provided that the Investigating Authority may, whenever necessary employ any auditor or actuary or both for the purpose of assisting him in any investigating under this section. [Section 33]

17.3 LIFE INSURANCE CORPORATION ACT, 1956

Life insurance business in India was nationalised with effect from January 19, 1956. On the date, the Indian business of 16 non-Indian insurers operating in India and 75 Provident Societies were taken over by Government of India. Life Insurance Corporation of India. Act was passed by the Parliament on June 18, 1956 and came into effect from July 1, 1956. Life Insurance Corporation of India Commenced its functioning as a corporate body from September 1, 1956. Its working is governed by the LIC Act. The LIC is a corporate having perpetual succession and a common seal with a power to acquire, hold and dispose of property and can by its name sue and be sued. Certain important provisions of the Act (as amended by IRDA Act, 1999) are discussed as follows:

Important Provisions of Life Insurance Corporation Act, 1956

1. Constitution;
2. Capital;
3. Functions of the Corporation;
4. Transfer of Services;
5. Set-up of the Corporation;
6. Committee of the Corporation;
7. Authorities;
8. Finance, Accounts and Audit; and
9. Miscellaneous.

Constitution

Establishment and Incorporation of Life Insurance Corporation of India (Section 3)

1. With effect from such date as the Central Government may, by notification in the Official Gazette, appoint, there shall be established a corporation called the Life Insurance Corporation of India.
2. The corporation shall be a body corporate having perpetual succession and a common seal with power, subject to the provisions of this Act to acquire, hold and dispose of property and may by its name sue and be used.

Constitution of the Corporation (Section 4)

1. The Corporation shall consist of such number of persons not exceeding sixteen as the Central Government may think fit to appoint thereto and one of them shall be appointed by the Central Government to be the Chairman thereof.
2. Before appointing a person to be a member the Central Government shall satisfy itself that the person has no such financial or other interest as is likely to affect prejudicially the exercise or performance by him of his functioning as a member, and the Central Government shall also satisfy itself from time to time with respect to every member that he has no such interest; and any person who is, or whom the Central Government proposes to appoint and who has consented to be a member shall, whenever required by the Central Government so to do, furnish to it such information as the Central Government considers necessary for the performance of its duties under this sub-section.
3. A member who is in any way directly or indirectly interested in a contract made or proposed to be made by the Corporation shall as soon as possible report to the Corporation.

Capital

The original capital of the corporation shall be five crores of rupees provided by the Central Government after due appropriation made by Parliament by law for the purpose, and the terms and conditions relating to the provisions of such capital shall be such as may be determined by the Central Government.

The Central Government may on the recommendation of the Corporation, reduce the capital of the Corporation to such extent and in such manner as the Central Government may determine (Section 5).

Functions of the Corporation

It is the general duty of the Corporation to carry on life insurance business, whether in or outside India, and the Corporation shall so exercise its powers under this Act as to secure that the life insurance business is developed to the best advantage of the community.

The Corporation also:

(a) Carries on capital redemption business, annuity certain business, or reinsurance business in so far as such reinsurance business appertains to life insurance business;
(b) Invests the funds of the Corporation in such manner as the Corporation may think fit and to take all such steps as may be necessary or expedient for the protection or realise of any investment, including the taking over of and administering any property offered as security for the investment until a suitable opportunity arises for its disposal;
(c) Acquires, holds and disposes of any property for the purpose of its business;
(d) Transfers the whole or any part of the life insurance business carried on outside India to any other person or persons, if in the interests of the Corporation it is expedient so to do;
(e) Advances or lends money upon the security of any moveable or immovable property or otherwise;
(f) Borrows or raises any money in such manner and upon such security as the Corporation may think fit;
(g) Carries on either by itself or through any subsidiary any other business in any case where such other business was being carried on by a subsidiary of an insurer whose controlled business has been transferred to and vested in the Corporation under this Act.
(h) Carries on any other business which may seem to the Corporation to be capable of being conveniently carried on in connection with its business and calculated directly or indirectly to render profitable the business of the Corporation; and
(i) Doing also such thing as may be incidental conducive to the proper exercise of any of the powers of the Corporation.

Transfer of Services

All the employees except chief agent will be vested into new life-business. The salary and terms of employment will remain the same unless insurance business thinks fit to change the terms of employment for the benefit of the policyholder. If any term is not acceptable to an employee, he can be terminated by paying three months' salary as compensation

Subject to such rules as the Central government may make in this behalf, every whole-time salaried employee of a Chief Agent of an insurer whose controlled business has been transferred to and vested in the corporation and

(a) who was employed by the Chief Agent wholly or mainly in connection with the controlled business of the insurer;
(b) whose salary on the appointed day did not exceed five hundred rupees per mensem; and
(c) who was in the employment of the Chief Agent for a continuous period of not less than one year immediately before the appointed day shall on and from the appointed day, become an employee of the Corporation and the provisions of Section 11 shall, so far as may be, apply in relation to such employee as they apply in relation to a whole-time employee of the insurer.

Provided that this section shall not apply except in cases where the Chief Agent of the insurer was required under the terms of his contract with the insurer to render the prescribed service to policyholders of the insurers. (Section 12)

Offices, Branches and Agencies (Section 18)

(i) The Central Office of the Corporation shall be at such a place as the Central Government may by notification in the Official gazette, specify.
(ii) The Corporation shall establish a Zonal Office at each of the following places, i.e. Bombay, Calcutta, Delhi, Kanpur and Madras and subject to the previous approval of the Central Government, may establish such other zonal offices as it thinks fit.
(iii) The territorial limits of each zone shall be such as may be specified by the Corporation.
(iv) There may be established as many divisional offices and branches in each zone as the Zonal Manager thinks fit.

Committee of the Corporation (Section 19)

The corporation may entrust the general superintendence and direction of its affairs and business to an executive committee consisting not more than five of its members and the executive committee may exercise all powers and do all such acts and things as may be delegated to it by the Corporation.

The Corporation may also constitute an Investment Committee for the purpose of advising it in matters relating to the investment of its funds, and the Investment Committee shall consist of not more than eight members of whom not less than three shall be members of corporations and the remaining members shall be persons (whether members of the corporation or not) who have special knowledge and experience in financial matters, particularly matters relating to investment of funds.

The Corporation may constitute such other committee as it may think fit for the purpose to discharge such of its functions as may be delegated to them.

Authorities

(a) Managing Director

The Corporation may appoint, one or more persons to be the Managing Director or Directors of the Corporation and every Managing Director shall be a whole-time officer of the Corporation, and shall exercise such powers and perform such duties as may be entrusted or delegated to him by the Executive Committee or the Corporation.

Corporation to be Guided by the Directions of Central Government

In the discharge of its function under this Act, the Corporation shall be guided by such directions in matters of policy involving public interest as the Central government may give to it in writing; and if any question arises whether a direction relates to a matter of policy involving public interest the decision of the Central Government thereon shall be final.

(b) Zonal Managers

The Corporation may entrust the superintendence and direction of the affairs and business of a zonal office to a person, whether a member or not, who shall be known as a Zonal Manager and the Zonal Manager shall perform all such functions of the Corporation as may be delegated to him with respect to the area within the jurisdiction of the Zonal Office.

The Corporation may constitute for each zone a Board consisting of such number of persons as it thinks fit to appoint thereto for the purpose of advising the Zonal Manager in respect of such matters as are referred to it under the regulations made by the Corporation.

The Corporation shall constitute in the prescribed manner for each zonal office an Employees and Agents Relations Committee consisting of such number of person as it thinks fit and every such committee shall consist of representatives of the Corporation and of its employees and agents.

Finance, Accounts and Audit

(a) Audit (Section 25)

The accounts of the Corporation shall be audited by auditors duly qualified to act as auditors of companies under the law for the time being in force relating to companies, and the auditors shall be appointed by the Corporation with the previous approval of the Central Government and shall receive such remuneration from the Corporation as the Central Government may fix.

Every auditor in the performance of his duties shall have at all reasonable time access to the books of accounts and other document of the Corporation.

The auditors shall submit their report to the Corporation and shall also forward a copy of their report to the Central Government.

(b) Actuarial Valuation (Section 26)

The Corporation shall, once at least in every two years, cause an investigation to be made of actuaries into the financial condition of the business of the Corporation, including a valuation of the liabilities of the Corporation and submit the report of the actuaries to the Central Government.

(c) Annual Report of Activities of Corporation (Section 27)

The Corporation shall, as soon as may be, after the end of each financial year, prepare and submit to the Central Government in such form as may be prescribed a report giving an account of its activities during the previous financial year, and the report shall also give an account of the activities, if any, which are likely to be undertaken by the Corporation in the next financial year.

(d) Surplus how to be Utilised (Section 28)

If as a result of any investigation undertaken by the Corporation under Section 26 any surplus emerges, 95% of such surplus shall be allocated to or reserved for the policyholders of the Corporation and the remainder may be utilised for such purposes and in such manner as the Central Government may determine.

(e) Reports to be laid before Parliament (Section 29)

The Central Government shall cause the report of the auditors under Section 25, the report of the actuaries under Section 26 and the report giving an account of the activities of the Corporation under Section 27 to be laid before both Houses of Parliament as soon as may be after each such report is received by the Central Government.

Miscellaneous

(a) Corporation to have the Exclusive Privilege of Carrying on Life Insurance Business (Section 30)

Except to the extent otherwise expressly provided in this Act, on and from the appointed day the Corporation shall have the exclusive privilege of carrying on life insurance business in India; and on and from the said day any certificate of registration under the Insurance Act held by any insurer immediately before the said day shall cease to have effect in so far as it authorises him to carry on life insurance business in India.

Exclusive Privilege of Corporation to Cease (Section 30A)

Notwithstanding anything contained in this Act, the exclusive privilege of carrying on life insurance business in India by the Corporation shall cease on and from the commencement of the Insurance Regulatory and Development Authority Act, 1999 and the Corporation shall, therefore, carry on life insurance business in India in accordance with the provisions of the Insurance Act, 1938.

Exception in the Case of Insurance Business in Respect of Persons Residing Outside India (Section 31)

1. Notwithstanding anything contained in Section 30 or in the Insurance Act, the Central Government may, by order, permit any person who has made an application in that behalf, to carry on life insurance business in India in respect of the lives of persons ordinarily resident outside India, subject to such restrictions and conditions as may be specified in the order and any such order shall be deemed to have effect as if it were a certificate of registration issued by the Authority to such person under Section 3 of the Insurance Act in respect of that class of business.
2. Nothing in sub-section (1) shall authorise any person permitted to carry on life insurance business of the nature referred to in that sub-section, to insure the life of any person ordinarily resident outside India, during any period of his temporary residence in India.

(b) Power of Corporation to have Official Seal in Certain Cases (Section 32)

The Corporation may have for use in any zonal office, divisional office or in any office outside India an official seal which shall be a fascimile of the common seal of the Corporation, with the addition on its face of the name of the zonal office, divisional office or other office where it is to be used, and any such official seal may be affixed to any deed or document to which the Corporation is a party.

(c) Requirement of Foreign Laws to be Complied with in Certain Cases (Section 33)

Where any property or rights appertaining to the controlled business of an insurer are transferred to and vested in the Corporation under this Act or would be so transferred and vested but for the fact that such transfer and testing are governed otherwise than by the law of India, the insurer shall comply with such directions as may be given to him by the Corporation for the purpose of securing that the ownership of the property or, as the case may be, that the right is effectively transferred to the Corporation.

(d) Revesting of Certain Shares Vested in the Administrator General (Section 34)

Notwithstanding anything containing in the Insurance Act, all shares which have vested in the Administrator General of any State under sub-section (8) of Section 6A of that Act and which have not been disposed of in accordance with the provision of that sub-section before the appointed day, shall, on payment of the amount of expenditure, if any, incurred by the Administrator General in relation to such shares by the persons who would have been entitled to those shares if the said sub-section had not been enacted, revest in such persons.

(e) Reputation of Assets and Liabilities in the Case of Foreign Insurers in Certain Cases (Section 35)

1. Any insurer incorporated outside India may, before the appointed day, make an application to the Central Government stating that among the assets appertaining to the controlled business of the insurer there are assets brought into India by the insurer for the purpose of building up his life insurance business in India which, notwithstanding anything contained in Section 7, should not be transferred to and vested in the Corporation.
2. On receipt of an application under sub-section (1), the Central Government shall determine the value of the assets of the insurer appertaining to his controlled business in existence on the 31st day of December, 1955, computed as at that date in accordance with the provisions contained in paragraph 3 of Part B of the First Schedule, and deduct therefrom the total amount of the liabilities of the insurer appertaining to this controlled business in existence on the 31st day of December, 1955, computed as at that date in accordance with the provisions contained in the Second Schedule; and if there is any excess, the Central Government may, by order, direct that such assets equivalent in value to the excess as may be specified in the order shall not be transferred to or vested in the Corporation, or where the order is made after the appointed day, that the Corporation shall be divested of the said assets.
3. In the case of any insurer incorporated outside India, the Central Government may also, by order, direct that any such liabilities in respect of life insurance policies expressed in any foreign currency issued on the lives of persons who are not citizens of India as are specified in the order together with any such assets necessary to meet the liabilities, as may be so specified, shall not be transferred to or vested in the Corporation or, if the order is made after the appointed day, that the Corporation shall be divested of such liabilities and assets as aforesaid:

4. The amount of liabilities in respect of the policies referred to in an order made under sub-section (3) shall be computed as at the 31st day of December, 1955:
   (a) in any case where in respect of the insurer concerned as order has been made under sub-section (2), in accordance with the provisions contained in clause (b) of the Second Schedule; and
   (b) in any other case, in accordance with method A specified in the Second Schedule.

   Explanation: In computing the amount of liabilities in respect of the policies referred to in this sub-section, allowance shall be made for receipts and payments in respect of such policies from the 31st day of December, 1955, up to the date of the order.
5. Every order made by the Central Government under this section shall be carried out by the Corporation in such manner as the Central Government may direct.

(f) Contracts of Chief Agents and Special Agents to Terminate (Section 36)

Notwithstanding anything contained in the Insurance Act or in any other law for the time being in force, every contract appertaining to controlled business subsisting immediately before the appointed day:

(a) between an insurer and his chief agent or between an insurer and a special agent; or
(b) between the chief agent of an insurer and a special agent;

shall, as from the appointed day, cease to have effect and all rights accruing to the chief agent or the special agent under any such contract shall terminate on that day.

Provided that in every such case compensation shall be given by the Corporation to the chief agent or the special agent, as the case may be, in accordance with the principles contained in the Third Scheduled, and the provisions of sub-Section (2) of Section 16 shall, so far as may be, apply in every such case.

(g) Policies to be Guaranteed by Central Government (Section 37)

The sums assured by all policies issued by the Corporation including any bonuses declared in respect thereof and, subject to the provisions contained in Section 14 the amounts assured by all policies issued by any insurer the liabilities under which have vested in the Corporation under this Act, and all bonuses declared in respect thereof, whether before or after the appointed day, shall be guaranteed as to payment in cash by the Central Government.

(h) Liquidation of Corporation (Section 38)

No provisions of law relating to the winding up of companies or

Corporations shall apply to the Corporation established under this Act, and the Corporation shall not be placed in liquidation save by order of the Central Government and in such manner as that Government may direct.

(i) Special Provisions for Winding-up of Certain Insurers (Section 39)

Where any insurer being a company (other than a composite insurer) whose controlled business has been transferred to and vested in the Corporation under this Act has in accordance with the provisions of this Act collected and distributed any moneys paid to him by the Corporation by way of compensation or otherwise and has also complied with any direction given to him by the Corporation for the purpose of securing that the ownership of any property or any right is effectively transferred to the Corporation, the Central Government may on application being made to it in this behalf by such insurer grant a certificate to the insurer that there is no reason for the continued existence of the insurer and where such a certificate has been granted shall cause the certificate to be published in the Official Gazette and upon the publication thereof the insurer shall be dissolved.

(j) Penalty for Withholding Property, etc. (Section 40)

If any person wilfully withholds or fails to deliver to the Corporation as required by Section 13, any property or any books, documents or other papers which may be in his possession or unlawfully retains possession of any property of an insurer which has been transferred to and vested in the Corporation under this Act or wilfully applies any such property to purposes other than those expressed in or authorised by this Act, he shall, on the complaint of the Corporation, be punishable with imprisonment which may extend to one year, or with fine which may extent to one thousand rupees, or with both.

(k) Tribunal to have Exclusive Jurisdiction in Certain Matters (Section 41)

No civil court shall have jurisdiction to entertain or adjudicate upon any matter which a Tribunal is empowered to decide or determine under this Act.

(l) Enforcement of Decisions of Tribunals (Section 42)

Any decision of a Tribunal may be enforced in any civil court within the local limits of whose jurisdiction the person against whom the decision is to be enforced actually and voluntarily resides or carriers on business or personally works for gain or owns any property, as if it were a decree passed by that court.

(m) Application of the Insurance Act (Section 43)

(1) The following sections of the Insurance Act shall, so far as may be, apply to the Corporation as they apply to any other insurer, namely:

Sections: 2, 2B, 3, 18, 26, 33, 41, 45, 46, 47A, 50, 51, 52, 110A, 110B, 110C, 119, 121, 122 and 123.

(2) The Central Government shall, as soon as may be after the commencement of this Act, by notification in the Official Gazette, direct that the following sections of the Insurance Act shall apply to the corporation subject to such conditions and modifications as may be specified in the notification, namely:
Sections: 2D, 10, 11, 13, 14, 15, 20, 21, 22, 23, 25, 27A, 28A, 35, 36, 37, 40, 40A, 40B, 43, 44, 102 to 106, 107 to 110, 111, 113, 114 and 116A
Section 42 of the Insurance Act shall have effect in relation to the issue to any individual of a licence to act as an agent for the purpose of soliciting or procuring life insurance business for the Corporation as if the reference to an officer authorised by the Controller in this behalf in sub-section (1) thereof included a reference to an officer of the Corporation authorised by the Authority in this behalf.

(3) The Central government may, by notification in the Official Gazette, direct that all or any of the provisions of the Insurance Act other than those specified in sub-section (1) or sub-section (2), shall apply to the Corporation subject to such conditions and modifications as may be specified in the notification.

(4) Every notification issued under sub-section (2) or sub-section (3) shall be laid for not less than 30 days before both Houses of Parliament as soon as possible after it is issued, and shall be subject to such modifications as Parliament may make during the session in which it is so laid or the session immediately following.

(5) Save as provided in this section, nothing contained in the Insurance Act shall apply to the Corporation.

(n) Act not to Apply in Certain Cases (Section 44)

Nothing contained in this Act shall apply in relation to:

(a) any insurer whose business is being voluntarily wound up or is being wound up under the orders of the court;

(b) any insurer to whom the Insurance Act does not apply by reason of the provisions contained in Section 2E thereof;

(c) any composite insurer in respect of the management of whose affairs an Administrator has been appointed under Section 52A of the Insurance Act;

(d) the scheme run by the Central Government known as the Post Office Life Insurance Fund;

(e) any approved superannuation fund as defined in clause (a) of Section 58N of the Indian Income-tax Act, 1922 which is in existence on the appointed day;

(f) any scheme in existence on the appointed day or any scheme framed after the appointed day with the approval of the Central Government whereby, in consideration of certain compulsory deductions made by Government from the salaries of its employee as part of the conditions of service, the payment of money is assured by Government on the death of the employee concerned or on the happening of any contingency dependent on his life.

(o) Special Provisions Regarding Transfer .of Controlled Business of Certain Composite Insurers (Section 45)

Notwithstanding anything contained in clause (c) of Section 44, the Central Government may, by notification in the Official Gazette, direct that on and with effect from such date as may be specified in the notification the assets and liabilities appertaining to the controlled business of a composite insurer in respect of the management of whose affairs an Administrator has been appointed under Section 52A of the Insurance Act shall be transferred to and vested in the corporation, and on the issue of such a notification the provisions of this Act shall, so far as may be, apply in relation to such insurer and to the transfer and vesting of the assets and liabilities of his controlled business in the Corporation subject to the modification that references in this Act to the appointed day shall be constructed as references to the day specified in the notification.

(p) Defects in Constitution of Corporation or Committees not to Invalidate Acts or Proceedings (Section 46)

No Act or proceeding of the Corporation or of any Committee of the Corporation shall be called in question on the ground merely of the existence of any vacancy or defect in the constitution of the Corporation or Committee, as the case may be.

(q) Protection of Action taken under Act (Section 47)

No suit, prosecution or other legal proceeding shall lie against any member or employee of the Corporation for anything which is in good faith done or intended to be done under this Act.

(r) Power to make Rules (Section 48)

(1) The Central Government may, by notification in the Official Gazette, make rules to carry out the purposes of this Act.

(2) In particular, and without prejudice to the generality of the foregoing power, such rules may provide for all or any of the following matters, namely:
   (a) the term of office and the conditions of service of members;
   (b) the manner in which the moneys and other assets belonging to any such fund as is referred to in Section 8 shall be

apportioned between the trustees of the fund and the Corporation;

(c) the services which the chief agent should have rendered for the purpose of the provision to Section 12;

(d) the jurisdiction of the Tribunals constituted under section 17;

(e) the manner in which, and the persons to whom, any compensation under this Act may be paid;

(f) the time within which any matter which may be referred to a Tribunal for decision under this Act may be so referred;

(g) the manner in which and the conditions subject to which investments may be made by the Corporation;

(h) the manner in which an Employees and Agents Relations Committee may be constituted for each zonal office;

(i) the form in which the report giving an account of the activities of the Corporation shall be prepared;

(j) the conditions subject to which the Corporation may appoint employees;

(k) the fees payable under this Act and the manner in which they are to be collected; and

(l) any other matter which has to be or may be prescribed.

(3) All rules made under this section shall be laid for not less than thirty days before both Houses of Parliament as soon as possible after they are made, and shall be subject to such modifications as Parliament may make during the session in which they are so laid or the session immediately following.

(s) Power to make Regulations (Section 49)

(1) The Corporation may, with the previous approval of the Central Government, by notification in the Gazette of India, make regulations not inconsistent with this Act and the rules made thereunder to provide for all matters for which provision is expendient for the purpose of giving effect to the provisions of this Act.

(2) In particular, and without prejudice to the generality of the foregoing power, such regulations may provide for:

(a) the powers and functions of the Corporation which may be delegated to the Zonal Managers;

(b) the method of recruitment of employees and agents of the Corporation;

(c) the number, term of office and conditions of service of members of Boards constituted under Section 22;

(d) the territorial limits of each zone established under this Act and the business to be transacted in each zone;

(e) the manner in which the fund of the Corporation shall be maintained;

(f) the maintenance of separate funds and accounts at each of the zonal office;

(g) the jurisdiction of each divisional office and the establishment of Councils representative of policyholders in each area served by a divisional office for the purpose of advising the divisional office in respect of any matter which may be referred to it;

(h) the conduct of business at meetings of the Corporation;

(i) the formation of Committees of the Corporation and the delegation of powers and functions of the Corporation to such Committees, and the conduct of business at meetings of such Committees;

(j) the form and manner in which policies may be issued and contracts binding on the Corporation may be executed;

(k) the classification of policies, whether issued by the Corporation or by any insurer whose controlled business has been transferred to and vested in the Corporation for the purpose of declaring differential bonuses, wherever necessary;

(l) the manner in which and the intervals within which the accounts of the various zonal offices, divisional offices and branch offices may be inspected and their accounts audited; and

(m) the conditions subject to which any payment may be made by the Corporation.

17.4 GENERAL INSURANCE BUSINESS (NATIONALIZATION) ACT, 1972

General Insurance Business (Nationalization) Act provide for the acquisition and transfer of shares of Indian insurance companies and undertaking of other existing insurers in order to serve better the needs of the economy by securing the development of general insurance business in the best interests of the community and to ensure that the operation of the economic system does not result in the concentration of wealth to the common detriment for the regulation and control of such business and for matters connected therewith or incidental thereto.

This Act governs the general insurance in our country. The Act contains provisions relating to the constitution, management and winding up of insurance companies and the conduct of all types of insurance business. All insurance business in India has been nationalised. The General Insurance Corporation of India carries on the general insurance business in India, its four subsidiaries besides a host of multinationals joining in the fray. The important provisions of the act are as follows:

Transfer to Public Ownership of General Insurance Business

Transfer of Shares of Indian Insurance Companies (Section 4)

(1) On the appointed day all the shares in the capital of every Indian insurance company shall, by virtue of this Act, stand transferred to and vested in the Central Government free of all trusts, liabilities and encumbrances affecting them.

(2) Out of the shares so transferred and vested, the Central Government shall, immediately thereafter, by notification, provide for the transfer of not less than ten shares of every such company to such persons as may be specified in the notification to enable the Indian insurance company to function as a Government company.

(3) Every notification made under sub-section (2) shall specify the names and description of the persons to whom the shares are transferred and the particulars of the shares which are transferred to each such person.

(4) A copy of every notifications made under sub-section (2) shall, as soon as may be after it is made, be sent by the Central Government to the concerned Indian insurance company, who shall, on receipt of such copy, and notwithstanding anything contained in the Companies Act or in its articles of association, forthwith rectify its register of members by including therein the persons mentioned in the notification as the holders of the shares specified therein.

(5) For the removal of doubts it is hereby declared that the transfer and vesting of shares effected under sub-section (1) shall not be deemed to affect any right of the Indian insurance company subsisting immediately before the appointed day against any shareholder to recover from him any sum of money on the ground that shareholder has not paid or credited to the insurer the whole or any part of the value of the shares held by him or on any other ground whatsoever.

Transfer of Undertakings of other Existing Insurers (Section 5)

(1) On the appointed day, the undertaking of every existing insurer who is not an Indian insurance company shall stand transferred to and vested in the Central Government and the Central Government shall immediately thereafter provide, by notification, for the transfer to and vesting in such Indian insurance company, as it may specify in the notification of that undertaking.

(2) Any notification made under sub-section (1) may provide that any of the undertakings aforesaid may be transferred to and vested in more than one Indian insurance company in such manner and

subject to such conditions as may be specified in the notification.

Effect of Transfer of Undertakings (Section 6)

(1) The undertaking of every such exiting insurer as is referred to in Section 5 shall be deemed to include all assets, rights, powers, authorities and privileges and all property, movable and immovable, cash balances, reserve funds, investments and all other rights and interests in, or arising out of, such property as were immediately before the appointed day in the ownership, possession, power or control of such existing insurer in relation to the undertaking whether within or without India, and all books of accounts, records and all other documents of whatever nature relating thereto, and shall also be deemed to include all borrowings, liabilities and obligations of whatever kind then subsisting of the existing insurer in relation to the undertaking.

(2) Unless otherwise expressly provided by this Act, all deeds, bonds, agreements, powers of attorney, grants of legal representation and other instruments of whatever nature subsisting or having effect immediately before the appointed day and to which any such insurer as in referred to in Section 5 is a party or which are in favour of such existing insurer shall be of as full force and effect against or in favour of the Indian insurance company in which the undertaking or the part to which the instrument relates has vested and may be enforced or acted upon as fully and effectually as if, in the place of the existing insurer referred to in Section 5, the Indian insurance company in which the undertaking or any part thereof as vested had been a party thereto, or as if they had been issued in its favour.

(3) If, on the appointed day, any suit, appeal or other proceeding of whatever nature in relation to any business of the undertaking which has been transferred under Section 5 is pending by or against any such existing insurer as in referred to in that section the same shall not abate, be discontinued or be in any way prejudicially affected by reason of the transfer of the undertaking or of anything contained in this Act, but the suit, appeal or other proceeding may be continued, prosecuted and enforced by or against the Indian insurance company in which the undertaking or the part to which the proceeding relates has vested.

(4) For the removal of doubts it hereby declared that in the case of foreign insurer or as the case may be, the Life Insurance Corporation, the provisions of Section 5 and preceding sub-sections shall only apply to the extent to which any property appertains, in the former case, to the general insurance business carried on in India and in the later case to the general insurance business carried on whether within or without India, and to

rights and powers acquired, and to debts, liabilities and obligations incurred and to contracts, agreements and other instruments made by the foreign insurer or the Life Insurance Corporation, as the case may be for the purpose of such general insurance business and to legal proceedings relating to these purposes, and the said provisions shall be construed accordingly.

(5) If any question arise as to whether any property appertains to any such general insurance business as in referred to in this section or whether any rights, powers, liabilities or obligations were acquired or incurred or any contract, agreement or other instrument was made by the foreign insurer or the Life Insurance Corporation, as the case may be, for the purposes of any such business or whether any documents relate to those purposes, the question shall be referred to the Central Government which shall, after giving an opportunity of being heard to the persons interested in the matter, decide it in such manner as it things fit.

Transfer of Service of Employees in Certain Cases (Section 7)

(1) Every whole-time officer or other employee of an existing insurer other than an Indian insurance company who was employed by that insurer wholly or mainly in connection with his general insurance business immediately before the appointed day shall, on the appointed day, become an officer or other employee, as the case may be, of the Indian insurance company in which the undertaking of that insurer or that part of the undertaking to which the service of the officer or other employee relates has vested, and shall hold his office or service under the Indian insurance company on the same terms and conditions and with the same rights to pension, gratuity and other matter as would have been admissible to him if there had been no such vesting, and shall continue to do so unless and until his employment in the Indian insurance company in which the undertaking or part has vested is terminated or until his remuneration, terms and conditions are duly altered by that Indian insurance company:
Provided that nothing in this sub-section shall apply to any such officer or other employee who has given, in writing, notice to the Central Government or to any person nominated in this behalf by that Government before the appointed day intimating his intention of not becoming an officer or employee of the Indian insurance company in whom the undertaking or part thereof to which his service relates has vested.

(2) If any question arises as to whether any person was a wholetime officer or employee, or as to whether any officer or employee was employed wholly or mainly in connection with the general insurance business of the existing insurer referred to in sub-

section (1), immediately before the appointed day, the question shall be referred within a period of two years from the appointed day and not thereafter, to the Central Government which shall, after giving an opportunity of being heard to the person concerned in the matter, decide it in such manner as it thinks fit and such decision shall be final.

(3) Notwithstanding anything contained in the Industrial Disputes Act, 1947 or in any other law for the time being in force, the transfer of the services of any officer or other employee under sub-section (1) shall not entitle any such officer or other employee to any compensation under that Act or such other law and no such claim shall be entertained by any court, tribunal or other authority.

Provident, Superannuation, Welfare and other Funds (Section 8)

(1) Where an existing insurer has established a provident, superannuation, welfare or any other fund for the benefit of his employees and constituted a trust in respect thereof (hereinafter in this section referred to as an existing trust), the moneys standing to the credit of such fund on the appointed day, together with any other assets belonging to such fund, shall stand transferred to and vested in the Indian insurance company on the appointed day free from any such trust.

(2) Where all the employees of the Life Insurance Corporation or any other existing insurer do not become employees of an Indian insurance company, the moneys and other assets belonging to any such fund as is referred to in sub-section (1), shall be apportioned between the trustees of the fund and the Indian insurance company in the prescribed manner; and in case of any dispute about such apportionment the decision of the Central Government thereon shall be final.

(3) Where the undertaking of an existing insurer has vested in more than one Indian insurance company, the Central Government may, by order, provide for the apportionment among such Indian insurance companies of moneys and other assets belonging to any existing trust relating to that undertaking in such manner as in its opinion may be appropriate.

(4) The Indian insurance company shall as soon as may be after the appointed day constitute in response of the moneys and other assets which are transferred to and vested in it under this section one or more trusts having objects as similar to the objects of the existing trusts in the circumstances may be practicable.

(5) Where all the moneys and other assets belonging to an existing trust are transferred to and vested in an Indian insurance company under this section, the trustees of such trust shall, as

from the appointed day, stand discharged from the trust, except as respects things done or omitted to be done before the appointed day.

General Insurance Corporation of India

Formation of General Insurance Corporation of India (Section 9)

(1) As soon as may be after the commencement of this Act, the Central Government shall form a Government company in accordance with the provisions of the Companies Act, to be known as the General Insurance Corporation of India for the purpose of superintending, controlling and carrying on the business of general insurance.

(2) The authorised capital of the Corporation shall be rupees two hundred and fifty crores, divided into two hundred and fifty lakhs fully paid up shares of one hundred rupees each, out of which rupees five crores shall be the initial subscribed capital of the Corporation.

(3) Notwithstanding anything contained in the Companies Act, 1956, it shall not be necessary to add the word "Limited" as the last word of the name of the Corporation.

Transfer to Corporation of Shares Vested in Central Government (Section 10)

All the shares in the capital of every Indian insurance company which stand transferred to and vested in the Central Government by virtue of Section 4 (with the exception of the shares transferred to any person under sub-section (2) of that section) shall, immediately after such vesting, stand transferred to and vested in the Corporation and every Indian insurance company shall forthwith give effect to such transfer of shares and rectify its register of members by including therein the Corporation as the holder of such shares.

Amounts to be for Acquisitions

Amounts to be Paid for Transfer and Vesting of Shares or Undertakings (Section 11)

(1) For the transfer of the shares of each Indian insurance company to, and vesting in, the Central Government, under Section 4, there shall be paid by the Central Government to the Corporation, for distribution to the shareholders of each such company, the amount specified against such company in the corresponding entry under column (3) of Part A of the Schedule.

(2) For the transfer to, and vesting in, the Central Government under Section 5, of the undertaking of each existing insurer, who is not an Indian insurance company, there shall be paid by the Central

Government to the Corporation, for payment to each such existing insurer, the amount specified against such insurer in the corresponding entry under column (3) of Part B of the Schedule.

Disbursement of Amounts by Corporation (Section 12)

(1) The total amount paid by the Central Government under Section 11 shall be treated as additional contribution to the subscribed capital of the Corporation and such additional subscribed capital shall stand allotted to, and vested in, the Central Government.

(2) The Corporation shall distribute the amount paid to it under Section II, to the shareholders or each Indian insurance company and to each existing insurer, who is not an Indian insurance company, in accordance with their rights and interests, and, if there is any doubt or dispute as to the right, or extent of the right, of any person to receive the whole or any part of such amount, refer such doubt or dispute to the Central Government for determination and thereafter act in accordance with the determination made by that Government.

(3) Save as otherwise provided in sub-section (2), the amount referred to in Section 11 shall be given in accordance with the provisions of Section 13, Section 14 or Section 15, as the case may be.

Mode of Payment (Section 13)

(1) Where the amount referred to in Section 11 is to be given:

(a) to the members of an Indian insurance company, the amount due to each such member shall be paid in full, where it does not exceed twenty-five thousand rupees, and where it exceeds twenty five thousand rupees, each such member shall be paid twenty-five thousand rupees and the balance of the amount due to such members shall be paid to him in three equal instalments, the first of which shall fall due on the appointed day,

(b) to a foreign insurer, it shall be given to him in cash within three months from the appointed day;

(c) to the Life Insurance Corporation, it shall be given to it in three equal annual instalments, the first of which within three months from the appointed day;

(d) to an existing insurer who is a co-operative society, it shall be distributed as soon as may be after the appointed day in accordance with the rules of the society which will apply in case of dissolution of the society;

(e) to an existing insurance not falling within any of the foregoing provisions, it shall be apportioned by the acquiring company among the individual policyholders of the insurer, whose policies with that insurer were in force on the appointed day and were comprised in the undertaking of such insurer in proportion to the premiums paid by the policyholders such policies and every such payment shall be made either:

(i) in cash, to be sent by postal money order, or

(ii) at the option of the policyholder, as a deduction in the premium due at the time of the renewal of the policy and such option shall be exercised by the policyholder before the expiry of three months from the appointed day (or within such further time not exceeding three months as the Central Government may, on the application of the policyholder, allow) and the option so exercised shall be final and shall not be altered or rescinded after it has been exercised:

Provided if any policyholder fails to exercise his option within the time allowed, he shall be deemed to have exercised his option in favour of payment in cash by postal money order.

(2) Where any amount is payable whether in instalments or otherwise under the provision of this section, the unpaid amount where the payment has become due shall carry interest at the rate of four per cent per annum from the appointed day.

Amount Payable to Shareholders may be Paid to Named Persons instead in Certain Cases (Section 14)

(1) Notwithstanding anything contained elsewhere in this Act, if a majority in number of persons, who, immediately before the appointed day, were registered in the books of an Indian insurance company as the members thereof, and representing two-thirds in value of the amount payable to the Indian insurance company, agree either in person or by proxy at a meting specially convened for the purpose that the amount so payable instead of being distributed among the members shall be given to any such person or body of persons as the members may nominate either at that meeting or subsequently for the purpose of carrying on any business, and the Central government is satisfied that due provision has been or will be made for the payment of the value of their respective shares to persons who have dissented from the resolution, the amount may be given to the person or body of persons so nominated in such manner and subject to such conditions as the Central Government may think fit.

(2) No resolution passed at any such meeting as is referred to in sub-section (1) held after the appointed day shall have any effect

unless the meeting has been convened after obtaining the approval of the Central Government.

Payment into Court in Case of Rival Claims (Section 15)

Where a claim to the amount payable under Section 11 is made by two or more persons adversely to one another, the Corporation may cause the amount to be deposited in any civil court having jurisdiction in that behalf and the court shall decide as to whom the payment shall be made.

Schemes for Mergers of Companies, etc. (Section 16)

(1) If the Central Government is of opinion that for the more efficient carrying on of general insurance business it is necessary so to do, it may, by notification, frame one or more schemes providing for all or any of the following matters:

(a) the merger in one Indian insurance company of any other Indian insurance company, or the formation of a new company by the amalgamation of two or more Indian insurance companies;

(b) the transfer to and vesting in the acquiring company of the undertaking (including all its business, properties, assets and liabilities) of any Indian insurance company which ceases to exist by reason of the scheme;

(c) the constitution, name and registered office and the capital structure of the acquiring company and the issue and allotment of shares;

(d) the constitution of a board of management by whatever name called for the management of the acquiring company;

(e) the alteration of the memorandum and articles of association of the acquiring company for such purposes as may be necessary to give effect to the scheme;

(f) the continuance in the acquiring company of the services of all officers and other employees of the Indian insurance company which has ceased to exist by reason of the scheme, in the same terms and conditions which they were governed immediately before the commencement of the scheme;

(g) the rationalisation or revision of pay scales and other terms and conditions of service of officers and other employees whenever necessary;

(h) the transfer to the acquiring company of the provident superannuation, welfare and other funds relating to the officers and other employees of the Indian insurance company which has ceased to exist by reason of the scheme;

(i) the continuance by or against the acquiring company of legal proceedings pending by or against any Indian insurance company which has ceased to exist by reason of the scheme, and the initiation of such legal proceedings, civil or criminal, as the Indian insurance company might have initiated if it had not ceased to exist;

(j) such incidental consequential and supplemental matters as are necessary to give full effect to the scheme.

(2) In framing schemes under sub-section (1), the object of the Central Government shall be to ensure that ultimately there are only four companies (excluding the Corporation) in existence and that they are so situate as to render their combined services effective in all parts of India

(3) Where a scheme under sub-section (1) provides for the transfer of any property or liabilities, then, by virtue of the scheme, the property shall stand transferred to and vested in, and those liabilities shall be transferred to and become the liabilities of the acquiring company.

(4) If the rationalisation or revision of any pay scale or other terms and conditions of service under any scheme is not acceptable to any officer or other employee, the acquiring company may terminate his employment by giving him compensation equivalent to three months' remuneration, unless the contract of service with such employee provides for a shorter notice of termination.

Explanation: The compensation payable to an officer or other employee under this sub-section shall be in addition to, and shall not affect, any pension, gratuity, provident fund or other benefit to which employee may be entitled under his contract of service.

(5) Notwithstanding anything contained in the Industrial Disputes Act, 1947 or in any other law for the time being in force, the transfer of the services of any officer or other employee of an Indian insurance company to the acquiring company shall not entitle any such officer or other employee to any compensation under that Act or other law, and no such claim shall be entertained by any court, tribunal or other authority.

(6) The Central Government may, by notification, add to, amend or vary any scheme framed under this section.

(7) The provisions of this section and of any scheme framed under it shall have effect notwithstanding anything to the contrary contained in any other law or any agreement, award or other instrument for the time being in force.

Schemes to be Laid before Parliament (Section 17)

A copy of every scheme and every amendment thereto framed under Section 16 shall be laid, as soon as may be after it is made, before each House of Parliament.

Functions and Management of Acquiring Companies

Functions of Corporation (Section 18)

(1) The functions of the Corporation shall include:
  (a) the carrying on of any part of the general insurance business, if it thinks it desirable to do so;
  (b) aiding, assisting and advising the acquiring companies in the matter of setting up of standards of conduct and sound practice in general insurance business and on the matter of rendering efficient service to holders of policies of general insurance;
  (c) advising the acquiring companies in the matter of controlling their expenses including the payment of commission and other expenses;
  (d) advising the acquiring companies in the matter of the investment of their funds; and
  (e) issuing directions to acquiring companies in relation to the conduct of general insurance business.

(2) In issuing any directions under sub-section (1), the Corporation shall keep in mind the desirability of encouraging competition amongst the acquiring companies as far as possible in order to render their services more efficiently.

Functions of Acquiring Companies (Section 10)

(1) Subject to the rules, if any, made by the Central Government in this behalf and to its memorandum and articles of association, it shall be the duty of every acquiring company to carry on general insurance business.

(2) Each acquiring company shall so function under this Act as to secure that general insurance business is developed to the best advantage of the community.

(3) In the discharge of any of its functions, each acquiring company shall act so far as may be on business principles and where any directions have been issued by the Corporation, shall be guided by such directions.

(4) For the removal of doubts it is hereby declared that the Corporation and any acquiring company may, subject to the rules, if any, made by the Central Government in this behalf, enter in such contract of reinsurance or reinsurance treaties as it may think fit for the protection of its interests.

Balance of Profit how to be Utilised (Section 20)

(1) After making provision for bad and doubtful debts, depreciation

in assets, provident, superannuation, welfare and other funds, debts due to Government and all other matters for which provision is necessary under any law or which are usually provided for by insurance companies, every acquiring company shall distribute the balance of profit as dividends.

(2) Any profit made by the Corporation and any sums received by the Corporation by way of dividends or otherwise shall be dealt with by it in such manner as may be prescribed.

Interim Provisions of Management of Indian Insurance Companies (Section 21)

(1) Notwithstanding anything contained in the Companies Act, or in the memorandum and articles of association of any Indian insurance company, or and from the appointed day and until a new board of directors of the Indian insurance company is duly constituted, the management of the company shall continue to vest in the Custodian incharge of the management of the undertaking of that company immediately before the appointed day by virtue of the provisions contained in the General Insurance (Emergency Provisions) Act, 1971 and the Custodian shall be entitled, subject to such directions as the Central Government may in this behalf, to exercise all the powers and do all acts and things as may be exercised or done by the company or by its board of directors.

(2) Nothing contained in sub-section (1) shall be deemed to prevent the Central Government from appointing any other person to take charge of the management of the undertaking of any Indian insurance company during period referred to in that sub-section if for any reason it becomes necessary so to so, and any person so appointed may exercise all the powers and do all acts and things which a Custodian may exercise or do under sub-section (1).

(3) The Custodian referred to in sub-section (1) and the person appointed under sub-section (2) shall be entitled to such salaries and other allowances as the Central Government may specify in this behalf and shall hold office during the pleasure of the Central Government.

Power of Central Government to Transfer Employee (Section 22)

The Corporation may at any time transfer any officer or employee from an acquiring company or the Corporation to any other acquiring company or the Corporation, as the case may be, and the officer or employee so transferred, shall continue to have the same terms and conditions of service as were applicable to him immediately before such transfer.

Power of Central Government to Issue Directions (Section 23)

The Corporation and every acquiring company shall, in the discharge of its functions, be guided by such directions in regard to matters of policy involving public interest as the Central Government may give.

Miscellaneous

Acquiring Companies to have the Exclusive Privilege of Carrying on General Insurance Business (Section 24)

(1) Except to the extent expressly provided in this Act, on and from the appointed day, the Corporation and the acquiring companies shall have exclusive privilege of carrying on general insurance business in India.

(2) Subject to the provisions of Section 36, any certificate of registration granted under the Insurance Act to any insurer other than an insurer referred to in sub-section (1) shall, on and from the appointed day, cease to have effect:

Provided that nothing in this sub-section shall apply to the carrying on by the Life Insurance Corporation of life insurance business and capital redemption and annuity certain business.

Properties in India not to be with Foreign Insurers Except with Permission of Central Government (Section 25)

(1) No person shall take out or renew policy of insurance in respect of any property in India or any ship or other vessel or aircraft registered in India with an insurer whose principal place of business is outside India save with the prior permission of the Central Government.

(2) If any person contravenes any provision of sub-section (1), he shall be punishable with imprisonment for a term which may extend to one year, or with fine which may extend to one thousand rupees or with both.

Acquiring Companies and Income-Tax (Section 26)

For the purposes of the Income-tax Act, 1961, every acquiring company shall be deemed to be an Indian company and a company in which the public are substantially interested.

Power to Reduce Amounts of Insurance in Certain Cases (Section 27)

An acquiring company may, having regard to its financial condition on the 13th day of May, 1971, or the financial condition on the said date of any exiting insurer whose undertaking has been transferred to and vested in it under this Act reduce the liabilities which have arisen under contracts of general insurance entered into before the said date in such manner and subject to such conditions as it thinks fit:

Provided that no such reduction shall be made except in accordance with specific proposals made by the acquiring company in this behalf and approved by the Central Government.

Right of Acquiring Company to Seek Relief in Respect of Certain Transactions (Section 28)

(1) Where an existing insurer has at any time within five years before the 13th day of May, 1971:
   (a) made any payment to any person without consideration,
   (b) sold or disposed of any property of the insurer without consideration or for an inadequate consideration,
   (c) acquired any property or rights for an excessive consideration,
   (d) entered into or varied any agreement so as require an excessive consideration to be paid or given by the insurer, and
   (e) entered into any other transaction of such an onerous nature as to cause a loss to, or impose a liability, on the insurer exceeding any benefit accruing to the insurer,

   and the payment, sale, disposal, acquisition, agreement or variation thereof or the transaction was not reasonably necessary for the purpose of the general insurance business of the insurer or was made with an unreasonable lack of prudence on the part of the insurer, regard being had in either case to the circumstances at the time, the acquiring company may apply for relief to the court in respect of such transaction, and all parties to the transaction shall, unless the court otherwise directs, be made parties to the application.

(2) The Court may make such order against any of the parties to the application as it thinks just having regard to the extent to which those parties were respectively responsible for the transaction or benefited from it and all the circumstances of the case.

(3) Where an application is made to the court under this section in respect of any transaction and the application is determined in favour of the acquiring company, the court shall have exclusive jurisdiction to determine any claim outstanding in respect of the transaction.

Duty to Deliver Possession of Property and Documents Relating Thereto (Section 29)

(1) Where any property appertaining to an existing insurer has been transferred to and vested in an Indian insurance company under Section 5:
   (a) every person in whose possession, custody or control any such property may be, shall deliver the property to the Indian insurance company forthwith, and

(b) any person who immediately before such vesting has in his possession, custody or control any books, documents or other papers relating to an existing insurer shall be liable to account for the said books, documents and papers to the Indian insurance company, and shall deliver them to that company or to such person as that company may direct.

(2) In particular, all the assets of an existing insurer appertaining to the undertaking help in deposit by the Reserve Bank of India under the Insurance Act or by trustees in trust shall be delivered to the Indian insurance company.

(3) Without prejudice to the other provisions contained in this section, it shall be lawful for each Indian insurance company to take all necessary steps for taking possession of all properties which have been transferred to and vested in it under this Act.

Penalty for Withholding Property, etc. (Section 30)

If any person wilfully withholds or fails to deliver to an Indian insurance company as required by Section 29 any property or any books, documents or other papers which may be in his possession or unlawfully retains possession of any property of an existing insurer which has been transferred to and vested in an Indian insurance company under Section 5 or wilfully applies any such property to purposes other than those expressed in or authorised by this Act, he shall, on the complaint of the Indian insurance company, be punishable with imprisonment for a term which may extend to one year, or with fine which may extend to one thousand rupees, or with both.

Officers and Employees of Corporation or of Acquiring Companies to be Public Servants (Section 31)

Every officer or other employee of the Corporation or of an acquiring company shall be deemed to be a public servant for the purposes of the Indian Penal Code.

Indemnity (Section 32)

Every officer of the Central Government and every officer or other employee of the Corporation and of any acquiring company shall be indemnified by the Central Government or the Corporation or the acquiring company, as the case may be against all losses and expenses incurred by him in, or in relation to, the discharge of his duties under this Act except such as have been caused by his own wilful act or default.

Dissolution of Corporation and Acquiring Companies (Section 33)

No provision of law relating to the winding up of companies shall apply to the Corporation or to an acquiring company, and neither the Corporation nor any such company shall be placed in liquidation save by order of the Central Government and in such manner as it may direct.

Reference to Existing Insurer in other Laws (Section 34)

Any reference to an existing insurer in any law other than this Act or any contract or other instrument shall, in so far as it relates to an acquiring company, be construed as a reference to that company.

Application of Insurance Act (Section 35)

Subject to such exceptions, restrictions and limitations, if any, as the Central Government may, by notification, specify in this behalf, the Insurance Act shall apply to or in relation to the Corporation and every acquiring company as if the Corporation or the acquiring company, as the case may be, were a insurer carrying on general insurance business within the meaning of that Act.

Exemption (Section 36)

(1) Nothing contained in this Act shall apply in relation to:
   (a) any general insurance business carried on by a State Government to be extent to which such insurance relates to properties belonging to it or undertakings owned wholly or mainly by the State Government; or to properties belonging to semi-government bodies, or any Board or body corporate established by the State Government under any statute or any industrial or commercial undertaking in which the State Government has substantial financial interest, whether as shareholder, lender or guarantor;
   (b) any general insurance business not falling within clause (a) which has been carried on by a State Government before the commencement of this Act, to the extent to which it is necessary to allow such business to run off:
   Provided that nothing contained in this clause shall be deemed to authorise the State Government to issue any new policies or renew any existing policies;
   (c) any insurer whose business is being voluntarily wound up or is being would up by a court;
   (d) the insurance business carried on by the Calcutta Hospital and Nursing Home Benefits Association Limited;
   (e) the insurance business carried on by the Export Credit and Guarantee Corporation Limited and the Deposit Insurance Corporation established under Section 3 of the Deposit Insurance Corporation Act, 1961; and
   (f) any scheme in existence immediately before the 14th day of May, 1971, or any scheme framed after the said day with the approval of the Central Government for the insurance of crops or of cattle or of flood risks or of war or emergency risks.

(2) If the Central Government is satisfied that an insurer, whether

established before or after the appointed day, carries on only such general insurance business as is not carried on ordinarily by insurers, it may, by notification, direct that nothing contained in this Act shall apply to such insurer.

Vacancies, etc., not to Invalidate Proceedings (Section 37)

No act or proceeding of the Corporation or of an acquiring company shall be called in question merely on the ground of the existence of any vacancy in or defect in the constitution of the Corporation or the company.

Protection of Action taken in Good Faith (Section 38)

No suit, prosecution or other legal proceeding shall lie against any officer of the Central Government or officer or other employee of the Corporation or of the acquiring company for anything which is in good faith done or intended to be done under this Act.

Power to make Rules (Section 39)

(1) The Central Government may, by notification, make rules to carry out the provisions of this Act.

(2) In particular, and without prejudice to the generality of the foregoing power, rules made under this section may provide for:

- (a) the manner in which the profits, if any, and other moneys received by the Corporation may be dealt with;
- (b) the conditions, if any, subject to which the Corporation and the acquiring companies shall carry on general insurance business;
- (c) the terms and conditions subject to which any reinsurance contracts or treaties may be entered into;
- (d) the form and manner in which any notice or application may be given or made to the Central Government;
- (e) the reports which may be called for by the Central Government from the Corporation and the acquiring companies;
- (f) any other matter which is required to be, or may be, prescribed.

(3) Every rule made under this section and every notification issued under Section 35 shall be laid, as soon as may be after it is made, before each House of Parliament, while it is in session, for a total period of thirty days which may be comprised in one session or in two or more successive sessions, and if, before the expiry of the session immediately following the session or the successive sessions aforesaid, both Houses agree in making any modification in the rule or notification or both Houses agree that the rule or notification should not be made, the rule or notification shall thereafter have effect only in such modified form or be of no

effect, as the case may be; so, however, that any such modification or annulment shall be without prejudice to the validity of anything previously done under that rule or notification.

17.5 CONSUMER PROTECTION ACT, 1986

A number of important changes such as checking of unfair trade practices, grant of interim injunction and grant of compensation were enacted in the 1984 Amendment of the Monopolies and Restrictive Trade Practices Act, 1969 (MRTP Act) however, to make it more effective and useful, nothing of much importance and use could come out of this exercise. Absence of time-bound disposal of cases, court-like proceedings of the MRTP commission's work, centralisation of MRTP Commission in Delhi, etc., continued to act as limitations of MRTP Act. Consequently, it was felt necessary to enact a more comprehensive legislation to protect the consumers' rights and the speedy, simple and inexpensive redressal of consumer disputes. In this background, the Consumer Protection Act, 1986 was introduced aiming at protection of the interests of consumers as stated in the preamble of the Act. It provides for the establishment of consumer councils and other authorities for the settlement of consumers' disputes.

Every human being is a consumer of one kind or other. In the distant past, the consumers were governed by the terms of contract between themselves and the traders. These terms were mostly one sided and obviously in favour of the traders. Moreover, the state showed least enthusiasm in coming to the rescue of consumers when they were deceived or cheated. The concept of absolute freedom of contract and the system of *laissez faire* appeared to be too bookish. All the more, for making huge profits or becoming rich overnight, the traders, businessmen, employers, producers and sellers, etc. at the cost of consumers' interest were adopting all sorts of abominable means and methods or malpractices. Even today, marketing of goods which are injurious to health and life, deception of the consumers through unfair trade practices such as, substandard quality, adulteration, non-supply of correct quantity, excess pricing, etc., are rampant in our society. The plight of the consumer in the country is worse confounded, because of his ignorance, illiteracy and weak economic position.

In order to protect the consumer from the unfair trade practices, the Union Government of India has enacted various legislations. But due to lack of proper co-ordination and integration among these legislations, it is observed that consumers are not fully and properly protected. Very prominently, this is because of poor and inadequate implementing machinery of the government, and rampant corruption and dishonesty.

A silver line was traced in the era of consumer protection during 1986 as it was the year of dawning of visible and tangible consumer movement in India. It was the year when the Consumer Protection Act came into force. It really gave pep to the existing consumer protection activities in the country.

Scope of the Consumer Protection Act, 1986 (COPRA, 1986)

The Consumer Protection Act, 1986 extends to the whole of India except the State of Jammu and Kashmir. The provisions of the Act are in addition to, and not in derogation of, the provisions of any other law for the time being in force. This Act applies to all types of goods and services unless specifically exempted by the central government by notification. The Act provides for setting-up of Consumer Protection Councils at Central and State levels and Consumers' Complaints Redressal Agencies at Central, State and District levels of the country wherein states include union territories also.

Consumer Protection Council

The central government is empowered to constitute the Central Consumer Protection Council which consists of the following 150 members, viz.:

1. The Minister in-charge of Department of Civil Supplies who shall be the chairman of the Central Council;
2. The Minister of State (where he is not holding independent charge) or Deputy Minister in the Department of Civil Supplies who shall be the vice-chairman of the Central Council;
3. The Minister of Food and Civil Supplies of Minister in-charge of consumer affairs in states;
4. Eight members of Parliament, five from the Lok Sabha and three from the Rajya Sabha;
5. The Commissioner from scheduled castes and scheduled tribes;
6. Representatives of the Central Government Departments, autonomous organisation concerned with consumer interest not exceeding twenty;
7. Representatives of the consumer organisations or consumers, not less than thirty-five;
8. Representatives of women, not less than ten;
9. Representatives of farmers, trade and industries, not exceeding twenty;
10. Persons capable of representing consumer interest not specified above, not exceeding fifteen; and
11. The Secretary in the Department of Civil Supplies shall be the member-secretary of the Central Council.

The term of the council shall be three years. The council may meet as and when necessary, but not less than three meetings of the council shall be held every year. Each meeting of the council shall be called by giving not less than 10 days' notices in writing to every member, specifying the time, place and agenda of the meeting. However, no proceedings of the councils shall be invalid merely by reasons of existence of any vacancy in or defect in the constitution of the council.

The council is empowered to constitute, from amongst its members, such working groups as it may deem necessary. Every working group so constituted shall perform such functions as are assigned to it by the central council. It seems that such working groups may prove to be more useful and effective in dealing with the specific problems allocated to them. The findings of such working groups are required to be placed before the council for its consideration. The resolutions by the council shall be recommendation in nature.

Objectives of the Central Council

The COPRA, 1986 provides that the objectives of the Central Council shall be to promote and protect the rights of the consumers, such as:

(a) The right to be protected against marketing of goods which are hazardous to life and property;
(b) The right to be informed about the quality, quantity, potency, purity, standard and prices of goods so as to protect the consumer against unfair trade practices;
(c) The right to be assured, wherever possible, access to a variety of goods at competitive prices;
(d) The right to be heard and to be assured that consumer interests will receive due consideration at appropriate fora;
(e) The right to seek redressal against unfair trade practices or unscrupulous exploitation of consumers; and
(f) The right to Consumer education.

The central council may have a significant role in the formulation of the Central Government's Economic Policy. In addition, it may respond to request for information and advice on particular issues relating to the protection of consumers. Though the decisions of the council are recommendation, they have a significant impact on several authorities concerned with the matters of Consumer Protection.

State Consumer Protection Councils

The state governments are also empowered to establish Consumer Protection Councils for their respective states. The State Councils shall consist of such members as may be notified by the state governments by notification from time to time. The objectives of every State Council (like Central Council) shall be to promote and protect within the state, the rights of the consumers as laid down in its clauses (a to b) of Section 6. So far, 22 States and Union Territories have set-up the Consumer Protection Councils under the Act. How far these councils have been successful in protecting the consumer interest is not free from doubt.

District Forum

A Consumer Disputes Redressal Forum to be known as the District Forum is required to be established by the state government with the prior approval of the central government in each district of the state.

(i) Composition of the District Forum

The Act provides that each district forum shall consist of a president, who is required to be a qualified to be a district Judge nominated by the state government. It shall consist of two members, among them one should be a lady social worker. The members may hold the office for a period of five years of up to the age of 65 years whichever is earlier and they are not eligible for re-appointment. Vacancy occurred by members' resignation may be filled by the state government and it has entire authority about deciding salary or honorarium to be paid to the members.

(ii) Jurisdiction of the District Forum

District Forum has the jurisdiction to entertain the complaints where the value of the goods or services or compensation claimed is less than Rs. 5,00,0000 (earlier it was Rs. 1,00,000). It can take complaints where opposite party/parties reside/s or carries on business in the district and the cause of action, wholly or in part, arises.

(iii) Procedure to be followed by the District Forum

Section 13 of the COPRA, 1986 lays down the procedure to be followed for the settlement of consumer dispute by the District Forum. After receiving a complaint from the complainant, it refers a copy of the complaint to the opposite party directing him to give his version within 30 days or such extended period not exceeding 15 days. If the opposite party denies or disputes the allegations contained in the complaint or omits or fails to take any action to represent his case within the time given by the District Forum, then the forum shall take the following if the complaint relates to goods. If complaint alleges a defect in the goods which cannot be determined by proper analysis, then the District Forum shall take a sample and send it to a laboratory with prescribed fee (from the complainant) and then it has to send a copy of the laboratory report to the opposite party of the complainant disputes with the correctness of report of the laboratory, then they may submit in writing their objections and then the District Forum gives a reasonable opportunity to the parties of being heard and issue an appropriate order.

If the complaint relates to service and where the opposite party on receipt of a copy of the complaint denies or disputes the allegations contained in the complaint, or omits or fails to take any action to represent his case within the time given by the Forum, the Forum shall proceed to settle the consumer dispute on the basis of:

(i) Evidence brought to its notice by the complainant and the opposite party denies or disputes the allegations contained in the complaint, or

(ii) Evidence brought to its notice by the complainant where the opposite party omits or fails to take any action to represent his case within the time given by the Forum.

If the District Forum is satisfied that the goods complained against any of the defects specified in the complaint or that any of the allegations contained in the complaint about the services are proved, it shall issue an order to the opposite party directing him to take one or more of the following things:

(i) to remove the defect pointed out by the appropriate laboratory from the goods in question;
(ii) to replace the goods with new goods of similar description which shall be free from any defect;
(iii) to return to the complainant the price, or as the case may be the charges paid by the complainant; and
(iv) to pay such amount as may be awarded by it as compensation to the consumer for any loss or injury suffered by the consumer due to the negligence of the opposite party.

The person (whether complainant or opposite party) dissatisfied with the order made by the District Forum may prefer an appeal against such order to the State Commission within a period of 30 days from the date of order.

State Commission

The State Commission is the consumer disputes redressal agency at the state level which is established by the state government with the prior approval of the central government. It consists of a president who is or has been a Judge of a High Court and two members—one of them is a woman.

(i) Jurisdiction of the State Commission

The State Commission can entertain the complaints where the value of the goods and compensation, if any, claimed exceeds Rs. 5,00,000 but does not exceed Rs. 20,00,000 (earlier it was Rs. 1,00,000 and Rs. 10,000,000 respectively). It can entertain appeals against the orders of any District Forum within the state and it can call for the records and pass appropriate order in any consumer dispute which is pending before or has been decided by any District Forum within the state, where it appears to the State Commission that such District Forum has exercised a jurisdiction not vested in it by Law or has failed to exercise a jurisdiction legally or with material irregularity. Hence, the jurisdiction of the State Commission is original as well as appellate.

(ii) Procedure

While disposing of the complaints, State Commission have to follow the Sections 12, 13 and 14 and the rules made thereunder with such modifications as may necessarily be applicable to it. Rule 10 of the Consumer Protection Act as are vested to the District Forum regarding the production documents, search and seizure. It may, however, be noted that the State Governments have yet to make their own rules in exercise of their powers under Section 30(2) of the Act. It is submitted that the State Government may adopt the similar rules as laid down by the central government, viz., Consumer Protection Rules, 1987. It will help in maintaining uniformity in Law all over the country.

Appeal against the Orders of the State Commission

Section 19 of the Act provides that the person aggrieved by an order made by the State Commission on a complaint may prefer an appeal against such order to the National Commission within a period of 30 days from the date of the order. The National Commission may entertain an appeal after the expiry of the said period of 30 days if it is within that period.

It may be noted that an order made by the State Commission on an appeal against the orders of the District forum is not appealable to the National Commission. Thus, provision exists only for a single appeal to the State Commission, from the order of the State Commission to the National Commission.

National Commission

This is the highest authority to settle the consumer disputes under the Act. It is an independent statutory body.

(i) Composition of the National Commission

The National Commission shall consist of a president appointed by the central government who is or has been a Judge of Supreme Court and four other members who are eminent in any field of knowledge—one of whom should be a woman. However, no sitting judge of the Supreme Court shall be appointed under the aforesaid provisions except after consultant on with the Chief Justice of India. The COPRA and the Rules have laid down many provisions to rescue the independence of National Commission. The terms and conditions of the service to the president and the members should be varied to their disadvantage.

(ii) Jurisdiction of the National Commission

Jurisdiction of National Commission is original as well as appellate. The original jurisdiction is limited to the complaints where the value of the goods or services and compensation exceeds Rs. 20,00,00 (earlier, it was Rs. 10,000,000). The appellate jurisdiction is confined to appeal against the orders of any State Commission. Further, the commission is empowered to call for records and pass appropriate orders in any consumer dispute where it appears that the State Commission has acted illegally or with material irregularity or exceeded its jurisdiction or has exercised its jurisdiction.

(iii) Procedure

The procedure to be followed in dealing with the complaints is specified by Section 22 of the COPRA which is similar to the powers of a civil court. It may also follow the procedure which is prescribed by the central government. Accordingly, the procedure has been laid down in the Rule 14 of the Consumer Protection Rules. These rules provide that a complaint containing the following particulars should be presented by the complainant in person or by his agent to the National Commission or be sent by registered post to the Commission:

(a) the name, description and address of the complainant;
(b) the name, description and address of the opposite party or parties;
(c) the facts relating to the complaint and when and where it arose;
(d) documents in support of the allegations contained in the complaint, and
(e) the relief which the complainant claims.

On receipt of a complaint, the National Commission has to follow the same procedure as is to be followed by the District Forum under Section 13 of the Act. The procedure to be flowered by the National Commission for hearing the appeal has been prescribed in Rule 15. Accordingly, a memorandum should be presented by the appellant or his agent to the National Commission in person or by post addressed to the commission. The memorandum must be set forth on the grounds of appeal without any arguments or narrative and must be accompanied by a certified copy of the order of the State Commission appealed against and such of the documents as may be received to support grounds of objection mentioned in the memorandum. However, under Section 19 of the Act, the appeal is to be preferred within a period of 30 days from the date of the order of the State Commission. When such an appeal is presented after the expiry of the period of limitation, the memorandum must also be accompanied by an application supported by an affidavit setting forth the facts on which the appellant relies to satisfy the National Commission that he has sufficient cause for not preferring the appeal within the period of limitation.

It is obligatory for the parties or agents to appear before National Commission on the date of hearing or any other day to which hearing may be adjourned. If the appealant/respondent or his agent fails to appear on such date, the commission may in its discretion either dismiss the appeal or decide expert on merits.

(iv) Appeal against the Order of the National Commission

A person dissatisfied with the order made by the National Commission may prefer an appeal against such order to the Supreme Court within a period of 30 days from the date of the order made by the National Commission and on an appeal preferred from the orders of the State

Commission shall be final and no further appeal against such orders should be preferred to the Supreme Court.

Filling of Complaints and Model Forms

Whoever wants to lodge a complaint either in the District Forum or State Commission or National Commission should use a form specifically meant for filling complaints in respective redressal agencies. They generally consist of name and addresses of both complainant(s) and the opposite party (ies), facts relating to the complaint, the value of the compensation claimed, and a declaration.

Concluding Remarks

The COPRA, 1986 was enacted to provide effective, inexpensive simple and speedy redressal to the consumer grievances. In fact, the three-tier redressal agencies envisaged in the Act have started functioning in almost all the states and have been providing effective redressal to consumers. The agencies in fact have done a lot, but still a lot more is to be achieved. They are facing problems in delivering speedy justice. Some of the pressing difficulties include shortage of funds, staff, lack of infrastructure, etc. which are putting hindrances in the smooth functioning of redressal agencies. Due to lack of these essential facilities, the redressal machinery is imitating rather than competing with the Civil Courts and, Civil Courts are known for giving adjournment dates. Strictly speaking, adjournment may be made a rare exception and not a rule.

However, there are still so many drawbacks in the implementation itself. The Amendment Act of 1993 remedied infact, some more shortcomings, and lapses in the original Act. It is shocking to note here that even after the lapse of 50 years of Independence, large number of consumers are lacking education and are ignorant about their rights and the Provisions of the Act. Eventually, they are exploited by the goods gesture of social organisation. However, the real protection to the innocent consumers can only be given by streamlining the efforts from all directions viz., voluntary consumer organisations, the business houses and the government. They have to play a collective role. Otherwise, the very purpose of the Act will be defeated.

17.6 SUMMARY

Insurance Act, 1938 was the first comprehensive legislation in India to regulate the business of insurance, when it was found that the earlier Indian company Act failed to meet the purpose. It was way back in 1912, when the Indian Life Insurance Companies Act and Provident Fund Insurance Societies Act, 1912 was passed, which was further modified and a new legislation was passed in 1928. In 1938 the Insurance Act was passed, which aimed to consolidate and amend the law relating to the business of insurance. The Act cause into force with effect from July 1939. The Act has been amended a number of times, the most important amendments being made in 1950, 1968 and 1999.

Life Insurance Corporation of India is a corporate body having perpetual succession and a common seal with power to acquire, hold and dispose of property and can by its name sue and be sued. It consists of not more than 16 members, appointed by the Government, one of whom shall be the Chairman. The corporation's duty is to carry out life insurance business to the best advantage of the community. According to Section 26, the corporation should make actuarial valuation once in every two years. At least 95% of the surplus disclosed by actuarial relation is to be distributed with profit among policyholders. The remainders shall be paid to the Central Government. Section 30 stated that LIC shall have exclusive privilege to transact life insurance business in India. The exclusive privilege has ceased to exist as a result of amendments made in 1999.

The General Insurance Corporation of India was formed on 22nd Nov. 1972 under the General Insurance Business (Nationalisation) Act, 1972 and by virtue of the same Act, 55 Indian general insurance companies became subsidiaries of the General Insurance Corporation of India and the undertaking of other erstwhile insurance were merged in undertakings of one or other four selected companies which were to operate in the nationalised set-up, viz. National Insurance Co. Ltd.; New India Assurance Co. Ltd., Oriental Insurance Company Ltd., and United India Insurance Co. Ltd. General Insurance Business (Nationalisation) Act, 1972 deals with the transfer of public ownership of general insurance business, formation and transfer of shares to corporation, amounts to be paid for acquisitions, schemes for reorganization of general insurance business and functions of the corporation and acquiring companies and their management.

17.7 REVIEW QUESTIONS

1. "Insurance Act, 1938 can be called as the pioneer in insurance business." Explain.
2. Discuss the important features of Insurance Act, 1938.
3. What are the conditions on insurer in respect to deposits as per Insurance Act, 1938.
4. Discuss the approved investments laid down in Section 27A of Insurance Act, 1938.
5. Discuss the functions of General Insurance Corporation of India Ltd.
6. Explain the important provisions of General Insurance Business (Nationalisation) Act, 1972.
7. Discuss the provisions relating to amounts to be paid for acquisition as per General Insurance Business (Nationalisation) Act, 1972.
8. Explain the various provisions with respect to transfer of public ownership of General Insurance Business (Nationalisation) Act, 1972.
9. Discuss the main functions of Life Insurance Corporation of India.

10. Highlight the important provisions of LIC Act, 1956
11. Who are the different authorities under LIC Act, 1956? Also state their duties.
12. Discuss the various provisions relating to Finance, Accounts and Audit as laid down in LIC Act, 1956.
13. Discuss the nature, scope, and limitations of COPRA, 1986.
14. What do you mean by consumer protection council? Explain the role and functions of state consumer protection council.
15. Write an essay on consumer dispute redressal agencies and their main functions.

18

CHAPTER

IRDA AND INSURANCE BUSINESS

LEARNING OBJECTIVE

The main objective of this chapter is to make the students learn about the brief profile of IRDA and its role and functioning in insurance business in India.

18.1 INTRODUCTION

The Government of India realized the necessities of setting-up Insurance Regulatory and Development Authority (IRDA) in 1999. The IRDA was set-up to provide for the establishment of an Authority, for protecting the interests of holders of insurance policies, to regulate, promote and insurer orderly growth of the insurance industry and for matters connected therewith or incidental thereto. With the birth of IRDA, the Government amended the Insurance Act, 1938, the Life Insurance Corporation Act, 1956 and the General Insurance Business (Nationalization) Act, 1972 for the sake of proper control at apex level.

Short Title, Extent, and Commencement

- This Act may be called the Insurance Regulatory and Development Authority Act, 1999.
- It extends to the whole of India.
- It shall come into force on such date as the Central Government may, by notification in the Official Gazette, appoint:
  Provided that different date as may be appointed for different provisions of this Act and any reference in any such provision to the commencement of this Act shall be constructed as a reference to the coming into force of that provision.

Definitions

In this Act, unless the context otherwise requires:

(a) "Appointed day" means the date on which the Authority is established under sub-section (1) of section 3;
(b) "Authority" means the Insurance Regulatory and Development Authority established under sub-section (1) of section 3;
(c) "Chairperson" means the Chairperson of the Authority;
(d) "Fund" means the Insurance Regulatory and Development Authority Fund constituted under sub-section (1) of section 16;
(e) "Interim Insurance Regulatory Authority" means the Insurance Regulatory Authority set-up by the Central Government through Resolution No. 17(2)/94-Ins-V, dated the 23rd January, 1996;
(f) "Intermediary or insurance intermediary" includes insurance brokers, reinsurance brokers, insurance consultants, surveyors and loss assessors;
(g) "Member" means a whole time or a part time member of the Authority and includes the Chairperson;
(h) "Notification" means a notification published in the Official Gazette;
(i) "Prescribed" means prescribed by rules made under this Act; and
(j) "Regulations" means the regulations made by the Authority.

Words and expressions used and not defined in this Act but defined in the Insurance Act, 1938 (4 of 1938) or the Life Insurance Corporation Act, 1956 (31 of 1956) or the General Insurance Business (Nationalization) Act, 1972 (57 of 1972) shall have the meanings respectively assigned to them in those Acts.

18.2 BRIEF PROFILE OF IRDA AND ITS FUNCTIONING

Establishment and Incorporation of Insurance Authority is:

(1) With effect from such date as the Central Government may, by notification, appoint, there shall be established, for the purposes of this Act, an Authority to be called "the Insurance Regulatory and Development Authority."
(2) The Authority shall be a body corporate by the name aforesaid having perpetual succession and a common seal with power, subject to the provisions of this Act, to acquire, hold and dispose of property, both movable and immovable, and to contract and shall, buy the said name, sue or be sued.
(3) The head office of the Authority shall be at such place as the Central Government may decide from time to time.
(4) The Authority may establish offices at other places in India.

Composition of Authority

The Authority shall consist of the following members, namely:

(a) A Chairperson;
(b) Not more than five whole-time members; and
(c) Not more than four part-time members.

To be appointed by the Central Government from amongst persons of ability, integrity and standing who have knowledge or experience in life insurance, general insurance, actuarial science, finance, economics, law, accountancy, administration or any discipline which would, in the opinion of the Central Government, be useful to the Authority.

Provided that the Central Government shall, while appointing the Chairperson and the whole-time members, ensure that at least the person is having knowledge or experience in life insurance, general insurance or actuarial science, respectively.

Tenure of Office of Chairperson and other Members

In IRDA:

(1) The Chairperson and every other whole-time member shall hold office for a term of five years from the date on which he enters upon his office and shall be eligible for reappointment:
Provided that no person shall hold office as a Chairperson after he has attained the age of sixty-five years.
(2) A part-time member shall hold office for a term not exceeding five years from the date on which he enters upon his office.
(3) Notwithstanding anything contained in sub-section (1) or sub-section (2), a member may—
  (a) Relinquish his office by giving in writing to the Central Government notice of not less than three months; or
  (b) Be removed from his office is accordance with the provisions of section.

Removal from Office

In IRDA:

(1) The Central Government may remove from office any member who—
  (a) Is, or at any time has been, adjudged as an insolvent; or
  (b) Has become physically or mentally incapable of acting as a member; or
  (c) Has been convicted of any offence which, in the opinion of the Central Government, involves moral turpitude; or
  (d) Has acquired such financial or other interest as is likely to affect periodically his functions as a member; or

(e) Has so abused his position as to render his continuation in office detrimental to the public interest.

(2) No such member shall be removed under clause (d) or clause (c) of section (1) unless he has been given a reasonable opportunity of being heard in the matter.

Salary and Allowances of Chairperson and Members

The salary and allowances payable to, and other terms and conditions of service of, the members other than part-time members shall be such as may be prescribed. The part-time members shall receive such allowances as may be prescribed. The salary, allowances, and other conditions of service of a Member shall not be varied to his disadvantage after appointment.

Bar on Future Employment of Members

The Chairperson and the whole-time members shall not, for a period of two years from the date on which they cease to hold office as such, except with the previous approval of the Central Government, accept:

(a) Any employment either under the Central Government or under any State Government; or

(b) Any appointment in any company in the insurance sector.

Administrative Powers of Chairperson

The Chairperson shall have the powers of general superintendence and direction in respect of all administrative matters of the Authority.

Meetings of Authority

In IRDA:

(1) The Authority shall meet at such times and places and shall observe such rules and procedures in regard to transaction of business at its meetings (including quorum at such meetings) as may be determined by the regulations.

(2) The Chairperson, or if for any reason he is unable to attend a meeting of the Authority, any other member chosen by the members present from amongst themselves at the meeting shall preside at the meeting.

(3) All questions which come up before any meeting of the Authority shall be decided by a majority of votes by the members present and voting, and in the event of an equality of votes, the Chairperson, or in his absence, the person presiding shall have a second or casting vote.

(4) The Authority may make regulations for the transaction of business at its meetings.

Vacancies, etc. not to Invalidate Proceedings of Authority

No act or proceeding of the Authority shall be invalid merely by reason of:

(a) Any vacancy in, or any defect in the constitution of, the Authority; or
(b) Any defect in the appointment of a person acting as a member of the Authority; or
(c) Any irregularity in the procedure of the Authority not affecting the merits of the case.

Officers and Employees of Authority

In IRDA:

(1) The Authority may appoint officers and such other employees as it considered necessary for the efficient discharge of its function under this Act.
(2) The terms and other conditions of service of officers and other employees of the Authority appointed under sub-section (1) shall be governed by regulations made under this Act.

Transfer of Assets, Liabilities, etc. of Interim Insurance Regulatory Authority

On the appointed day:

(a) All the assets and liabilities of the Interim Insurance Regulatory Authority shall stand transferred to, and vested in, the Authority. *Explanation*: The assets of the Interim Insurance Regulatory Authority shall be deemed to include all rights and powers, and all properties, whether movable or immovable, including, in particular, cash balances, deposits and all other interests and rights in, or arising out of, such properties as may be in the possession of the Interim Insurance Regulatory Authority and all books of account and other documents relating to the same; and liabilities shall be deemed to include all debts, liabilities and obligations of whatever kind;
(b) Without prejudice to the provisions of clause (a), all debts, obligations and liabilities incurred, all contracts entered into and all matters and things engaged to be done by, with or for the Interim Insurance Regulatory Authority immediately before that day, for or in connection with the purpose of the said Regulatory Authority, shall be deemed to have been incurred, entered into or engaged to be done by, with or for, the Authority;
(c) All sums of money due to the Interim Insurance Regulatory Authority immediately before that day shall be deemed to be due to the Authority; and
(d) All suits and other legal proceedings instituted or which could

have been instituted by or against the Interim Insurance Regulatory Authority immediately before that day may be continued or may be instituted by or against the Authority.

Duties, Powers and Functions of Authority in IRDA are:

(1) Subject to the provisions of this Act and any other law for the time being in force, the Authority shall have the duty to regulate, promote and ensure orderly growth of the insurance business and re-insurance business.

(2) Without prejudice to the generality of the provisions contained in sub-section (1), the powers and functions of the Authority shall include:

(a) Issue to the applicant a certificate of registration, renew, modify, withdraw, suspend or cancel such registration;

(b) Protection of the interests of the policyholders in matters concerning assigning of policy, nomination by policyholders, insurable interest, settlement of insurance claim, surrender value of policy and other terms and conditions of contracts of insurance;

(c) Specifying requisite qualifications, code of conduct and practical training for intermediary or insurance intermediaries and agents;

(d) Specifying the code of conduct for surveyors and loss assessors;

(e) Promoting efficiency in the conduct of insurance business;

(f) Promoting and regulating professional organizations connected with the insurance and re-insurance business;

(g) Levying fees and other charges for carrying out the purposes of this Act;

(h) Calling for information from, undertaking inspection of, conducting enquiries and investigations including audit of the insurers, intermediaries, insurance intermediaries and other organizations connected with the insurance business;

(i) Control and regulation of the rates, advantages, terms and conditions that may be offered by insurers in respect of general insurance business not so controlled and regulated by the Tariff Advisory Committee under Section 64U of the Insurance Act, 1938 (4 of 1938);

(j) Specifying the form and manner in which books of account shall be maintained and insurers and other insurance intermediaries shall render statement of accounts;

(k) Regulating investment of funds by insurance companies;

(l) Regulating maintenance of margin of solvency;

(m) Adjudication of disputes between insurers and intermediaries or insurance intermediaries;

(n) Supervising the functioning of the Tariff Advisory Committee;
(o) Specifying the percentage of premium income of the insurer to finance schemes for promoting and relegating professional organizations referred to in clause (f);
(p) Specifying the percentage of life insurance business and general insurance business to be undertaken by the insurer in the rural or social sector; and
(q) Exercising such other powers as may be prescribed.

Grants by Central Government

The Central Government may, after due appropriation made by Parliament by law in this behalf, make to the Authority grants of such sums of money as the Government may think fit for being utilized for the purposes of this Act.

Constitution of Funds

(1) There shall be constituted a fund to be called "the Insurance Regulatory and Development Authority Fund" and there shall be credited thereto:
   (a) All Government grants, fees and charges received by the Authority;
   (b) All sums received by the Authority from such other source as may be decided upon by the Central Government; and
   (c) The percentage of prescribed premium income received from the insurer.
(2) The Fund shall be applied for meeting:
   (a) The salaries, allowances and other remuneration of the members, officers and other employees of the Authority; and
   (b) The other expenses of the Authority in connection with the discharge of its functions and for the purposes of this Act.

Accounts and Audit

(1) The Authority shall maintain proper accounts and other relevant records and prepare an annual statement of accounts in such form as may be prescribed by the Central Government in consolation with the Comptroller and Auditor-General of India.
(2) The accounts of the Authority shall be audited by the Comptroller and Auditor-General of India at such intervals as may be specified by him and any expenditure incurred in connection with such audit shall be payable by the Authority to the Comptroller and Auditor-General.
(3) The Comptroller and Auditor-General of India and any other person appointed by him in connection with the audit of the audit of the accounts of the Authority shall have the same rights,

privileges and authority in connection with such audit as the Comptroller and Auditor-General generally has in connection with the audit of the Government accounts and, in particular, shall have the right to demand the production of books of account, connected vouchers and other documents and papers and to inspect any of the offices of the Authority.

(4) The accounts of the Authority as certified by the Comptroller and Auditor-General of India or any other person appointed by him in this behalf together with the audit-report thereof shall be forwarded annually to the Central Government and that Government shall cause the same to be laid before cash House of Parliament.

Power of Central Government to Issue Directions

The Central Government is empowered to take action without prejudice to the foregoing provisions of this Act, the Authority shall, in exercise of its powers or the performance of its functions under this Act, be bound by such directions on questions of policy, other than those relating to technical and administrative matters, as the Central Government may give in writing to it from time to time. Provided that the Authority shall, as far as practicable, be given an opportunity to express its views before any direction is given under this sub-section. The decision of the Central Government, whether a question is one of policy or not, shall be final.

Power of Central Government to Supersede Authority

(1) If at any time the Central Government is of the opinion:

(a) That, on account of circumstances beyond the control of the Authority, it is unable to discharge the functions or perform the duties imposed on it by or under the provisions of this Act; or

(b) That the Authority has persistently defaulted in complying with any direction given by the Central Government under this Act or in the discharge of the functions of performance of the duties imposed on it by or under the provisions of this Act and as a result of such default the financial position of the Authority or the administration of the Authority has suffered; or

(c) That circumstances exist which render it necessary in the public interest so to do, the Central Government may, by notification and for reasons to be specified therein, supersede the Authority for such period, not exceeding a six months, as may be specified in the notification and appoint a person to be the Controller of Insurance under section 2B of the Insurance Act, 1938 (4 of 1938), if not already done:

Provided that before issuing any such notification, the Central

Government shall give a reasonable opportunity to the Authority to make representations, if any, of the Authority.

(2) Upon the publication of a notification under sub-section (1) superseding the Authority,—
   (a) The Chairperson and other members shall, as from the date of suppression, vacate their offices as such;
   (b) All the powers, functions and duties which may, by or under the provisions of this Act, be exercised or discharged by or on behalf of the Authority shall, until the Authority is reconstituted under sub-section (3), be exercised and discharged by the Controller of Insurance; and
   (c) All properties owned or controlled by the Authority shall, until the Authority is reconstituted under sub-section (3), vest in the Central Government.

(3) On or before the expiration of the period of suppression specified in the notification issued under sub-section (1), the Central Government shall reconstitute the Authority by a fresh appointment of its Chairperson and other members and in such case any person who had vacated his office under clause (a) of sub-section (2) shall not be deemed to be disqualified for reappointment.

(4) The Central Government shall cause a copy of the notification issued under sub-section (1) and a full report to any action to be laid before each House of Parliament at the earliest.

Furnishing of Returns, etc. to Central Government

(1) The Authority shall furnish to the Central Government at such time and in such form and manner as may be prescribed, or as the Central Government may direct to furnish such returns, statements, and other particulars in regard to any proposed or existing programme for the promotion and development of the insurance business during the previous financial year.

(2) Copies of the reports received under sub-section (2) shall be laid, as soon as may be after they are received, before each House of Parliament.

Chairperson, Members, Officers and Other Employees of Authority to be Public Servants

The Chairperson, members, officers and other employees of Authority shall be deemed, when acting or purporting to act in pursuance of any of the provisions of this Act, to be public servants within the meaning of Section 21 of the Indian Penal Code (45 of 1860).

Protection of Action Taken in Good Faith

No suit, prosecution or other legal proceedings shall be against the

Central Government or any officer of the Central Government or any member, officer or other employee of the Authority for anything which is in good faith done or intended to be done under this Act or the rules or regulations made thereunder:

Provided that nothing in this Act shall exempt any person from any suit or other proceedings, which might, apart from this Act, be brought against him.

Delegation of Powers

(1) The Authority may, by general or special order in writing, delegate to the Chairperson or any other member or office of the Authority subject to such conditions, if any, as may be specified in the order such of its powers and functions under this Act as it may deem necessary.

(2) The Authority may, by a general or special order in writing, also form committees of the members and delegate to them the powers and functions of the Authority as may be specified by the regulations.

Power to make Rules

(1) The Central Government may, by notification, make rules for carrying out the provisions of this Act.

(2) In particular, and without prejudice to the generality of the foregoing power, such rules may provide for all or any of the following matters, namely:

(a) The salary and allowances payable to, and other terms and conditions of service of, the members other than part-time numbers under sub-section (1) of section 7;

(b) The allowances to be paid to the part-time members under sub-section (2) of section 7;

(c) Such other powers that may be exercised by the Authority under clause (q) of sub-section (2) of section 14;

(d) The form of annual statement of accounts to be maintained by the Authority under sub-section (1) of section 17;

(e) The form and the manner in which and the time within which returns and statements and particulars are to be furnished to the Central Government under sub-section (1) of section 20;

(f) The matters under sub-section (5) of section 25 on which the Insurance Advisory Committee shall advise the Authority; and

(g) Any other matter which is required to be, or may be, prescribed, or in respect of which provision is to be or may be made by rules.

Establishment of Insurance Advisory Committee

(1) The Authority may, by notification, establish with effect from such date as it may specify in such notification, a Committee to be known as the Insurance Advisory Committee.

(2) The Insurance Advisory Committee shall consist of not more than twenty-five members excluding *ex-officio* members to represent the interests of commerce, industry, transport, agriculture, consumer forum, surveyors, agents, intermediaries, organizations engaged in safety and loss prevention, research bodies and employee's association in the insurance sector.

(3) The Chairperson and the members of the Authority shall be the *ex-officio* Chairperson and *ex-officio* members of the Insurance Advisory Committee.

(4) The object of the Insurance Advisory Committee shall be to advise the Authority on matters relating to the making of the regulations under section 26.

(5) Without prejudice to the provisions of sub-section (4), the Insurance Advisory Committee may advise the Authority on such other matters as may be prescribed.

Power to make Regulations

(1) The Authority may, in consultation with the Insurance Advisory Committee, by notification, make regulations consistent with this Act and the rules make thereunder to carry out the purposes of this Act.

(2) In particular, and without prejudice to the generality of the foregoing power, such regulations may provide for all or any of the following matters, namely:

(a) The time and palaces of meetings of the Authority and the procedure to be followed at such meetings including the quorum necessary for the transaction of business under sub-section (1) of section 10;

(b) The transactions of business at its meetings under sub-section (4) of section 10;

(c) The terms and other conditions of service of officers and other employees of the Authority under sub-section (2) of section 12;

(d) The powers and functions which may be delegated to committees of the members under sub-section (2) of section 23; and

(e) Any other matter which is required to be, or may be, specified by regulations or in respect of which provision is to be or may be made by regulations.

Rules and Regulations to be Laid Before Parliament

Every rule and every regulation made under this Act shall be laid as soon as may be after it is made, before each House of Parliament, while it is in session, for a total period of thirty days which may be comprised in one session or in two or more successive sessions, and if, before the expiry of the session immediately following the session or the successive session aforesaid, both Houses agree in making any modification in the rule or regulation or both Houses agree that the rule or regulation should not be made, the rule or regulation shall thereafter have effect only in such modified form or be of no effect, as the case may be, so, however, that any such modification or annulment shall be without prejudice to the validity of anything previously done under that rule or regulation.

Application of Other Laws not Barred

The provisions of this Act shall be in addition to, and not in derogation of, the provisions of any other law for the time being in force.

Power to Remove Difficulties

(1) If any difficulty arises in giving effect to the provisions of this Act, the Central Government may, by order published in the Official Gazette, make such provisions not inconsistent with the provisions of this Act as may appear to be necessary for removing the difficulty. Provided that no order shall be made under this section after the expiry of two years from the appointed day.

(2) Every order made under this section shall be laid, as soon as may be, after it is made, before each House of Parliament.

18.3 SUMMARY

Insurance Regulatory and Development Authority (IRDA) has come to stay for the smooth management and control of insurance business in India. The performance of IRDA is being debated and appreciated both within and outside the nation. So far, the IRDA has been trying very hard to streamline the business procedures in insurance sector with an utmost caution on the quality of service by the both new and old players in the field.

It would be too early to comment over the performance of IRDA but one thing is sure that the emergence of IRDA has been widely appreciated by the insurance experts, professionals, and insurance business players. However, the success of the IRDA may be tested in the long-run when the policies sold by the private business players get matured.

18.4 REVIEW QUESTIONS

1. Discuss and illustrate the powers, duties, and scope of IRDA.
2. Write short note on:
   (a) Finance, Accounts and Audit of IRDA.
   (b) Powers of Central Government in IRDA functioning.

PART C

INSURANCE PROCEDURES

19

CHAPTER

LIFE INSURANCE PROCEDURES AND DOCUMENTATIONS

LEARNING OBJECTIVE

The objective of this chapter is to discuss the procedure for obtaining a life insurance policy and the documentation in life insurance policy.

19.1 INTRODUCTION

The life insurance product is intangible, i.e. nobody can feel and see it. Moreover, the contract between the parties is a long-term contract. Therefore, it is essential to understand:

(i) the various products of Life Insurance, and
(ii) various documents to be prepared to get the insurance policy.

Firstly, the various basic products of the Life Insurance are discussed. Throughout the world, the Life Insurance products fall under four broad categories and most Insurance plans are basically of the following types:

1. Term Assurance, which provide for benefit if death occurs within policy term.
2. Pure Endowment, which provides only for payment on survival of policy term.
3. Combination of Term Assurance and Pure Endowment known as Endowment Plans providing for benefits both on deaths during term or on survival at the end of term.
4. Annuities to take care of surviving too long, i.e. beyond the income-earning period of the assured.

19.2 TERM ASSURANCE

Under this type of life insurance contract, the sum assured is payable only in the event of death during the term. In case of survival, the contract comes to an end at the end of term. There is no refund of premium. These policies are usually non-participating. Since only death risk is covered, the premium is low and the contract is simple. However, some companies do offer participating policies under term insurance plans. In contrast with others life insurance contracts, which are usually long, even up to 40 years or more, the term insurance contracts are usually registered for short periods (as one year or two years). They help to provide collateral security for loans. Some insurers offer term insurance policies for longer terms of 3, 5 or 6 years with fixed (level) premium payable each year. Such contracts can be renewed for further equal periods till the life assured reaches the age of 65 years.

19.3 WHOLE LIFE ASSURANCE

This is also a different type of term assurance. Under whole life plans, life insurance protection is available throughout the lifetime of the life assured. It is effectively a long-term insurance plan with a 'level' premium and the sum assured is payable only on the death of the insured and premiums are payable till death.

In the early years of life insurance, a whole life policy was deemed to have matured once the life assured reached the age of 100. The sum assured was paid to him at the age of 100 as mortality tables were available only upto age 100. Nowadays, insurance companies waive payment of further premiums under a whole life plan, if the premiums are paid for say, 35 or 40 years or the life assured has attained the age of 75 or 80 years.

The following products are available in the market:

Name of the Company	*Type of Plan*
1. Life Insurance Company	Whole Life Plan, Whole Life Single Plan, Whole Life Limited Plan
2. Allianz Bajaj Life Insurance	Life Time Care Plan
3. HDFC Standard Life Insurance	NIL
4. ICICI Prudential Life Insurance	NIL
5. TATA AIG Life Insurance	NIL
6. Birla Sun Life Insurance Company	Flexi Life Line/While Life Plan
7. SBI Cardiff Life Insurance Company	NIL
8. Max New York Life Insurance	20 years Endowment

Pure Endowment

Life Insurance plans, which provide for payment of policy monies only on survival of the specified period, are called pure endowment. In case a person dies then his legal heirs are not entitled for any amount. These plans are not popular as they only cater to the saving element of insurance and there are better alternatives available in the market.

Endowment Assurance Policy

Endowment insurance plans are a combination of Term Assurance and Pure Endowment and provide for the payment of the Sum Assured (SA) in case of death during the term (term assurance), or on survival of the term (pure endowment). This plan is a combination of term 'level' premium plan and 'pure endowment' plans. Since the SA is payable on death or on survival, the premium charged under endowment plans are higher than term or whole life insurance plans.

This is a form of saving plans under which contribution in form of premium are accumulated on basis of compound interest and this money is made available on survival up to particular term. Generally premiums are payable during the entire term of an endowment policy but under limited payment endowment plans premium paying period is fixed and less than the term of the policy. The payment of premiums stops at the end of this period, but the SA is payable on survival of the term or on earlier death.

19.4 MONEY BACK ENDOWMENT PLANS

To meet the need of the insured, the insurer have devised endowment plans wherein part of Sum Assured is made payable periodically during the term of the policy. Notwithstanding the payments at periodic intervals, the Sum Assured atleast continues to be the same till the end of the term and it is called money back endowment plan.

The following products are available in the market:

Name of the Company	*Type of Plan*
1. Life Insurance Company	Endowment
2. Allianz Bajaj Life Insurance	Save Care, Cash Care
3. HDFC Standard Life Insurance	Single Life Classic Endowment, Joint Life Endowment
4. ICICI Prudential Life Insurance	ICICI Pru Cash back, ICICI Pru Save 'n' Protects
5. TATA AIG Life Insurance	Assure 10, 20, 30 years' security
6. Birla Sun Life Insurance Company	Flexi Save Plus, Flexi Cash Flow
7. SBI Cardiff Life Insurance Company	NIL
8. Max New York Life Insurance	Endowment Participating Insurance

19.5 ANNUITIES

The Annuity is a reverse of the life insurance principal. When a person purchases a Life Insurance contract he agrees to make a series of payments (premiums) to the insurer and in return the insurer agrees to pay a specified sum to the beneficiaries, in case of death of life assured or on maturity. If a person buys an Annuity Contract he pays the insurer a specified capital sum (Purchase Price), may be in instalments or lump sum and in return the insurer promises to make a series of payments to him as long as he lives. The various types of annuities are broadly available in the following two plans namely immediate annuity and deferred annuity.

19.6 OTHER INSURANCE PRODUCTS

Based on the above-mentioned broad categories, the life insurance products are formulated with some modifications as per need of the different sections of society. As the need grows and more and more new players enter the insurance market, the life insurance product formulation will grow simultaneously. Some of the products are classified as follows:

1. Individual and Group Policies

In the case of individual insurance, the contract is with the individual policyholder. The decision to take out the policy is voluntary and the amount as well as plan of insurance is decided by the individual. The individual pays the premium and has the right to seek determination or alternation of the contract.

In the case of group insurance, the contract is with the employer or with the group/association. A single master policy is issued covering all the members, as per agreed terms. The individuals covered under the master policy are not parties to the contract. The amount and terms of insurance are negotiated by the employer or group, and apply equally to all members. The premium is paid by the employer or group with/without being collected from the members.

The members of the group will be covered for insurance evidenced by the master policy. The master policy will stipulate which member is covered and for how much. It is customary to allow existing members an option to join the cover or not. The option is important if the members have to contribute to the cover or if he has to forego some other benefit in lieu of coverage. The premium may sometimes have to be shared by the members also.

2. With Profit and Without Profit Policies

The life insurance companies carries out an actuarial valuation of its liability in all policies in its books periodically (now normally annually). The assets of the business are also valued. The prescribed rules as per accounting practices are laid down by IRDA for both the valuations. The excess of the value of assets thus arrived at over the amount of the total policy liabilities is called valuation surplus.

The With Profit Policies allow the policyholder to participate in valuation surplus. Should such a surplus exist, the company will first provide for any special contingencies it may foresee or contributes towards a general reserve (as prescribed) and the balance, if any, will be distributed among those policyholders who have 'with-profit' or 'participating' policies.

The non-profit (without-profit) policy does not carry a right to receive bonus. The whole life and endowment policies are often with-profit policies whereas the temporary assurance policies are customarily non-profit contracts.

3. Female Insurance

Females by nature are more susceptible to every type of death. This is generally a standard adopted by Insurer's world over and females are not considered very favourable insurance prospects. It is because of this condition that Indian Insurance Industry considers insurance underwriting of females under special conditions. From Insurer point of view Indian female should have genuine need for life insurance.

The lives of females have to be considered in relation to their income, employment, educational standards, socio-economic background and marital status. Keeping the above consideration, the insurance for women has been classified into the following three main categories.

Category I Women who have earned income through employment in Institutions are eligible for Life Insurance in NMS (Non-Medical Scheme). This also covers Government, Quasi Government and professionals like Doctors, Lawyers, Architects, Engineers and Insurance Agents.

Category II Women with unearned income means those who are assessable under Income Tax, having large properties and investments which result in income and are covered by Income Tax, fall in Category II. In these cases, proof has to be obtained of their being Income Tax payee such as:

A. Proof of Income Tax assessment order in last 3 years.
B. Certified copies of Income Tax filed in last 3 years.
C. C.A. certificate showing GIR/PAN number.

There may be cases, where three years' return or detail is not available, then the following standard is adopted:

A. Where proof of income is available for one year, then insurance provided is three times the annual Income.
B. Where proof of income is available for a period of two years or more than two years the insurance provided is five times the average annual return.

Category III This is that class of women who are not covered under Category I and II and the classification is as under:

A. Single woman
B. Married woman

Female Sum Assured

Category I Depending on income at par with man.

Category II Rs. 30 lakhs subject to financial underwriting: for Rs. 20-30 lakhs, the total cover should be about 7 times the average income for last 3 years and minimum educational qualification should be Matric/SSC and have PAN No. Husband and children also should be adequately Insured.

Category III (a) Single Woman—Rs. 4 lakhs subject to financial position, social status and adequate Insurance on rest of family members.

(b) Married Woman: Max. Rs. 7 lakhs or equal to husband's insurance, whichever is less.

Pregnant woman can be insured on following conditions:

(a) Only on Medical Basis.
(b) Medical Health Report by competent authority.
(c) If there is no case history of complications or abnormality.
(d) Gynaecologist Report in prescribed Form to be obtained.
(e) In cases of Insurance of over Rs. 5 lakhs special test Report has to be obtained.
(f) All cases are normally handled at Regional Office level.

4. Policies for Children and Physically Handicapped

(a) Children Policy

In earlier times Life Insurance companies did not handle policies fo children as children were considered bad risks because of high mortalit factors or in other words high death rate because of existing diseases lik small pox, diphtheria and other child-related diseases. As of today the healt structure has improved the survival rate among children thereby forcing th insurance companies to take out policies which take care of both male an female children. In some of the policies the adopted risk is deferred till th age of maturity which is normally 18 years.

These are Insurance plans where the father or mother proposes fc insurance on the life of the minor child and pays the premium. However, th risk on the life of the child will begin only after the child reaches a specifie age. The period during which there is no risk is called the Deferred Dat The risk may continue after the deferred date for a predetermined tern either as a Whole Life or an Endowment Policy. The original policy cove the entire term including the deferment period. The risk will commenc without medical examination on the deferred date, unless the defermer period is less than 10 years.

The main advantage of this plan is that a policy for a relatively larg amount can be taken for a relatively low premium. This premium wi continue even after the deferred date, irrespective of the state of health of tl child then. The proposer has the option to say that the policy will n continue after the deferred date. In that case, the policy terminates on th date and cash payment is made to the proposer, which is not exactly the total amount of premium paid. It could be more or less.

In earlier years, risk cover would be allowed only after the child attained the age of 18. However, Insurance companies nowadays, do allow risk cover even from younger ages under certain plans.

With a view to making the life assured, viz. the child, the absolute owner of the policy after the deferred date, a special provision is made by which the policy automatically vests in the life assured on the deferred date. Thereafter, the life assured becomes the absolute owner of the policy. The policy is deemed to be a contract between the insurance company and the life assured. That is why the vesting age has to be at least 18 years. Otherwise, the assured would remain a minor and there cannot be a valid contract with the assured.

Under Children Assured plans, there are special provisions to cover contingencies before the deferred date. Premiums may be waived if proposer dies before vesting date. The proposer, different from the life assured, can terminate the policy, in which case the premium will be refunded, subject to conditions. If the life assured dies before the deferred date, the benefits (return of premiums) follow different specifications. Participation, in surplus, normally will commence after the deferred date, but can be effective retrospectively from an earlier date. There are variations in these matters between different policies.

(b) Handicap Policy

Policy for the handicapped was started in 1995. This policy is mainly for dependents that are handicapped. Under this an individual of Hindu Undivided Family can take a policy on his own life so as to provide lump sum amount or an annuity to a handicapped person, who may be his dependent. The normal term period range is 10 to 35 years, with multiples of 5 up to term of 35 years.

The Benefits are 20% immediately on death of assured and balance 80% will be used to provide annuity certain for 15 years. In case of death of handicapped person the assured can keep the policy being reduced to paid up sum assured or have return of premium.

Double Accident Benefit (DAB) is available subject to existing conditions and is payable on death only.

19.7 LIFE INSURANCE PROCEDURES AND DOCUMENTATION

Now, let us discuss the procedure for obtaining the Life Insurance policies. As stated earlier that the Life Insurance contract is long-term contract for an intangible product, therefore, all terms and conditions in various Insurance documents should be well defined to make them understandable to the customer to avoid any legal battle at latter stage.

The following documents are involved to enter into any Insurance contract:

(A) Prospectus;
(B) Proposal Form;
(C) Deposit Receipts;
(D) Policy Documents;
(E) Endorsement;
(F) Renewal Notice; and
(G) Bonus Notice.

(A) Prospectus

When the parents want to admit their ward in school or college then they have to buy the prospectus of the school or college to know the facilities available there and other special features of the school or college. Similarly in the life Insurance business the company provides information about itself and the product through the prospectus. Therefore, prospectus is a document, which gives details regarding set-up of the life Insurance company, plans or features of the life Insurance products and other terms and conditions. Though, the prospectus provides a lot of information to the client to decide about the product/policy but he would like to take the advice and guidance of a salesperson. At the same time the prospect (a person who wants to buy the insurance) would like to know the price (premium) to be paid by him for any particular product. To calculate the premium the following procedure is to be followed:

Firstly, we should find out the age of the proposer as the premium will depend on the age of the prospects. On the date of the proposal, the age may be defined as—

(1) Age nearer to the birthday;
(2) Age on next birthday; and
(3) Age on last birthday.

If a person was born 22 years 8 months earlier. Then

(1) Age nearer to the birthday is 23;
(2) Age on next birthday is 23; and
(3) Age as on last birthday is 22.

If a person is 22 yrs. 5 months 29 days then the age nearer birthday will be 22 yrs. and if the age is 22 yrs. 5 months 30 days the age nearer birthday will be 23 yrs.

Examples

(1) If a person is born on 1/1/80, then on 1/8/2000 he is 20 yrs. 7 months and 1 day old, therefore:
(a) his age nearer to his birthday 21 yrs.
(b) his age as per last birthday 20 yrs.

(c) his age as per next birthday 21 yrs.

(2) If a person is born on 1/1/80, then on 11/4/2000 he is 20 years 3 months and 11 days old, therefore:

(a) his age nearer to his birthday 20 yrs.

(b) his age as per last birthday 20 yrs.

(c) his age as per next birthday 21 yrs.

After calculating the age the premium will be calculated as follows:

1. Tabular premium for the age concerned.
2. Loading proposal for reason of health and/or physical impairments: Extras on adverse health features or adverse Medical report, e.g. Blood pressure, sugar, diabetic, smokers, etc.
3. Extra for occupation: There are extra premiums on hazardous or extra-hazardous occupations, e.g. Aviation and defence, mining and other occupational risks.
4. Extra for accident benefits (if asked and if allowed): To get additional benefit on account of accidental death, the extra premium is to be paid for Double Accident Benefit (DAB) and Extended Permanent Disability Benefit (EPDB).
5. Extra for premium waiver benefit: If a person becomes disabled then he will not be able to pay the premium because he may not be able to earn because of his disability. Therefore, the company waives off the premium on payment of additional premium.
6. Rebate for large sum assured Adjustments are made for higher sum assured. The different insurers follow different rates but the oldest Insurance company in India, i.e. LIC follows the following discounts structure:

   (1) Rs. 25,000-Rs. 49,999 Rs. 1.00 less than tabular premium

   (2) Rs. 50,000 and more Rs. 2.00 less than tabular premium
7. Mode of payment: Similarly the adjustments are there also for different mode of payment as per details given below:
   If the mode of payment is yearly 3% less than the table rate.
   If the mode of payment is half-yearly 1.5% less than the table rate.
8. Extra for monthly mode of payment except salary saving scheme. For monthly payment 5% more than the table rate.

Where the premiums are payable on half yearly or yearly basis, there is saving in administrative expenses compared to quarterly mode. In half-yearly or yearly mode the insurer issues less number of notices and fewer collection receipts and consequential accounting entries would also be less. This would result in saving in administrative cost. Moreover, the insurer can earn more interest. While for monthly payment the extra premium is to be charged to cover up additional administrative expenses.

In short, we can say:

Lesser number of instalment of premium: Higher amount but more discount. More number of instalment of premium: Lower Amount but less discount.

Premium Amount = Sum Assured x Premium Rate/1000

Examples

1. Premium Calculation for yearly payment

Sum Assured	Rs. 50,000
Term	30 yrs.
Age	25 yrs.
Tabular Premium/1000 (Qtly. Mode)	Rs. 40
Rebate for large Sum Assured	Rs. 2 per 1000
Rebate for yearly payment	3%
Premium Calculation	*Rs.*
Tabular Premium (Qtly. Mode)/1000	40.00
Less Rebate for large Sum Assured	–2.00
Less Rebate for yearly payment (3% of Rs. 40)	–1.20
TOTAL	36.80
Premium = 36.8 x 50,000/1000	= Rs. 1840

2. Premium Calculation for Half-yearly payment

Sum Assured	Rs. 50,000
Term	30 yrs.
Age	25 yrs.
Tabular Premium/1000 (Qtly. Mode)	Rs. 40
Rebate for large Sum Assured	Rs. 2 per 1000
Rebate for half-yearly payment	1.5%
Premium Calculation	*Rs.*
Tabular Premium (Qtly. Mode)/1000	40.00
Less Rebate for large Sum Assured	–2.00
Less Rebate for half-yearly payment (1.5% of Rs. 40)	–0.60
TOTAL	37.40
Premium = 37.40 x 50,000/1000	= Rs. 1870
Half-yearly Instalment	1870/2 = Rs. 935

3. Premium Calculation for Quarterly payment

Sum Assured	Rs. 50,000
Term	30 yrs.

Age	25 yrs.
Tabular Premium/1000 (Qtly. Mode)	Rs. 40
Rebate for large Sum Assured	Rs. 2 per 1000
Rebate for quarterly payment	NIL

Premium Calculation	*Rs.*
Tabular Premium (Qtly. Mode)/1000	40.00
Less Rebate for large Sum Assured	–2.00
Total	38.00
Premium—38 X 50,000/1000	= Rs. 1900
Quarterly Instalment = 1900/4	= Rs. 475

4. *Premium Calculation for monthly payment*

Sum Assured	Rs. 50,000
Term	30 yrs.
Age	25 yrs.
Tabular Premium/1000 (Qtly. Mode)	Rs. 40
Rebate for large Sum Assured	Rs. 2 per 1000
Add for monthly payment	5%

Premium Calculation	*Rs.*
Tabular Premium (Qtly. Mode)/1000	40.00
Less Rebate for large Sum Assured	–2.00
Add for Monthly Mode 5% on Rs. 40	+2.00
	40.00
Premium = 40 x 50,000/1000	= Rs. 2000
Monthly Premium = 2000/12	= Rs. 166.66

From the above illustrations you must have observed that if the number of instalments are more then the yearly premium will be more and if the number of instalments are less then the yearly premium will be less.

	No. of Instalments	*Each Instalment (Rs.)*	*Yearly Premium (Rs.)*
Yearly	1	1840	1840
Half-yearly	2	935	1870
Quarterly	4	475	1900
Monthly	12	166.66	2000

Very Important: The rebates and loading are always on the basic tabular premium.

(B) Proposal Form

After selecting the product to be taken by the prospect the next stage in the contract of Life Insurance begins with the proposal. The Indian Contract Act says, "When one person signified to another his willingness to do or to abstain from doing anything with a view to obtaining assent or that other such act or abstinence, he is said to have made a proposal."

In Life Insurance the proposer through a standard printed proposal form of the insurer makes the proposal. Before the life insurer considers it for acceptance, the insurer obtains several forms duly completed. These forms provide relevant data for the purpose of assessment of the risk.

As the literacy rate is low in our country, therefore, the proposal form should be in simple language, which can be easily understood by the person and he is able to complete it and answer the questions clearly without any scope for ambiguity. It will be better if the proposal forms are in the regional languages at the respective offices.

Where the life to be insured has to be medically examined, the questions in the proposal form have to be carefully framed. The question, which can be answered by the medical examiner after professional examination should not be included in the proposal form. It is best to include in the proposal form only questions of fact, which are in the knowledge of the proposer. The criteria for selection of questions for inclusion in the proposal and medical examination form should aim at avoidance of any duplication, questions of fact should be included in the proposal form and details arising out of medical examination should be left to the medical examiner.

The statements made and the answers given in the proposal form are the basis of the contract of assurance in terms of the declaration made at the foot of the proposal form. For this reason it is essential that the proposer should give complete information about the identity, occupation, family history, personal history, health and habits of the life to be insured.

The proposal form would contain the following information:

(1) Name

The name of the proposer is to be filled carefully. Any error in giving the full and correct name may create difficulties at a later date. In the event of death of the life assured, the first thing to be established is that it is the life assured under the policy who has died.

(2) Nationality

The nationality of the life to be insured is very important because under RBI rules, life Insurance policies on the lives of foreigners can be issued only under special circumstances and subject to certain conditions. Furthermore, the rules and regulations of some countries permit their nationals to buy a policy of life Insurance only under certain circumstances and subject to certain rules. Therefore, if the nationality is not correctly stated it may create complications after the policy is issued and in some cases even the Insurance contract may have to be cancelled, thus causing avoidable inconvenience to both the parties.

(3) Occupation

The occupation of the life to be insured is very important for assessing the risk. Therefore, the full nature of the occupation detailing the duties should be stated. The designation such as manager, engineer, craftsman, operator, manufacturer and businessman do not convey the exact nature of duties and often there is tendency to use them to camouflage hazardous risk, which calls for acceptance at extra premium. If the occupation had been wrongly stated in the proposal whether knowingly or even innocently the double accident benefit and even the claim for the basic sum assured may be denied under certain circumstances in the event of claim by death. If the occupation is hazardous the proposer is required to fill in a special query form giving full information regarding the exact nature of duties.

(4) Age

Since the Insurance premiums are worked out on the basis of age at entry, it is important to give the exact date of birth. Generally, the insurer insists that proof of age must be submitted along with proposal and the following types of age of proofs would be generally acceptable to the insurer:

(a) Certified extract from Municipal or other records made at the time of birth. In most of the cases children name is not generally mentioned in the birth certificate when a birth certificate is produced, it is normally insisted that the person who produces it should be requested to confirm that it pertains to the life assured. Tallying of the father's name as given in the birth certificate with that given in the proposal is also done.

(b) Certificate of Baptism or certified extract from family Bible if it contains age or date of birth.

(c) Certified extract from school or college records if age or date of birth is stated therein. The certificate should be on the letter head of the School or College.

(d) Certified extract from service register in the case of Government employees and employees of quasi-Government institutions including Public undertakings.

(e) Passport issued by Government of India.

If any of the above mentioned proof is not available then any of the following proof is acceptable:

(i) Marriage certificate in case of Roman Catholics issued by the Roman Catholic Church.

(ii) Certified extracts from service records of small commercial institutions or industrial undertakings, provided it is specifically mentioned in such an extract that conclusive evidence of age was produced at the time of recruitment of the employee.

(iii) In case of Defence personnel, identity card issued by the Defence Department.

(iv) A true copy of the university certificate such as Matriculation or Higher academic examination.

(v) A true copy of SSC certificate issued by a Board set-up by the Central or State Government attested by a Development Officer.

If any of the above age proof is not available the following non-standard proofs are accepted:

(a) Horoscopes prepared soon after birth can be accepted provided they are genuine and the genuinity of the horoscopes will be determined by the insurer.

(b) The insurer may admit age on the basis of elder's declaration. The elder's declaration being executed by a considerably elder relative or friend who has personal knowledge of the life assureds' date of birth. The elder's declaration is required to be executed and it must be signed by the declarant in the presence of a Magistrate or an officer empowered to administer oath. In case the age stated in the proposal and the age as per declaration differ the higher age will be admitted.

(c) The age of the party as given by him or assessed by the medical examiner whichever is higher would be acceptable.

(d) If the proposer is from the rural areas, the insurer would admit age on the basis of a declaration by the proposer himself counter-signed by the secretary or a member of the Panchayat or the Tehsildar or Block Development Officer.

(e) Where the age of proof does not indicate the exact date of birth, the date of birth would be assumed to be the first July of the year of birth in case only the year of birth is given and in the case where month and the year are given, the date of birth would be assumed as 15th of that month.

The proposals in respect of which non-standards proofs only are available are accepted with modified terms.

(5) Nominee

It should be ensured that the nominee is appointed to receive the claim amount in the event of death. This will also avoid expenses in obtaining evidence of legal title and delay in settlement of claim.

(6) Hazardous Employment

This information is a must to assess the risk if proposer is in hazardous employment, e.g. a person in the armed forces, pilot, etc.

(7) Details of other Life Insurance Policies

It is very important from the insurer's point of view. Firstly, the information is obtained from the assured as to whether he has simultaneously applied to other insurer. If it happens that assured has submitted proposals to different Insurance companies keeping one company in dark then the contract is breach of the doctrine of *uberrima fides*. Secondly, the insurer gets information as regard to the total risk covered on the life both with respect to the quantum and with respect to nature of acceptance of work.

(8) Additional Information for Female Proposer

If the proposer is female then the qualification, average monthly income, source of income along with the husband's information, if married, like source of income, monthly income, other policies, so that relevant details of the risk to be covered can be found out. At the time of proposal, she should not be in an advance stage of pregnancy. The details of earlier deliveries whether those have been normal etc. are also asked for.

(9) Family History

The family history of a proposer is also sought to find out about the longevity in the family. The state of health of the living members and the cause of death of those who have predeceased the proposer. The extra mortality rating arises if parents have died of heart attack. It also helps to find out whether there have been hereditary, infectious or contagious diseases in the family of the proposer.

(10) Details of Personal Health

The details of personal health are also obtained to know if there are any adverse signals, i.e. infectious diseases which an ordinary medical examination cannot detect.

(11) Name of Medical Attendant (Regular)

The name of regular Medical Attendant is to be given so that any information about the medical history can be obtained. In case of premature death, the Medical Attendant would be a useful source of information.

(12) Declaration

At the end of the form, the proposer has to declare that he has disclosed true and accurate state of affairs in reply to various queries. By virtue of this declaration, the doctrine of *uberrima fides* operates.

Medical examination report is also obtained but not in all cases depending upon the age and the sum assured. The medical report is a confidential report and has the following information:

(a) Name and Address of the proposer;
(b) Signature of the proposer;
(c) Identification mark of the proposer;
(d) Appearance of the proposer; and
(e) Details of various body parts/system:
- Mouth, eyes, ears, throat;
- Respiratory system;
- Cardiovascular system;
- Abdomen;
- Gentio urinary system;
- Nervous system;
- Pregnancy details (For female proposer); and
- Operation, if any, details.

The medical examiner should be qualified and having experience as a general practitioner or a consulting physician.

Agent's Confidential Reports

Agent being the only person who has seen the proposer in flesh and blood, therefore, should accept the responsibility for recommending a good life to the best of his knowledge. He should exercise due caution. If the risk is proved to be bad one then disciplinary action can be taken against him.

The report should contain the following information:

1. Name, Age, Address of the proposer;
2. How long he has known the proposer;
3. Name of the Medical examiner and date of medical examination;
4. Appearance;
5. Monthly Income and its source; and
6. Details of previous policies, if any.

The details in the above-mentioned forms are indicative and the same can vary from insurer to insurer as well as product-wise.

Deposit Receipt

Along with the proposal form the first instalment of the premium as calculated above is to be deposited to the insurance company. Only after getting the first payment of the premium the proposal will be scrutinized by the insurance company.

(D) Policy Documents

After scrutiny of the proposal form, if it is found in order then the policy document is issued. This Policy document is a very important document.

This document is to be kept in safe custody, and should be handed over in a neat manner. It should not be left unattended, should not be misplaced or soiled otherwise there will be a lot of inconvenience at the time of:

(a) Taking loan against it;
(b) Passing any endorsement;
(c) Giving it as collateral security; and
(d) Taking claim.

It is like a Pronote or Registry. A policy document is the proof of contract. It mentions conditions of contract and also the rights of the policyholder. However, the policyholder seldom goes through the policy document. The assured should know the rights he enjoys and also the conditions he has to fulfil, so that the benefits under the contract are maintainable.

The policy document consists of the following seven important parts:

(a) Heading

The name of the company is given on top of the policy document.

(b) Preamble or Recital Clause

This part states that the statements in the proposal and the declaration form the basis of the contract and that the first premium has been received. This implies that if any of the statements are proved to be not true, the contract is vitiated or is considered ineffective from the legal point of view. The standard wording of this clause is as follows:

> "The Insurance Company has entered into this contract of insurance on the basis of proposal and declaration received from the proposer for effecting a life insurance contract on the life of the person named in schedule."

(c) Operative Clause

This part mentions that the assured agrees to pay the premium as per schedule and in consideration of the event on the happening of which the sum assured is payable subject to: (i) proof of the happening, (ii) title of claimant, and (iii) proof of age, if not admitted earlier.

(d) Proviso Part

This part states that the policy of assurance is subject to conditions and privileges printed on the back of the policy and further the policy schedule and every endorsement made on the policy shall be part of the policy. (This is necessary because the signature/attestation of the Insurer's official is on the first page, while the conditions and privileges are printed on the following pages).

(e) Schedule Part

This part states the policy number, name, address and occupation of the life assured, date of commencement, the sum assured amount, to whom and when payable, whether with or without profits, the premium payable, mode of payment, date of maturity, date of final payment of premium, plan of assurance, dates of proposal and personal statement, date of birth and whether the age is admitted, and other special conditions.

(f) Attestation Part

This part testifies that the insurer has entered into the contract. This is signed by an authorized official of the insurer.

(g) Conditions and Privileges

These are printed on the back of the policy and are part of the policy.

Policy Conditions

Following conditions are part of the life assurance contracts. If the conditions are not fulfilled, the benefits are either not payable or payable subject to some restrictions. In order to get full benefit, one should be aware of these conditions:

(i) Forfeiture in Certain Events

If the premium is not paid, as per the contract on the due date the policy lapses. This means that the assured loses risk cover. Even premium paid in the past are lost if the policy has not acquired paid-up value. The insurer company issues notices of premium, although it is not legally bound to do so.

If any of the conditions mentioned in the policy or subsequent endorsement is not complied with, then also the contract may get terminated resulting in losing of the risk cover and also the amounts paid in the past. The same happens if it is found that untrue or incorrect statements have been made in the proposal or the personal statement or material information has not been disclosed. All benefits will cease and all money forfeited. These penalties are subject to section 45 of Insurance Act, 1938.

(ii) Proof of Age

Age is the very basis which governs risk level and its pricing in Life Insurance. Thus, age is important for determining the risk involved and the premium amount. The life insurance companies will insist on proof of age at the time of submitting the proposal.

If the age is found to be lower, the difference is refunded without interest. Similarly, if the age is found to be higher, the difference is charged with interest or adjustment done either in sum assured or subsequent premiums or claim settlement (on case to case basis).

(iii) Travel, Residence or Occupation

The policies of life insurance are free from all restrictions as to travel, residence and occupation, except where a proposer has at the time of proposal, an intention to take up a hazardous occupation or the proposer is a student. The policies are free from war risk restriction. For covering aviation risks extra premium is charged wherever necessary. If the assured does not want to pay extra premium, the policy is issued subject to a restrictive clause.

(iv) Suicide

If the life assured commits suicide before the expiry of one year from the date on which the policy is issued, the policy will be null and void. However, if the policy has been assigned for valuable consideration in good faith and the notice of such an assignment has been given at least one calendar month before death, the claim amount will be paid to the extent of the interest of the assignee.

(v) Instalment Premium

The premium has to be paid in advance. If the mode of payment is monthly, quarterly or half yearly and if death takes place before all the premiums for the policy year are paid, the unpaid instalments for that policy year are deducted from the claim amount.

(vi) Privileges of the Assured (Days of Grace)

Premium must be paid on the due date. However, a maximum of one calendar month but not less than 30 days of grace period is allowed for payment of yearly, half yearly and quarterly premium. For monthly premium the grace period is 15 days. If the premium is paid within the grace period, it will be accepted without any late fee. Further, if death takes place within grace period and the premium remains unpaid, the claim amount is paid in full subject to deduction of unpaid premium in case of yearly mode of payment and subject to all outstanding premiums in the policy year in case of other modes of payment.

(vii) Revival of Lapsed Policies

1. Ordinary Revival Scheme

(a) If the premium is not paid, within the grace period, the policy lapses. It can however be revived (means brought back into full force) during the life time of the life assured, but within a period of five years from the date of the first unpaid premium and before the date of maturity. (The requirements for revival vary according to the period elapsed from the default in premium payment.)

(b) If the revival is completed within 30 days from the expiry of the grace period only a simple revival charge of Re. 1 is made.

(c) If the revival is made within a period of six months from the due date of the first unpaid premium, no evidence of health is required. The assured has to pay arrears of premium with interest, subject to a minimum payment of Re. 1.

(d) If the policy is to be revived after six months but before the expiry of 5 years from the date of first unpaid premium the requirements would be as under:
- Evidence of good health and habits of the life assured including a medical report from the medical examiner, which may be called for depending on sum assured. For determining whether non-medical basis will apply or not, the sum assured in question will be taken as the original sum assured less the paid up value, as on the date of lapse.
- Evidence to show that there has been no adverse change in personal or family history or occupation.
- Payment of premium in arrears with interest.

It is open to the insurer to modify the original terms and conditions while granting revival. This will depend upon the new circumstances as revealed by the information submitted. The insurer can also decline to revive the policy if he finds that circumstances have so changed as to make the life uninsurable.

Under this scheme, all the arrears of unpaid premium with all other requirements have to be submitted. The revival will be effective from the date of lapse on full payment made in one go.

Special Revival Scheme

If the policyholder is not in a position to pay all the arrears of premium at the same time, revival can be effected under this alternate scheme, provided:

(i) The policy had not acquired any surrender value at the time of lapse.

(ii) Application for revival is received after six months but before 3 years from the date of lapse.

(iii) Revival of the same policy under this scheme had not been done before.

Under this Scheme

1. A new policy will be issued in which the date of commencement will be shifted to a date prior to the date of revival by the period for which premiums were received under the original policy. The plan and the period of insurance will be the same as those under the original policy, but the premium ceasing or the maturity age

would not exceed the maximum allowable under the plan. (The period for backdating will be not less than three months).

2. The revised rate of premium would be calculated on the basis of the age at commencement of the new policy.
3. The assured will have to pay the accumulated difference between the revised premium and the old premium with interest.

Revival by Instalment Methods

If a policyholder cannot pay arrears in one lump sum and if the policy cannot be revived under Special Revival Scheme, he can make use of Instalment Revival Scheme. In this scheme, on the date of revival he has to pay:

(a) 6 monthly premiums, if mode is monthly;
(b) 2 quarterly premiums, if mode is quarterly;
(c) 1 half year premium, if mode is half yearly; and
(d) Half of the yearly premium, if mode is yearly.

The balance of revival amount is paid in instalments spread over two years along with normal interest on premium instalments. Other requirements regarding health are as required in Ordinary Revival Scheme.

(viii) Claim Concession

If premium is not paid within the grace period the policy lapses and if death takes place subsequently, only the paid up value if acquired, is paid.

(ix) Non-Forfeiture Regulations

If payment of premium is stopped after at least three full years premium have been paid the policy will not be wholly void, but it will be treated as paid up for a reduced sum assured—

(i) This reduced sum assured will bear the same ratio to the full sum assured as the number of premiums actually paid bears to the total number originally laid down or in other words by application of proportionate rule.
(ii) Such reduced sum should however, not be less than Rs. 250 (excluding bonus, if any) for policies of sum assured of Rs. 1,000 or over.
(iii) The paid up value is payable on death or on expiry of the term as the case may be as per the original contract.
(iv) A paid up policy does not participate in the profits disclosed in the valuation.
(v) As a policy becomes automatically paid up, no separate communication or endorsement is necessary.

(E) Endorsement

Writings on or on the back and forming part of policy is a contract:

- Endorsement may be alteration, assignment or pledging, etc.
- Endorsement refers to all amendments to master policy documents.
- It is a document attached to the policy. It is through this document the original terms are modified in the original policy document.
- Endorsement remedies the more general provisions in the policy itself.
- Endorsement is a memorandum added to a policy indicating the alterations to the terms of policy.
- In case where nomination is not effected in policy in the beginning it can be made by making endorsement on the policy. Policyholder can cancel the earlier or previous nomination.
- In case the space is not available it is done on separate piece of paper and pasted on policy with signatures of the assured and attestation of same by insurance company officials.
- Endorsement is necessary if the nominee is minor and policy names an appointee. This is done by obtaining signatures of appointee.
- In case of Group policies, the endorsement is necessary in following cases:
  (a) Revision of Benefits due to:
    (i) New Membership;
    (ii) Increase in Benefits; and
    (iii) Termination of membership.
  (b) Change in Rules.
  (c) Revision in Table Rates leading to revision in premium rates.

(F) Renewal Notice

Normally the policies in non-life insurance are for a period of 12 months but in case of life Insurance the yearly premiums are paid based on term of the policy, i.e. for number of years. Though there is no binding on insurance company to send intimation for renewal to the policyholder, but if due to some reason the policyholder forgets to deposit premium it is not only loss to the insured but also to the insurer who has incurred expenses on maintenance of policy and the relevant documentation. Thus, the life insurance company has evolved the system of sending renewal notice to the policyholder. This is done in advance so that policyholder deposits the premium, which is as per agreed terms and conditions. Thus, renewal notice is beneficial to company as well as policyholder.

(G) Bonus Notice

Bonus Notice is the intimation about bonus earned by the policy.

This is a source of information to the policyholder by which he comes to know regarding how much premium he has deposited and what is the amount of bonus his policy has accumulated. This helps him to have an idea about the status of his policy and he can keep in mind the health status of his policy.

19.8 SUMMARY

Life Insurance is purchased to mitigate the adverse consequences that may follow either on early death of a person or on his living too long. Every possible consequence that requires to be taken care of constitutes a need for insurance. To meet the needs of the people the insurers have developed different type of products such as:

Term Assurance

The sum assured is paid only on death during the term of contract.

Whole Life Insurance

The sum assured is paid only on the death of the insured which means only his legal heirs will get the benefit.

Endowment Assurance

The benefit is paid either on death or maturity which ever is earlier.

Annuities

It is the reverse of life assurance and benefit is paid till the person survives.

The above-mentioned plans can be for an individual or for a group. These plans can also be with profit or without profit. There are different plans for Female, Children, and Handicapped Children.

Insurance contract is a long-term contract, therefore, terms and conditions should be well defined to avoid any legal battle at future date. To avoid any problem for the legal heirs the following documents are used to issue the policy and subsequent changes:

(1) Prospectus,
(2) Proposal form,
(3) Deposit Receipt,
(4) Policy,
(5) Endorsement,
(6) Renewal notice, and
(7) Bonus notice.

Out of the above, the policy document is the most important document which clearly defines the terms and conditions of the policy. The term and conditions may be defined under three broad categories, namely:

(1) Mandatory terms and conditions, (2) Prohibited terms and conditions, and (3) Permissible terms and conditions

The following terms and conditions fall under the above-mentioned broad categories:

(1) The payment of premium,
(2) Days of grace,
(3) Age Proof,
(4) Suicide,
(5) Forfeiture in certain events,
(6) Travel Residence Occupation,
(7) Revival of Lapsed policy,
(8) Claim concession, and
(9) Non-forfeiture.

19.9 REVIEW QUESTIONS

1. Comment on the following Statement: "A man who owns a large amount of Term Insurance and is saving money regularly elsewhere should convert some of his term policies to Whole Life or Endowment Insurance.
2. It has been said that in buying Insurance, one should apply the following rule: "Buy as much premature death protection as you need and pay as much for it or you can afford." Explain the reasoning behind this and whether or not you agree with it.
3. Why should one buy an annuity policy?
4. Calculate the premium

(1)	Date of Birth	1/2/1980
(2)	Sum Assured	Rs. 75,000
(3)	Term of the policy	30 years
(4)	Large Sum Rebate	Rs. 2 per thousand
(5)	Tabular Premium (Qtly. Mode)/1000	
	Age 19 yrs.	Rs. 37
	Age 20 yrs.	Rs. 38
	Age 21 yrs.	Rs. 39
	Age 22 yrs.	Rs. 40

(A) Calculate the premium if premium payment is monthly mode. (Add 5%)

(B) Calculate the premium if premium payment is quarterly. (No Rebate)

(C) Calculate the premium if premium payment is half-yearly mode. (Rebate 1.5%)

(D) Calculate the premium if premium payment is yearly mode. (Rebate 3%)

(i) If the policy is taken on 25/3/2000.
(ii) If the policy is taken on 21/9/2000.
(iii) If the policy is taken on 2/9/2001.

5. Some of the terms and conditions of the typical life Insurance policy are designed to protect the company whereas other are designed to protect the insured. Classify the provisions according to the parties protected.

20
CHAPTER

SETTLEMENT OF CLAIMS IN INSURANCE

LEARNING OBJECTIVE

The objective of this chapter is to discuss the procedure for settlement of claims under insurance and a number of imperative issues associated to the claim settlement process.

20.1 INTRODUCTION

Insurance, in actuality is an arrangement by which the losses suffered by a small number of insured are spread over many, exposed to similar risks. Insurance is a protection against financial loss arising on the happening of an unexpected event. Insurance companies collect premium to provide security for the purpose. As loss is paid out of the premium collected from the insuring public and the insurance companies act as trustees to the amount so collected. Insurance companies have standard proposal forms, which are to be filed up giving the details of insurance required and presented to insurance company. Depending upon the answers given in proposal form insurance companies assess the risk and quote the premium. On payment of premium and acceptance thereof by insurance company the insurance is affected. However, unless premium is paid there is no insurance cover. In case of unexpected incident the insurance companies give the claim. The life insurance claim can arise either:

- On the death of the policyholder (death claim), or
- On the maturity of the policy (maturity claim), or
- Survival up to a specified period during the term (survival benefit).

During the insured period from the date of taking the Life Insurance policy to date of settling the claim the policy earns bonus, if the premium is paid in time, and the policy may lapse if the premium is not paid. However, under non-forfeiture option the insurance company does not forfeit the amount and the policy is converted into paid-up value or surrender value along with the bonus so accrued on such policy.

20.2 BONUS

Financial soundness of a company is determined by comparing all assets with all liabilities. In a valuation of a life Insurance company, the liabilities pertaining to life Insurance policies are worked out. Other liabilities, like outstanding capital, etc. are already determined clearly and don't have to be estimated or assessed every time. The policies liabilities as determined by the valuation have to be compared with all the assets less what is earmarked for other liabilities, which are known. The net figure of assets is equal to what appears as "life fund" on the liabilities side and is the fund set aside for meeting the claim of policyholders. There is surplus if the actual life fund exceeds the liabilities shown by the valuation, which means that the fund set aside for policyholders is more than the need. If the fund is less there is deficit.

If a surplus is shown in a valuation, it has to be distributed amongst the policyholder. Any bonus distribution system should be equitable to existing and new policyholders, simple to operate, easy to understand and flexible. Following are the main systems of distribution of bonus:

1. Reversionary Bonus

Under this system, bonus is given as uniform percentage additions to the basic sum assured and is payable with the sum assured. It is called Simple Reversionary Bonus. If the bonus is calculated as a percentage of the basic sum assured plus any existing bonus previously declared it is known as Compound Reversionary Bonus.

2. Tontine Bonus

Under this system the bonus is reserved only for those policyholders who survive a period of years and bonuses are not paid to those policyholders who die during the deferred period.

3. Contribution Bonus

The bonus is allotted to policyholder taking into account the contribution made by the policyholder towards the surplus. The bonus payment is generally made either by paying cash or applying it to reduce future premium.

4. Interim Bonus

Generally the bonus vests on policies that are in force on the date of valuation. Policies resulting into claims by death or maturity subsequent to the policy year containing the date of valuation will not have any bonus that year. Therefore, interim bonus may be declared to be paid along in such claims. This is with a view to facilitate settlement of claims that may arise before the next valuation is completed and avoid reopening of all these cases at a later date.

5. Terminal Bonus

This benefit is payable on policies which are in force for the full sum assured for a minimum period of 15 years before resulting into claim by death or maturity. This bonus is in addition to the reversionary or interim bonus, if any. Terminal Bonus is not payable for paid up policies, surrendered, or discounted policies. The bonus is always paid on Sum Assured.

20.3 SURRENDER VALUE

Under Section 113 of Insurance Act, 1938, the policy of life Insurance under which the whole of benefit become payable on a contingency, which is bound to happen, shall if all premiums have been paid for at least 3 consecutive years, acquire a guaranteed surrender value to which shall be added the surrender value of any subsisting bonus already attached to the policy.

Further Section 113(2) provides that a policy which has acquired surrender value shall not lapse by reason of non-payment of further premiums but shall be kept alive to the extent of paid-up sum assured and such paid-up sum shall include in full all subsisting reversionary bonuses that have already attached to the policy. Such amount shall not be (Excluding attached bonuses) less than the amount bearing to the total period for which premiums have already been paid bears to the maximum period for which premiums were originally payable.

The paid-up value is calculated as under:

$$\text{Paid-up Value} = \frac{\text{No. of Instalments Paid} \times \text{Sum Assured}}{\text{Total No. of Instalments Payable}} + \text{Bonus (if any)}$$

$$\text{Surrender Value (SV)} = \text{Paid-up Value} \times \text{Surrender Value Factor}/100$$

The Surrender Value factor depends upon the following:

- Rate of interest earned by the Insurer.
- The payment made in advance for number of years.

To illustrate the paid up and surrender value the examples are given below:

Example

Sum Assured	= Rs. 50,000
Age	= 35 years
Date of Commencement	= 1/4/90
Term	= 20 years
Mode of payment	= (a) Yearly, (b) Half-Yearly, (c) Quarterly, (d) Monthly
Last Premium Paid	= 1/4/2001
Surrender Value Factor	= 60%

You are to calculate paid up value and surrender value:

(a) If mode of payment is yearly

No. of Instalments paid	= (1/4/2001-1/4/90) + 1 = 12

(Note: Because the instalments on 1/4/90 is also paid)

Total Instalments payable	= 20
Paid up value	= 12/20 × 50,000 = Rs. 30, 000
Surrender Value	= 30,000 × 60% = Rs. 18,000

(b) If the mode of payment is half-yearly

No. of Instalment paid	= (1/4/2001-1/4/90) × 2 +1 = 11 x 2 + 1 = 23

(*Note*: We multiplied by 2 because of half-yearly mode and added 1 because the instalment on 1/4/1990 is also paid).

Total Instalments payable	= 20 × 2 = 40
Paid up value	= 23/40 × 50,000 = Rs. 28,750
Surrender Value	= 28,750 × 60% = Rs. 17,250

(c) If the mode of payment is quarterly

No. of Instalments paid	= (1/4/2001-1/4/90) × 4 + 1 = 11 × 4 + 1 = 45

(*Note*: We multiplied by 4 because of quarterly mode and added 1 because the instalment on 1/4/1990 is also paid).

Total Instalments payable	= 20 × 4 = 80
Paid up value	= 45/80 × 50,000 = Rs. 28,125

Surrender Value = 28,125 × 60%
= Rs. 16,875

(d) If the mode of payment is monthly

No. of Instalments paid = (1/4/2001-1/4/90) × 12 +1
= 11 X 12 + 1 = 133

(Note: We multiplied by 12 because of monthly mode and added 1 because the instalment on 1/4/1990 is also paid).

Total Instalments payable = 20 × 12 = 240

Paid up value = 133/240 × 50,000
= Rs. 27,708

Surrender Value = 27,708 × 60%
= Rs. 16,250

Guaranteed Surrender Value

The minimum surrender value is equal to 30% of the total amount of premiums paid excluding first year premium and additional premiums for additional benefits. In addition, cash value of existing accrued bonus will also be allowed subject to surrender value factor. This is known as "Guaranteed Surrender Value." As per the provisions of Insurance Act, the surrender value formula has to be mentioned in policy documents.

Minimum (guaranteed) surrender value allowable = 30% of the total premiums paid:

(a) excluding the First year Premium,
(b) all extra Premiums, and
(c) additional premiums for D.A.B.

The surrender of policy would mean cancellation of the contract.

Restriction on Surrender of Policy

(1) Policy cannot be surrendered if any one of the assignees is a minor even with the consent of his natural or appointed guardian as the guardian is empowered only to collect all debts due but he is not authorized to dispose of by selling or mortgaging etc. property of the minor except with the permission of the court. If the court is satisfied that the policy should be surrendered in the interest of the minor it may allow surrender of the policy.

(2) Similarly, if the policyholder or the assignee has become insane or has been adjudicated as insolvent, the policy cannot be surrendered.

(3) In case of a lunatic, the manager or committee, appointed under Indian Lunacy Act may surrender the policy.

(4) In case of an insolvent the receiver can surrender the policy.

(5) If a prohibitory or an attachment order has been served on the insurer attaching the policy then the surrender value cannot be paid.

20.4 LOANS

The insurer also grants loans under the policies under the following terms and conditions:

(i) The maximum loan value is 90% of the surrender value including bonus.
(ii) The policy is to be assigned in favour of insurer.
(iii) The nominee is entitled to get the sum payable under the policy less the loan and loan interest falling due.
(iv) Each policy is taken independent of other policy therefore separate application is made for the loan.
(v) Before paying loan any unpaid premium is recovered from the loan amount.
(vi) The interest is charged at fixed rate and compounded half yearly.
(vii) Loans are granted minimum for six months. If the loan is paid early even then interest of minimum six months will be charged. However, if a policyholder dies during this period then the minimum period of six month is not applicable.
(viii) If a policyholder is repaying regularly the loan amount then the additional loan can also be granted but the maximum limit will be 90% of the surrender value.

Generally the repayment of loan is in lump sum but it can be paid in instalments on special request of the policyholder.

20.5 LIFE INSURANCE DEATH CLAIMS

Death claim can further be classified as follows:

(i) Premature claim: where the insured dies within three years of taking out of policy or revival as the case may be.
(ii) Other claim where the insured dies after three years of taking out of the policy.

Under the death claim the following procedure is to be followed:

1. Intimation of Death

The intimation of death is to be given by a proper person. While intimating about the death the following information must be sent:

(a) Policy number;

(b) Name of the life assured;
(c) Date of death;
(d) Cause of death; and
(e) Claimants relationship with the deceased.

2. Proof of Death

(a) A certificate issued by the Municipal Corporation;
(b) Certificate from local board or Panchayat;
(c) Attending Doctor may also give the death certificate;
(d) Sometimes none of these certificates are available because the death has taken place due to:
   (i) Plane crash;
   (ii) Train accident;
   (iii) Washed away in water;
   (iv) Buried under the tons of earth and stone in a landslide; and
   (v) In a fire the dead body is not recovered or is beyond recognition.

   Under these circumstances, the insurer has to take the judicious decision and ask for satisfactory proof of death; and
(e) Under the Indian evidence Act, a person who has disappeared is presumed to be dead only if he has not been heard of for 7 years by those who would normally have heard of him if he had been alive.

When the intimation of the disappearance of the assured is received, the claimant should be informed that unless premiums are paid regularly until such time the decree from the court is obtained presuming the death of life assured, the policy would lapse. Thus, as per evidence act one has to wait for 7 years in case of presumption of death. The insurer may pay the claim if the death is due to the following reasons:

- During war defense personnel may be reported missing and may be presumed dead. In such case the certificate from officer commanding and enquiry report, if any, may be considered as sufficient proof of death.
- When the assured is reported missing on the high seas, one should ascertain whether the person was on board the ship at the last port of call.
- If the ship had sunk the list of survivors should be verified
- When a person has been drowned in the sea, river, tank or well the body is found decomposed beyond recognition and the possibility of suicide is ruled out or suicide clause is not applicable then claim for the basic sum assured only should he paid.
- When the assured is killed during hunting, mountain-climbing or

by an attack by a wild beast in a forest and the dead body is either not recovered or found mutilated beyond recognition the evidence produced by the claimant should be carefully examined and the basic sum assured only should be paid.

If an insurer feels that it is a premature claim then he may call for the following information:

- The claimant may give the factual data about the cause of death, date of death, terminal illness, the particulars of doctors consulted by the deceased during last three years and particulars of other policies held by life assured.
- The certificate from the doctor who attended on the assured during his terminal illness or who certified the death.
- The certificate from the hospital where he was hospitalized.
- The details of leave availed by the life assured during last one year for his treatment from his employer.

Proof of Title

Once the proof of death is submitted to the insurer then next step is to determine to whom the claim is payable on the death of the life assured. Generally while filling the proposal form at the time of taking a policy, the name of the nominee is given. Upon the death of the life insured the amount is payable to the nominee given in the proposal form or the assignee if the endorsement is issued in favour of the assignee. The distinction between the nomination and assignment is as follows:

Difference Between Nomination and Assignment

Nomination

1. Can be made:
   (a) Before issue of the policy by naming his age, relationship and address in the proposal form or by a letter giving details, or
   (b) By an endorsement on the policy.
2. Deed not applicable.
3. Policyholder only can appoint nominee.
4. It is affected where Insurance Act, 1938 applies, or where similar enactments apply, viz. in Pakistan and Sri Lanka.
5. Assured retains control and can deal with the policy in any manner he likes.
6. Need not be supported by a consideration.
7. May be witnessed.
8. Notice is required to safeguard the nominee interest.
9. Nominee has no right to sue under the policy.
10. It can be cancelled without any reason.

11. Where nominee is a minor, appointment of the life appointee by the life assured only is required.
12. Appointee can be appointed in the wording of the nomination.
13. No vested interest in favour of nominee is created.
14. Nominee's right is only to collect policy moneys on the death of the assured and when paid by the insurer.
15. If nominee dies, rights under the policy revert to the life assured or his legal representatives.
16. If the nominee dies after the life assured and before settlement of the claim, the policy moneys would be payable to the heirs of the life assured.

Assignment

1. Can be effected by endorsement.
2. By separate deed on stamped paper.
3. The absolute owner of the policy may be "whether proposer or the life assured or the absolute assignee to the extent of his interest. Or the person having requisite authority from such owners can assign assignment.
4. It can be executed anywhere in the world. It can be altered by the life assured during the currency of the policy by Cancellation of nomination or by a new nomination or by an assignment.
5. Assured loses control over the policy. Absolute assignee is the owner of the policy and can deal with it.
6. Must be supported by a consideration.
7. Notice is required to enable the assignee to acquire priority over other assignees.
8. Assignee has right to sue under the policy.
9. It cannot be cancelled by the assignor. The assignee has to first reassign the policy.
10. When assignee is a minor, guardian is to be appointed.
11. Guardian cannot be appointed in the wording of the assignment.
12. Assignee acquires interest.
13. On receipt of the notice, the insurer has to recognize the assignee as the person legally entitled to receive the benefits.
14. If a conditional assignee dies, the right under the policy reverts to the life assured, depending upon the terms of assignment. If an absolute assignee dies, the right devolves upon his/her heirs.
15. If the assignee (absolute or conditional) dies after the life assured and before settlement, the policy moneys would be payable to the heirs of the assignee.

In case the life assured dies leaving no nomination or assignment under the policy the insurer calls for the evidence of legal title to the estate of the deceased, i.e.:

(a) Letters of Administration.
(b) Succession certificate.
(c) Certificate issued by the Administrator General.

To moderate the hardship of the legal heirs the insurer can waive the proof of title provided—

(a) There is no dispute in the family and heirs are of one mind.
(b) Payment on indemnity bond can be made only to heirs. The deceased has left behind no will.

Claim Amount

(i) After getting all the documents as mentioned above the insurer pays the nominee the claim amount equivalent to the sum assured alongwith the bonuses after deducting any loan or unpaid premium if any.
Example: A policy was taken at the age of 35 under endowment plan for a Sum Assured of Rs. 2,00,000. The Risk date was 14/10/1985 and the annual premium instalment was of Rs. 10,000. The premium was not paid on 14/10/1998. The person expired on 05/02/1999. The bonus accrued Rs: 60,000 as on date. The claim amount will be as follows:
Claim Amount = 2 lakh (+) 60,000 (–) Rs. 10,000 = Rs. 2,50,000
(ii) If the policy has lapsed because of non-payment of premium then the paid-up value along with the bonus after deducting the loan amount is paid to the nominee or the legal heirs.
(iii) Claim Concession: Sometimes the Insurer pays the policy amount as if the policy was in full force:
   (a) If the policyholder dies within six months from the due date of the first unpaid premium, provided at least three full years premium has been paid.
   (b) In respect of policies where the premiums are paid for five years or more the claim concession is extended to the period of one year, instead of six months from the due date of first unpaid premium (FUP).

This will be subject to:

(i) Deduction of the unpaid premium with interest thereon up to date of death, and
(ii) Deduction of the premiums falling due before the next anniversary of the policy.

This is being explained with the help of following examples:

Example 1

The particulars of Mr. Ashok	
Sum Assured	Rs. 2, 00,000
Term	20 Years
Date of commencement	1/5/1985
Mode of Payment	Yearly
Yearly Premium	Rs. 10,000
Last Premium paid	1/5/1999
Died on	1/10/2000

Claim Amount

The premium not paid for 1/5/2000 but died on 1/10/2000, i.e. within 5 months from the date of first unpaid premium, therefore under claim concession clause, Mr. Ashok's beneficiary will be entitled for the full sum assured i.e. Rs. 2,00,000 plus Bonus, if any, but the premium unpaid on 1/5/2000 will be deducted along with the interest upto 1/10/2000.

Example 2

The particulars of Mr. Alok Nath	
Sum Assured	Rs. 5,00,000
Term	20 Years
Date of commencement	1/5/1985
Mode of Payment	Yearly
Half-yearly Premium	Rs. 13000
Last Premium paid	1/1/1989
Died on	1/8/90

Claim Amount

The premium not paid for 1/5/90 but died within 3 months from the date of first unpaid premium, therefore, under claim concession clause Mr. Alok's beneficiary is entitle for the full claim of Rs. 500,000 plus bonus, if any, after deducted the premium amount of Rs. 13,000 along with the interest.

Example 3

The particulars of Mr. Anand	
Sum Assured	Rs. 400,000
Term	20 Years
Date of commencement	1/5/1985
Mode of Payment	Yearly
Yearly Premium	Rs. 20,000
Last Premium paid	1/5/1990
Died on	1/8/1992

Claim Amount

Mr. Anand's beneficiary is entitled only for the paid-up amount, i.e. Rs. 1,20,000 plus bonus if any (6/20 × 4,00,000) not the full amount because A died after more than one year from the first unpaid premium.

Attachment of Policy

1. If the office receives a prohibitory order from a Court of Law, careful note of the same should be taken on the claim card, stating that no payment shall be made till the prohibitory order is vacated.
2. If the prohibitory order is received attaching a certain specified amount which is less than the policy money due, the claim will not be settled by keeping the sum attached in suspense account and by paying the balance amount to the claimant unless the attaching authority approves of such action as there is a risk of attaching authority issuing a decree at a later date in favour of the plaintiffs for a sum higher than the original sum attached.
3. An income tax notice under Section 226(3) is on a different footing from a prohibitory order. If the policy stands in the assured's own favour and if the Income Tax Officer demands payment of the arrears of income tax in respect of the income of the deceased, payment has to be made provided satisfactory proof of death and age of the assured have been duly furnished. On the other hand, if the policy is assigned before the notice, payment can be made to the Income Tax Officer only provided the assignee gives consent to the same. Otherwise, the Income Tax Officer should be informed that the policy having been duly assigned belongs to assignee and not to the assured assessee and that the Company cannot, therefore, make payment thereof to the Income Tax Officer but will pay the same to the rightful owner, viz. the assignee of the policy. The position is, however, entirely different where only a nomination has been made under Section 39 of the Insurance Act. Nomination confers the right or title to the policy on the nominee subject to all encumbrances thereon. As such, payment has to be made to the Income Tax Officer, ignoring the nomination. The nominee should, however, be informed about the demand of the Income Tax Officer adding that the payment will be made thereunder to the Income Tax Officer unless the income-tax notice is withdrawn.

Accident Benefits

If the policy is issued under the accident benefit scheme then the insured amount is doubled therefore every care is taken before paying the accident benefit. The payment of accident benefit depends on the following important factors:

(1) There must be an accident caused by outward, violent and visible means.
(2) The life assured must sustain bodily injury resulting solely and directly from the accident.
(3) Such injury must result in death within 120 days of its occurrence. Some insurers may stipulate periods shorter than 120 days.
(4) Such injury should, solely, directly, independently of all other causes, result in death of the life assured.
(5) The claimant must intimate the death as a result of accident and produce evidence to the satisfaction of the insurer, about the conditions being met. The period of 120 days (or 90 days) is to ensure the linkage between accident and death. In some cases insurer may consider the claim, even if the period of 120 is exceeded.

But all accidents are not covered and exclusions are as follows:

(1) Suicide or attempted suicide or intentional self-inflicted injury whether sane or not at that time.
(2) Under influence of drugs or alcohol, narcotics or psychotropic substance not prescribed by a Medical Professional.
(3) War, Invasion, Civil War, Riots, Revolution or any war like operation.
(4) Criminal or unlawful act.
(5) Service in the military or police.
(6) Flying activity other than as a paying passenger.
(7) Racing vehicle.

Permanent Disability Benefits

In case of permanent disability arising out of an accident, the following benefits are provided for in the Insurance policy:

(a) An additional sum equal to the sum assured will be paid in monthly instalments spread over 10 years.
(b) The future premiums are waived. In case of claim (Death or maturity) before 10 years the disability benefit instalments, which have not fallen due, will be paid along with the claim. The maximum limit is Rs. 5.00 lakhs or Rs. 10.00 lakhs depending upon the insurer and exclusion clauses are the same as under accident benefit.

The basic pre-conditions for granting the benefit are:

1. That the disability should be solely and directly as a result of

accidental injury.

2. The disability must be total and permanent.
3. The accidental injury and the resultant disability should take place before the assured attains the age of 65 years.

Generally the policy defines the disability in physical terms viz. loss of sight of both the eyes, amputations of both the hands at or above the wrist, or amputation of both the legs at or above ankles, etc. It is also stated that the disability must be total and permanent and such that the life assured then or in future, would not be able to do any work, occupation or profession to earn or obtain any wages, compensation or profit.

Immediately after the disability, the life assured must intimate the Insurance company giving full details and within a specific period say 120 days or less or more depending upon different insurer, provide proof of disability to the satisfaction of the company.

If the claim is admitted the waiver of premium should be allowed from the due date of the premium following the date of accident, which brought about the disability. If the decision is not taken then the premium is to be paid till the final decision. However, these premiums will be refunded on admitting the claim.

20.6 LIFE INSURANCE MATURITY CLAIMS

1. A Maturity claim is payable as per the terms of the contract, at the end of the term of the policy, if the life assured lives upto that date. It includes the sum assured and any other specified sum plus vested bonuses. Any debt or charge under the policy, like loans, outstanding premia (due but not paid), etc. will be deducted.
2. Settlement of maturity claims is usually free from complications relating to title, as policy moneys are paid to the life assured himself/herself. In case the policy is absolutely assigned, then the settlement is made in favour of the absolute assignee.
3. Insurers generally inform the policyholders well in advance of the maturity date and even send the form of discharge with a request to return the same duly stamped, signed and witnessed along with:
   (a) The policy document for cancellation;
   (b) Proof of age, if age is already not admitted; and
   (c) If there is an assignment executed on a separate stamped paper, the document of assignment.
4. If there is a loan subsisting, the policy document would already be with the insurer, as the policy has to be assigned in favour of the insurer before getting the loan. If the policy remains paid up (automatically or on request), the paid up value, which will include the vested bonus as on that date, will be the claim amount.

5. The discharge voucher will show the gross amount of claim, the deductions, if any, and the net amount payable. The gross amount normally consists of the basic sum assured or paid up value, the vested bonus and interim bonus payable, any deposit lying in the said policy account and return of excess premiums collected, if any. For example, the extra premium for double accident benefit was lowered by the LIC a few years back, but it was decided to refund the excess premiums at the time of settlement of claim.
6. The deductions from the gross amounts normally consist of loan amount, outstanding interest on the loan, unpaid premium, if any, (monthly in respect of salary savings scheme policies) and X-charge, if any. The X-charge facility is provided by the LIC so as to help the policyholder, when the renewal premium paid is less than the correct amount. Instead of keeping the lesser amount in deposit and asking for the balance premium, the amount is straight away adjusted and renewal premium receipt issued, after debiting the balance amount needed to an X-charge account. Of course, this facility is used only to meet very small shortfalls. The X-charge account is verified at the time of claim and the total outstanding amount is deducted from the gross claim amount.
7. Proof of age does not cause a problem because age is admitted in most of the policies at the commencement. If at the time of claim, the original policy document is not found, the procedures required for issue of duplicate policy may not be gone through in full. Insurers may be willing to settle the maturity claim on the basis of an indemnity bond unless the circumstances warrant more caution.
8. If the life assured dies after the date of maturity but before settlement of claim, the policy vests in the deceased life assured's estate. The claim amount is then payable to the legal heirs of the life assured as per the law applicable. The nomination under section 39 is valid only in case of death of life assured before date of maturity not on or after. The insurer may settle the claim in favour of all the legal heirs of the life assured on joint discharge, on the basis of an indemnity. However, if the amount of claim is large, a succession certificate or other proofs of title may be called for. Wills have to be probated.

Attachment of Policies

1. If a prohibitory order is issued by the Court, the assured will be advised that no payment can be made to him until the prohibitory order is vacated.
2. If an income tax notice is received before the date of maturity, but has not been withdrawn, the Income Tax Officer should be informed about the date of maturity and about the status of the

person (i.e. assured, assignee) to whom the money will fall to be paid on the date of maturity on assured's surviving that date. An enquiry should be made whether he has realized the arrears of income tax from the assured and whether he still claims the policy moneys on the date of maturity or whether he would withdraw the notice served on the Insurer. If the Income Tax Officer replies that the notice will stand, he should be asked to serve on or after the date of maturity a fresh notice with necessary challan.

3. If a policy has been effected under the Married Women's Property Act, 1874 the policy moneys have to be paid to the special trustees if trustees have been appointed; otherwise to the Official Trustee. However, if all the beneficiaries are major and competent to contract and if no special trustees have been appointed, the Insurer would be prepared to pay the policy moneys to the beneficiaries directly after obtaining a joint discharge form from them. A declaration is also obtained from these beneficiaries along with the discharge from which *inter-alia* gives their ages and where they declare that they are capable of giving a valid discharge to the Insurer.

Example of Maturity Claim

Sum Assured = Rs. 2 lakh
Plan Endowment with profit
Date of Commencement = 14/10/1985
Mode of Payment = Yearly
Bonus = Rs. 1 lakh
Term = 15 Years
Maturity Amount = 2 lakh (+) 1 lakh [Bonus] = 3 lakhs

20.7 LIFE INSURANCE SURVIVAL CLAIMS

Some policies are entitled for the survival benefit before the expiry of the full term of the policy but on survival of the life assured. For example, in the Money Back plans of the LIC say of 15 years term, 1/4th of the sum assured becomes payable on the life assured surviving 5 years, further ¼ of the sum assured becomes payable on his surviving 10 years and the balance ½ of the sum assured becomes payable on his surviving to the end of the term of the policy, viz. 15 years. The risk (death cover), however, is for the full SA during the entire term. Bonus additions continue to be on the full sum assured till, the policy is finally determined.

Settlement of the survival benefit is even easier than settlement of maturity claim. The insurer sends advance intimation and the discharge voucher and the life assured is required to return the same duly stamped, signed and witnessed and send the original policy document also for necessary endorsement. The gross amount is the instalments of the sum assured payable (1/4 in the example cited) and the net amount is arrived at after deduction of the outstanding loan interest, outstanding premium, X-charge, etc.

Example

Sum Assured = Rs. 4 lakh
Money Back Policy
Date of Commencement = 14/10/1980
Mode of Payment = Yearly
Bonus = Rs. 2 lakh
Term = 20 Years
Survival Benefits
25% of the Sum Assured at the end of 5 yrs.
25% of the Sum Assured at the end of 10 yrs.
25% of the Sum Assured at the end of 15 yrs.
25% of the Sum Assured at the end of 20 yrs.
Amount payable on maturity = Rs. 1,00,000 (25% of 4 lakh) + Rs. 2 lakh = 3 lakhs.

It is important to note that the Claim amount along with the bonus received by the beneficiary or policyholder is exempted under Section 10 (10D) of Income Tax Act. But the annuity/pension amount received by the policyholder will be taxable under the heading Salary provided the purchase price of annuity is exempted under Section 80CCC of Income Tax Act, 1961.

20.8 SUMMARY

While the policy with profit is in operation, the policyholder is entitled for the bonus. The bonus can be paid out of the surplus earned by the insurer. The bonus can be paid either as simple reversionary bonus or compound reversionary bonus. If the policy is for more than 15 years then the Insurer also pays terminal bonus.

If the policy has been lapsed because of non-payment of premium the policy will be converted into paid-up value under the non-forfeiture option. The policy can also be surrendered wherein the contract will be terminated and the surrender value will be paid to the Insured.

The purpose of taking a Life Insurance policy is predominantly to provide for protection against financial problems that may be faced in case the life assured dies too young or lives too long. Details of the contingencies under which the benefits are payable, are specified in the policy. When these contingencies occur, the benefits have to be claimed by the policyholder or the beneficiaries, as determined under various provisions of the policy and the law.

Claims may arise because of survival up to the end of the policy term, which is the date of maturity (Maturity Claims), survival up to a specified period during the term (Survival Benefits), death of the life assured during the term (Death Claims).

While settling the claim the insurer desires the certain documents like proof of death, cause of death, proof of title, the certificate of disability and any other document to pay the sum assured amount along with the bonus after deducting unpaid premium if any to the legal heirs. The Insurer will also verify that there is no attachment of policies from the Court or Income Tax Department.

20.8 REVIEW QUESTIONS

1. Explain and illustrate the terms Paid-up Value, Surrender Value and Guaranteed Surrender Value?
2. What is the process of getting insurance claims in case of the death of the person?
3. Explain the provisions of the Claim Concession?
4. How are the benefits under Accident and Disability being paid?
5. Calculate paid-up value and surrender value.
   Sum Assured = Rs. 4 lakh
   Endowment Plan
   Term = 20 years
   Mode of Payment = Half Yearly
   Date of Commencement = 10/08/1982
   Last Premium Paid = 10/08/1996
   Surrender Value Factor = 72%
6. From the following particulars, calculate the amount of claim payable, if the insured died on 27th August 2000:
   Date of commencement = 13/07/1984
   Sum Assured = Rs. 60,000
   Table Term = Money Back (with profit) 25 years
   Last Premium paid due = 13/07/1999
   Three instalments of Rs. 12,000 each had been paid in 1989, 1994 and 1999
   (Assume that total bonus declared from 3/85 till 3/2000 is Rs. 800 per thousand sum assured and that premium is Rs. 2500. Ignore interest, if any.)
7. Mr. A has a whole life policy for Rs. 7.00 lakhs. His tenth annual premium is due on 1st Aug. 2001. He fails to pay the premium and dies on 31/07/2001. How much does his beneficiary get? Suppose he dies on 2/8/2001, how much does his beneficiary get?

21

CHAPTER

NON-LIFE INSURANCE PROCEDURES

LEARNING OBJECTIVE

The objective of this chapter is to acquaint the students about the documents normally required for obtaining non-life policies and other important issues concerning to these policies.

21.1 INTRODUCTION

Insurance policy is a legal document that sets forth in writing the contract between the insured and the insurer. It describes the main characteristics of property in detail and the perils against which the property is covered and the conditions of insurance. Since it is a written contract between the two parties it should, therefore, fulfil the essential conditions for a valid contract. These are, namely:

(i) Offer and acceptance. Corporate agreement (a consensus and indemnity) being reached by the parties.
(ii) Absence of fraud or misrepresentation.
(iii) Capacity of the parties.
(iv) Legality the Object must be legal.
(v) Consideration.

These conditions have already been discussed.

21.2 WHO CAN INSURE?

Every person cannot obtain a non-life insurance policy. Only persons who are having insurable interest in the subject matter of insurance can obtain this policy. They may or may not obtain such a policy.

1. Absolute owner of property.
2. Wife can insure property of her husband and *vice-versa* till such time they are living together.
3. $1/64^{th}$ owners of a ship can insure ship up to his interest in the ship.
4. A person can insure his life as he has interest in his own life.

But those who must obtain such a policy include the following:

(a) Under Statute

It includes the following:

(i) Certain ecclesiastical corporations.

(ii) Tenants for life or other limited owners of land. Such persons are required to insure at their own expense buildings, which have been erected, improved or added to out of funds raised by means of charges on the settled land.

(b) Persons under a Disability

A person of unsound mind or an infant may own a property and it has to be insured on his behalf by his guardian, trustees as the case may be.

(c) An Agent

An agent who is not having insurable interest in the subject matter of insurance and is not even in possession of it may as an agent, insure on behalf of its owner. The agent must have the authority to insure, or the insurance must be ratified or adopted by the principal subsequently.

The above listed category of persons for obtaining a non-life insurance policy may contact the office of insurance company directly or through an agent. The insurance companies have devised a printed proposal form for every type of cover required by the insuring public to make an application or offer for insurance cover. These proposal forms have been devised in such a manner that through questions contained in it elicit all material facts about the particular risk proposed for insurance. The nature of questions varies according to the particular class of insurance concerned.

In fire insurance the proposed forms are not used compulsorily. The practice varies from company to company. However, where pre-survey has been conducted by the company's officer or by the surveyor for big industrial risk, it is not used. The proposal forms are required in case of small risks. Therefore, sometimes the declaration is not there in fire proposal forms. As already pointed out earlier lesson that when the insured signs below the declaration he certifies the correctness of the answer given to the questions asked for in the proposal form. It means that the duty of observance of good faith on the part of the proposer becomes far stricter. When the pre-survey is conducted by the insurance company then in that case insurer will not blame the proposer for this duty later on at the time of payment of claim.

In Marine Cargo insurance proposal form is not used instead a questionnaire or declaration form is used which has to be completed by the proposer. However, in Marine Hull insurance the proposal is invariably used. Questionnaire extracts all information, which is required by the insurers to accept the risk, and in case it is to be accepted then on what rate of premium and conditions. The questionnaire contains the following questions:

1. Name and address of the proposer.
2. Description of goods to be insured.
3. Place where goods originally manufactured or produced.
4. Details of packing.
5. Details of Voyage or transit by Rail/Road.
6. Basis of valuation.
7. Estimated value of goods to be shipped/railed during one year.
8. Maximum value to be sent by any one shipment/railing.
9. Type of insurance cover required.
10. How long has proposer previously been handling this type of business?
11. With which company previously insured. Type of cover grated, rate charged and premiums.

Material Facts

A material fact is a fact, which would influence the mind of a prudent insurer to accept or not to accept the risk. If it is to be accepted then on what rate and conditions.

If a fact is material, is known or aught to be known to the proposer, and has not disclosed it honestly believing not to be material to the risk then he cannot be excused later on. The test is whether a reasonable man would have considered the fact material. In *Joel* v. *Law Union and Crown Insurance Co.* (1908) Fteleher-Moulton L.J. said: "*The disclosure must be of all you ought to have realized to be material, not of that only which you did not in fact realize to be so.*" Material facts relate to the subject matter of insurance and any fact, which reveals that the physical hazard is above normal, is material to the insurers.

There are certain facts, which are connected with, insured himself known as moral hazard which may be material. While accepting a risk of burglary insurance the insurer's mind would be influenced in case he knows that the proposer has just spent a long period in prison on conviction of a fraud. In *Horne* v. *Poland* (1922) it was found that the insured was an alian for Eastern European Country where standard of business conduct were not as good as that of United Kingdom. Moreover, the insured assumed on English name, this was held as a material fact in the case. But it does not mean that the nationality of a proposer in every case is a material fact. In the course of his judgement J. Lush said: "*I can not agree with the view —— that the mere fact that a person is a foreigner and not a British subject is in all cases a material fact, so that the non-disclosure of it invalidates the policy —— each case must depend on its circumstances."* A fact, which has not been disclosed, may be material though the insurer agrees that, had he known it, he might still have accepted the risk on the same premium,. terms and conditions. The insurer must be in possession of all the material fact that could reasonably influence his mind except the facts, which need not be disclosed stated below:

The Common Law duty of disclosure is based on common sense. Therefore, there are certain facts which if asked for from the proper will be unreasonable. They are expressed in Porter's "Laws of Insurance": *"The insured need not mention what the insurer knows, or what he waives of, nor what lessons the risk agreed and understood to be run by the express terms of the policy, nor general topics of specialization, as for instance, the insurers are bound to know every cause which may occasion perils—as the probability of lighting, hurricanes, earthquakes, etc."* In short, the proposer must disclose all material facts which are in his reach of knowledge or known to him, but he is not expected to disclose the following facts:

(i) Facts, which lesson the risk.
(ii) Facts of common knowledge, e.g. the existence of state of riots.
(iii) Facts, which have been waived by the insurers by their conduct.
(iv) Facts, which the insurers in the ordinary course of their transacting business know or should know.
(v) Facts, which can or should be inferred by the insurer from the information given by the proposer.
(vi) Facts, which are not known to the proposer on which he is expected to know.
(vi) Facts which a proposer could not reasonably be expected to know to be material.

21.3 DOCUMENTS REQUIRED FOR NON-LIFE INSURANCE POLICY

A policy is the written legal evidence of contract between the insured and the insurers. The following documents are required in non-life policy:

1. The Proposal or Questionnaire

This is an offer of the proposer to insurer for the coverage of his property, interest, life, or liability against certain risks against which he is exposed. The insurer use printed proposal forms for various types of covers and insert questions according to particular class of Insurance concerned to elicit all material facts concerning the risk. They are devised in such a manner that almost all information required by the insurers for the proposed risk is drawn out and there is little scope that any material fact is left out. If the proposer feels that still some of the material facts have been left out, he is required to spell them out. The proposer is required to answer all questions of the proposal form correctly and fully otherwise he will be guilty of non-observation of utmost good faith which can render the contract voidable at the option of the insurers. The proposal contains a declaration as follows:

> "I do hereby declare that the answers given in the proposal form are true to the best of my knowledge and belief, and I further agree that this proposal and declaration shall be the basis of the contra.. between myself and the insurers."

The proposer by signing this unqualified declaration of the truth of the statements thereby warrants them. He agrees that they shall be the basis of the contract. Whenever statements are warranted, they must be absolutely true. If they are not, the contract will be void from its commencement because the statements are the very basis of the insurance contract.

In Marine Hull and Miscellaneous insurance the proposal form is invariably used but in Marine Cargo insurance instead of proposal form Questionnaire is used. Though in questionnaire declaration is absent yet it does not mean that the proposer will not observe utmost good faith, since it is imperative in the part of the proposer to observe utmost good faith always whenever he is seeking an insurance contract.

2. Cover Note

The second important document is cover note. It is issued when the negotiations are on or a big risk is being pre-surveyed by either company's officer or the surveyor, to afford temporary insurance protection to the insured. Once the insurers accept the proposal with advance premium either a letter is issued to the insured confirming acceptance of the risk or a cover note is issued. Sometimes policy is also issued straightaway. Cover note provides immediate protection to the insured and contains all necessary particulars, name and address of the insured, sum insured, cover granted, basis of valuation and subject matter of insurance. Cover note is also made subject to tariff warranties and conditions of the policy. Since it is an unstamped document hence it is always followed by a stamped policy within the time limit prescribed.

3. Certificate of Insurance

The third document is used in non-life insurance policies is certificate of insurance. It is used in Motor Insurance being made Compulsory under Motor Vehicles Act, 1939 and last amended in 1988. The Motor Vehicle Act says that the Motor Policy shall have no effect until or unless certificate of insurance is issued in a prescribed format.

Instead of insurance policy, certificate of insurance is the only evidence of existence of valid insurance required by Motor Vehicles Act, acceptable to the R.T.O. and the Police Authorities. Certificate of Insurance contains serial number, particulars of the vehicle, viz. Registration number, Engine chassis number, Model and make of the vehicles and cubic capacity. In addition name and address of the insured, date of commencement of insurance and its expiry date and the use of the vehicle. Certificate of insurance is also issued in Marine Cargo policies under open cover and declaration policies.

Marine declaration policies are of two types, viz. declaration policy and special declaration policy. These policies are issued mainly for internal transit of goods within India.

(i) Open Declaration Policy

An open declaration policy is also known as 'floating policy'. It is issued to take care of all sending during a particulars period and is worded in general terms. It is issued for one year and for an amount that an insured estimates in advance the total sending in a year. Whenever the insured sends a consignment he is required to declare it to the insurer through a declaration and the sum insured go on reducing. In case it is fully declared before its expiry then either the insured can enhance the policy for further sum insured through endorsement or can take a fresh policy. Full premium is paid on the entire sum insured at the time of taking out the policy. This policy can be extended as many times as the insured desires by an endorsement during the year.

At the end of the year in case any balance is there, the entire premium on the balance sum insured is refunded to the insured. After the expiry of the policy a fresh policy has to be taken. It is to be noted that once the insured has taken a declaration policy for a particular period he should not take another policy with other insurer.

(ii) Marine Special Declaration Policy

It works on the same lines as declaration policy except it can not be granted for less than 2 corers. In case it is taken for 5 corers reduction in basic premium to the extent of 20% is applicable to the insured. A slab of further discount is given for every five crore and it goes on upto 45%. The policy can only be issued if the approval of the Regional Office of the company has been obtained. Normally previous 3 yrs. premium and claim experience is taken into consideration for granting this policy.

If this policy is cancelled by the insured or no goods have been dispatched during the entire period of policy minimum premium of Rs. 5000 will be deducted and only the balance premium will be refunded.

Some times the insured requires certificate of insurance under open policies also for particular sendings. Since the original policy is with the insured hence certificate of insurance contains all particulars of policy, i.e. type of cover granted, basis of volution, name and address of the insured, sum insured of particular consignment for which certificate is issued, etc. for the benefit of those whom certificate of insurance is being sent, i.e. bankers or financiers, etc. Since the original policy is duly stamped therefore, certificate of insurance need not be stamped.

4. The Policy

As already discussed, the contract is completed when an offer is followed by unqualified acceptance. The contract is normally in common form and there are no real negotiations between the insured and the insurers about all the terms and conditions of the policy in details. However, there is a clear agreement about the essential features of the contract. The parties must be determined, the insured must have agreed to a particular insurer and insurer must have agreed to insure a particular insured. Both the parties must be 'ad idem' about the subject matter of insurance, period of insurance, the sum to be insured and the premium to be paid.

A policy is normally divided into the following parts:

(i) Heading;
(ii) Preamble or Recital Clause;
(iii) Operating Clause;
(iv) Schedule (description of subject matter);
(v) Exceptions;
(vi) Signature;
(vii) Conditions; and
(viii) Endorsements.

Each of the above headings will be dealt with one by one. The students are advised to obtain a specimen copy of policy and go through it to know how it is made up.

(i) Heading

The heading gives the name of the insurance company and the address of its Registered office. This is the practice till now but after denationalization of life and general insurance business you will find the other details for example a statement that the company is associated with another company, which may guarantees fulfilment of the contract.

(ii) Preamble (or Rental Clause)

This introduces the parties to the contract, i.e. insured and the insurer. It refers to the proposal with declaration in case the contract is based upon it. This clause also refers to the premium paid by the insured as consideration.

(iii) Operation or Insuring Clause

This clause sets out the nature of the insurance, which the company is granting. It contains the essence of the contract. It contains the perils covered under the policy and the circumstances under which the company will be liable to make payment of claim to the insured. There are certain perils, which are excluded from the scope of the policy, are also mentioned in this clause. A reference is also made to sum insured and other limits of liabilities of the company.

Non-life insurance policies usually run for a year, subject to continuation through renewal. However, short period policies (i.e. less than a year) and are known as short-term policies. Some policies are also issued and for more than one year like long-term Mediclaim, long-term JPA, Cattle and Erection policies.

(iv) Schedule

It contains all type written information applicable to the particular contract. The schedule describe the subject matter, i.e. property insured completely for the purpose of identification. For example, fire policy schedule provides the following particulars:

(i) Policy No.;
(ii) Agency;
(iii) Date of issue;
(iv) Name, address and occupation of the insured;
(v) Perils covered and rate of premium;
(vi) The dates of commencement and termination of insurance; and
(vii) Detail description of subject matter of insurance.

It should be remembered that the insurance do not undertake to indemnify the insured against loss by peril insured against, but only against loss arising from the destruction of the particular object insured and the identity of the object can only be established by referring it to the description in the contract.

Therefore, the subject matter of insurance must be described by the insured in a very clear of fair manner in the proposal form so that there should not be any ambiguity left about its identification.

Further there is no need to mention the insurable interest of the insured in the policy except:

(i) For insurance of profit.
(ii) For insurance against third party liability.
(iii) For insurance of rent.
(iv) Where the insured specifically call for it.

(v) Exceptions

The exceptions are limitations of the cover. Exceptions begin with the words such as "Provided that the company shall not be liable for." Exceptions are also known as proviso.

Exceptions are found in the operative clause, or among the conditions. They can be found listed by themselves also. Exceptions must be written in clear terms and there should not be ambiguity about them. In case there is any doubt it will go against insurer's interest.

(vi) Signature

The policy is signed on behalf of the company by manager or any other officer authorized by the company. In other words, it is under hand.

(vii) Conditions

Conditions governs the contract. Normally they are printed on the back of the policy. In fact they should be printed on the face of the policy above the signatures to make sure that the conditions are incorporated in and form part of the policy itself.

The conditions are provisions or terms of the contract. All insurance policies are variably subject to conditions that define or limit the contract and the liabilities of the parties particularly of insurers.

First of all it is necessary to distinguish between condition precedent and stipulation.

A condition precedent, a breach of which renders the contract voidable whereas breach of stipulation does not render the contract voidable, but gives the right to the aggrieved party to sue for damages. A stipulation does not become condition precedent merely because it comes under the heading 'conditions' in the policy.

There are two types of conditions: Implied conditions and written conditions. Both conditions are further divided into:

(i) conditions precedent to contract,
(ii) conditions subsequent to the policy, and
(iii) conditions precedent to liability.

(i) Implied Conditions

These conditions are the result of judicial judgements or of common law. Although these are not written in the contract yet they are implemented with full force. These conditions are implied in all contracts of insurance.

(a) Utmost Good Faith

Both parties must observe utmost good faith towards each other at all times.

(b) Existence of Subject Matter

The subject matter must exist at the time when the contract is made.

(c) Insurable Interest

The insured must have legal relationship with the subject matter of insurance.

(d) Identification

The subject matter of insurance must be capable of identification.

Express Conditions

These conditions are expressed (written) in the contract. An express condition can extend or limit the scope of the implied condition, for example, subrogation or contribution conditions. In case they are in conflict with each other then written condition will overrides the implied condition. Sometimes the implied condition itself is given the shape of a written condition to draw the attention of the insured. The written conditions impose addition obligation on the insured.

(i) Condition Precedent to the Contract or Policy

In case this condition is not observed by the insured the contract will be ineffective *ab-initio,* for example, non-observance of utmost good faith by the insured, lack of insurable interest in the subject matter, etc.

(ii) Conditions Subsequent to Contract

These conditions are to be observed after the policy has been issued and will continue to be observed during the entire period of the policy, for example, the insured will not make any material alterations in the subject matter of insurance as stated in the policy.

(iii) Conditions Precedent to Liability

These conditions are to be observed when the loss occurs under the policy which is payable by the insurer, e.g. immediate notice or within stated period in the policy a notice of particular loss is to be given to the insures so that they can make arrangements for assessment of loss or completion of claim form and other formalities to be completed by the insured in connection with the loss.

All the above three types of conditions are conditions precedent but if conditions under (i) and (ii) are not observed by the insured no loss is payable subsequent to their breach whereas under (iii) the breach will only affect of a particular loss where timely notice is not given to the insurer. In case subsequent losses take place they are payable provided notice of these losses are given to the insurers timely.

The effect of breach of above conditions varies with the nature of the condition but following points are to be noted:

(i) Breach of condition precedent to the contract avoid the policy from its commencement but in the absence of fraud the insured can claim refund of premium paid by him in full for failure of consideration.

(ii) Breach of condition subsequent to the contract avoid the policy from the day the breach was manifested. In this case the premium will not be refunded to the insured either part or full as there is no failure of consideration.

(iii) Breach of condition precedent to liability does not avoid the policy. The insurer will not pay a particular loss where either notice has not been given or it is given after a considerable lapse of time to the insurers. All subsequent losses will be considered by the insures if timely notice of loss is given to the insures.

(iv) Onus of proof is on the insurers to prove that the condition has been breached.

21.4 WARRANTIES

In addition to the implied and express conditions, there are also express warranties incorporated in the policy. These warranties may be either printed on the policy itself or contained in a separate form shape which are attached to the policy. To ensure that the risk remains the same throughout the currency of the policy as accepted by the insurers on certain rates and terms and conditions, warranties are inserted in the policy.

Warranties protect the insurers against the introduction of any feature that may increase the risk during the currency of the policy.

A warranty is a representation by the insured that a particular state of affairs exists or will exist, or an undertaking by the insured that he shall do or shall not do a particular act. A warranty is in fact a condition precedent. All warranties must be complied with strictly. In case insured has broken any of the warranty the insurers are free to disown the liability. However, the insures may ignore any breach of warranty by the insured and allow the contract to remain enforce.

A warranty may or may not be a continue warranty. If it is a continue warranty such as the proposer states in the proposal that all the statements made by him are not only true but remain true throughout the period of the policy then the insures will have to state clearly in the policy itself. The insurers, therefore, by incorporating the proposal by reference in the policy makes the insured statements in the proposal as continuing warranty.

In certain cases the warranty will specify certain circumstances as essential to the contract, for example:

(i) After every show, the cinema hall must be swept and in case sweeping of cinema hall after every show is not carried out, the warranty is broken and the contract will depend upon the circumstances:

(a) If the sweeping of cinema hall has never been done after every show from the beginning, the policy is avoided "ab initio."

(b) If the sweeping of cinema hall is carried out after every show for 3 months and then the practice was abandoned, the policy would be avoided from the day the sweeping was stopped. Until that day the contract would be of full effect.

(c) If the sweeping was regularly carried out but on a particular day it was not carried out and there was a loss. The position is the same as in (b) above. The insurer would not be liable for the loss.

(d) If the sweeping was regularly carried out but on one day it was not carried out and no loss occurred, but this fact came to light later following a loss at a time when sweeping of hall was carried out. Strictly speaking, the insurer can avoid the policy from the day the warranty was broken and may avoid the later loss.

The representation has already been dealt with. The distinction between representations and warranties has been clearly manifested in a legal case *Dehanh* v/s *Hartley* by Ford Mansfield as follows:

> "There is a material distinction between a warranty and a representation. A representation may be equitably and substantially answered, but a warranty must be strictly complied with. Supposing a warranty to sail on the Ist August and the ship did not sail until 2nd August, the warranty would not be complied with. A warranty in a policy of insurance is a condition or a contingency; and unless that be performed, there is no contract. It is perfectly immaterial for what purpose a warranty is introduced; but being inserted, the contract does not exist unless it be literally complied with."

21.5 CONSTRUCTION OF POLICIES

The insurance policy is a legal document and therefore, great care is taken by the insurer to draft it, but still sometimes disputes arise about the interpretation of the policy. The object of the construction is to find out the intention of the parties and record them into the contract because it is the contract in which the original suggestions of the parties have been clearly mentioned. In case parties intentions are clear then there is no necessity of rules of construction but sometimes the intentions are not clear and the courts use these rules of contraction as a guide in deciding the cases. The main task of the law is to know the intentions of the parties which must prevail. Some of the rules are given below:

1. *Parol (Oral) evidence*: It is not admitted to vary or contradict the terms and conditions of a written contract except under certain circumstances which are as follows:
   (i) To identify the subject matter or the parties to the contract.
   (ii) To resolve an ambiguity which is obvious and not merely latent?
   (iii) To prove that the policy was obtained by fraud hence voids.
   (iv) To prove a parol condition on the basis of which a party entered into the contract.
2. The typed or hand written words will override the printed portion of the policy as they show special intentions of the

parties. Therefore, an endorsement may contradict or modify the printed part of the policy.

3. The policy being drafted by the insurer will be construed strictly against them in case there is an ambiguity in the wording in the policy. The interpretation more favourable to the insured will be taken. Since the wording of the policy is of the insurers, it is their duty that the meaning of the words is clear. If they fail in their duty it will go against them rather than in their favour.
4. Words are assumed to have been used in their ordinary popular sense except for legal terms that are construed according to their strict legal meaning in the policy.
5. The ordinary rules of grammar and punctuation will apply. There can be omission of commas and error in punctuation in the documents and the judges has the discretion to correct it. It is a golden rule that the application of commas should be omitted or minimize in the policy.

21.6 ENDORSEMENTS

Endorsement governs the contract. They may limit or emphasize the risks granted by the printed form of policy. They may be printed, typed or hand written on the policy itself. They are issued during the currency of the policy to effect changes in the policy. Sometimes they are attached at the time of issue of a policy. Whenever the cover is to be restricted or certain other changes are to be made during the currency of the policy, the insurer's consent in writing is required to be obtained by the insurers. The insurers should call for the policy and affix the endorsement thereon themselves only then the policy will give true and complete picture of the contract. Sometimes this practice is not followed by the insurers which later on results unnecessary litigation.

In some classes of tariff business, the endorsements are compulsorily attached to the policy. The motor tariff provides wordings of the endorsements that are used by the insurers as circumstances demands. Likewise workmen tariff provides that in case a particular rate of premium is charged, then the relative endorsement must be applied in the policy. Usually endorsements are used during the currency of the policy under following circumstances:

1. Change in insurable interest by way of mortgage or sale of the property insured.
2. Change in sum insured (increase/decrease).
3. Change in the risk, e.g. change of contraction of building or its occupation in fire insurance.
4. Extension of insurance to cover additional perils.
5. Change in address.
6. Transfer of goods to another location.

7. Cancellation of insurance.

Unauthorized Alteration

Where one party to the written contract makes material changes in the subject matter of insurance without the written consent of the other party, the affected party may avoid the contract if so desired. The alteration has no other effect.

21.7 DURATION OF THE CONTRACT

The policies may be issued for:

(i) A short period.
(ii) A period of one year.
(iii) Long-term policies.

(i) A Short Period

Short period policies are those policies that are issued for less than a year. Those businessmen who are dealing with seasonal crops like cotton, jute, etc. take these policies generally. Since these policies are for a short period, there is no provision for renewal of such policies. Moreover, instead of prorata premium a higher premium is changed known as short period scale because they are taken sometimes when the risk is greater.

(ii) A Period of One Year

Most of the policies are issued for one year. They are known as annual policies. There is a provision for renewal of such policies. Policies can be extended or prorata basis to bring the renewal date to a particular day or some other mutually convenient date.

(iii) Long-term Policies

Policies issued for 2 or more years are termed as long-term policies. They are issued for completion of big projects, dwelling losses, and building in course of construction and Janta Personal Accident policies.

Under annual policies there is a provision for renewal of the policy for further period of one year. The renewal to be effective the insured must pay the premium and the insurers accept it. The consent of both the parties is necessary. If this provision is not there the policy will terminate automatically on the expiry date of the policy. It is to be noted that renewal of policy constitutes a fresh contract. In case there is change in the subject matter or any other change then it will constitute a fresh offer and the insurer must agree to the changes.

The offer for renewal may come either from insurers by inviting renewal of the policy through renewal notice to the insured and the insured must pay the premium or the offer may come from insured for renewal of his policy and the insurers must accept it by renewing the policy. The general practice is that well before the expiry of the policy the insurers send renewal notice indicating the premium and consent to renew the policy. However, there is no obligation on the insures to send renewal notice. If the renewal notice is not received by the insured he may tender the premium to the insures; which they may accept or refuse at their discretion.

21.8 AMENDMENTS TO THE CONTRACT

Where identity of the subject matter of insurance is destroyed or alterered in such a way that it no longer represents the subject matter intended to be insured by a policy during its currency. In such a case, without any express condition the policy will not be effective unless the consent of the insurers has been obtained of the new risk. Normally a condition is inserted in the policy by which the insurers prohibit the alternations in the subject matter of insurance during the policy period to protect their interest which may either—

(a) Provide that the insurers will not be liable for any loss if there is any change in the subject matter.

(b) Require that the insurers should be notified in case of any change takes place. The condition does not give the right to refuse the acceptance of change to the insurers once it is notified. Therefore, the wording of the endorsement provides that:

   (i) The policy shall cease until notice is given.

   (ii) The insures are at liberty to accept or reject the alteration desired by the insurers.

   (iii) In case the alternation is accepted, the insurer can charge extra premium or impose new conditions.

Alterations in the Policy

During the course of the policy the need may arise for a change in the original contract, the circumstances have been explained under the head endorsements above. It is not one sided, either party may desire to amend it. The insurer if they have committed a mistake while issuing a policy, which comes in their knowledge subsequently, can correct the contract also. The general rule is that to give effect to any material alteration both parties must agree. On reaching a mutual agreement the alteration is given effect by endorsement by a separate memorandum, which will then read in conjunction with the policy.

Mistake and Rectification of the Policy

The need to rectify the policy arise when one or both the parties has made a mistake, as a result of which the contract does not correctly express the intentions of the parties. If rectification of the contract is possible, neither party can repudiate the contract.

Normally the insurers prepare the policy and it is, therefore, their duty to see to it that it properly states the terms of the contract. For satisfaction of the contract one should not move the court direct unless unsuccessful approach has in the first instance been made to the other party.

Almost all insurers include a note in their policies impressing upon the insured to read the policy document thoroughly and carefully and in case he notices any mistake, it should be returned to the insurers for rectification. In case insured fails in his duty, he is debarred from claiming rectification. Although every case has its own merits.

21.9 ASSIGNMENT

Generally a contract cannot grant any profit to or impose any liability upon, a third person. This rule is modified and in certain circumstances, a third person may take the place of one of the original parties to the contract.

Assignment is legally recognized passing of interest in property or in a right (including right under a contract) from one person to another when a policy covers specific property or liability arising from the possession of such property, the subject matter may be assigned by the insured in two ways.

(i) Voluntary

When the insured voluntarily assigns the subject matter of insurance by way of sale, mortgage or gift, the policy remains enforce only to the extent to cover the remaining interest of the insured if any. In case no interest of the insured is left, the policy is terminated immediately as soon as the assignment takes place. However, when the contract of sale of subject matter is entered into between the insured and the intending purchaser, the policy covers the interest of the purchaser until the completion of the sale. To protect the insured it is necessary that the transfer of subject matter of insurance and assignment of policy should take place simultaneously and the insurer also agree to affect the transfer in the policy.

It will not be out of place to mention here that fire insurance policy is a personal contract between the insured and the insurer. Therefore, the insured cannot assign the policy to the new owner of the subject matter without the express consent of the insurers. The insurer can refuse their consent without giving any reason.

(ii) Through the Operation of Law, as in the Case of Bankruptcy or Death

When the assignment takes place by operation of law or by will of the insured, on his death and the interest in his property passes on to his legal heirs, the policy remains valid to cover the new interest. This has been provided in policy condition.

Apart from assignment of the subject matter or the policy, the insured sometimes desires to transfer the amount payable to the third party under a policy, when a claim arise. This assignment of proceed of the policy may be made by the insured either before or after the claim has arisen. The insurers can not refuse unless the policy provides otherwise.

21.10 Termination of the Contract

Once the policy is issued, it will normally continue till its expiry. However, under the following circumstances the contract is terminated before its expiry:

Cancellation of Policy

(i) By order of the court.
(ii) By destruction of subject matter
(iii) By breach of a condition of the policy which makes it voidable.
(iv) By material alterations made by the insured without the consent of the insurers.
(v) By payment of total loss by the insurers.
(vi) By mutual consent.
(vii) Insurers exercising their power to cancel the policy as per authority given to insurers by cancellation clause in the policy or the insured exercise this option to cancel his policy.
(viii) By an assignment by the insured of his entire interest in the subject matter.
(ix) By commencement of proceedings for liquidation or winding up of the insurers.

21.11 REFUND OF PREMIUM

Once the premium is paid the insured is not entitled to either whole of part of the premium. However, there are number of exceptions to this rule which are as follows:

1. Cases where Insured is Entitled for the Refund of Full Premium

(i) Where the contract is *utra vires.*
(ii) Where the risk never attached e.g. the subject matter destroyed before the contract is concluded.
(iii) Where the policy is void 'ab initio' by innocent misrepresentation.
(iv) Where the contract is illegal but the policy stands issued and the insured is not aware of the illegality of the contract.

In the above cases there has been no consideration from the insurers but once the policy has run and the insurers are bound to pay the claim then the insured is not entitled for the refund of the premium.

2. Cases where the Insured is Entitled to Partial Refund of Premium

(i) When the policy is cancelled by mutual consent or by the insured under cancellation clause, the insured is entitled for refund of premium on prorata basis if insurers cancel the policy and on short period scale if the policy is cancelled on insured's request.

(ii) If more than one policy has been effected on the same subject matter for double sum insured inadvertently (fraud being absent) and a claim is reported both policies will refund the premium on prorata basis.

(iii) In case the insurance company has gone into liquidation, the premium for unexpired risk is refundable.

(iv) In case of fraud on the part of the insurers.

3. Cases where Insured is not Entitled for Any Refund of Premium

(i) When the policy is terminated during its policy period in the circumstances given in (ii), (iii), (iv), (iv), (v) and (viii) under the head cancellation of policy.

(ii) When the insured has committed fraud.

(iii) When the contract is illegal and the insured was fully aware about it before completion of the contract.

Adjustments of Premium

Under Fire and Marine declaration policies on stocks or workmen compensation policies a provisional premium is paid by the insured at the inception of the policy. At the end of the policy period average sum insured is worked out under fire and marine declaration policies. Under workmen compensation policies actual total wages paid to the employees during the policy period are known and then premium actually chargeable is calculated. In case the provisional premium is found to be in excess then the excess premium is refunded to the insured. Alternatively if the premium is short then it is called for from the insured. Similar is the position of consequential loss policies

21.12 RENEWAL NOTICE

The preamble of the Miscellaneous and fire policies states that the indemnity will be provided under these policies 'during the period of insurance named in the schedule or of any subsequent period in respect of the insured shall have paid and the insurers shall have accepted the premium required for renewal of these policies.

There is no legal obligation on the part of the insurer to send renewal notice to the insured reminding him about the expiry of his policy. Still as a matter of maintaining good and healthy relationship with the insured, the insurer send renewal notice to the insured well in advance of the expiry date of the policy, preferably a month. The insured's attention is invited in the renewal notice towards any alteration if made should be intimated to insurers. In Motor policies he is also advised to fix the sum insured in such a way that should represent the market value of his vehicle. The statutory provision is also stated in it that no risk can be assumed unless the premium is paid in advance.

21.13 SUMMARY

It is not that every person can obtain a non-life insurance policy. Only those persons can obtain who have insurable interest in the subject matter of insurance and that too to the extent of their interest. In addition to it one should have the capacity to enter into a contract. Further the object must be legal because an illegal object will render the policy void *ab initio*.

In case one fulfil these requirement then one has to make an application (offer) in the form of printed proposal form to any insurance company of his choice for obtaining insurance protection of any thing which has intrinsic value. While completing of proposal form one has to exercise utmost good faith towards insurance company by answering each and every question of the proposal form and then send it to insurance company along with premium (consideration). After the proposal is accepted as proposed the insurance company either issue· a cover note, which is followed by a stamped policy, or policy is issued straightway. In this way the contract of a non-life policy is obtained.

There are various documents which are to be used, viz. proposal form, cover note, certificate of insurance, warranties and endorsements to obtain a non-life insurance policy. Their necessity and importance has been explained in detail in the lesson. In addition to it the different heads in which the policy has been divided is also explained.

The various aspects of policy, i.e. its construction, duration, amendments and how it can be assigned or terminated before the normal expiry date has been dealt with in detail.

The warranties, endorsements which are used while issuing or after the issue of the policy their definitions and importance are also considered at length and the various circumstances under which the insured can claim refund of full or part premium and necessity of renewal notice is explained at length.

21.14 REVIEW QUESTIONS

1. Who can insure? Narrate the common questions in all the proposal forms. What is effect of declaration?
2. What is the difference between a 'condition' precedent to the policy and condition precedent to liability?
3. What constitutes a valid assignment of policy?
4. What do you understand by the following terms:
   (a) Warranty;
   (b) Condition Precedent; and
   (c) Condition subsequent to liability.

5. Under what circumstances the insured can claim refund of premium under his policy.
6. Distinguish between the assignment and property insured, assignment of policy and assignment of Policy proceeds.
7. Under what circumstances the policy is terminated before its normal expiry date.
8. What is material fact and its importance from the point of view of insurers?

GLOSSARY

A

Accident: One time event which is unintended, unforeseen and unexpected. It is something that is definite in time and place.

Accidental Death and Dismemberment Insurance: A form of insurance providing benefits in the accidental death, or the accidental loss of sight or members (such as an arm or a leg).

Accidental Death Benefit: A lump sum payment for loss of life due to an accident that was the direct cause of death. The cause of the mishap must be accidental for a benefit to be payable under the policy.

Act of God: An event beyond human origin or control. Lightning, windstorms, and earthquakes are examples. The damage from which would not be the responsibility of a bailee, although the bailee might be responsible for many other calamities. Acts of God are excluded by the usual bill of landing as well as by some insurance policies, unless specifically included.

Actual Cash Value: The basis of loss settlement in property insurance policies which takes into consideration such factors as replacement value less depreciation, market value, rental value, the use of the building, the area in which it is located, obsolescence, assessed validation and any other factor which would have an effect upon the value. A working rule-of-thumb definition, however, is "replacement cost new at the time of loss, less depreciation." See Replacement Cost Value.

Actuary: A social mathematician who uses mathematical skills to define, analyze and solve complex business and social problems involving insurance and employee benefit programs.

Additional Living Expense Insurance: Insurance for the extra amount it costs and insured to live until repairs are made to the insured's dwelling

Additional Vehicle: A vehicle acquired during the policy period in addition to those already listed in the Declarations

Adjuster: One who determines the amount of loss suffered. A "company" or "independent" adjuster represents the company. A "public" adjuster represents the policyholder.

Admitted Company: A foreign or alien insurance company which has been licensed by the insurance department of the state in question, and thereby is authorized to conduct business within that state to the extent licensed. Also know as an authorized company.

Adverse Selection: The insuring of one or more risks with a higher chance of loss than that contemplated by the applicable insurance rate. The selection of such risks is adverse because the rate is inadequate.

Age Change: The halfway point between birthdays when the age of the applicant changes to the next higher age. In some insurance companies, the age is based upon the applicant's age at his nearest birthday. In others, it is based on the age of his last birthday.

Agent: One who has authority to act for another. The insurance language, an agent is the person who sells insurance by contacting the policyholder, and by contract and by law is endowed with many of the powers of the company itself.

Aggregate Limit: In a policy such an aggregate limit, the maximum amount the insurer will pay during the policy period, irrespective of the policy's limit of liability.

Agreed Amount Clause: A condition of a policy stating that the insurer agrees to waive the coinsurance requirement in consideration of the insured's maintaining insurance equal to the amount agreed upon at the inception of the policy.

All-Risk Policy: A policy which covers loss caused by any peril which is not excluded, as contrasted to "named peril" policies which protect against certain perils named in the policies.

Annuitant: A person during whose life an annuity is payable. Generally, an annuitant is the person who receives the monthly income payment.

Annuity: A contract providing periodic income payments for a fixed period of time or during the lifetime of an annuitant. It may be defined as the systematic liquidation of an estate.

Annuity, Cash Refund: A life annuity contract which provides that upon the death of the annuitant, the beneficiary (or his estate) will receive a lump sum payment which represents the difference between the amount the annuitant paid to the insurance company and the total income payments received by the annuitant.

Annuity, Certain: Payable for a minimum specified period and continuing thereafter throughout the life time of the annuitant.

Annuity, Deferred: Payments commence more than one year after the payment of the first (or single) premium to the insurance company, usually at a selected retirement age.

Annuity, Instalment Refund: Similar to a cash refund annuity, except that money is refunded in instalment payment and the insurance company makes payments to the designated beneficiary until the total of the payments made to the annuitant and the beneficiary equals the consideration paid.

Annuity Joint and Last Survivor: An annuity issued on the lives of two or more persons, which is payable as long as one of them survives.

Application: A form filled out and signed by a prospective insured which becomes part of the policy.

Appraisal Clause: The clause in a policy that sets forth the conditions under which a disputed loss is decided by appraisers.

Appraiser: (1) A person who determines the value of property, or (2) A party who determines the amount of a disputed loss.

Assessment: The charge levied by an insurer writing an assessable policy (as sold by some mutual insurers), in addition to the policy premium, in the event the insurer becomes unable to pay its total losses.

Assignee: A person, firm, of corporation to whom the rights under contract are assigned in their entirety or in part.

Assignment: Transferring property rights to another. Insurance policies may thus be assigned or transferred to another, but usually this requires the consent of the insurer.

Assumed Liability: Contractual liability, which arises from agreement between people as opposed to liability which, arises from common or statute law.

Assured: The person or party protected by a policy of insurance. Same as insured.

Attained Age: An age which a person or insured has attained on a given date. For life insurance purposes, the age is based on either the nearest birthday or the last birthday, depending on the practices of the insurance company involved.

Automatic Premium Load (Automatic Premium Advance): A provision in a life insurance policy that states that if an insured fails to pay a premium by the end of the grace period, the amount of the premium due will be loaned to the insured automatically. However, the loan value of the policy must be sufficient to cover the loan plus interest. Generally, the insured must request that the clause be made a part of the policy at the time of application.

Aviation Clause: A clause that limits the liability of the insurance company if certain types of aviation accidents cause the death of an insured.

B

Bailee: One who has custody of the property of another to be held and returned to the owner in good condition. The owner who delivers the property is called the bailor; the one who receives it is the bailee.

Bailor: A person entrusting goods to another.

Barratry: Wilful and illegal sinking, casting away, or damaging a ship at sea or its cargo.

Beneficiary, Contingent (Secondary): A parson who is entitled to benefits only after the death of a primary beneficiary.

Beneficiary, Irrevocable: The insured may not change the designated beneficiary without the beneficiary's consent.

Beneficiary, Primary: A person who is entitled primarily to benefits upon the death of an insured.

Beneficiary, Revocable: The designated beneficiary may be changed at the insured request without the consent of the beneficiary.

Beneficiary, Tertiary: The person who entitled to the policy benefits if the primary and contingent beneficiaries predecease the insured.

Bid Bond: A bond intended to guarantee that the bidder on a construction, supply or service contract would enter into the contract if successful as a bidder.

Binder: An oral or written agreement to insure which serves as evidence of coverage prior to the issuance of a policy.

Binding Authority: The right one party (usually an agent) has to represent another (usually the insurer) in effecting or creating an insurance contract.

Binding Receipt: Insurance becomes effective on the date of the receipt and continues for a specified period of time until the company disapproves the application.

Blanket Insurance: A single amount of insurance covering several items (e.g. one amount of insurance to cover two buildings, or one building and its contents)

Blanket Position Bond: A fidelity bond, which insures an employer against loss from dishonest acts by employees.

Bodily Injury: Injury, sickness, or disease sustained by a person, including death at any time resulting therefrom.

Bond, Fidelity: An insurance policy that reimburses an employer for employee theft, embezzlement, or dishonesty. May be written to cover specific employees or all employees.

Bond, Surety: A written agreement wherein on part, called the surety, obligates itself to a second party, called the obligee or beneficiary, to answer for the default of a third party, call the principal.

Broker: A licensed, legal representative of the insured who negotiates with underwriters on behalf of the insured. Nevertheless, the broker receives a commission from the insurer (underwriter).

Builders Risk: A special form dealing with the unique loss exposure of property under construction.

Burglary: Theft by forcible and illegal entry, evidenced by visible signs made by tools, explosives, electricity, or chemicals.

Business: A trade, profession or occupation.

Business Use: The use of a vehicle for the purposes of the business or occupation.

By Order of Civil Authority: A directive of city officials cr other civil authority that a building may be destroyed by the fire department to present the spread of conflagration.

C

Cancellation: The termination of a contract before its normal ending.

Captive Agent: An agent who, by contract, represents only one company and its affiliate. Sometimes called "exclusive or controlled agent."

Cargo: Goods being transported by rail, plane, truck, ship, or other conveyance, excluding the equipment needed to operate the conveyor.

Cash Surrender Value: The amount (stated in the policy) which is available in cash upon the surrender of a policy for cancellation before or after the policy matures (as in death claim or otherwise). This is one of the three non-forfeiture options.

Cede: To pass on to another insurer (the reinsurer) all or part of the insurance written by an insurer (the ceding insurer) with the object of reducing the possible liability of the latter.

Certificate of Insurance: A document containing information concerning the master policy of a group indicating that the individual is covered.

Civil Commotion: A disturbance among, or a popular uprising of, a large number of people.

Claim: An amount requested of an insurer, by a policyholder or a claimant, for an insured loss.

Claims-Made: A liability insurance policy version covering losses from claims asserted against the insured during the policy period.

Coinsurance Clause: In property insurance, a clause require in the insured to maintain insurance at least equal to stipulated percentage of value in order to collect partial losses in full.

Collision: The impact of a vehicle with another object or vehicle, or the upset of a vehicle.

Collision Coverage: Covers damage to a covered auto caused by collision with another object or vehicle.

Collision Insurance: Coverage for the loss resulting from the striking of another object by a moving vehicle.

Commissions: Payments made by the insurance company to the agent for the sale and servicing of a policy. Commissions are calculated as a specific percentage of the premium paid and the percentage determined in accordance with the contract between the agent and his insurance company.

Common Disaster Clause: This clause defines the method of the payment of the proceeds of the policy by the insurance company if the insured and the named beneficiary die simultaneously in a common disaster. It protects the contingent beneficiary since it would consider the primary beneficiary predeceased the insured.

Comparative Negligence: Under comparative negligence, the damages collectible in relation to another person are diminished in proportion to one's degree of negligence.

Comprehensive Automobile Coverage: "All-Risk" Physical damage protection for automobiles, except for loss by collision or upset (which may be added).

Concealment: In insurance, a failure to disclose a material fact, which may void an insurance policy.

Condition: Something established or agreed upon to be necessary to make a policy of insurance effective.

Conditional Receipt: A receipt given for the payment of the initial premium (accompanying the application) which makes coverage effective under the contract if the risk is approved as applied for, subject to the other conditions set forth in the receipt.

Consideration: One of the elements of a valid contract. The premium and the statements made by the prospective insured in the application are construed as the insurer's consideration. The insurance company's consideration is its promise to pay a valid claim.

Contract Bond: In general terms, a surety bond guaranteeing the performance of a contract, usually associated with construction work, but possible for almost any kind of contract. Sometimes called a performance bond.

Contributory Negligence: A common law defense in which the plaintiff must be entirely free from fault in order to recover from a negligent defendant.

Contributory Plan: A term applied to employees benefit plans (such as group insurance or group annuities) under which both the employees and the employer contributes.

Conversion Privilege: The right granted to the insured to change his coverage from a group policy to an individual policy. If a member of a group resigns therefrom, he is given an opportunity to secure an individual policy within a specified period thereafter regardless of whether or not he is in good health at that time. This term is also applied to the right of an insured to convert from a convertible term policy to a permanent form of insurance.

Coverage for Damage to Your Covered Auto (Physical Damage Coverage): Insures against damage to an insured auto caused by collision and other than collision losses.

Coverage Territory: Geographic region where coverage is available under the Personal Auto Policy. Includes the United States and its territories and possessions, Canada and Puerto Rico. Coverage is also provided if the auto is damaged while being transported between these ports.

Credit Life Insurance: Life insurance designed to pay the balance of a loan (usually payable in instalments) if the insured dies before the loan has been paid in full. Generally, a bank department store, or a finance company handles credit life insurance. Usually this form of insurance is written on a group basis, but it may also be written on an individual basis.

D

Death Benefit: The amount that is paid to a beneficiary as the result of the death of an insured.

Death Claim: Proof of the insured's death and the beneficiary's application that are filed with the insurance company in a request for payment under the policy.

Declarations: Section of the Personal Auto Policy that shows who is insured, what property is covered, when and where coverage is effective, and how much coverage applies.

Deductible: In a policy providing a deductible clause, the amount which must first be subtracted from the total damage incurred before determining the insurance company's liability. Of several types used, the straight deductible establishes the insurer's liability above the deductible but not below it; the franchise deductible establishes the insurer's liability for the entire amount of damage once the deductible amount is exceeded in a loss; and the disappearing deductible establishes the insurer's liability for an increasing proportion of the loss, as the total damage rises above the deductible, until the deductible finally "disappears." The insurer is liable for the entire amount. The deductible may be in the form of an amount of dollars, a percent of the loss, a percent of the value of the insured property, or a period of time, as in health insurance.

Depreciation: The reduction in value of tangible property caused by physical deterioration, obsolescence, or wear and tear.

Directors & Officers: Coverage for directors and officers.

Direct Writer: A company which sells insurance to the public either through employees licensed as agents or through licensed agents, compensated on a commission basis, who represent only one company; but not through independent agents representing more than one company.

Disability Benefit: A feature added to some life insurance policies which provides for the waiver of premiums upon the furnishing of proof that in insured has become totally and permanently disabled and/or for the payment of monthly income benefits to the insured.

Dividend: A refund of part of the premium under a participating policy of a share of policyholder's surplus funds apportioned for distribution. They are derived from savings in mortality and expenses and interest earned in excess of the assumed rate used in the calculation of the premium in the policy reserves.

Dividend Options: The insured is given the option to apply dividends as follows: (1) He may receive the dividend in cash. (2) Apply the dividend toward the payment of any premium due on the policy. (3) Apply the dividend toward the purchase of paid-up additional insurance. (4) Leave the dividend with the insurance company to accumulate an interest.

Domestic Company: An insurance company incorporated or organized under state law is a domestic insurer in that particular state.

Double Indemnity: A clause providing payment of twice the face amount of the policy if loss of life is due to an accident.

Dwelling: A house in which people live, as distinguished from a store, a factory, or any other commercial type building.

E

Effective Date: The day upon which a policy first becomes eligible to pay covered losses.

Endorsement: A document with language attached to and becoming part of a basic policy for the purpose of amplifying or modifying it, either at its inception or during its term.

Endowment Insurance: A policy that (after a specified number of years) pays a stated amount to the insured. If the insured dies during the endowment period, the face amount of the policy is paid to the designated beneficiary. An endowment pays at the earlier of death or a specified period.

Evidence of Insurability: Any statement or proof of a person's physical condition that may affect acceptance for insurance.

Exceptions: Provisions in a policy that eliminate coverage for specified causes of death and/or disability. Also known as exclusions.

Excess Insurance: An amount of protection that bears all or a portion of a loss after the loss exceeds an agreed amount.

Exclusion: (1) That which is not covered by the insurance as stated in the policy. (2) A clause in an insurance policy which specified that which is excluded from the policy's coverage.

Exclusive Agent: An agent who, by contract, represents only one company and its affiliates. Sometimes called a "captive agent."

Experience Rating (Group Insurance): The premium is computed on the basis of past losses and expenses incurred by the insurance company in the settlement of claims and other expenses involving a particular group of risk.

Extended Coverage Insurance: Protection against loss or damage caused by windstorm, hail, smoke, explosion, riot, civil commotion, vehicles, and aircraft.

Extended Term Insurance: A non-forfeiture option, under which the face amount of the policy is continued in force for a specified additional period of time after default in the payment of a premium.

F

Face Amount: The amount of insurance stated on the face of the policy that will be paid upon the death of the insured (or in some cases at the maturity of the policy). It does not include any amount that has been added through dividend additions or additional insurance payable in the event of accidental death.

Facility of Payment Clause: A provision in a policy which permits the insurance company to pay insurance proceeds to persons other than the insured, the designated beneficiary, or the estate of the insured.

Fair Plan: A program to provide "Fair Access to Insurance Requirements" for property owners who experience difficulty in buying insurance on property located in blighted or deteriorating urban areas.

Family Income Benefits: Under this form of life insurance, on the death of the insured, a monthly income is paid to the beneficiary (ies) to the end of the family income period stipulated in the policy in addition to the lump sum payment (face amount). For example, it could run for a period of 10 years starting with the inception date of the policy, or it could run for 15 years, 20 years, or to age 65. Usually, it is a decreasing term insurance provision that is combined with whole life insurance. If the insured survives the family income period, the family incomplete protection ceases. The policy reverts to the face amount (usually, payable in a lump sum upon the death of the insured).

Family Member: A person related to the named insured or his or her spouse by blood, marriage or adoption who lives in the named insured's household.

Family Maintenance Policy: This type of policy combines ordinary life insurance and level term insurance. It affords the payment of a monthly income during a stated period of 10, 15 or 20 years or to age 65 as pre-selected by the insured. The monthly income is payable from the date of death to the end of the pre-selected period. The payment of the face amount of the policy is payable at the end of such pre-selected period.

Farm Owners—Ranch Owners (FO-RO): A package policy for farming and ranching risks which can be described as homeowners policy adapted for farm and ranch properties. Basically the policy provided property and liability insurance to which may be added appropriate additional coverage such as animal collision, employer's liability, custom farming, etc.

Federal Crime Insurance Program: Administered by the Federal Insurance Administration to provide limited burglary and robbery coverage for property owners who experience difficulty in buying insurance on property located in blighted or deteriorating urban areas.

Fidelity Bond: An insurance policy that reimburses an employer for employee theft, embezzlement, or dishonesty. May be written to cover specific employees or all employees.

Fiduciary: A person who occupies a position of trust, especially one who manages the affairs of another. For example, the guardian of a minor is a fiduciary.

Financial Responsibility Laws: State laws that require owners or operators of autos to provide evidence that they have funds to pay for automobile losses for which they might become liable.

Fire: Combustion manifested in light, flame and heat for useful purposes (friendly fire) or destruction purposes (hostile fire). Insurance covers loss from only the latter.

Floater: A policy that covers property at many locations, even world-wide and in the course of transit.

Flood: Overflow of water from its natural boundaries. More specifically defined by the National Flood Act of 1968 as "a general and temporary condition of partial or complete inundation of normally dry land areas from: (1) The overflow of inland or tidal waters. (2) The unusual and rapid accumulation or runoff of surface waters from any source.

Foreign Company: In insurance, a company doing (authorized) business in one state but incorporated in another.

Form: A document providing the specifics of the insurance issued, either separate unto itself or attached to other descriptive language.

Fortuitous Cause: An accidental and unexpected cause of loss. A happening by chance.

Fraternal Insurance: A cooperative type of insurance provided by a social organization for its members (e.g., life insurance offered by the "Knights of Columbus").

Free of Particular Average (EPA): A clause which exempts the company insuring cargo from partial losses, usually limited to apply only if the amount be less than an agreed sum, or if some other described condition exists.

G

Garage Policy: Protects garage or service station operators from claims alleging bodily injury or property damage caused by the operator's negligence in business operations and the use of automobiles.

General Average: In ocean marine insurance, a loss that is common to all interests (i.e., the hull owners, the cargo owners, and receivers of the freight and charges, etc.), that may arise due to a peril to the entire venture, that requires a sacrifice or expenditure for the benefit of all.

Grace Period: A specified period after a premium payment is due during which the protection of the policy continues even though the payment for the renewal premium has not yet been received.

Group Certificate: Certificate given to employees participating in a group insurance plan which sets for the protection to which they are entitled.

Group Insurance Policy: A policy protecting a group of persons, usually employees of a firm generally called a "master policy."

H

Hazard: A condition that may lead to a PERIL, thus creating a loss (e.g., oily rags leading to a fire).

Hold Harmless Agreement: A contractual arrangement in which one party agrees to assume certain liability which otherwise would be borne by the other party.

Homeowners' Policy: A "Package" policy for dwelling and contents risks combining fire and allied line coverage with comprehensive personal liability and theft insurance for homeowners and tenants.

Hull: The ship itself as distinguished from its cargo.

I

Implied Warranty: An indirect expression or inference, not in writing, by the policyholder that certain conditions exist or will be met (e.g., that a building is not on fire when insured, or that a vessel is seaworthy).

Improvements and Betterments: Additions made to real estate enhancing its value and amounting to more than mere repairs or replacement of waste. When made by a tenant, such additions are normally included in the tenant's own property insurance.

Inchmaree: A clause used in ocean marine policies to identify additional named perils beyond the basic marine perils.

Incontestable Clause: A clause that makes the policy indisputable (except for non-payment of premium and the operation of the war clause exclusion) regarding the statements made by the insured in the application after a specified period of time has elapsed (usually one, two, or three years).

Increase in Hazard: The standard fire insurance policy is suspended from liability while the hazard in a risk has been increased beyond what was contemplated at the time the policy was written.

Indemnify: To pay for loss suffered.

Independent Agent: A property-liability insurance producer who sells insurance as an independent contractor while representing one or more insurers of that agent's choosing on a commission basis, owning the expiration records of customers served.

Indirect Damage: Loss resulting from or as a consequence of, an insured direct loss.

Individual Insurance: Policies that afford protection to the policyholder and/or his family (as distinct from group insurance). Sometimes it is referred to as personal insurance.

Industrial Policy: A Policy with a face amount of $ 1000 or less for which the premiums are usually payable weekly or monthly and collected in person.

Inherent Explosion: Explosion caused by the normal process of a risk (as opposed to one caused by external causes), e.g., a dust explosion in a grain elevator

Inherent Vice: The characteristics of any physical property which are expected to cause deterioration or damage to that property without help, e.g., milk sours eventually, and wooden houses depreciate over time. Excluded by most insurance policies.

Injury: An act that damages or destroys a person or property.

Inspection Report: A report that contains general information regarding the health, habits, finances, and reputation of an applicant made by a firm that specializes in rendering this type of service.

Insurable Interest: A potential for financial loss from a certain event that a person must have before acquiring insurance against that event.

Insurance: The transfer of risk from the insured to the insurer. The insurer promises to pay the insured or beneficiaries an amount of money, services, or both for economic losses sustained from an unexpected and accidental event, during a period of time for which the insured makes a premium payment to the insurer.

Insurance Clause: A clause that defines and describes the scope of the coverage afforded and the limits of indemnification.

Insurance Company, Alien: One that was organized under the laws of a country other than the United States.

Insurance Company, Domestic: One conducting business in the state in which it was organized. A company who has its home office in the state in which it is conducting business.

Insurance Company, Foreign: One conduction business in a state other than the state in which it was organized. A company having its home office in a state other than the one(s) in which it is conducting business.

Insurance Services Office (ISO): A voluntary, non-profit association of property and casualty insurance companies providing a great variety of services on a national basis.

Insured: The person(s) or party(ies) protected by an insurance policy, synonymous with assured. Some property-liability policies distinguished between the named insured another insured.

Insuring Clause (Agreement): The portion of a policy that describes the risk that the insurer has agreed to assume.

Intermediary: One who arranges reinsurance between companies. A reinsurance broker.

J

Jettison: In ocean marine insurance, the voluntary throwing overboard of part of the cargo or gear of the vessel to lighten the load and save the vessel from conditions of stress at sea.

Jewelers Block Insurance: Broad policies insuring jewelers against all loss to their stock in trade. Generally considered too be a type of inland marine insurance.

Joint Life Insurance: Insurance on the lives of two or more persons with the face amount payable in the event of death of either (or any one) of them.

Joint Ownership Coverage: The purpose of this coverage is to provide coverage for individuals, other than husband and wife, residing in the household or non-resident relatives who jointly own a private passenger auto or a pickup or van that has a gross vehicle weight of less than 10,000 lbs. and is not used for the delivery or transportation of goods and materials.

Juvenile Insurance: Life insurance policies written on the lives of children within specified age limits.

K

Key Person Insurance: An individual policy designed to reimburse an employer for the loss of a key person's service due to his or her death. Usually, the employer pays the premium and is the beneficiary.

L

Lapse: The termination of a policy for non-payment of premium; used more commonly in life insurance. If the insurance contract becomes void for other reasons, it is also said to have lapsed.

Larceny: Theft of personal property. Modern Criminal laws include obtaining property under false pretense and embezzlement, which common law did not include in theft.

Law of Large Numbers: A mathematical concept that postulates that the more times an even is repeated (in insurance, the large number of homogeneous exposure units), the more predictable the outcome becomes. In a classic example, the more times on flips a coin, the more likely the results will be 50% heads, 50% tails.

Legal Liability: Liability imposed by laws, as opposed to liability arising from an agreement or contract.

Legal Reserve Life Insurance Company: An insurance company that operates under insurance laws that specify the minimum amount of reserves that the insurance company must maintain on its policies.

Level Premium: A premium that remains unchanged throughout the life of the policy.

Level Term Insurance: A term Contract whose face amount remains level throughout the life of the contract but whose premium increase according to the age of the insured.

Libel: To publish defamatory statement about another. The general distinction between libel and slander is that the first must be in writing or similar permanent form, while the later is oral.

Liability Coverage: Covers damage for Bodily Injury (BI) or Property Damage (PD) for which an insured becomes legally responsible because of an auto accident.

Life Expectancy: The average number of anticipated years of life remaining for individuals who are the same age in accordance with the mortality table indicated in the policy.

Life Insurance: Insurance upon the lives of human beings that create an immediate and guaranteed estate at the death of an insured.

Limited Pay Life Insurance: A plan of permanent life insurance under which the premiums are payable for a specified number of years (5, 10 years or to age 65). After which the policy can continue to remain in effect for life without it being necessary for the insured to make any additional payments.

Limit or Limit of Liability: According to the terms of a given policy, the most an insurer will pay for any one loss.

Lloyd's of London: A collection of individuals who assume policy obligations as the individual obligation of each.

Loading: An amount that is added to net premiums in order to cover the insurance companies operating expenses and possible contingencies. The cost of acquiring new business, collecting expenses, and general management expenses constitute loading.

Loan Value: The amount specified in a policy that the insurance company will lend to an insured at the rate of interest which the insurance company may charge for such loans (as indicated in the policy).

Loss: (1) The amount the insurer is required to pay because of a happening against which it has insured. (2) A happening that causes the company to pay (e.g., any reduction in quantity, quality, or values of insured property resulting from an insured peril. (3) The over-all financial result of some operation, as opposed to "profit." (4) The amount suffered by a person or property, with or without insurance.

Loss of Use Insurance: Insurance that compensates the policyholder for inability to use property destroyed or damaged by an insured peril.

Loss Payee: Party besides the insured (such as a lending institution) that has an insurable interest in the vehicle insured. Also called a Lienholder.

M

Malpractice: Improper actions or failure to exercise proper skill by a professional or others involved with the care of the human body; such as a physician, dentist, blood bank, etc.

Marine Insurance: One of major divisions of insurance (life, health, property, marine, casualty, surety), primary written for property in transit. If my sea, "ocean" marine (or "wet" marine); otherwise, "inland" marine.

Material Fact: Information having objective reality that influences an insurer in granting or not granting insurance coverage.

Maturity: The date on which a policy becomes payable due to the death of the insured, or as a result of an insurer's living to the end of an endowment period.

Medical Payment Coverage (Med): Pays medical expenses incurred in an auto accident for the insured and passengers in the insured's car.

Mercantile Risk: A property location used for the selling of merchandise, as distinguished from a habitational risk or a manufacturing risk in which goods are processed.

Merit Rating: A system of rating in which the experience of the individual risk is a factor in determining the rate.

Minimum Premium: The lowest flat or eared policy charge for which a policy will be issued or for which coverage will be provided.

Misrepresentation: Misleading the company as to material facts affecting a policy or the settlement of a loss, either by directly or indirectly lying. Misrepresentation as to material facts voids policies.

Mobile Home Insurance: A special policy has been designed to meet the needs of mobile home owners or occupants, covering physical damage to the home, contents and personal liability while the home used as a permanent residence.

Moral Hazard: A condition or characteristic by which an insured intends to profit from an insured loss.

Morale Hazard: The condition that exists when an insured becomes lax in matters of safety and fire prevention because insurance is in place to pay for a loss which may occur.

Mortality Table: A statistical table that indicated the probability of death and survival at each age.

Multi-Peril Insurance: Synonymous with multi-line insurance, a policy including both property and casualty coverage (e.g., a homeowner's policy).

Mutual Insurance: Protection written by an incorporated insurer having no capital stock and directed by policyholders that are its owners.

Mutual Life Insurance Company: A life insurance company owned and controlled by its policyholders. Mutual Life Insurance Companies issue participating policies.

Mysterious Disappearance: The vanishing of insured property in an unexpected manner.

N

Named Insured: The person designated in the policy as the insured, as opposed to someone who may have an interest in a policy by not be shown by name.

Named Peril Policy: One that specifies the exact cases of loss for which the insurer will pay, as contrasted with a policy that insures against "all risks" (and then lists only exclusions, modifications, and conditions).

National Flood Insurance Act of 1968: An act establishing a basis for flood insurance as a joint venture between the private insurance industry and the Federal Government. The Federal Government has since taken over the entire program.

Negligence: The Failure to exercise the care that an ordinary prudent person would exercise: either doing that which a prudent person would not do, or failing to do that which a prudent person would do.

Net Amount at Risk: The difference between the face amount of a policy and the reserve.

Net Premium: (1) The gross (paid) premium less any return premium or dividend. (2) The premium less the commission.

No-fault Insurance: Form of automobile insurance where each insurance company pays the damage of its own insureds, regardless of who was at fault for the accident.

Non-contributory Plan: A group employee benefit under which the employer pays for the full cost of the benefits for his employees.

Non-forfeiture Values (Options): Benefits required by law to be made available to the insured (or his beneficiary) in the event that he discontinues his premium payments. These provide that he does not forfeit or. lose all that he has invested in the policy.

Non-medical Life Insurance: Insurance that is issued without requiring the applicant to submit to a medical examination. The insurance company relies on the applicant's answer to the questions rewarding his physical condition, personal references, and inspection reports. However, the insurance company retains the right to require a medical examination, if an investigation indicates a need for one.

Non-owned Vehicle: An auto that is not furnished or available for the regular use of the insured or any family member.

Non-participating Life Insurance: Insurance that does not pay dividends to the policyholders.

Non-renewal: Decision made by the insurance company not to extend coverage for another policy period after the current policy period expires.

O

Obligee: The party in whose favour a bond runs, i.e., the party protected from loss under the bond.

Obligor: One bound by the obligation covered by a bond. Also called the "principal."

Occupancy: (1) The use to which a building is put. (2) The type of contents a building contains.

Occurrence: In insurance, the term may be defined as continual, gradual, or repeated exposure to an adverse condition which is neither intended nor expected to result in injury or damage, as contrasted with an accident, which is a sudden happening.

Omnibus Clause: A part of an automobile or yacht liability policy which extends coverage to persons and organizations other than the named insured, such as members of the insured's family, servants and others using the automobile with the owner's permission.

Optional Benefit: An additional benefit that may be included in a policy at the applicant's request.

Ordinary Life Insurance: Insurance policies of $ 1,000 or multiples thereof that provide coverage for the entire life of the policyholder and for which the premiums are payable until death. It is also referred to as whole life insurance or straight life insurance, and is different from term insurance in that it includes a cash value build-up.

Other Insurance: A Personal Auto Policy provision that describes how much the insurer will pay when more than one insurance policy or coverage applies to the same loss.

Other Than Collision Coverage (OTC): Covers damage to a covered auto caused by something other than collision coverage, such as hail, glass breakage and theft. Also called Comprehensive Coverage.

Over Insurance: Coverage in amounts greater than the value of the property insured or the amount of loss sustainable by the insured (e.g., several policies of hospitalization insurance for a total amount in excess of daily room charges).

P

Package Policy: A combination of property-liability coverages of two or more separate policies in on contract with one premium.

Paid-Up Additions: An additional amount of insurance purchased through dividends (single premium insurance) which increase the amount of protection afforded.

Paid-Up Insurance: Life Insurance on which future premium payments are not required. Frequently, the term is used to identify a 20-payment life insurance policy on which 20 annual premiums have been paid. Fractional paid-up insurance is the term applied to the policy that is issued under the non-forfeiture option.

Pair-and-Set Clause: An Inland marine policy provision which requires the insurer, at the insured's option, to restore or pay for the entire pair or set of jewelry or fine arts when only part has been lost, destroyed, or damaged.

Partial Loss: Is one involving less than all of the values insured or calling on the policy to pay less than its maximum amounts.

Participating Insurance: Insurance that entitles the policyholder to share in the divisible surplus of the insurance company through dividends.

Particular Average: In ocean marine insurance, a loss (partial or total) which falls on one or more property(ies) or interest(s) being shipped, as opposed to a General Average.

Payor Clause: A clause that provides for the waiver of premiums on a child's policy following the death or the total disability of the adult applicant for the child's policy.

Penalty of the Bond: In a surety bond, the amount guaranteed or the limit of the company's liability.

Peril: The cause of loss (e.g., fire, explosion, accident).

Perils of the Sea: Causes of loss unique to the operation of ships and their cargoes, i.e., sinking, stranding, heavy weather, etc., but not fire lighting, or theft.

Personal Articles Floater: World-wide coverage on an "all-risk" basis for scheduled, valuable personal property.

Personal Auto Policy: Coverage designed to replace both the family auto policy and the special package auto policy as the "standard" form for insuring private passenger autos and certain types of non-business trucks.

Personal Effects Floater: An inland marine policy that insures articles (usually accompanying travelers) against "all-risk" while away from home.

Personal Injury Protection (PIP): Also known as no-fault insurance, providing insurance for medical costs, loss of earning, additional living expenses, and funeral costs for occupants of the insured automobile and pedestrians other than those insured under other policies.

Physical Hazard: Danger of loss or liability arising from the condition, occupancy, or use of property, as opposed to such danger arising from the character of the policyholder.

Pilferage: Theft in small quantities, e.g., not limited to the taking of a whole package or all of the property insured.

Piracy: Robbery on the high seas, typically the seizure of a vessel and cargo.

Policy: The printed document issued by the insurance company to the insured that is the insurance contract.

Policy Fee: A small fee charged by some insurance companies for the first year (or portion thereof) in addition to the regular premium.

Policy Form: Document used to assemble an insurance policy that describes the policy coverages, exclusions and conditions.

Policyholder: The party to whom a policy is issued, and who pays a premium to an insurer in consideration of the patter's promise to provide insurance protection.

Policy Loan: A loan made by an insurance company to an insured under his policy (not in excess of its cash value). Policy loans may be assessed. a fixed interest rate or an adjustable rate.

Policy Period: Period of time listed in the Declaration when coverage under the policy is in effect.

Policy Term: The period of time for which the policy will normally remain in existence.

Premises: The building (or section of a building) insured or containing the insured property. Depending on policy conditions, it may also include an adjacent area.

Premium: The amount of money an insurance company charges to provide coverage.

Primary Insurance: When two or more coverages or policies apply to the same loss, the one that pays first, up to its limit of liability or the amount of the loss, whichever is less.

Principal: In suretyship, the principle is the one whose honesty, fidelity, or ability to perform is guaranteed.

Private Passenger Auto: A four-wheel motor vehicle, other than a truck, owned or leased for at least six continuous months.

Proceeds: The net amount of money that is payable by the insurance company at the death of an insured or when the policy matures.

Product Liability: The liability that a merchant or a manufacturer may incur as the result of some defect in the product sold or manufactured.

Profits Insurance: Coverage for the loss of profit that the policyholder could have earned that the merchandise destroyed in a fire (or by a covered peril) been sold otherwise.

Proof of Loss: A written statement of a claim giving the pertinent facts and data that may be in the form of an affidavit.

Property Damage (PD): Physical injury to, destruction of or loss of use of tangible property.

Pro Rata Cancellation: Termination of a policy by the insurer, for which the return premium due the policyholder is the full proportionate part for the un-expired term.

Proximate Cause: That which brings about a result without the intervention of any other force. Important in insurance since it establishes which policy(ies) will pay for a loss; e.g., the one insuring the perils which was the proximate cause of the loss.

Public Adjuster: One who, for a fee, represents policyholders in the adjustment of their losses with insurance companies.

Punitive Damages: Damages awarded to a plaintiff that are meant to punish the defendant for anti-social actions rather than reimburse the plaintiff for loss.

Q

Quota Share Reinsurance: A form of pro rata reinsurance (proportional) in which the reinsurer assumes an agreed percentage of each insurance policy being insured and shares all premiums and losses accordingly with the reinsured.

R

Rate: The price for a unit of insurance; all units in a given policy, multiplied by the rate per unit, produce the premium. In fire insurance, the price per $ 100 of insurance for one year. The basis for pricing other types of insurance varies greatly, i.e., payroll is used in workers' compensation insurance, area of retail floor space or sales volume is used in certain types of general liability insurance, etc.

Rating: A method under which an insurance company can issue a policy for a subsequent risk by increasing the premium based on the increased risk involved.

Rating Factor: Characteristics that differ depending on the individual risk that is being rated, such as the type of vehicle to be insured and the age and sex of the insured driver. For most personal auto coverages, they are used to modify the finished rate.

Rebating: Paying, offering, or giving anything of value (or any valuable consideration not specified in the policy) to any person as an inducement to purchase a policy of insurance. Rebating is illegal and both parties are guilty of it when it is done knowingly.

Reduced Paid-up Insurance: A non-forfeiture value (option) in a policy that provides for the continuation of the insurance but at a reduced amount (sometimes called Fractional Paid-up Insurance).

Reinstatement: The resumption of coverage under a policy that lapsed.

Reinsurance: (1) The transaction whereby an insurance company (the reinsurer), for a consideration, agrees to indemnify another insurance company known as the ceding company (the reinsured) against all or part of a loss which the latter may sustain under a policy of policies it has issued. (2) When referred to as "a reinsurance," the term means the relationship between reinsured and reinsurer.

Removal: The taking of property to some place other than at which it was insured. The standard fire insurance policy used in most states insures against damage done in removing the insured property from the path of the fire.

Renewable Term Insurance: Insurance that may be renewed at the end of the term, for another term, without evidence of insurability. The rates increase at the end of each term and are based on the attained age of the insured at the time.

Renewal: Continuance of coverage under a policy beyond the initial period.

Rental Value Insurance: Insurance which reimburses the owner-occupant of a building for the cost of renting some other place if the building is rendered unusable by some peril insured against.

Rent Insurance: Insurance that reimburses a building owner against loss of rental income if the building is not usable by a tenant because of some peril insured against.

Replacement Cost Insurance: Protection that pays the cost to restore or replace damaged or destroyed property without deduction for depreciation. Automatically included in homeowner's forms.

Replacement Vehicle: A vehicle the insured acquires during the policy period that replaces one shown in the Declarations.

Representation: Information communicated by the prospective insured to an insurer that will influence the latter's underwriting decision.

Reserve: A sum (required by law) set aside by an insurance company to assure the payment of future claims.

Retention Clause: A clause in a policy of reinsurance by which the ceding company agrees to retain for its own accounts a certain part of the line.

Rider: Another word for Endorsement.

Risk: (1) Defined variously as uncertainty of loss, chance of loss, or the variance of actual from expected results. However defined, its existence is the reason people by insurance. (2) The subject matter of an insurance contract, e.g., the building, cargo, or liability exposure insured.

Robbery: the taking of property by violence or threat of violence.

Running Down Clause: The clause in an ocean marine hull policy which covers damage done to another ship by collision, and other property damage caused by collision.

S

Safe Burglary Insurance: Protection against loss of property caused by forcible entry into a safe or vault. Damage to safes, vaults, and other property on the premises resulting from burglary is also covered unless caused by fire.

Salvage: Property in a loss saved from further loss.

Schedule: A list of insured properties, and the amount of insurance on each, which is attached to a "schedule" policy, as distinguished from a "blanket" policy.

Schedule Bond: A fidelity bond covering a number of named individuals or positions (irrespective of who occupies them), as contrasted with a blanket bond, which covers all.

Schedule Policy: A listing of two or more items of property in a policy, with specified amounts of insurance applying to each item.

Self-insurance: The retention of sufficient exposure units by an entity to permit the operation of the Law of Large Numbers. Self-insurance is a term often mistakenly used to describe the situation when an entity decided to retain its own risks.

Settlement Options: Methods (other than immediate payment in lump sum) by which an insured (or beneficiary) may choose to have the proceeds of an insurance policy paid.

Short Rate Cancellation: Termination of a policy by the policyholder before its stated expiration. The insurer refunds the policyholder a return premium in less amount than the pro rata part that is still unearned to compensate the insurer for expenses incurred to that point, (since the termination is at the request of the policyholder).

Single Limit of Liability: Policy limit that applies to all bodily injury and property damage arising from a single accident.

Single Provisions: Certain provisions that must be included in a Life Insurance Policy.

Social Insurance: Insurance provided by government.

Split Limit of Liability: Policy that has separate limits per person and per accident for Bodily Injury and a per accident limit for property damage.

Stated Amount Insurance: Insurance written to cover an item of property for a specific amount of insurance.

Stock Life Insurance Company: A Life Insurance Company owned and controlled by its stockholders who share in its divisible surplus. Generally, Stock Insurance Companies issue Non-Participating Life Insurance. However, some of them also issue Participating Life Insurance.

Subrogation: In insurance, the substitution of one party (insurer) for another party (insured) to pursue any rights the insured may have against a third party liable for a loss paid by the insurer.

Substandard Risks: Risks that do not met minimum underwriting criteria.

Sue and Labour Clause: Language in marine and inland marine policies requiring the policyholder in event of loss to take all necessary means to save the property from further loss and recover from others who caused the loss. The insurer agrees to pay the costs, even if they exceed the policies limit of liability.

Suicide Clause: A provision specifying that in the event the insured commits suicide within two years from the date the policy was issued, the insurance company's liability is limited to the payment of a single sum equal to the premium(s) actually paid (less any indebtedness due to the insurance company).

Supplemental Contract: An Agreement between an insurance company and an insured under which the insurance company retains the lump sum payable (under a Life Insurance Policy) and makes payments to the insured or the beneficiary in accordance with the settlement option selected by the insured.

Surety Bond: A written agreement wherein on part, called the surety, obligates itself to a second party, called the obligee or beneficiary, to answer for the default of a third party, call the principal in failing to perform specified acts within a stated time.

Surplus: The remainder after a company's liabilities are deducted from its assets.

Systematic Premium Plan (Check-O-Matic Plan): A plan under which the insured authorizes a bank to deduct the necessary funds from this account each month to pay a premium that is forwarded to his insurance company by the bank.

T

Temporary Substitute Auto: An auto or trailer that the named insured does not own that is used as a temporary substitute for a vehicle that is out of normal use because of breakdown, repair, servicing, loss, or destruction.

Tenants Policy: A form of homeowner's policy sold to persons who rent their living quarters or are co-op apartment owners.

Term Insurance: Insurance that is generally designed to afford coverage for a limited number of years. Usually no provision is made for cash values. It can be described as "Pure Protection."

Theft: A broad term meaning the wrongful taking of the property of another.

Third Party: The claimant under a liability policy, so-called because the first two parties are the insured and insurer, who enter into the insurance contract which pays the third party's claims.

Total Disability: An illness or injury that prevents an insured continuously performing every duty pertaining to his occupation or from engaging in any other type of work for remuneration. (This working varies from one insurance company to another.)

Total Loss: (1) Loss of all the insured property. (2) Under a given policy, a loss involving the maximum amount for which the policy is liable.

Towing and Labour Coverage: Coverage that pays for charges incurred by the insured for towing and labour charges.

Trailer: Vehicle designed to be pulled by a private passenger auto, pick-up or van.

Treaty, Reinsurance: A reinsurance agreement between an insurance company and a reinsurer, usually for one year or longer, which may be divided into two broad classifications: (1) The participating type which provides for sharing of risks between the ceding company and the reinsurer. (2) The excess type that provides for indemnity by the reinsurer only for loss which exceeds some specified predetermined amount.

Twisting: Inducing an insured to cancel his present insurance and replace it with insurance in the same or another insurance company by misrepresenting the facts or by presenting an incomplete comparison.

U

Umpire: A person selected by two appraisers to help settle disputes in property insurance claims.

Unauthorized Insurance: Insurance written by an insurer no licensed by the country or state in which the risk is located (non-admitted company).

Underwriter: One who accepts or rejects risks for an insurer (originally, by writing the person's name under the contract of insurance being issues).

Underwriting: The analysis of information pertaining to an applicant which was obtained from various sources and determination of whether or not the insurance should be: (1) Insured at request. (2) Offered at higher premium. (3) Declined.

Unearned Premium: The portion of the premium representing the un-expired portion of the policy term.

Underinsured Motorists Coverage (UIM): Coverage that reimburses the insured for the difference between the actual damage sustained for bodily injury and the amount of liability insurance carried by the at-fault driver if the at-fault driver's limits are less than the insured's.

Uninsured Motorists Coverage (UM): Pays for bodily injury sustained by the insured that is caused by an uninsured motorist.

Uninsured Motor Vehicle: A vehicle that has no Liability coverage; has Liability coverage that does not meet the state's financial responsibility requirement; is driven by an unidentified hit-and-run driver; or has invalid Liability coverage because the insured is insolvent or denies coverage.

Unoccupied Building: The temporary absence from a building of an occupant, but with the occupant's furniture and personal effects remaining, as opposed to a Vacant Building, which has neither occupants nor contents.

V

Vacant Building: A building with nothing in it. If the furniture is in the building and the owner intends to return, the building is Unoccupied.

Valued Policy: A policy in which the company agrees that the property insured is worth the amount of insurance, and therefore in the event of total loss, pays the face value of the policy without need of proof of the value at the time.

Vandalism: Damage done maliciously, included in the extended coverage endorsement. Also called "malicious mischief."

W

Waiver: The intentional relinquishment of a known right.

Waiver Endorsements: An agreement that waives the liability of the insurance company for a loss that would normally be covered under the policy.

Waiver of Premium: A provision included in many policies that waives the payment of premiums after an insured has been totally disabled for a specific period of time (usually 6 months)

War Clause: A clause in a policy that limits an insurance company's liability if a loss is caused by war.

Warranty: A statement by the insured on the literal truth of which the insurance contract depends.

Warranties and Representations: Most state laws specify that all statements by the applicant in the application (or to the medical examiner) are considered (in the absence of fraud) to be representations and not warranties. A warranty must be literally true. A breach of warranty may be sufficient to void a policy whether the warranty is material or not and whether or not such breach of warranty had contributed to the loss. A representation needs only to be substantially true. Generally, a representation would be material to the risk and that the applicant made with fraudulent intent.

Whole Life Insurance: Insurance policies of $ 1,000 or multiples thereof that provide coverage for the entire life of the policyholder and for which the premiums are payable until death. It is also referred to as Ordinary Life Insurance or straight life insurance, and is different from term insurance in that it includes a cash value build-up.

Wholesale Insurance: Group insurance written for small groups of employees, usually less than fifty. Each employee applies for and receives an individual policy. Usually, this type of insurance is written without a medical examination and the premiums are on a renewable term basis, but higher than on regular group insurance.

Windstorm Insurance: Protection against damage done to property by unusually high winds, cyclones, tornadoes, or hurricanes. Today, windstorm insurance is not available except under an extended coverage endorsement.

Workers' Compensation Insurance: Protection which provides benefits to employees for an injury or contracted disease arising out of and in the course of employment. All states have laws that require such protection for workers, and prescribe the length and amount of such benefits provided.

Written Premiums: The premiums on all the policies that a company has issued in a period of time, as opposed to earned premium.

Y

Your Covered Auto: Vehicles listed in the policy Declarations and, under certain circumstances, newly acquired autos and replacement autos.

BIBLIOGRAPHY

ALCI, *Life Insurance Fact Book, 1999*, American Council of Life Insurance, Washington, 1999.

Bedi, S.K., "Some Issues Concerning Privatization and Regulation of Insurance Sector." Paper presented in National Conference on Privatization of Insurance Sector: Corporate Challenges and Strategies. Nov. 5, 2001, Rohtak.

Belth, J.M., The Financial Strength of Life Insurance Health Companies, *The Insurance Forum*, Sept. 1999.

Bennett, C., *Dictionary of Insurance*.

Boora, A.S. and Chaudhary, R., "Indian Insurance Sector: Past, Present and Future." Paper Presented in National Conference on Nov. 5, 2001, Rohtak.

Boora, S.S., "Insurance Sector: Plunging into Uncertainty." Paper Presented in National Conference on Nov. 5, 2001, Rohtak.

Chhabra and Suri, *Management Process and Perspectives*, Kitab Mahal, Allahabad, 2000.

Chidambaram, K. and Alagappan, V., *Business Environment*, Vikas Publishing House Pvt. Ltd., New Delhi, 1999.

Crawford, M.L., *Life and Health Insurance Law*, McGraw Hill, Irwin, 1998.

Draft Regulations of Insurance Broker.

Ganguly, Anand, *Insurance Management*, New Age Publishers Ltd., Delhi, 2002.

Garg, M.C., "New Paradigms in Indian Insurance Industry" *Yojana*, April 2001, pp. 27-31.

General Insurance Compendium, *The Insurance Times*, Kolkata, 2000.

Gupta, A., "Privatisation of General Insurance Sector—How much Rationale", *The Management Accountant*, Oct. 1998.

Harrington, S.E. and Gregory, R.N., *Risk Management and Insurance*, McGraw Hill, Irwin, 1999.

Insurance Act, 1938. (Amended up to date)

Insurance Information Institute Fact Book, 2000, III, New York, 2000.

Insurance Institute of India, *Insurance Business Environment*, Mumbai.

Insurance Institute of India, *Principles of Insurance*, Mumbai.

Insurance Regulatory & Development Authority Act, 1999.

Jain, M.K., Determination of Capital required in a Life Insurance Business, *The Chartered Accountant*, Sept. 2001.

Jain, Rajiv, *Insurance Law and Practice*, Vidhi Publications, New Delhi, 2001.

Jha, R.N., *Insurance in India*, Bharat Book Bureau (International), Mumbai, 1999.

Lekhi, R.K., *Public Finance*.

Life Insurance Compendium, *The Insurance Times*, Kolkata, 2000

Meder, R.C., Changes in the Global Insurance Market, *ICFAI Reader*, May 2001.

Mishra, M.N., *Insurance—Principle and Practice*, S. Chand & Co. Ltd., New Delhi, 2001.

Pant, N., "Insurance Regulation and Development Bill: An Appraisal", *Economic and Political Weekly*, Nov. 6, 1999.

Parera, R.I., "Challenges and Opportunities: Privatization of Insurance", *The Chartered Accountant*, January, 2001.

Paresh Parasnis, "Distribution of Life Insurance—An Industry in Transition", *Chartered Secreatry*, Aug. 2001.

Pritam, S.P., "Evolution of Distribution Channels and Modern Marketing Techniques," *Yogakshema*, May 1999.

Raj, Aggarwal and Diwan, Parag, *Business Environment*, First Edition, Excel Book, Delhi, 2000.

Ranade, Ajit and Ahuja, Rajeev, "Issues in Regulation of Insurance", *Economic and Political Weekly*, Jan. 29, 2000.

Ranade, Ajit and Ahuja, Rajeev, "Three Questions about Insurance Liberalisation", *Decision*, Jan.-March 1997.

Regulations of Surveyor and Loss Assessor.

Regulations of Third Party Administrator in Health Service.

Rejda, G.E., *Principles of Risk Management and Insurance*, Pearson Education, Delhi, 2002.

Sachar, Rajender, "Insurance Bill: Ominous Oportents", *Mainstream*, Nov. 6, 1999.

Sighania, V.K., *Direct Tax Planning and Management*, Taxman Publishers, New Delhi, 2002.

Srivastva, D.C. and Srivastva, Shashank, *Indian Insurance Industry—Transition and Prospects*, New Century Publications, Delhi, 2001

Underwriting Mannuals of Insurance Companies.

Underwriting Practices of Motor, Fire, Marine and Miscellaneous by Federation of Insurance Institute of India.

Vats, R.M., *Law Relating to Insurance*, Universal Law Publishing Co. Pvt. Ltd., Delhi, 1999.

Vaughan, E.J. and Vaughan, T.M., *Fundamentals of Risk and Insurance*, John Wiley and Sons Incls., 1996.

Internet

www.aira.org <http://www.aira.org>

www.bimaonline.com

www.gicoi.com

www.healthinsuranceohio.com

www.iii.org <http://www.iii.org>
www.indiainfoline.com
www.insuranceinstituteofindia.com
www.insure.com <http://www.insure.com>
www.insweb.com
www.irda.org
www.irdaindia.org
www.irdaindia.org
www.knowledgedigest.com
www.law.cornell.edu <http://www.law.cornell.edu>
www.licihdia.com
www.nolo.com <http://www.nolo.com>
www.quickeninsurance.com <http://www.quickeninsurance.com>
www.rims.org
www.singhania.com <http://www.singhania.com>
Yoga Kshema, a Journal published by central office of LIC of India, Mumbai.

INDEX